DECISION MAKING IN CRIMINAL JUSTICE

Toward the Rational Exercise of Discretion

SECOND EDITION

LAW, SOCIETY, AND POLICY

Series Editors: Joel Feinberg, Travis Hirschi,
Bruce Sales, and David Wexler
University of Arizona

A Continuation Order Plan is available for this series. A continuation order will bring delivery of
each new volume immediately upon publication. Volumes are billed only upon actual shipment. For
further information please contact the publisher.

DECISION MAKING IN CRIMINAL JUSTICE
Toward the Rational Exercise of Discretion

SECOND EDITION

Michael R. Gottfredson

Department of Management and Policy
University of Arizona
Tucson, Arizona

and

Don M. Gottfredson

School of Criminal Justice
Rutgers University
Newark, New Jersey

Plenum Press • New York and London

Library of Congress Cataloging in Publication Data

Gottfredson, Michael R.
  Decision making in criminal justice.

  (Law, society, and policy; v. 3)
  Bibliography: p.
  Includes index.
  1. Criminal justice, Administration of—United States—Decision making. 2. Police
discretion—United States. 3. Judicial discretion—United States. 4. Sentences (Criminal
procedure)—United States—Decision making. 5. Probation—United States—Decision
making. 6. Parole—United States—Decision making. I. Gottfredson, Don M. II. Title.
III. Series. HV9950.G68   1987   364   87-7260
ISBN 0-306-42525-4

First Printing—November 1987
Second Printing—April 1989
Third Printing—March 1990

© 1988 Plenum Press, New York
A Division of Plenum Publishing Corporation
233 Spring Street, New York, N.Y. 10013

Printed in the United States of America

PREFACE

The study of decisions in the criminal justice process provides a useful focus for the examination of many fundamental aspects of criminal justice. These decisions are not always highly visible. They are made, ordinarily, within wide areas of discretion. The aims of the decisions are not always clear, and, indeed, the principal objectives of these decisions are often the subject of much debate. Usually they are not guided by explicit decision policies. Often the participants are unable to verbalize the basis for the selection of decision alternatives. Adequate information for the decisions is usually unavailable. Rarely can the decisions be demonstrated to be rational.

By a *rational decision* we mean "that decision among those possible for the decisionmaker which, in the light of the information available, maximizes the probability of the achievement of the purpose of the decisionmaker in that specific and particular case" (Wilkins, 1974a: 70; also 1969). This definition, which stems from statistical decision theory, points to three fundamental characteristics of decisions. First, it is assumed that a choice of possible decisions (or, more precisely, of possible alternatives) is available. If only one choice is possible, there is no decision problem, and the question of rationality does not arise. Usually, of course, there will be a choice, even if the alternative is to decide not to decide—a choice that, of course, often has profound consequences. Choosing to do nothing (report a crime, make an arrest) has its impact; and the prison inmate whose case is "continued" for later parole consideration would no doubt agree that "delay is the deadliest form of denial" (Parkinson, 1971: 119). Second, it is assumed that some information is available for use in arriving at the decision. Again, the idea of a rational decision made wholly without information would hardly occur to us. Ordinarily it is expected that if a decision is to be made, some information will be available. Third, there is assumed to be a goal or a set of goals, purposes, or objectives to be achieved (or maximized or minimized). If it is not known what is sought to be achieved, then it is not possible to assess the rationality of any particular decision choice.

There is no requirement that we prefer rationality, but we assume that rational decisions generally are preferred and sought in the criminal justice system. We admit the preference and the assumption.

It is clear that increased rationality in criminal justice is likely to be achieved only after it has become possible to identify more explicitly, with adequate operational definitions, the specific objectives of each phase of the apparatus intended to reduce, control, or at least cope with problems of delinquency and crime (or in some other sense to provide justice). A second requirement must be the identification, the adequate description, and perhaps the elaboration of additional alternative decision choices at each step. The third necessity, of course, is the requirement of information. By the term *information* we do not refer to mere data, no matter how carefully collected or how reliable, but to those data that, by demonstrable relevance to objectives, reduce uncertainty in the decision under consideration. Thus, having information implies having knowledge of the relation of the datum in question to the decision objectives and such knowledge is often wholly lacking in the criminal justice system.

If the decision maker, whether victim, policeman, or judge, is unclear about the objectives of a given decision, that person can hardly be expected to behave rationally in the sense of maximizing the probability of achieving that undefined purpose. Of course, people do have objectives in making decisions, but often the objectives are only vaguely felt and difficult to express. A profound lack of clarity of definition and of adequate measurement of objectives abounds in the criminal justice system.

Moreover, these objectives are sometimes conflicting. Given a mixed set of criminal justice goals, including such possibly conflicting aims as retribution, deterrence, rehabilitation, reintegration, or desert, it is not surprising to find absent a clear consensus on objectives among the members of a criminal justice agency. At each step in the processes of these systems, which require decisions with remarkably profound impact on the subsequent lives of the persons involved, fundamental conflicts may be perceived readily. The most basic conflict, perhaps, is that between perceived essentials of just desert (punishment or reward) and various utilitarian perspectives that stress crime reduction. In this book we emphasize utilitarian aims; these are compatible with the rational, pragmatic, and probabilistic frame of reference that we have sought to employ.

Authors who set out to describe and to analyze major decisions in the criminal justice process are confronted quickly with a critical decision themselves: which decisions, among the scores that occur between the initial definition of conduct as illegal and the decision to release a punished person from state control, should serve as examples for the inquiry? Compelling arguments could be made that nearly every decision in the juvenile and criminal justice processes ought to be regarded as critically in need of careful study. Most juvenile and criminal justice decisions can be regarded rightly as vitally affecting both the lives of those about whom the decisions are made and the welfare of the community. In part, our decisions were made pragmatically: we assumed the juvenile justice system decisions generally to be beyond a reasonable scope for our efforts, and the decision points to be discussed are those about which most recent research has been concerned (and, consequently, about which most is known). It was our further aim, however, to select those decisions made by individual actors in the criminal justice system that have the greatest impact on the system as a whole. For that reason, we begin in Chapter 2 with a discussion of the decision to report a crime to the police.

The decision of the victim of crime as to whether or not to report the offense to the police is of such a critical nature that the victim may be regarded fairly as a principal gatekeeper to the criminal justice system. Yet if we ask how much is known of the objectives of the victim (in calling or not calling the police), we find the answer to be, surprisingly little. How often, and in what circumstances, does the victim seek mere retribution? When, in reporting a crime, is the victim concerned to achieve the offender's incapacitation? Is deterrence sometimes an aim in crime reporting, as it is, apparently, in sentencing or parole decisions? What objectives are sought by the victim when an event is *not* reported?

The decisions made by police are similarly complex and not yet well understood, although more research has been done on this topic. If a crime is reported to them or discovered by them, it is they who ordinarily must decide what is to be done next. Generally, they must decide whether to invoke the law. This involves deciding whether a crime apparently has occurred. It may involve deciding on legal issues such as reasonable suspicion or probable cause. In deciding whether to make an arrest, the police officer may have various discretionary choices—for example, arrest, issue a citation, refer to a social agency, offer counsel, do nothing.

Again, the objectives may be diverse. General goals are subject to debate. Information to guide general policy or individual decisions may be lacking.

The discretion in decision making exercised by prosecutors has been perhaps less often noticed in the past, less in the public eye, than that of police or judges. Nevertheless, it is very broad; and the decisions have profound consequences for the rest of the criminal justice system. Prosecutors, too, must decide whether to invoke the law. Is the defendant to be charged? If so, what specific offense or offenses will be alleged? Shall the accused be brought to trial or should a plea of guilty to a lesser offense be negotiated? What resources should be brought to bear on the necessary investigation? Again, the prosecutor may have a variety of goals: increasing convictions, winning cases, "cracking down" on specific kinds of offenses, or, more generally, aims of deterrence, incapacitation, rehabilitation, or desert. Some recent research has focused on the information needs of the prosecutor to aid in the selection of alternative courses of action in pursuit of diverse objectives.

Should an accused person be held in custody before trial? A foundation of American law traditionally has been the presumption of innocence before trial. Bail may be used to help ensure the availability of the defendant in court, but the Constitution of the United States prohibits that it be excessive. Some have advocated, nevertheless, the preventive detention of some accused, not for what they have done but for what they may do. Within this context, we seek to examine the goals and information needs of the court for decision making on bail and release on recognizance. Again, both general policy and individual case decisions are involved. Fundamental issues of liberty and crime control are at stake.

The judge, in passing sentence, traditionally has had much autonomy and much discretion. Yet he or she is dependent upon the police, the prosecutor, and the probation officer (among others) as sources of information. The often conflicting goals of the entire criminal justice system are those typically expressed by individual judges: desert, rehabilitation, incapacitation, deterrence—in short, the provision of both deserved punishment and crime control. Thus, the aims may be derived from moral principles or from utilitarian purposes of crime reduction. Alternative dispositions, once the determination of guilt has been made, are increasingly complex. They generally must be selected within legal constraints that vary markedly among jurisdictions. And these decisions generally must be made in the absence of clear consensus on the aims of sentencing, without an explicit, clearly articulated policy guiding the exercise of discretion. They are made also in the absence of a systematic procedure for feedback on the consequences of decisions, even in terms of the later criminality of those sentenced. Also absent, therefore, is convincing evidence of the relation of a given disposition to deterrence, incapacitation, or rehabilitation. In short, most present sentencing decisions involve complex goals, much data but little information, diverse alternatives, considerable discretion, and little structured policy.

At present, nearly every prison and jail in the United States is overcrowded. Incarcerated populations are at an all-time high. The administrator of a correctional institution must run a distinctive kind of hotel without benefit of a reservation service. Typically, the jail or prison administrator has little to say about who comes to stay or for how long. Within the institution, however, there are many decisions to be made. These, as elsewhere in the system, are of two general types: policy decisions and individual decisions. General policy decisions may involve, for example, the development of appropriate (and presumably effective) programs of treatment for different kinds of offenders. Individual decisions may be required with immediacy (for example, assign to suicide prevention watch or place in protective custody); or they may appear more mundane (select work assignment, place where beds are available, decide initial custody classification), or they may be critical to rehabilitative aims (place in educational programs or in vocational training, recommend counseling, place in institution nearest family). The aims are similarly complex. Often they appear to conflict, as when concerns of custody and security and those of treatment are at odds. Some correctional research may help to inform these decisions, but much remains to be done to sort mere data from useful information to guide correctional decisions to greater rationality.

Probation, although typically an "arm of the court," also may be considered to be a part of corrections, namely, corrections in the community. Parole, which generally refers to supervision in the community after a period of incarceration (rather than in lieu of it) may be regarded in the same way. Probation decisions do not end with the placement by the judge of the convicted offender in that dispositional category. Rather, a process of decisions by probation staff is then initiated. Some of these have to do with placement, for example, in caseloads of varying size, methods, or levels of intensity of supervision or surveillance. Others, of course, address the question of whether an assertion of probation violation (to the court) or parole violation (to the paroling authority) is to be made. The objectives, alternatives, and information needs are, in general, similar to those that obtain in other parts of the system.

Paroling decisions are highly visible, much discussed, and widely debated. Goals of parole board members tend to reflect a variety of differing perspectives: sanctioning, treatment, fairness, citizen representation, and gatekeeping (reservation service). Like judges, parole boards have been subject to much criticism for alleged arbitrary and capricious decision making, for disparity in the granting or denial of parole, and for ineffectiveness. As with sentencing decisions, much research has been done and much remains to be learned. Similar needs for consensus on goals, for structured policies governing the exercise of discretion, and for information demonstrably relevant to both policy and individual decisions are apparent.

These are all complex decisions, and our title, given both this complexity and the importance of the topic, is presumptuous. Our goals are more modest: to examine some of this complexity, to discuss some of the recent research relevant to the concept of rationality in decision making, and to point to some areas in which further inquiry is most needed. Each of the critical decision points examined involves a large topic in itself.

When the criminal justice system is considered from a perspective of decisions, it is apparent immediately that decisions are the stuff of that system. Thus, few aspects of criminal justice are found to be outside the plausible scope of discussion. It might be argued that the greatest omission in this book is a chapter on the decision of the offender to commit a crime. There is a reason, however, for omitting such a chapter, in addition to the obvious one that the topic involves much of criminology, sociology, psychology, psychiatry, and related disciplines. It is that we have sought to focus on information needs, objectives, and choices within the criminal justice system, toward the end of better reasoned and more logical dealing with the problem of crime after it has occurred.

This book differs from many discussions of criminal justice decision making not only in its emphasis on rationality, but also in its primary reliance on scientific social research. To be sure, some legal analysis is undertaken, principally in the context of discussions of decision goals. But our concern with the idea of *information* leads us to examine research that attempts to discover how decisions actually are made in the criminal justice system and whether they are made in ways compatible with purported aims. Traditionally, these areas of inquiry have fallen into the realm of social science

We stress rationality and we urge a scientific outlook, but we trust we will not be mistaken as seeming to propound these modes as the only force for progress toward criminal justice. Rather, in agreement with Bertrand Russell (1962:260) we would note that "the impulse toward scientific construction is admirable when it does not thwart any of the major impulses that give value to human life, but when it is allowed to forbid all outlet to everything but itself it becomes a form of cruel tyranny." Science increases knowledge, and knowledge brings power. It is apparent that the increased rationality that is sought through social science may be exercised safely only in a context of values beyond the scope of discussion here. That suggests a further limitation of this book, but indeed it stems from a limitation of science. Russell concluded his essay on science and values: "The dangers exist, but they are not inevitable, and hope for the future is at least as rational as fear (1962:269)."

We have not attempted to review all of the research bearing on the decisions discussed. Rather, we have been selective in our attempt to review those studies that best inform about the concepts of information, goals, and alternatives. And we limit our analyses to studies of routine cases in the system; all too often discussions of decisions in criminal justice focus on the unique, exceptional cases, to the detriment of an understanding of how decisions typically are made. Despite these omissions, we have sought to deal with areas of particular importance to criminal justice if the decisions of significant actors in that system—and hence procedures and programs—are to be made more rationally.

We have tried to write for our colleagues in criminal justice research and in criminal justice administration, at the same time hoping that the book will be useful to students. These are in some respects diverse audiences, and we are aware that going down the middle of the road may disrupt traffic both ways. We have sought, however, to refer the reader elsewhere for more detailed, more technical, or more thorough discussion of critical points.

In the final chapter we identify ten requisites for increased rationality in decision making in criminal justice. These requisites are derived from our analyses of the decisions discussed in this book. We also attempt a reconciliation among the apparently conflicting goals that seem to abound in the criminal justice system. In this final chapter we assert that the application of scientific methods to criminal justice decision making offers the greatest hope for improvement of our system of justice. We are well aware that to argue in favor of a central role for facts in a world of values will be seen as shortsighted by some, naive by others— a dangerous reversion to an inglorious and thoroughly discredited earlier era or an embarrassingly optimistic faith in the potential for change. Our consolation lies in our belief that the alternative position rests on the implicit supposition that progress will be made when presumptions are regarded as facts, when untested hunches are acted upon with vigor, when goals are unspecified, and when fashionable alternatives are accepted for their novelty alone.

The theme of the book involves goals, alternatives, and information as three legs of the stool on which the decision maker sits. If goals are unclear or confused, if alternatives are unrelated to them, or if information is irrelevant—if any one leg is weak—he or she who sits upon the stool must sit with trepidation.

In the first edition of this book we noted with gratitude our debt to two of our colleagues with whom we enjoyed a lengthy collaboration over the years and whose work greatly influenced our concepts and analyses, Michael J. Hindelang and Leslie T. Wilkins. Although this edition is markedly revised to include more recent research related to our theme, it continues to reflect the impact of these two scholars on our thought and work.

Our gratitude is expressed to Shirley Jackson, who typed and edited the manuscript, kept track of the project, and greatly simplified our task by her fine work.

We each continue to thank the other for accepting the responsibility for the errors in the book.

CONTENTS

Chapter 1

OVERVIEW

This chapter presents an overview of decisions in the criminal justice system: what they are, who makes them, how they are made, and with what consequences. Its aims are to identify the themes that will serve as the focus of detailed discussions in subsequent chapters, to familiarize the reader with the decision point frame of reference, and to highlight our analytical method. Later, we put flesh on these bare bones; our purposes here are to provide the context for our later detailed investigations, to define our terms, and to give a glimpse of our conclusions. The justification for these conclusions comes, we believe, in the remainder of the book.

When a crime occurs, the event may or may not be reported to the police or other law enforcement officials. If the victim or other observers do not report the crime, the criminal justice system is not invoked; but when a crime is reported, a complex sequence of decisions may ensue. These decisions are critical events in the lives of the persons affected, and they are the central features of the criminal justice system.

The report to the police of a bicycle theft, a rape, or a robbery may, for example, be the stimulus to decisions such as:

- Should a police car be dispatched?
- Should the event be regarded as an offense?
- Should an arrest be made?
- Should an alleged offender be held or released?
- Should a citation be issued?
- Should an alleged offender be prosecuted? With what priority?
- Is the offender guilty?
- If guilty, what should be the sentence? Fine, jail, or prison? Should the offender be placed on probation?

- Any special conditions?
- If sentenced to confinement, where? For what purpose?
- How long?
- What degree of custodial security is required?
- To what programs should the persons be assigned?
- Should the offender be paroled from custody?
- Should parole be revoked?
- Should the offender be discharged?

These, of course, are but a few of the decisions (although they are important ones) made at every step in the criminal justice process. Many are clearly of extreme importance to the individuals affected. They deal with loss of liberty and other serious intrusions and interventions in individual lives. They are obviously critical to the efficient, effective, and humane functioning of the criminal justice system. If that system is to serve society well, such decisions should be made rationally, ensuring the fair, efficient, effective, and humane system widely sought for the control and reduction of crime.

These decisions are of two general kinds. Some are made about persons—that is, individual decisions. Others are agency or institutional decisions (Cronbach and Gleser, 1957) including questions of general policy. As will be seen, however, it is not easy to separate the two general kinds of decisions, since decisions as to general policy provide the context, including constraints, within which individual decisions are made.

THE NATURE OF A DECISION

Any decision has three main components. There is first a *goal* (or a set of goals) that the decision maker would like to achieve. It is reasonable and useful for analysis to assume that the decision maker (such as police officer, prosecutor, or judge) has some objective or objectives that may be specified. That is, if there is a decision problem, the decision maker wishes to bring about some change in the state of affairs or has a desire to optimize some result. For example, the prosecutor may wish to achieve a conviction of the alleged offender in court; the judge may desire an optimal sentence for both the protection of society and rehabilitation of the offender.

Second, there are some *alternatives*. If there is no choice, there is no decision problem. Ordinarily, the decision maker in the criminal justice system has a variety of choices, although he or she may often wish for more or for better ones. It is very important to note that the decision maker usually has, within the law and agency rules or regulations, considerable *discretion* in choosing a course of action.

Third, the decision maker has some *information* to guide the selection among alternatives. In order to qualify as information in this sense, the data available about alternatives must be related to the goals of the decision—that is, the data must be relevant. The definition of relevance in this context is that the data must reduce uncertainty about the consequences of the decision.

It is clear that decisions may not be evaluated very thoroughly if the goals of the decisions are unknown. Similarly, it is difficult to see how decisions might be improved in the absence of clear and explicit specifications of those goals, because no means for assessing the information value of data about alternatives would be available. The information value of a datum is determined by the relation of the datum to the consequences of the alternative choices; if there is no relation, then there is no information. We shall see that decisions about crime, offenders, and alleged offenders often are made with much data but little information.

Increased rationality in the criminal justice system thus requires the improvement of information available for decisions. This is a central theme of this book. In one of his *Unpopular Essays*, Bertrand Russell (1962:71) said: "Man is a rational animal—so at least I have been told. Throughout a long life, I have looked diligently for evidence in favor of this statement, but so far I have not had the good fortune to come across it, though I have searched in many countries spread over three continents." Citing Aristotle as perhaps the first to proclaim man as a rational animal, Russell did not find Aristotle's reason for this view very impressive—"It was that some people can do sums" (1962:72).

Rationality in decision making about persons caught up in the criminal justice system may be assumed to be a requirement for "improved," "more efficient," or "more effective" decisions. If this is accepted, then there will be further requirements. There must be some agreed-upon objectives for the decisions, relevant information about the person, possible choices and knowledge of the probable outcome once decisions are made. In the criminal justice system now, however, clear agreement on objectives is not easily found. Usually, little information is available to the persons with responsibility for the decisions, and often evidence on the likely consequences of alternatives is entirely lacking. Given these difficulties, it may not be expected that Russell's observation may be easily refuted or that we will readily find much better support for Aristotle's claim of man's rationality than his own. Nevertheless, the analysis of decisions, including an assessment of the sometimes conflicting, usually poorly articulated goals in this field and of information needs may provide a basis for progress toward a more rational system.

The concept of rationality is, of course, a complex one. Philosophers have debated its definition from many points of view. For the purposes of this book, however, the concept of a rational decision may be defined more readily. Note the definition offered in the preface: We assume that a "rational decision is that decision among those possible for the decisionmaker which, in the light of the information available, maximizes the probability of the achievement of the purposes of the decisionmaker in that specific and particular case" (Wilkins, 1975:70).

This definition again calls attention to the three main components of a decision:—goals, alternatives, and information. The definition of information, as distinct from data (observations), is critical: information is data that reduce uncertainty (that is, provide guidance as to the probabilities) of achievement of desired decision objectives.

These concepts are central to the analyses of decisions presented in this book. We seek to examine, for each of the decision-making problem areas discussed, aspects of these three decision components—goals, alternatives, and information—and to review selected empirical studies pertinent to them. From this examination, we then seek to identify some requisites for increased rationality in decision making.

CRIMINAL JUSTICE DECISIONS

The system of criminal justice may be portrayed schematically quite well by a flow diagram showing the series of points at which decisions may be triggered by a report of a crime. Police officers, prosecutors, judges, wardens, and parole board members have in common that they all make decisions about offenders or alleged offenders against the law. They have in common also the fact that the decisions they make have consequences for other parts of the system. Thus, decisions by police affect the workload of the prosecutors, whose decisions in part determine cases to be tried in court. The correctional administrator must make numerous decisions about inmate placements, although he or she has no control over intake or discharge, these critical workload requirements being determined by decisions of judges and paroling authorities. The complex tree of decision points that may be envisioned thus also depicts the interrelated nature of the component parts of the system, such as police, prosecution, the courts, and corrections.

The trigger event for the entire system, the reporting of a crime, is examined in Chapter 2. The decision by a victim to report or not report the crime is critical to the entire system of criminal justice. Yet, it is known that many or most crimes are not reported. This decision represents a somewhat neglected area of study, but we seek to examine available evidence concerning it before considering the decisions made by functionaries of the system.

Police decisions are addressed in Chapter 3. It is the police who first decide, in any event that is allegedly, apparently, or actually a crime, whether to invoke the law. It has been asserted that police officers "have, in effect, a greater degree of discretionary freedom in proceeding against offenders than any other public official" (Bittner, 1970:107). They decide, for example, whether an offense has occurred, whether to arrest, whether to issue a citation, whether to hold persons in custody, and whether to refer persons to other social agencies. They decide whether to press for the invoking of the criminal law or to forget it. The police do not merely apply and enforce the law; rather, and to a great extent, they use discretion in invoking the law (Goldstein, 1969; Kadish, 1962; Packer, 1964).

If a person is arrested and accused of a crime, the tradition in the United States is that he or she is presumed innocent until proven guilty. But what is to be done pending trial or some other disposition of the case? In these circumstances, regarding accused adults, there has been an expansion of interest in extending release, while trial is awaited, to large numbers of persons while maintaining assurance of the defendant's availability for trial. Traditionally, release on money bail has been the principal, and often the only, method for avoiding confinement of the accused while awaiting trial (despite its obvious discrimination against the poor).

In many parts of the United States programs of release on the person's "own recognizance" now have been added. The decision as to the disposition of the alleged offender now thus commonly includes alternatives to financial bail. The presumption of innocence, together with a concern for community security, provide a context of conflict of aims typical of many critical criminal justice decisions. The issue is joined by the need for striking a balance between the concern for the protection of society and the desire to guarantee maximum freedom for the person. The desire to prevent future crimes opposes the desire to allow the suspect to be free before trial. Thus, the analysis of this decision (Chapter 4) provides a particularly challenging setting for the examination of the concept of rational decision making.

Once a person has been arrested, a variety of decisions may be made before that person leaves the adjudicatory system or is sentenced. Those decisions focus on whether to press the case—that is, to file charges (and the specific nature of the charges) and, if the decision is to prosecute, on the degree of vigor with which to prosecute. Generally, across the country, too little is known of the criteria that provide the basis for these decisions. Even careful descriptions of the processes in various jurisdictions are lacking. Worse, there is even less information available concerning the effects of these decisions, either in terms of impact elsewhere in the criminal justice system or in respect to the later activities of the persons accused.

Prosecution decisions are discussed in Chapter 5. Typical decisions include the prosecutor's decision whether to file charges at all and, if it is decided to do so, the selection of the specific charge. The latter decision includes the issue of *plea bargaining*, that is, a negotiated plea. Prosecutors may be involved also in decisions by a lower court, such as the need for a municipal judge to determine whether a defendant should be held to answer to a higher court (for example, to a superior court on a felony charge), tried on a misdemeanor charge, or dismissed. If there is plea bargaining, are inducements offered by the prosecutor or the court to encourage guilty pleas? If so, what inducements are involved?

A related decision is that taken by the defendant: Does he or she decide to plead guilty or to go to trial? If the latter, is the choice that of a trial by the court (that is, by the judge) or by a jury? Finally, of course, there is the finding of the court as to guilt.

If the defendant is found guilty, then there is the problem of sentencing. That central feature of criminal justice decision making is discussed in Chapter 6. The sentencing decision is at present guided unsystematically by goals of retribution, rehabilitation, community protection, deterrence, and equitable treatment. It is a decision that must be made within constraints imposed by law and by resources (that is, alternatives). It is a decision that typically must be made in the absence of information provided systematically to assist the judge in making equitable sentencing decisions, assuring that similarly situated offenders are similarly treated in the selection of sentencing alternatives. Moreover, it is a decision that must be made with little systematic knowledge of the consequences of previous decisions in similar cases. The attention given thus far to analyses of sentencing does not match the importance of the problem. It would be difficult to find other decision problems critically affecting the liberty and future lives of large numbers of people in which decisions are made with so little knowledge of their likely results.

Presentence reports, usually completed by probation officers, are employed in most jurisdictions when penalties of more than one year may ensue and in some jurisdictions when lesser penalties may result.

Typically, these reports follow from an investigation by the probation officer. Ordinarily he or she has talked to the defendant and, possibly, to family, friends, employers, or others. The report usually is intended to present a comprehensive assessment of the defendant and that person's life situation. It often includes a recommendation concerning the court's disposition. Commonly, some identifying and demographic data are included, and official and defendant's versions of the offense are summarized, as is the prior criminal record. Frequently, the report includes: a brief life history; descriptions of the defendant's home and work situations; assessments of interests, attitudes, aptitudes, and physical and mental health; and other personality assessments. All are intended to clarify the factors resulting in the defendant's present difficulty and to assist in the court's decision as to disposition.

The judge may be presented in this way with a great mass of data concerning the offender before him, and this may provide the judge with an increased feeling of confidence in the decision. But although the courts typically keep records of decisions taken, they ordinarily do not keep score on the outcomes. As a result, information on the relevance of most of the assembled case data to rational decision making for disposition (placement) of the offender is unavailable. Thus, presented with a wealth of data never assessed for its empirical relevance to his or her decision problem, the judge may have exhaustive data but little information.

After sentencing, the next critical points of decision depend, of course, upon the outcome of the sentencing process. Typically, these will include placement decisions affecting the offender's program in jail, under probation supervision, or in prison; they may include the decision as to whether to parole; and they often include determination of the length of time to be required in custody or under supervision. In each case, the decision makers are confronted with the usual, sometimes conflicting, demands of the criminal justice system for punishment, societal protection, and rehabilitation of the offender.

Decisions on the offender's program are made by probation officers, correctional classification officers, wardens, parole board members, parole officers, and others. Like the judge, these decision makers typically lack the basis from painstaking record keeping, analysis, and feedback that is requisite to a truly well-informed decision process. Analysis of these correctional decisions is to be found in Chapters 7 and 8.

Little work has been done toward developing classification methods for use in jails, and little systematic study has been completed that could give probation administrators an increased confidence that their charges will be provided with the kind and degree of treatment most appropriate in each case. To the extent that each jail inmate and each probationer is unique, no amount of experience can assure such confidence; but to the extent that similar persons respond similarly to differential program placements, that experience could guide future decisions and thus could improve the results of jail and probation programs.

Much more research has been done with persons sentenced to prisons or to correctional facilities for youth, and much of this material has relevance to classification problems in the area of jail and probation. Except in those research studies, the term *classification* typically refers to procedures for the assignment of persons to institutions or to institutional programs.[1] In some systems (for example, in California) the newly arrived prisoner is observed and studied intensively for a period of two or three months, in specially designed reception–guidance centers. Such study may include interviews with the inmate that together with materials assembled from inquiries of others (usually including the presentence report) provide a basis for a social history. Vocational counseling may be provided, and recommendations may be made concerning the offender's needs for education and training. Group and sometimes individual psychological testing may be included in the assessment procedures. Sometimes they include observations of behavior in housing units, recreational facilities, and counseling sessions. And (more rarely) they may include psychiatric evaluations or individual psychological diagnostic study.

The objectives typically are determination of the institution in which the prisoner will serve at least the first part of his or her term, the degree of custody and security (that is, physical restraint and surveillance) required, and the treatment program judged appropriate in terms of rehabilitative aims. In correctional systems with sophisticated treatment resources, program placement alternatives may be diverse, each with ardent advocates claiming rehabilitative value. They may include, for example, educational regimes, vocational training for numerous occupations, group and individual counseling and psychotherapy from diverse theoretical frames of reference, occupational therapy, forestry or road camp programs, and school or work furlough placements. The data collected to aid in these decisions sometimes are compiled with painstaking accuracy. Ordinarily, however, even when such data are collected carefully there is little evidence of their validity in terms of any objectives of the correctional process. Hence, again, much data, little information.

There are indeed beliefs among correctional staff responsible for these decisions in the validity of certain kinds of data in predicting program outcomes. Such beliefs are regarded most usefully as hypotheses to be tested through follow-up studies. Those found valid can be retained and used in educating other decision makers to increase the likelihood of helpful program placements. Those not supported by the evidence can be rejected. Without such a process of systematic study and feedback to the decision makers, improvement in the decisions cannot be expected. Rather, that which was "reasonably supposed," "assumed," or "thought likely" is apt to be accepted increasingly as if it were supported by evidence—indeed, to be mistaken for "fact." Presumptions concerning relations of offender data to desired outcomes thus may in time achieve the status of folklore. These concepts then may provide a basis for implicit classification models. In this way, implicit classification methods based on tradition and folklore may become the chief tools of the correctional decision maker.

Many useful starts toward more explicit and reliable classification methods have have been made, and validation studies, with respect to a variety of correctional purposes, have begun to be reported. These classification methods, from psychological, sociological, or psychiatric perspectives, are not equally valuable for all purposes. Some have more direct treatment implications than others. Some are demonstrably more reliable than others. Some are more helpful in generating testable hypotheses than others. In only a few instances has the relevance of the classification for treatment placement been demonstrated clearly. The need is great for development of theoretically sound, clinically useful, testable classification systems, with enunciation of the probably etiology, for proposed treatment or control measures and for demonstration of the effectiveness of differential treatment placements.

Offenders are not the only proper subjects for classification efforts. Other components of intervention strategies may be classified as well. These may include environmental settings, workers (treaters), and treatment methods. One may then proceed to seek to sort out the optimal "matches" for greatest effect in terms of desired outcomes.

Parole decisions, discussed in Chapter 9, may be broken into three generic classes. First, there is the decision when to release from custody (the discretionary release component). Second, there is a series of decisions relating to supervision that must be made—what size caseload, what conditions, and so forth (the supervision component). Third, parole also at times involves decisions about return to custody (the revocation component). Parole provides a good basis for discussion of our present knowledge of decision making and of the contributions and limitations of classification and prediction methods. Related to each of these components has been a long line of research efforts, many of which have had their principal focus on classification studies with a predictive purpose.

IMPORTANCE OF THE STUDY OF DECISIONS

Increased rationality in criminal justice is likely to come about only after it has become possible to identify explicitly, with adequate operational definition, the specific objectives of each phase of the various parts of the apparatus designed to reduce, control, or at least cope with problems of crime. A second requirement must be the identification and adequate description of the alternative decision choices at each step. The third necessity, about which we have perhaps the least evidence, is the requirement of information.

It is far easier to conceptualize the information needs for more rational decision making than to achieve them in practice. One reason is the present lack of consensus on objectives at each of the decision points that define the flow of persons through the process. Another is lack of knowledge generally of relative effectiveness of the available alternatives in terms of the objectives chosen, especially as measures of effectiveness may differ for different classifications of persons. The third reason is that agency information systems with appropriate relations with other agencies in the system do not exist. These are needed in order to provide the follow-up studies of persons that are essential to estimation of the branching probabilities of objective achievement along the tree of decisions.

The definition and measurement of objectives is an obvious requisite to improved effectiveness, efficiency, and justice. These values can be known to be attained only in terms of those definitions and measurements. The global concept of justice is the most elusive of consensual definition, but there appears at least to be much agreement that equity may be regarded as a necessary (though insufficient) condition of justice. Examples will be given throughout the book to illustrate the formulation of rules for decisions with respect to specific classifications of persons in order to provide a plausible means for increased equity in decision making.

Similarly, we assume that efficiency and effectiveness are values widely sought and that their achievement requires the study of alternatives and the development of information. Knowledge that an alternative choice exists does not by itself provide the decision maker with information. That is, the availability of the alternative does not reduce uncertainty about the probable consequences of selection; that requires knowledge of the relation of that choice to the decision objective. This is a principal reason for the need for program evaluation at each stage in the criminal justice process, and it is why such research is critical to the improvement of individual decision making. In the final chapter we outline a system that permits the evaluation of these many decisions in light of their central components—goals, information, and alternatives.

TOWARD MORE RATIONAL DECISIONS: POLICY CONTROL GUIDELINES

Methods now exist to improve measurably the decision making in the criminal justice system. The methods we have in mind have come to be called guidelines and studies of their implementation and effects now are available for a variety of criminal justice decisions. Throughout subsequent chapters we will draw on the research bearing on the creation and use of decision guidelines to make more rational criminal justice decisions. But the term *guidelines* has many uses and we wish to restrict its meaning in this book to a specific method of policy control. Therefore we must define what we mean by guidelines.[2]

The decision policy models that we refer to as guidelines and which are described in subsequent chapters all have indispensable common features. The essential aspects of the general policy control method include:

1. A general policy for decision making, including a statement of the goals sought, articulated in explicit terms, within which individual case decisions are made.
2. Explicitly defined criteria for decision making, with the specific weights to be given to these criteria, also explicitly defined.
3. Within the general policy model, guidelines in the form of a chart (matrix or grid) are used in the process of arriving at a particular decision. The most important policy concerns, decided by those responsible for the decision-making policy, are reflected in the dimensions of the grid. In most models one axis reflects the seriousness of the offense and the other reflects characteristics of the offender. The intersection of the appropriate columns and rows for the two axes provides an expected decision for cases possessing the attributes used in classifications for the chart.

4. The guidelines grid is intended to structure the use of discretion but not eliminate it. There are two ways in which discretionary judgments are required of the decision maker:

   a. Some discretion must be exercised within the cells of the two-dimensional grid. For example, a range of sentence durations may be suggested within which a choice may be made.

   b. Considering the facts of each case, the decision maker is expected sometimes to reach a decision that is a departure (that is, an exception) from the suggested decision outcome.

5. When departures are made, the decision maker must provide explicit reasons for the exception from the usual decision for offenders or accused persons in the classification that applies.

6. There is an established system of monitoring to provide periodic feedback to the authorities responsible for the decision policy, giving the percentage of decisions falling outside each guideline category and the reasons given for these decisions.

7. The authorities may modify the guidelines at any time.

8. The general policy, including the guidelines incorporated within it, is not regarded as a "once and for all" statement of a "right" policy; rather, the policy statement and the procedures are designed to facilitate an evolutionary system of policy development changing in response to experience, resultant learning, and social change.

9. The policy in general, and the guidelines specifically, are open and available for public review, criticism, and debate.

These are general features of the policy control (guidelines) models we advocate. Additional features of similar models, which lead to variation among them, are not included in our list, since these features are not critical to the use of guidelines models. For example, models may and do differ as to whether they have been devised, at least initially, from research aimed at a description of current practice or whether they were constructed as a result of normative judgments as to desired policy (e.g., decisions of ethics and values and of the jurisprudence of sentencing). Both kinds of models already have been used with success in a variety of settings.

Examples of such guidelines and recent research bearing on their effectiveness will be presented throughout subsequent chapters. The most notable existing guideline models concern bail, sentencing, and parole decisions and therefore these chapters contain the most fully developed examples. Much of the justification for our advocacy of guidelines models comes from the research now available about how decisions are made in the criminal justice system, the focus of most of this book.

Applying the guidelines perspective to what is known about criminal justice decisions leads, in our final chapter, to the identification of ten requisites for increased rationality in criminal justice. We claim that rationality can be more nearly approached by increased attention to the specification of clear, consistent purposes; by the identification or invention of adequate alternatives; by the identification of more relevant information; by using adequately flexible decision policy structures; by mechanisms for the control of unbridled discretion; by differentiation of policy and case decision making; by development of explicit policy and decision rules; by provision of adequate feedback systems; by improved measurement and classification processes; and by the insistence on decision policy and procedures within a system for evolutionary development toward more rational decisions.

NOTES

1. In research literature about classification, this usually would be called *assignment* or *allocation,* reserving the word *classification* to refer to the allocation of initially undefined classes in such a way that individuals in a class are in the same sense similar or close to each other. See Cormack, 1971:321.
2. For a defense of this guidelines method and a summary of criticisms, see Gottfredson and Gottfredson (1984).

Chapter 2

THE VICTIM'S DECISION TO
REPORT A CRIME

The occurrence of a crime signals the potential involvement of the criminal justice process. It is the triggering mechanism for discretionary actions on the part of victims and possibly of criminal justice functionaries. These discretionary actions are the very basis of the criminal justice system (Remington *et al.*, 1969).

The occurrence of a crime is by no means a sufficient condition for the involvement of the criminal justice system. A series of decisions must take place before the criminal justice system becomes involved. First, the behavior in question must be noticed, and the decision to define it as a crime must be made. This discovery and definition may be made by a citizen (as a victim or a witness) or by the police. Second, someone must decide that the behavior in question is properly within the realm of the criminal justice system. Third, the decision to enter the event into the criminal justice process must be made. This chapter is concerned principally with this last decision, the decision to report a crime to the police. Only recently have studies become available that permit an examination of this decision. The earlier decisions of discovery and definition, although of great interest, have received less research attention.[1]

VICTIMS' DECISIONS TO INVOKE THE CRIMINAL
JUSTICE SYSTEM

The victim of criminal behavior may be the most influential of all criminal justice decision makers. By virtue of the decision as to whether or not to report a criminal victimization to the police, the victim is a principal "gatekeeper" of the entire criminal justice process. This is true especially for the crimes of common theft and assault.[2] In the overwhelming majority of cases, if the victim does not report the crime to the police, the event will not be dealt with by the criminal justice system. This generalization is supported by observational research on police behavior and by survey data on victimization. In a study of a large urban police department, for example, Reiss (1971) found that 95% of the criminal incidents known to the police came to their attention through citizen initiative.[3] The fact that the vast majority of crimes were not discovered by the police, but rather were reported to them, suggested to Reiss that urban policing is much more a reactive than a proactive process. Results from victimization surveys (discussed subsequently) also support the notion that victim behavior is the main determinant of input to the criminal justice system. When representative samples of the population were interviewed about their victimization experience, only 3% of the victimizations they reported as known to the police came to the attention of law enforcement because the police were on the scene (Hindelang and Gottfredson, 1976).

Victims thus serve as a preliminary filter for the crimes of common theft and assault with which the criminal justice process will be concerned. The cases that they report to the police may proceed through the system, although this is not certain. Numerous later decisions, each of which serves in turn as the filter for later decisions, are made about the case. But those cases not reported by victims to the police have almost no chance of proceeding through the process.

It is therefore difficult to overestimate the influence that these victimized decision makers have over the nature of the criminal justice process. The decision of the victim is obviously bound inextricably with the major questions and issues that confront the whole of society about the criminal justice system.

A moment's reflection will indicate that the victim's decision whether to report a crime may have considerable impact on the goals of the criminal justice system. One of the principal aims of the system, for example, often is thought to be general deterrence—the prevention of crime in the general population by the imposition of penalties on those committing criminal acts. Deterrence theorists typically argue that there are two important determinants of deterrence: the certainty and the severity of punishment. Clearly, the victim plays a vital role in relation to the concept of certainty. If the victim decides not to report a crime to the police, the probability of a sanction's being imposed upon the offender is reduced to nearly zero. Similarly, victims' discretion may influence critically the equity of the criminal justice system. If, all things being equal, some types of offenders are more likely to be brought to the attention of the police by victims than are other types, then, because all future decisions (for example, to arrest, to convict, to punish) are predicated on the victim's decision, equity is reduced. Thus, a study of how victims exercise their discretion to report crimes to the police has important implications for the attainment of equity in the process as a whole.

Other overall aims commonly ascribed to the criminal justice process might be analyzed similarly. Are victims' decisions made consistently with these goals? What factors appear to influence these decisions, and are they compatible with the goals of the process?

Apart from the gatekeeping influence of the victim's decision to report a crime, affecting the nature of the entire criminal justice process, the decision has critical implications also for the key participants in the system. For the victim, the decision has obvious importance. A report to the police clearly and authoritatively (although not irrevocably since the victim can decide later not to press charges) indicates that a situation has arisen in the life of the victim that is perceived as demanding official state recognition and action. It may be motivated by a desire on the victim's part for officially sanctioned retribution, by a more general sense of social obligation, or by hope of restitution. For many victims it signifies the beginning of an involvement with the various agencies within the criminal justice system—an involvement that may make substantial demands on the victim's time and resources.

Alternatively, the decision to report a crime to the police may be simply the perceived solution to an immediate crisis. In many cases a call to the police in and of itself may terminate a victimization in which the victim's only desire is to find a peaceful resolution (for example, in a domestic assault). Thus, rather than necessitating full processing through arrest and conviction, the consequence desired by the victim may be only the cessation of victimization. For still other victims, the decision to report to the police may be more a matter of practical concern. Many theft insurance policies, for example, require that the police be notified prior to the awarding of a claim.

Thus, a report to the police may reflect a feeling of societal obligation, a desire for retribution, or an effort to deal with a crisis. It may be a result of dispassionate assessment of the financial benefits that will accrue. It may be a combination of these.

The consequences of the decision for the victim, then, include the issue of how well these objectives actually were met: Was retribution satisfied? Was the immediate crisis resolved? Was the social obligation seen as fulfilled? The ultimate determination of the consequences important to the victim may turn, in part, on the activities and decisions of still other criminal justice actors: Did the police decide to proceed with the case? Was the accused convicted? Was the disposition seen by the victim as a just one? It may readily be seen that the question of the importance of the decision to victims is complicated, and it is one that might require a number of answers depending on the individual circumstances of the victim and the goals he or she is seeking to attain. It may also be seen that the research issues posed are formidable.

No less complex and difficult are the questions that may be raised by considering the societal consequences of victims' decisions. What are the implications for crime prevention, justice, and equity of this highly discretionary and extremely low visibility decision? Can a society that seeks lower levels of crime be satisfied by less than full reporting of crimes by victims when an unreported crime necessarily means an unapprehended offender? If crimes committed by some offenders, or some classes of offenders, are usually reported whereas others tend not to be, does this imply a corresponding reduction in equity and in justice?

Consider, however, the implications of full reporting of criminal victimization. Can an already overtaxed system of justice accommodate such an increase in the numbers of crimes reported to the police? Is justice truly better served if all events that can be brought to the attention of the police are reported to them?

As with the importance of the victim's decision for the victim and for the criminal justice system, the potential consequences to society depend in a large part on the characteristics of these decisions as they now are made. That is, in order to assess the effects of these decisions for the victim, for the criminal justice system, and for society it is necessary first to understand how the decisions are made.

CHARACTERISTICS OF THE DECISION TO REPORT A CRIME TO THE POLICE

Until quite recently, the victim's decision to report a crime was not regarded widely as a central component in the criminal justice process. Rather, considerable emphasis was placed on the police as initiators of the system.[4] Perhaps the single most important influence on viewing the victim, rather than the police, as the principal gatekeeper of the process was a development in the field of statistics, the victimization survey.

Although it has long been realized that not all crimes come to the attention of the police, until the advent of victimization surveys there were no systematic data available by which either the extent or the characteristics of crime unknown to the police could be assessed. In 1967, researchers working under the auspices of the President's Commission on Law Enforcement and Administration of Justice undertook a series of studies to determine the utility of assessing this "dark figure" of crime. They interviewed representative samples from the general population about criminal victimizations that those questioned had experienced, whether or not the persons interviewed had reported them to the police. These early surveys and subsequent similar ones revealed that a very large proportion of the victimizations reported to the interviewers had not been reported to the police. For many kinds of crime, over half had not been reported. These surveys demonstrated that, for whatever reason, a vast number of victims of crimes of theft and assault decided not to invoke the criminal justice process.

Since these early victimization surveys there has been a good deal of developmental work on the method. In 1972 the United States Bureau of the Census began a program to produce annual estimates of criminal victimization for the nation.[5] This project is referred to as the National Crime Survey (NCS).

In these surveys a multistage cluster sampling is used to select representative samples of Americans twelve years old or older. They are asked questions about common assault and theft victimizations that they may have experienced during the six months before the interview. About 130,000 persons are interviewed each year. The responses are then weighted (according to a commonly used procedure) to yield national estimates for the year. These data give the basis for the best available estimates of the extent to which victims of certain crimes, in exercising their discretion, decided not to invoke the criminal process. Also, they provide some clues to the ways in which this discretion is exercised.

Some results from the National Crime Survey are displayed in Figures 1 and 2. These data show, for a ten-year period, the proportion of victimizations of various types that the victim says were not reported to the police. Three important facts are apparent. First, large numbers of crimes go unreported every year; for some kinds of crime over half are not reported. Second, different forms of crime have different rates of reporting. Vehicle theft is much more likely to be reported to the police than is, say, larceny. Third, the nonreporting rates are relatively stable from year to year.

Two other important results should be noted. In general, victimi-

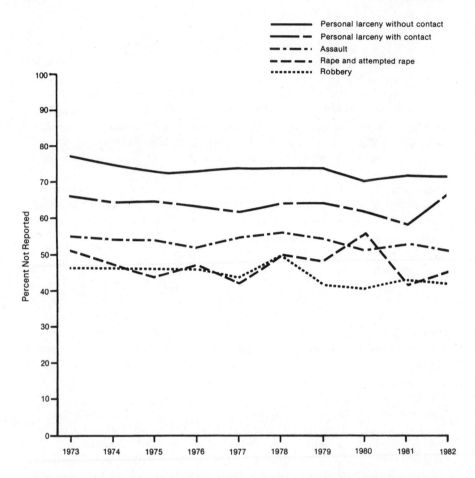

FIGURE 1. Estimated percent of personal victimizations not reported to the police, by type of victimization, United States, 1973–1982. SOURCE: This figure was constructed by the *Sourcebook* staff from data provided by the U.S. Department of Justice, Bureau of Justice Statistics.

zations of businesses are more likely to be reported to the police than are either personal or household victimizations. And completed crimes are more likely to be reported than are those merely attempted.

The vast number of unreported crimes demonstrates the critical role of the victim's decision and raises the question of the major influences on the decision. Studies of victim discretion have used essentially two

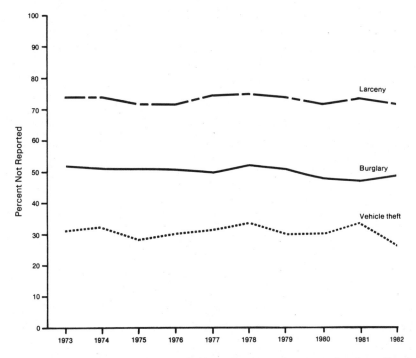

FIGURE 2. Estimated percent of household victimizations not reported to the police, by type of victimization, United States, 1973–1982. SOURCE: This figure was constructed by the *Sourcebook* staff from data provided by the U.S. Department of Justice, Bureau of Justice Statistics.

methods in seeking answers to this question. The first has been to ask victims directly why they did or did not report their victimization to the police. The second has been to study various aspects of the victimization—characteristics of the victim, the offender, and the event—as they relate to whether the victimization was reported to the police.

REASONS FOR NOT CALLING THE POLICE

Data from the 1981 National Crime Survey on the reasons that victims gave for not reporting their crime to the police are summarized in Table 1. In general, the reasons most often given for not reporting a crime to the police are that "nothing could be done" and "victimization not important enough." One-fifth of the survey-reported rapes, nearly two-fifths of the robberies, three-fifths of the larcenies, and one-half of

TABLE 1. Percentage of Victimizations Not Reported to the Police, by Reason for Not Reporting

	Private/ personal matter	Nothing could be done/lack of proof	Not important enough	Reported to some- one else	Police wouldn't want to be bothered	Too incon- venient	Fear of reprisal	All other reasons	Not given
Crimes of violence									
Rape	35%[a]	18%	4%	8%	–%[b]	2%	16%	42%	2%
Robbery	15	21	15	9	9	6	7	39	5
Aggravated assault	31	10	22	11	7	3	5	22	4
Simple assault	32	8	30	14	7	2	3	14	3
Crimes of theft									
Burglary	9	23	23	7	10	2	1	44	2
Larceny	8	23	39	3	10	2	1	32	2
Motor vehicle theft	12	18	16	8	8	3	—	52	1

SOURCE: Bureau of Justice Statistics National Crime Survey, 1981.
[a] Percentages add to more than 100% for each type of crime because some people gave more than one reason for not reporting.
[b] 0 or less than 0.5%.

the household burglaries that were not reported to the police were not reported, according to the victims, because the victims believed that "nothing could be done" or that it was "not important enough."

There is some revealing variation in the reasons that people gave for not reporting their victimizations to the police. For some types of crime, most notably rape and assault, a large proportion of victims who did not report the event to the police explained that the victimization was a "a private matter." "Fear of reprisal" (although infrequently given as a reason for not reporting to the police generally) was cited in nearly one in six rapes.

It would be easy to infer too much from these reasons given by victims for not calling the police. The data reflected in Table 1 are subject to the numerous limitations involved in the survey method used. These include problems in sampling and in the accuracy of recall. They concern issues about the willingness of respondents to participate and the sensitivity of the subject matter.[6] These categories of reasons for not reporting a crime are, moreover, rather broad and ambiguous. For example, "nothing could be done" has several possible interpretations. After an assault, for instance, giving this reason may reflect the victim's belief that the physical harm done cannot be rectified. Alternatively, it may be based on his or her belief that an unknown assailant, whom the victim might not be able to identify could not be apprehended. The response "police wouldn't want to be bothered" may mean that the victimization was so minor that the victim was reluctant to request police involvement; on the other hand, it could mean that the victim believed that the police would simply be uninterested in his or her victimization, even if it were relatively serious. Also, "victimization was reported to someone else" may have various meanings. Perhaps it was reported to a representative of a different social agency, such as a private security guard or a teacher. Maybe it was reported to a friend or relative who, it was believed, would take matters into his or her own hands. Finally, the "other" category contains a large proportion of the reasons given, indicating that more refinement of the response categories would be informative.

These data on the reasons given by victims of crime for not reporting the event to the police are nevertheless informative as to how this discretion may be exercised. Many victims apparently believed that the crime was not worthy of official state action either because it was seen by the victim as not being important or because the victim perceived the police as being uninterested. Thus, it may be that victims frequently divert from the criminal justice system what they perceive as relatively trivial victimizations. The fact that attempted crimes are less often reported to the police than are completed crimes is consistent with this interpretation (Hindelang and Gottfredson, 1976). Many other victims claimed that they did not report their victimizations to the police because it was not appropriate to do so; the event was not seen as one falling properly into the realm of official recognition and sanction. Many victimizations were "reported to someone else," or they were considered to be "private matters." Thus, in dealing with many of these events, the victims chose either to ignore them (an important decision outcome) or to use nonlegal mechanisms. Included are a sizable proportion of the rapes and attempted rapes and assaults that were not reported to the police. Thus, although the data reviewed thus far suggest that victims' discretion operates largely on the basis of the perceived worthiness of bringing the event to the attention of the police, a sizable proportion do not do so because it is seen as an inappropriate response.

Hindelang (1976) studied the ways in which these reported reasons for failing to report a crime to the police were related to the nature of the crime, to the characteristics of the victim, and to the victim–offender relationship. For crimes between strangers, compared with those between nonstrangers, the reason for not reporting the crime was more likely to be that "nothing could be done." For crimes between non-strangers, the reason given for not reporting was more likely to be that it was a "private matter." Victims of completed crimes (and victims of crimes involving weapons) were less likely than victims of crimes only attempted to give as a reason for not reporting that it was "not important."

It might reasonably be expected that such characteristics of the victims as age, race, sex, or income would be related to the reasons given for not reporting the crime to the police. Hindelang found, however, that once the type of victimization was taken into account, they generally were not. The implication appears to be that the nature of the harm suffered by a victim of crime determines the victim's decision more than these classifications. He did find, however, that the victim–offender relationship conditions, to some extent, the reason for failing to report. Not surprisingly, people victimized by acquaintances are more apt to view the event as a private matter than as a public concern; but people victimized by strangers often believe that the police will be unable to do anything about it anyway.

Unfortunately, most research on the reasons for the invocation of the criminal justice process by victims is based on the reasons given for not calling the police. Seldom have victims who have reported the event to the police been asked why they did so. One exception is a study by Smith and Maness (1976) who, in a telephone survey of eighty-eight burglary victims, found that the reason most frequently given for reporting the burglary was that it was an "obligation." The authors interpreted this as a "sense of civic duty," citing some of the responses placed in this category as: "It's just the first thing you do"; "It's the proper thing to do"; "It's the natural thing to do"; and "It's the only way we can have law and order."

Other responses in the same survey had more distinctively personal utilitarian implications. About a third (32%) said they had called the police in order to "catch the person," 23% to "recover property," and 27% for "personal protection."

These data suggest that for many victims the decision to report a crime to the police may be influenced more by a sort of personal cost–benefit analysis than by a more general sense of social obligation. Is the time and energy required by reporting the event worth the benefit received by way of insurance money, freedom from continued victimization by the offender, or personal retribution? National Crime Survey robbery data on the relation between reporting to the police and whether the victim was covered by theft insurance, displayed in Table 2, lend some support to this cost–benefit notion. There is a strong association between insurance coverage and reporting to the police. Eighty-five percent of the robbery victims with theft insurance reported it to the police, but only 51% of those without it did so. Skogan (1984) reports similar data from the NCS and for victimization surveys from other countries.

There is another category of events that may fall within such a cost–benefit explanation, but here few data are available. These are crimes

TABLE 2. Robbery Victimizations Reported
and Not Reported to the Police, by Insurance
Coverage, United States, 1973–1977

Theft insurance[a]	Reported to police	
	No[b]	Yes
No	49% (1,163,564)	51% (1,810,863)
Yes	15% (53,705)	85% (304,347)

SOURCE: Analysis of data tapes from the National Crime Survey, Household Portion, 1973–1977.
[a] Excludes victims who responded "Don't know" to the question, "Was there any insurance against theft?"
[b] Includes victims who responded "No" and "Don't know" to the question, "Were the police informed of this incident in any way?"

for which the victim either shares some culpability or was breaking a law or social norm at the time of victimization. In these cases, the victim may be subject either to legal action or to great embarrassment should the crime be brought to the attention of the authorities. Some "victim-precipitated" assaults may fall into this category, as may some victimizations that take place during a "victimless crime." Examples of the latter would include "johns" robbed by prostitutes, homosexuals assaulted by their partners, drug dealers robbed and beaten by their customers, and illegal abortions resulting in harm to the women. It frequently has been suggested that the low probability of the victim's reporting such crimes to the police, which makes the offender virtually immune from the law, increases the frequency of their occurrences (Humphreys, 1970).

CORRELATES OF THE DECISION TO CALL THE POLICE

There now have been several studies of the correlates of calling the police using victimization survey data. The survey approach to studying this problem probably is preferable, for the crimes of common theft and assault, to alternative methods for several reasons.

First and foremost, the general population survey has the goal of obtaining representative samples of the population upon which to base estimates. Of course, such a goal is an ideal seldom achieved fully in practice. For the National Crime Surveys, some sampling biases are known to exist, but they probably are much less severe than the biases typically encountered in other procedures such as observational methods.

Second, with the survey method it is possible to ensure that standard instruments are used, in order to enhance the reliability of responses. For the National Crime Surveys, the reliability of responses is known to be very high (Hindelang, Gottfredson, and Garofalo, 1978).

Third, given the relative infrequency of victimization, extremely large sample sizes are required to obtain sufficient numbers of victimizations so that the correlates of calling the police can be determined reliably. For example, for 1976, it is estimated that the rate (per 1,000 persons twelve years old or older) in the United States for personal robbery was 7 and for assault it was 25. Clearly, large retrospective samples using general survey techniques are required to study the correlates of such statistically rare phenomena.

The surveys of the ways in which victims exercise their discretion to call the police are, however, certainly not without some shortcomings. These problems fall into two rather general categories related to potential response biases and to the scope of coverage.

Response bias refers to the circumstances in which, for a variety of reasons, the answers given by the respondent are not valid. The various response biases involved in the National Crime Survey (NCS) have been reviewed by Hindelang, Gottfredson, and Garofalo (1976) and Skogan (1981). They include such phenomena as memory effects and questionable veracity of responses. Perhaps the most important known bias is the apparent inability in these surveys to elicit many instances of assault. The evidence suggests that this inability is related to the victim–offender relationship. Assaults between nonstrangers are less likely to be identified in the survey than are other types of crime.

The victimization surveys are limited in their scope of coverage to the personal crimes of rape, robbery, assault, and theft; to the household crimes of burglary and theft; and to the business crimes of burglary and robbery. Other forms of crime—such as employee crime, consumer fraud, and victimless crimes—are not feasible targets for the survey approach, because the victim either will not or cannot report the event to an interviewer. For example, many consumer fraud victims are unaware of their victimization, a situation that makes the survey approach unsuitable. As a consequence, the best available information on the ways victims use their discretion to notify the authorities of crime is for the crimes of common theft and assault, and very little is known about other forms of crime.

One of the major dimensions on which reporting to the police varies is the nature of the offense suffered by the victim. In general, the more serious the crime, in terms of greater bodily harm or financial loss, the more likely is the event to be brought to the attention of the police. Thus, victims of completed crimes are more likely to call the police than are victims of attempted crimes, victims of aggravated assault are more likely to call the police than are victims of simple assault, and so on. The gravity of the harm done to the victim serves as a major determinant in the decision to invoke the criminal justice process. This can be inferred from most of the studies that have investigated the issue. For example, Gottfredson (1976) analyzed data on an estimated 208,000 personal victimizations in the NCS city surveys and found that factors associated with the concept of gravity of harm were the best predictors in the data of whether the police were called. When a weapon was involved in the incident (particularly, a gun), when the victim was injured (particularly, seriously), and when there was financial loss to the victim (particularly, great loss), the likelihood of a call to the police increased. When these factors were found to be present in a victimization in combination, the probability of a report to the police was very high.

Regardless of the type of crime, elements of the offense that increased the gravity of the harm to the victim were found by Hindelang

(1976) to be associated with the decision to call the police. He analyzed victim reporting to the police within specific crime categories, and this general result held not only for personal victimizations but for the household crimes of burglary and larceny and the business crimes of burglary and robbery as well. As was found in Gottfredson's study, when elements that increased the gravity of the harm to the victim (such as weapons, amount of loss, or assault) were present in an offense in combination, the probability of a call to the police increased within each type of crime.

Similar findings on the relation between the seriousness of the victimization and the probability that it would be reported to the police were reported by Schneider, Burcart, and Wilson (1976). Using data from a small victim survey in Portland, Oregon, conducted in 1974, they scaled the victimizations according to the Sellin–Wolfgang (1964) seriousness index. (This index was derived, using magnitude estimation procedures, to permit the ranking of crimes according to estimates of their seriousness.) They reported that "the seriousness of the crime is one of the most important factors explaining why some crimes are reported and others are not" (1976:97). Of the crimes categorized as of "low seriousness," only 24% were reported to the police, whereas of those classified as of "high seriousness," 80% were reported. Similar results have been reported by Ennis (1967) and Bloch (1974) from their analysis of the survey data from the President's Commission on Law Enforcement and the Administration of Justice, by Sparks and his colleagues in a survey conducted in London (1977), and in the British Crime Survey by Hough and Mayhew (1983).

Aggregating three years of the National Crime Survey national data on personal crimes, Gottfredson and Hindelang (1979a) classified all of the victimizations reported in the survey according to the Sellin–Wolfgang seriousness scale. They also found an association between seriousness and the report of the event to the police. For the four categories of seriousness used, the percentage of victimizations reported to the police ranged from 38% for the least serious events to 74% for the most serious.

Skogan (1984) reviewed the evidence about reporting crimes to the police that is available from victimization surveys conducted in many different countries, including the United States. His main conclusion was that

> most of the explainable variance in reporting is related directly to characteristics of the incident. Whether an offense was completed or only attempted, if there was an injury or financial loss, and other elements of seriousness are by far the strongest predictors of reporting. (1984:120)

Results like these have been confirmed for incidents of spousal violence. Berk and colleagues (1984) studied about 200 victims in spouse abuse shelters and victim assistance programs. Despite the obvious potential for selection bias in such samples, they discovered that nearly half did not report a call to the police (either by themselves or by a bystander). The important factors in these calls appeared to be the seriousness of the incident, past spousal assaults, and the presence of other relatives.

CHARACTERISTICS OF THE VICTIM

Other things being equal, are some victims more likely to notify the police than are others? This question bears directly on the issues of victim decisions and general criminal justice system goals. Are some kinds of victims—perhaps because of fear or distrust of the police or because of an inability or unwillingness to take the time to comply with the demands made by the criminal justice system that attend reporting a crime— substantially less likely to invoke the criminal process by calling the police? If so, is equity, from the standpoint of these victims at least, reduced? Does differential access to the criminal justice system imply a differential general deterrent effect? Because the decision to call the police determines so substantially the nature and the effects of the entire criminal justice process, it is important to know whether some classes of victims are less likely to invoke the law when victimized. Two broad groups of victim characteristics have been studied to determine whether they are associated with the decision to report a crime. In this section we examine some results of studies of demographic variables such as age, sex, and race. In the next section, we will discuss attitudinal variables, such as attitudes toward the police.[7]

Hindelang's study of the National Crime Survey city data showed that there were slight associations between demographic characteristics of the victim and reporting to the police. For personal crimes, whites were slightly less likely to report the offense to the police than were blacks and other minority group members (44% versus 50%), and younger persons were less likely to report the offense than were older persons (54% for persons sixty-five or older versus 33% for persons twelve to nineteen years old). Males were less likely to report the offense than were females (42% versus 51%).

Hindelang recognized that these differences in reporting may be a result of differences in the types of victimization experienced by these groups. He therefore analyzed the data for the relations between demographic characteristics and the decision to report the crime, controlling for the type of crime experienced by the victim. The relation between the victim's age and reporting to the police generally maintained when this was done. That is, the proportion reported to the police increased as age increased. When age and type of victimization were controlled, however, racial differences in reporting behavior were inconsistent. When racial differences did exist, sometimes whites and sometimes blacks and other minority group members were more likely to call the police. On the other hand, when controls for age and type of victimization were introduced, men generally were less likely to call the police then were women—often markedly so.

The relation between victim characteristics and the decision to report a crime was analyzed by Gottfredson and Hindelang (1979) using the NCS national data aggregated for the years 1974–1976. These data provided an estimated eighteen million personal victimizations for analysis. This study involved an examination of victim characteristics at both the individual and the community level, controlling for the seriousness of the victimization.

They found little relation between the victim's family income and reporting to the police. That is, roughly the same proportion of crimes were reported to the police for the poor as for the wealthy. The same was found to be true on the community level. They categorized the respondents according to the wealth of the neighborhood in which they lived and found little difference in the proportions of crimes reported to the police in wealthy compared with poor neighborhoods.

Similarly, there was only a slight difference in the proportions of crimes reported to the police according to whether the victim was victimized by a stranger or by someone known to the victim. The proportions of reported crimes done by strangers was 48%; for nonstranger crimes it was 42%.

They also examined the proportions of crimes reported to the police across differing levels of urbanization. Again, little difference in the rate of reporting was found, although as population density increased, the proportion reported decreased.

Various other associations were studied. Married victims were more likely than the never married to call the police. Employment status was not related to the decision. There was a slight association between education and reporting: the more education, the more likely the event was to be reported to the police.

By far the strongest correlate of the decision to call the police was the seriousness of the crime experienced by the victim. Across all victim characteristics studied, the seriousness of the crime (as measured by the

Sellin–Wolfgang seriousness scale) maintained a moderately strong relation to reporting to the police. Judging by victimization surveys, demographic and social characteristics of victims appear to play little role in the decision to call the police. Skogan (1984:124) has succinctly summarized the evidence:

> A consistent finding of victim surveys is that crime reporting is relatively independent of the personal attributes of victims. Within major crime categories there are few impressive differences between blacks and whites, men and women, or high- and low-income families, in the extent to which they mobilize the police when victimized. Nonreporting also is not particularly related to the size or type of community in which victims live. One might expect crime reporting to be higher in urban areas, where informal mechanisms of social control are weaker and the police are often relied upon to regulate conflict and resolve disputes. However, Laub (1981) found no important differences between reporting rates by type of crime in urban, suburban, and rural jurisdictions.

ATTITUDES TOWARD THE POLICE AND THE DECISION TO REPORT A CRIME

If the victim of a crime of common theft or assault does not report the event to the police, it is unlikely that the crime will be processed through the criminal justice system. We therefore have stressed that the victim is an important gatekeeper to the system. The studies discussed thus far suggest that this critical reporting decision depends substantially upon some characteristics of the victimization.

An important concern of the criminal justice system is embedded in the concept of equal access to the law. The studies so far reviewed can be regarded as preliminary assessments of the extent to which equal access to the police is achieved. From this perspective it is reassuring to find that there is relatively little variability in reporting to the police that is associated with victim characteristics studied thus far. When differences exist, further research is needed to determine their origins, but some plausible hypotheses might be advanced. For example, the disproportionate underreporting by men relative to women might be explained by differential sex role socialization that encourages males in our society to handle their own problems. And the inverse relation between age and reporting to the police may be a result of the availability of alternative social control mechanisms for handling disputes among younger people, such as those provided by school authorities and parents.

One important victim characteristic that may have some bearing on the notion of equal access to the law is the victim's attitude toward the police. Do people who fear or mistrust the police or those who have had negative experiences with the police fail to report their crimes more often than those without these attitudes or experiences? The issue was posed directly by the President's Commission on Law Enforcement and Administration of Justice (1967:144): "People hostile to the police are not so likely to report violations of the law, even when they are victims . . . yet citizen assistance is crucial to law enforcement agencies if the police are to solve an appreciable portion of the crimes that are committed." If some segments of society are markedly distrustful or suspicious of the police or simply believe them to be ineffective and if these attitudes are manifested in lower rates of reporting to the police, then clearly, the goal of equal access will not be met.

The ways in which the attitudes of victims of personal crimes were associated with the decision to report the crime were studied by Garofalo (1977), using the National Crime Survey city data. He focused on the responses given to the question, Would you say, in general, that your local police are doing a good job, an average job, or a poor job? The findings were similar to those of other public opinion surveys. There was little variation in responses to this question, with most people giving their local police favorable ratings. (The exceptions to this general finding are that blacks and other minority group members and young people tend to give somewhat less favorable ratings.) Garofalo found that these evaluations of the police were not related to recent victimization experiences. Moreover, it was found (as seen in Table 3) that the overall ratings of police performance in the cities studied were not strongly related to whether or not a victim reported the crime to the police. As Table 3 shows (row percentages), Garofalo found only minor variation in the proportion of crimes reported to the police being associated with the victim's ratings of the police. Referring to the similarity in the column percentages for each level of police rating, Garofalo reported (1977:31) that, "given the close correspondence between these two response distributions, apparently we can discount the possibility that the experience of contact with the police, that results when a victimization is reported to them, has any significant effect on subsequent ratings of the police."

Because he had found that ratings of police varied systematically by race and age, Garofalo analyzed these same data within age and race categories. His results were much the same. When, however, the data were analyzed according to the seriousness of the crime (as measured by the Sellin–Wolfgang scale), an interesting pattern was revealed. For victimizations of moderate and great seriousness there was no association between the victim's attitude toward the police and whether the

TABLE 3. Proportions of Personal Victimizations Reported and Not Reported to the Police by the Victim's Rating of the Police, 1975 National Crime Survey: City Surveys

Rating of police[a]		Reported (percentage)	Not reported (percentage)	Estimated number[b]
Positive	1	51[c]	49	(71,671)
		8[d]	7	
	2	49	51	(279,608)
		31	29	
	3	46	54	(362,257)
		38	40	
Negative	4	47	53	(223,173)
		24	24	
Estimated number[b]		(446,709)	(490,000)	(936,709)

SOURCE: Garofalo (1977: Table 16).
[a] Respondents who did not expresss an opinion on the evaluation of police performance question were not given a scale score.
[b] Estimated number of victimizations.
[c] Row percentages.
[d] Column percentages.

victim reported the incident to the police; but for victimization with low seriousness scores, there was a consistent increase in the proportion of events reported to the police as the rating of the police grew more favorable.

A somewhat different approach to the assessment of the relation between attitudes and the decision to report a crime was taken by Schneider and her associates (1976). They administered a series of opinion questions in conjunction with a victimization survey in Portland. Unlike the NCS (which provided the data analyzed by Garofalo), the questions asked were quite specific. Thus, for the scale they named "Trust in Police" they asked the victims whether the police would give serious attention to their complaints, treat them as well as others, believe them, and try to find out who committed the crime, and they also asked victims about their general attitude toward the police. They also collected data on their respondents' perceptions of police–community relations, police effectiveness, and attitudes toward the courts.

Schneider also found a substantial relation between the seriousness of the victimization and reporting to the police. This relation generally was maintained regardless of the victim's reported trust in the police or perception of police–community relations, police effectiveness, or attitude toward the courts.

As Garofalo found, Schneider *et al.* reported that the attitudinal items were somewhat more highly correlated with the reporting decisions for the least serious crimes than for the most serious crimes. In their study of spousal violence, Berk *et al.* (1984) found no influence for a variety of attitudinal measures on whether the police were called.

Thus, it consistently has been found that, overall, demographic characteristics of victims (whether measured at the individual or the aggregate level) are less strongly correlated with the decision to report a crime than is some measure of the gravity of the crime. Similarly, a consistent finding has been that the influence of attitudes on reporting may depend on the nature of the crime experienced by the victim. The implication is that for the victim of a crime of relatively low "seriousness," factors other than the nature of the harm itself may become influential in the decision to report to the police, whereas when the harm done to the victim is grave, then characteristics of the victim play a much less influential role.

REPORTING DECISIONS FOR OTHER FORMS OF CRIME

Victimization surveys, which provide the best available data about the reporting decisions of victims, unfortunately do not include many important forms of criminal activity. In large part this is a limitation of the method. It is simply not feasible to employ retrospective surveys to uncover victimizations of certain types. And for crimes of which the victim is unaware of victimization (for example, consumer fraud), the method obviously is not valid. Thus, for many forms of crime we do not have the essential basis needed for study of this crucial decision. We may know how many and what types of events are reported to the police, but we lack data on those that occurred but were not reported. In view of the vast numbers of crimes that do go unreported, inferences about the decision-making process made only from data on the reported group are extremely hazardous.

One exception to this bleak state of ignorance is found in the case of shoplifting, about which some clever and interesting research has been done. Shoplifting differs from the crimes already discussed in that the victim is an organization rather than an individual. It is also a crime of extremely low visibility. It often is not known whether inventory losses are due to shoplifting, employee theft, delivery fraud, or simply poor inventory accountability.

It might be thought that when an organization rather than an individual is the victim of criminal behavior there would be less discretion exercised about informing the police. Studies of police referral of apprehended shoplifters indicate, however, that this is not the case. Hindelang (1974) obtained the records of a security firm that serviced retail stores by keeping track of the persons apprehended for shoplifting in the area. Staff of the participating stores filled out a form that included information about the shoplifter, the type of goods stolen and their value, and whether a police referral was made. By studying these records, Hindelang was able to determine the factors most highly predictive of a call to the police once an apprehension had been made by store employees. Studying the records of more than 6,000 apprehended shoplifters during a three-year period, he found that only 26% had been reported to the police. Thus, even for the case of organizational victims, these data indicated that discretion about invoking the criminal justice process is large, with remarkable consequences.

A large array of factors about the shoplifter (such as age, sex, race), the merchandise stolen (for example, type and retail value), and the method of shoplifting (including under clothing, price switching, professional) were available for analysis. By far the apparently most influential variable in the decision to call the police was the value of the stolen property. Of secondary importance were what was stolen (stealing liquor tended to be reported more often), who stole it (men and older persons were more likely to be reported), and how it was stolen. The ability of these few factors to discriminate between those who were referred to the police and those who were not was remarkable. Hindelang's multivariate analyses show, for example, that shoplifters who stole articles of small value (not liquor and less than $1.90) under their clothes were referred to the police only 10% of the time, whereas those who stole fresh meat of a large value under their clothes were referred to the police 85% of the time.

The possible emphasis on the value of the shoplifted merchandise as a criterion for referral to the police is consistent with the importance of offense seriousness as already discussed. That is, the value of the merchandise may be taken as an indicant of the gravity of harm. Hindelang (1974:590–591) offered some plausible explanations for the other apparent criteria:

> It is likely that the interpretation placed on the act of theft by the store personnel plays an important role in moderating the probability of referral to the police. For example, if the items stolen are those which the store personnel believe are to be resold—liquor, cigarettes, and perhaps fresh meat—they may take a firmer position in favor of referral. Similarly, if the items stolen are viewed by the store personnel as items which are not essential to survival.

The method of shoplifting may also be considered by the store personnel to verify intent. For example, although one may absentmindedly or temporarily place a small object in a coat pocket while one continues to shop, or may pick up an object that has an incorrect price tag affixed to it, it is unlikely that placing an object under one's clothes or into another bag could be construed as accidental.

In a similar study of shoplifting referrals, Cohen and Stark (1974) studied 371 case history records completed by store detectives in a large department store in Los Angeles. (This study thus differed somewhat from Hindelang's work. Whereas the referrals to the police in Hindelang's data were made largely by store employees, such as clerks and managers, the Cohen and Stark data were derived from private security guards.) Again, the question investigated was whether the apprehended shoplifter was turned over to the police or released. The amount of discretion exercised was again vast, with over half the apprehended shoplifters not reported to the police. A wide range of attributes of the shoplifters and of the offenses was studied in an effort to determine the principal determinants of the police referral decision. For the most part, the characteristics of the shoplifter (such as sex and race) were not found to be strongly related to the decision. The one major exception was employment. Unemployed shoplifters were referred more often, other things constant, than were those who were employed. The interpretation of this finding offered by Cohen and Stark was that the store detectives might perceive that unemployed shoplifters are more apt to be persons who steal for a living and hence pose threats in the future, whereas the employed may be only occasional thieves.

The value of the shoplifted merchandise again proved to be a strong correlate of the decision to call the police. Shoplifters stealing less than thirty dollars worth of goods were referred to the police only a third of the time, whereas those stealing more than thirty dollars worth were referred three-fourths of the time.

Hindelang's study was replicated by Lundman (1978) on a sample of 664 shoplifting cases from the records of a nationwide department store chain. In these stores, as in the Cohen and Stark study, the referrals were made by security personnel rather than regular store employees. Similar data about the shoplifters, their methods, and the merchandise stolen were collected. Again, the retail value of the shoplifted goods was the single strongest correlate of the decision to call the police. When the amount of the theft was taken into consideration, the shoplifter's sex was unrelated to police referral, but the shoplifter's age and race were associated with the decision to report. Older persons and non-whites were more likely to be referred than younger persons and whites. Lundman's (1978:400) conclusion was that

> [a]lthough offender characteristics are important, the seriousness of the alleged offense is clearly the most critical determinant of whether or not an

apprehended shoplifter is referred to the police. Whatever the exact magnitude of the contributions of offender characteristics to the decision to refer, they occur within limits imposed by the seriousness of the offense.

There are, of course, many plausible interpretations for the consistent finding that the single strongest correlate of the decision of shoplifting victims to call the police is the value of the stolen merchandise. It may reflect the desire to focus on professional thieves, who may be expected to steal items of larger value. Or it may be believed that the occasional shoplifter will be deterred by the apprehension itself, and it may be thought that the costs to the store in time and money associated with prosecution might therefore be avoided. The number of persons apprehended for shoplifting would make universal referral and prosecution prohibitively costly. Thus, there is a practical need to screen the cases and refer only those thought necessary. The value of the shoplifted articles may be a useful indicant of necessity in the sense of preventing professional thefts. Other decision criteria can be inferred from these studies. There appears to be a clear reluctance to refer young offenders to the police for shoplifting and a preference to refer those with a prior record of shoplifting. Also, the fear of lawsuits apparently leads some stores to refer all those apprehended shoplifters who refuse to sign a confession.

Apart from these few studies, knowledge about how nonstreet crime victims decide to invoke the law is very meager. A large gap in knowledge exists in the are of consumer fraud. The lack of reliable data about consumer fraud generally, not even indicating the scope and characteristics of the problem, contributes to our ignorance of the factors influencing victims' decisions to invoke the law. Consumers may complain about suspected fraudulent activities to various authorities (such as to the police, to better business bureaus, to newspaper columns, or to consumer complaint offices of attorneys general), and this makes compilation of accurate data difficult.

One of the major difficulties faced by victims of consumer fraud is that they, like those responsible for enforcing the law, may have great difficulty distinguishing fraud from aggressive business practices. Thus, the victim of consumer fraud may face ambiguity, unlikely for victims of armed robbery, in deciding whether an event is indeed a crime and thus merits reporting to the police or other agencies.

There is some evidence that among those who do report fraudulent business practices the desire for restitution rather than punishment predominates (Steel, 1975). That is, victims complaining of consumer fraud generally want their money back or the product repaired satisfactorily, rather than wanting the offending business punished in some way.

There are indications that knowledge or ignorance of the appropriate legal channels plays a large role in who reports consumer frauds. Thus, studies generally find that it is members of the middle class who most often report consumer fraud to the authorities (Steele, 1975), although some have suggested that the poor are most often its victims (Caplovitz, 1967).

Victims of crimes that occur within the context of the victim's participation in criminal activity may be the least likely to be reported to the police. Obviously, however, few data are available that permit study of the question. It is not uncommon for police departments to receive reports of robberies and assaults from customers of prostitutes or from prostitutes themselves, but most such occurrences undoubtedly go unreported because of the victim's fear of embarrassment or criminal prosecution. Similarly, it is not uncommon for such complaining victims to fail to follow up on prosecution.

The interesting issue of those persons who suddenly decide to report the ongoing criminal activities in which they themselves or their colleagues are engaged—the so-called whistle blowers—is also in need of study. There are documented cases of such activities in many walks of life: government bureaucrats involved in kickback schemes, organized crime figures, doctors involved in organized Medicaid frauds, and "customers" of illegal gambling and drug operations. The forces that lead a person who is implicated in ongoing criminal activity to report the activity are in need of study.

THE DECISION TO REPORT A CRIME: SOME IMPLICATIONS OF THE EVIDENCE

The studies reviewed in this chapter demonstrate quite convincingly that the citizen's exercise of discretion as to whether to notify the police of a crime profoundly circumscribes the cases that will serve as the basis for all of the subsequent criminal justice decisions.[8] All of these data strongly reinforce the assertion at the beginning of this chapter of the impact of the victim's decision to report a crime. The vast discretion exercised by citizens in invoking the law plays a central role in the definition of the goals of the criminal justice process and in their achievement. It is clear form the evidence that the criminal justice system depends on the selection by the victims of crime of the cases and persons that will flow through the system and that a good deal of selection does go on. For many forms of criminal processing the criminal justice system begins with victim initiative. Thus, all of the issues of interest in this book that may be raised about criminal justice decision making must be raised also about this fundamental trigger event to the application of the law.

It is important, therefore, that the limitations of our knowledge about victim decisions be underscored. Although the victimization surveys provide us with some hitherto unavailable information about how the victim's discretion to report a crime is exercised, there are many problems in using the results from that method for this purpose. Not all victimizations that occur are reported to the survey interviewers, and it is known that some types may be less likely to be reported to the interviewers than others. Crimes between people known or related to each other (such as child abuse and assaults between spouses) are probably underrepresented in such surveys. Also, some events reported to the interviewers may not in fact be crimes, and there is undoubtedly some degree of invalidity in answers to the question about whether the event was reported to the police. Although there has been some study of the reasons victims give for not invoking the law, there is very little evidence that bears directly on why victims did choose to call the police. Less yet is known about whether, after calling the police, they were satisfied with their decision. Finally, it must be stressed that the information available about the decisions of victims of common theft and assault is very great when compared to the nearly absent information about the decisions of victims of other forms of criminal activity.

The issues raised by the vast exercise of victim discretion are fundamental to the criminal justice system. As Reiss (1971:70) puts it, "citizens may be regarded as enforcers or non-enforcers of the law and its moral order . . . at issue, are the questions of when is one obligated to call the police and what are the consequences of citizen discretion for moral order." An answer to these questions might best be addressed by an analysis of the victim's decision in terms of the three essential components of rational decisions discussed in Chapter 1—goals, information, and alternatives.

GOALS OF THE VICTIM

The evidence suggests that the goals sought by victims in relation to their decisions to report a crime are many, that any one decision may embody several of them, and that there is a considerable likelihood that many of these goals may conflict with those of other key criminal justice decision makers. Subsequent chapters will demonstrate that a growing body of literature exists addressing the goals of others in the system, but almost no attention has been given either to the theoretical goals of the victim as a decision maker or to the ways in which these goals may be compatible or in conflict with the goals of other criminal justice decision makers.

In attempting to identify the salient goals of victim reporting it might first be useful to examine the criteria apparently used in the decision. Victims of crime, at least partially, appear to operate along a "seriousness dimension." Most studies suggest this interpretation, where *seriousness* is defined by monetary loss or physical harm. Both individuals and organizations appear to decide to call the police partly on the basis of the gravity of their loss. Hence, it may be that the first "filter" for the entire criminal justice process tends to screen out the less serious events from further processing.

The substantial nonreporting of victims raises the important issue of whether a system of justice can operate fairly or achieve other goals set for it when it is able to process only those cases selected for it by individual citizens. Obviously, for a large body of crimes the offenders will never be held accountable in the criminal justice system. If not all offenders are formally processed by the criminal justice system, is there necessarily a reduction in equity? If one function of the justice system is to acknowledge and reaffirm, in a formalized fashion, the legal values of society, and yet it is denied that opportunity due to the reluctance of citizens to inform the legally constituted authorities that they have been victims of a transgression of those legal values, can the system realistically be expected to fulfill that function?

Clearly, these questions have profound implications for fundamental purposes of the criminal justice system. Although their answers are bound to be complex and cannot be answered entirely with the data studied here, the data available on reporting to the police may begin to address them. For example, although it may be thought that full reporting is a requisite for an efficient and equitable criminal justice system, there may be distinct and proper advantages in a citizen-based discretionary system for invoking the criminal process. The burden that full reporting (more than doubling the number of offenses now reported) would place on an already overtaxed system of justice should be noted. Were an effort to be made to involve the full machinery of the criminal justice system (or even that of the police stage) in every victimization, the system would be less able (with its limited resources) to deal efficiently, effectively, and fairly with the more serious cases. In any case, given the low visibility of the decision, it never would be possible to ensure full reporting.

Of more concern is not whether all crimes should or should not be reported to the police but, rather, whether the reporting process operates fairly and in a way compatible with the central aims of the criminal justice system. It is possible to have less than full reporting and still have an equitable decision process. This requires, however, that criteria used in the decision by victims do not include invidious discrimination on the basis of offender characteristics unrelated to criminal justice aims. Equity requires also that no groups of victims be shut off systematically from the criminal justice system because of fear or mistrust of the police.[9] By and large, the nature of the harm suffered by victims appears to be more important than are the characteristics of the offender or attitudes toward the police in explaining variation in reporting behavior. This fact suggests that it may be possible to achieve equity without full reporting.

Some of the studies reviewed, however, do suggest inequity in reporting to the police. Offenders known to the victims, for example, are less likely, other things equal, to be reported to the police. Several explanations, of course, may be offered. For some, the victim may believe (perhaps correctly) that resolution of the victimization problem would best be achieved outside the context of the criminal justice system. Calling the police when someone within the household is involved may aggravate the situation later on. Or, alternative social control mechanisms—a call to the parents of the offender, for example—may be sufficient.

Of more concern are the victims of nonstrangers who suffer serious physical or psychological harm yet are afraid to involve the police lest the situation become aggravated. Abused children and spouses may fall disproportionately into this category. In recent years attempts have been made, through special units of police departments and various "crises lines," to alleviate this problem. The problem may be seen as one of expanding the decision alternatives available to these crime victims in a way that is compatible with their goals. These often emphasize simply the cessation of the victimization, rather than retribution or general crime prevention. Unfortunately, adequate evaluations of these programs are lacking, and such evaluations are a pressing research need. The fact that one in six rape victims who failed to report to the police says that she did not do so because she was afraid of reprisals is evidence of the need for demonstrably effective alternatives for the victim.

Various other arguments would support the use of seriousness as a criterion by victims in their decision to report. For example, many trivial offenses may be resolved best by the parties involved, and the invocation of the criminal justice process would be both wasteful of scarce resources and even detrimental to an amenable settlement of the dispute. Examples might be an assault between playmates over a bicycle or a youngster who steals candy from the neighborhood drug store.

The emphasis in victim decision making on the gravity of the harm suffered cannot be interpreted in light of any single goal. Depending on the circumstances, it may reflect a concern for general deterrence, since the greater the harm done, the more important the victim may believe it to be that the offender should be caught and punished in order to prevent others from suffering the same criminal act. Many street robbery victimizations may fall into this category. It may, on the other hand, reflect an incapacitative aim. For example, the personnel of the stores in the shoplifting studies clearly desired that the professional shoplifters be given special attention. Reporting to the police as a means of stopping an ongoing victimization between nonstrangers may be seen also as pursuit of an incapacitative goal. The more serious the personal harm, the greater may be the likelihood that the victim seeks personal revenge or retribution for the crime by calling the police.

Available studies strongly imply that for many victims the decision to report a crime is made for personal, utilitarian reasons. The relation between the status of the victim's theft insurance and frequency of reporting to the police, the high rate of reporting stolen automobiles, and Reiss's finding that many businessmen said they reported crime for insurance purposes all clearly suggest a motive of personal gain.[10] This raises some important issues relative to the goals of the criminal justice process. For example, Reiss (1971:68) argues that

> these data on insurance coverage strongly suggest that one's civic obligation to mobilize the police against crimes of property is often subverted by question of personal gain. . . . These relationships are based on conceptions of personal gain, generally monetary gain or the avoidance of loss in time and effort. The effort is not worth the cost. . . . Given the absence of a sense of civic responsibility to mobilize the police, and the essentially reactive character of much policing of everyday life, the citizenry has enormous power to subvert the system by its decisions to call the police or not.

And, as Skogan (1984:114) remarks on the basis of his worldwide review of reporting:

> In every jurisdiction there is a great deal of unreported crime—even in the most "civil" places, where cooperation with the police was presumed to be high—and everywhere the decision to report seems to be dominated by a rational calculus regarding the costs and benefits of such action.

The characterization of the goal sought by many victims in their reporting decision as one of personal gain can be supported in a number of other ways. It finds support in the factors associated with nonreporting: the greater the personal financial loss, the more likely the event will be reported to the police; and the greater the gravity of the injury, the more likely it is that it will be reported. The fact that school children have been found to have a very low rate of reporting (Gottfredson, 1976) may be a function of a social code that warns against informing on one's peers and hence may also be viewed as a personal gain decision. Additionally, the reasons most commonly given in the National Crime Surveys for not reporting a crime to the police ("Nothing could be done" and "Victimization not important enough") may be interpreted under a personal gain model of decision making: it may be perceived that the effort and time (cost) involved in dealing with the police are just not worth the results, personally (gain).

The victim decision goals best suited for the achievement of the traditional aims of the criminal sanction are far from clear, and they may be expected to vary according to the specific aim in question. As Reiss suggests, there may be a profound contradiction between those goals and their goal of personal gain. Under the classical deterrence position, for example, the ultimate goal is thought to be achieved if punishments are administered both certainly and severely. If, however, no part of the criminal justice system is notified of a crime, there can be no opportunity to administer the penalties, and thus the certainty of punishment is diminished. If the victim sees no personal payoff in reporting a crime, perhaps because the personal loss is not substantial, then the goals of the two decision models will conflict. On the other hand, there might be substantial compatibility between such personal utilitarian goals of the victim and other aims of the criminal justice process. One is the already discussed initial screening on the basis of seriousness, which may be functional for an overtaxed system of justice. Alternatively, if retribution is thought to be a major goal served by the criminal sanction, and if the victim is seen as the important focus of a retributive philosophy, there may be little conflict between the aims of the criminal sanction and the personal gain decision model, at least for some types of victimization.

The question therefore arises as to how victims' decisions are to be evaluated. Are they to be evaluated by the proportion of victimizations that are reported to the police, as a purpose of deterrence would seem to indicate? Or should some measure of personal satisfaction be developed that allows for a considerable degree of discretion on the part of the victim?

Suppose, for example, that the extent of victim reporting were to be selected, as adoption of a deterrence aim would suggest, as the measure of "successful" victim decisions. Furthermore, suppose that an active effort were made to increase substantially the level of reporting in furtherance of the deterrence goal. Given the low levels of the current ability of the police to "do something" about many victimizations, as measured by clearance rates that approximate 20% for many property crimes, then it is probable that victim satisfaction would decrease with a successful increase in reporting. This might be true particularly if the victims were led to believe that in reporting the crimes to the police there would be a meaningful personal gain.

DECISION ALTERNATIVES AND INFORMATION

Currently, the decision alternatives available to the victims of crime are quite limited. The major choice, of course, is either to report to the police or to do nothing. The importance of such alternatives should not be minimized, however; the power vested in victims is fundamental. It is the power to invoke the law and its corresponding sanction and the power not to do so. In many respects, the decision not to call the police is indeed the fundamental exercise of control over the criminal justice process.

The victim as a criminal justice decision maker is in some ways in a position analogous to the police as decision makers. Neither has complete control over the consequences of their decisions. As Reiss and Bordua (1967) pointed out, the police do not have command over the output of their decisional alternatives. If the main concern is justice, then in using their discretion not to arrest a suspect the police may feel, on the basis of the individual characteristics of the case, that justice has been served. If, however, the decision is to arrest, then control over the decisional output is taken from the hands of the police and placed in the hands of the prosecutor, the judge, or both. Thus, if the latter's decision is not to proceed with the full impact of available criminal sanctions, then the police may believe that justice has not been served and hence that their decision has been subverted.

A similar analysis may be relevant to the victim's decision. In deciding not to notify the police about a crime, many victims may believe that justice is better served. But when the decision is made to notify the police, the victim loses control over the decisional output, since the disposition of the case is taken from the victim's control. The fact that victims do not control the output of the process may have important implications, not necessarily consciously recognized in the individual case, for the ultimate purposes thought to be served by reporting a crime to the police. It may be that this inability to control directly the decision output is a main factor in the victim's use of what may best be called a personal gain goal in decision making, rather than one or more of the classic criminal law goals.

The issue of the time and effort that may be involved in reporting a crime and the requirements of other significant criminal justice goals, such as general deterrence, are, in the context of this analysis, information requirements. Victim decision makers, like many of their counterparts in the rest of the criminal justice system, lack information about the consequences of their decisions. And in relation to many of the potential consequences such information simply does not exist because the relevant studies have not been undertaken.

The large proportion of crimes that go unreported may have implications for the expansion of decision alternatives for the victim. Those who fail to report, for example, because it is a personal matter or because of fear of reprisal may profit by the existence of nonlegal dispute resolution mechanisms (such as neighborhood counseling centers). Or it may be useful to establish strong incentives for those who may encounter victims who are seriously injured (physically or psychologically) but who do not report to call the incident to the attention of the authorities. Doctors, dentists, clergy, and others provide examples but may require structures that are designed to avoid the violation of patient–client confidence.

Further studies of the ways in which victim decisions may affect the goals of the criminal justice process and studies of the personal requirements of victims (many of which may conflict sharply with the goals of crime prevention and even justice) are needed both to understand the decision more fully and to design suitable alternatives. Probably no criminal justice participant has a greater amount of discretion or is in a role more capable of influencing the character of the entire system of justice.

NOTES

1. One major exception involves studies of police decisions to file a report of behavior as crime. These are discussed in Chapter 3.
2. This chapter will focus mainly on crimes of common theft and assault, since it is about these crimes that most research has been done and for which the victim is the principal initiator of the criminal justice process. For other types of crime (such as many forms of consumer fraud or victimless crimes), the victim probably is less active as the initiator of the process. There are several possible reasons for this: (1) for many consumer fraud and white collar offenses the victim may be unaware of the victimization; (2) there may be more uncertainty on the part of the victim over the definition of the

questionable behavior as crime; (3) there may be less certainty as to the proper authority to receive the report (e.g., police, consumer fraud bureaus, better business bureaus); (4) in the case of victimless crimes (e.g., gambling, narcotics, or prostitution), if there is indeed a victim he or she might be implicated in criminal activity if a report were to be made. Portions of the text discussion draw upon Hindelang and Gottfredson (1976).

3. Reiss was one of the first researchers to recognize that citizens are the principal initiators of the process—i.e., that victim decisions are fundamental to an understanding of the criminal justice process.

4. See, for example, Miller *et al.*, 1971: Ch. 1.

5. For a thorough discussion of early victimization surveys see Hindelang (1976). A good general introduction to the NCS is provided by Garofalo and Hindelang (1977). Recent reviews of the method include Skogan (1981); Gottfredson (1986); and Sparks (1981, 1982).

6. For a discussion of the limitations of these survey data see Hindelang, Gottfredson, and Garofalo (1978: Ch. 10); Skogan (1981); and Sparks (1981, 1982).

7. As noted above, Hindelang (1976) found that demographic characteristics of victims were unrelated to the reasons given for not calling the police once the type of crime and the victim–offender relationship were taken into account

8. The influence of the victim in the police decision to arrest once a complaint has been made has also been found to be considerable, as will be discussed in the next chapter.

9. It should be stressed that the victims' discretion does not rest solely with calling the police. Perhaps more important is the decision to regard some behavior as criminal in the first place. Most of the evidence suggests that it is the victim, rather than the police, who must apply the criminal law to behavior in the first instance (the police can, of course, decide later not to regard some behavior as a crime). Variability in this decision demands a good deal of study, since it might bear directly on the equity of the process.

10. Reiss (1971) also suggests that insurance coverage may inhibit some victims from reporting for fear that their policies will be cancelled.

Chapter 3

THE DECISION TO ARREST

Police decisions have not been a neglected area of study and commentary by social scientists and legal scholars.[1] On the contrary, the literature about police work is vast, diverse, and impossible to summarize briefly without violating its complexity.[2] Our purposes, however, do not require a thorough review. Rather, we seek to investigate the information requirements, goals, and alternatives of the decision to arrest; to review studies bearing on the ways in which arrest decisions are made routinely; and to offer some comments on directions for the enhancement of rationality. This itself is no small task, for no single aspect of police work has received more scholarly attention recently than has the decision to arrest. Our review must therefore be selective, including only the most informative studies and commentaries.

The focus of this chapter is on arrest—the decision by a police officer to take physical custody, by virtue of the authority of the law, of a person who is suspected of having violated a law.[3] The focus is restricted further, initially, by considering only arrests made in the absence of warrants (that is, by officers acting without prior specific authorization by a court). This latter restriction does not preclude the vast majority of arrests, although it does exclude investigation of issues unique to the warrant situation.

A focus on the decision to arrest excludes from consideration most of what the police do routinely. As Bittner (1974) tells us on the basis of considerable observation, "when one looks at what policemen actually do, one finds that criminal law enforcement is something that most of them do with the frequency located somewhere between virtually never and very rarely." Similarly, Reiss (1971) has noted, on the basis of sustained observation of patrol practices, that for a policeman "the modal tour of duty does not involve an arrest of any person." Studies of calls to the police for assistance discover uniformly that the vast majority of citizens' requests for police help do not involve crime-related matters (Bercal, 1970; Cumming, Cumming, and Edel, 1965; Reiss, 1971; Wilson, 1965). Accordingly, this is not a chapter about police work; rather, it is a chapter about a narrow slice of routine police work, albeit a critically important slice: the decision whether to invoke the law of arrest.[4]

An appreciation, however, of the routine daily activities of police work—the context within which arrest decisions are made—facilitates a study of the goals that may be pursued by arrest decisions. Two aspects of routine police work that are particularly critical in shaping the aims of arrest merit comment at the outset: the dependency of the police on citizen demands and cooperation and the maintenance of order function of most routine police work. We will describe these "contexts" of the arrest decision here briefly, developing their significance to arrest decisions throughout the chapter.

In our discussion of victims' decisions to report crimes to the police, we stressed that the evidence documented the assertion that it is the victim of crime rather than the police officer who is the principal initiator of the criminal law. That is, of the crimes that come to the attention of the police, most do so as a result of citizen initiative. This observation of how criminal events generally become police business led Reiss (1971) to characterize police involvement as a great deal more reactive than proactive. As described in more detail later in this chapter, Reiss has also discovered that citizens control arrest practices not only in calling the police in the first instance but also through their preference about arrest once the police arrive. As a matter of empirical reality, it appears that the arrest decision is largely circumscribed by citizen initiation.[5] Therefore, whatever goals are pursued by the decision to arrest, their achievement must be measured within a context that is principally police-reactive and citizen-initiated.[6]

Students of the police role also have asserted repeatedly the dominance of the responsibility of the police for maintenance of order in relation to that of enforcing the law (e.g., Wilson, 1965). Arrest decisions are thus seen as one of the available techniques for carrying out the task of preserving order; in this respect the decision to arrest is one of several possible responses to threats to the public order and one that is the least often employed. Other techniques that fall under the rubric of order maintenance include hospitalization, talk, traffic direction, physical presence, issuing an order to move on, requesting that a radio be turned down, and so forth. Each technique has the central aim of restoring order where there is disorder (Wilson, 1965).

Bittner has developed this conceptualization of the context of arrest decisions most fully. It is the capacity of the police (and the public expectation of this capacity) to intervene in pressing problems and to compel a resolution that defines the context of police work. Bittner's thesis is

> that the police are empowered and required to impose, or, as the case may be, coerce a provisional solution upon emergent problems without having to brook or defer to opposition of any kind, and that further, their competence to intervene extends to every kind of emergency, without any exceptions whatever. (1974:18)

Bittner (1974:30) summarizes the special competence of the police as being responsible for events characterized as "something-that-ought-not - to - be - happening - and - about - which - someone - had - better - do - some-thing-now!"

Throughout the following discussion of arrest decisions these contexts within which these decisions are made must be kept in mind. Arrest decisions are, to a large degree, constrained by citizen input; the police, like all subsequent actors in the criminal justice system, are dependent upon earlier decisions for input. Their information, goals, and alternatives are thus influenced strongly by the cases made available by others for their decisions. In addition, these decisions take place as a part of a larger role played by the police, the central feature of which is dealing with a wide range of problems, with authority, that have eluded alternative resolution. Solving pressing interpersonal crises involves the use of numerous tools, the ultimate of which is arrest.[7] And much evidence suggests that arrest is the tool of last resort; at least one observer concludes: "And no policeman who is methodical in his work uses it in any other way" (Bittner, 1975:113).

The nature of these contexts within which routine arrest decisions are made most certainly does not derogate the importance of the decisions. Indeed, the decision to arrest involves a fundamental application of the coercive power of the state, one with extensive consequences for both the accused and society. To whom and for what purposes such power is applied are issues of paramount importance not only to the efficient, effective, and just administration of justice but to society as a whole. It is a decision, like others considered in this book, with profound implications for the rationality of the entire criminal justice process.

THE DISCRETIONARY NATURE OF ARRESTS

We noted in Chapter 1 that in the absence of alternatives there is no decision problem. That is, there must be a choice of actions available, even if that choice is only to decide not to take any form of action. Do the police indeed have a decision problem with respect to arrest? Is discretion at this phase of the criminal justice process permissible?

Only relatively recently has the discretionary nature of the arrest decision been acknowledged widely. Historically, statutes, police administrators, and scholarly commentary all have been in agreement with the position that the police were not empowered to decide whether or not to enforce the law in all cases that come to their attention. Full enforcement, it was asserted, was both desirable and the legal requirement. Accordingly, there was no discretion involved in arrest. If the circumstances fit the letter of the statute, then an arrest must be made (Goldstein, 1969).

Admittedly, this is something of a caricature of the "no discretion" position. Although it is argued subsequently that discretion in arrests is both inevitable and proper if adequately controlled, a well-reasoned position can be sustained to strive for extremely limited discretion in these decisions. The arguments of J. Goldstein (1969) are especially noteworthy in this respect.

Goldstein stressed that police decisions not to invoke the criminal law are of low visibility. That is, if the decision is made not to arrest, the decision is not known publicly. This circumstance prohibits the possibility of review on a regular basis to ensure that this discretion is not abused. Goldstein does not argue for "total enforcement" in all situations. Total enforcement is precluded by due process restrictions regarding searches, arrests, and so forth. These constraints, however, define an area of full enforcement in which the police are authorized and expected to enforce the law. Thus, within this area, according to Goldstein, the police have not been delegated discretion.

Practically, such a position creates problems (for example, legal ambiguities, personnel and time constraints, and outmoded statutes) that Goldstein acknowledges. His recommended solution, however, focuses on the legislature, rather than on the police. Legislatures should redefine the common areas of selective enforcement in such a way that the police are not delegated discretion not to invoke the criminal law. The statutes should be cleared, by elected representatives, of obsolete laws, and the situations in which it is preferable not to arrest should be written explicitly in the law. Such a solution, it is argued, removes the power of the criminal law from the whim of each police officer and puts it with elected representatives.[8]

Considerable progress undoubtedly could be made in the control of police discretion were legislatures to revise the criminal codes substantially, deleting obsolete statutes and specifying more precisely the acts that are not intended to fall within the purview of the criminal law. Greater specificity is needed particularly in the realm of the so-called victimless crimes. But it is both unrealistic and ill-advised to argue that discretion in arrest decisions be eliminated. It is unrealistic, given the complexity and variability of behavior that, in any circumstances, can be considered criminal. It is ill-advised because individualized judgment, taking account of the immediate circumstances of the behavior in question, is a necessary component of just decision making.[9]

By way of illustration, consider a case of assault between spouses. A neighbor calls the police to the scene, where they witness a physical assault and heated argument. Should they make an arrest? Of both parties? As an alternative should they seek to engage the couple in professional counseling? Does the presence of children matter? What if the victim refuses to sign a complaint? Does the presence of a weapon matter? Suppose the parties become reconciled on the spot? What if one of them turns to attack the officers?[10]

Obviously, the contingencies surrounding the event (as well as the available alternatives) may have a lot to do with the appropriateness of an arrest. Countless other examples could be constructed that illustrate essentially the same point: discretion is a central and important feature of arrest decisions. An awareness of this has led, in H. Goldstein's (1977:94) words, to "a steadily growing recognition of police discretion and increasing support of the contention that it is not only necessary and desirable, but should be openly acknowledged, structured, and controlled."[11] Similarly, the President's Commission on Law Enforcement and Administration of Justice argued for the legitimacy of arrest discretion:

> The police should openly acknowledge that, quite properly, they do not arrest all, or even most, offenders they know of. Among the factors accounting for this exercise of discretion are the volume of offenses and the limited resources of the police, the ambiguity of and the public desire for nonenforcement of many statutes and ordinances, the reluctance of many victims to complain and, most important, an entirely proper conviction by policemen that the invocation of criminal sanctions is too drastic a response to many offenses. (1967:106)

Only when the "false pretense of full enforcement," to use Davis's (1975:52) words, is put to rest and the acknowledgment made that the police do have a decision problem (that is, a choice) with respect to arrest can the goals, alternatives, and information requirements of arrest decisions be defined clearly.

GOALS AND ALTERNATIVES FOR ARREST DECISIONS

If it is agreed that police do not serve a purely mechanical function of invoking the law whenever they have the opportunity to do so, then the question arises as to the decision goals that are pursued by arrest or its alternatives (including doing nothing) in individual cases. A moment's reflection demonstrates that each of the classic aims of criminal law—desert, incapacitation, treatment, and general deterrence—often can be the aim of the decision.[12] Adding to the complexity of decision goals are the requisites of practicality, personal utility, and efficiency. Wilson describes the often conflicting goals and the immensely difficult balancing problem in an arrest decision as a cost–benefit analysis.

> His actual decision whether and how to intervene involves such questions as these: Has anyone been hurt or deprived? Will anyone be hurt or deprived if I do nothing? Will an arrest improve the situation or only make matters worse? Is a complaint more likely if there is no arrest, or if there is an arrest? What does the sergeant expect of me? Am I getting near the end of my tour of duty? Will I have go to court on my day off? Will the charge stand up or will it be withdrawn or dismissed by the prosecutor? Will my partner think that an arrest shows I can handle things or that I can't handle things? What will the guy do if I let him go? (1965:84)

Ignoring for the moment the idiosyncratic aims of the decision, the achievement of both utilitarian aims (crime control) and desert aims (punishment) clearly are involved in many arrest decisions. That is, the general questions posed by Wilson may be analyzed according to the specific aim of intervention. Concern for the future behavior of the suspect if no arrest is made might be construed as the pursuit of the goal of incapacitation. If the suspect is not taken into custody, will he continue to offend? Consider again the case of a domestic assault. A principal concern in the police intervention typically is whether an arrest is needed to preclude future (perhaps imminent) violence by the offender.

Treatment (rehabilitation) might similarly be a crime control aim of specific arrest decisions. Does the officer's observation indicate that, as an alternative to arrest, family counseling will reduce future domestic disturbances? Should a young person be arrested so that the family court can take appropriate treatment intervention? Should a youth apprehended for shoplifting be arrested, or will a talk with his parents suffice to prevent future occurrences?

General deterrence—the prevention of crime in the general population by means of sanctions applied to offenders—commonly is regarded as a dominant aim of the criminal law. Certainly it has been central to many analyses of arrest decisions and to police work generally.[13] It clearly is an aim in many arrest decisions, as when an officer decides to arrest a youth for vandalism in an area with recent widespread vandalism. A deterrence aim may be pursued more generally as one component in most arrests for serious crimes.

Although most of the commentary on the goals of arrest decisions has focused on these crime reduction or utilitarian aims, desert is surely a major goal as well. Put simply, people should not be arrested unless they deserve it on the basis of their behavior.

But what does it mean to *deserve* an arrest? Part of the meaning of desert in this context must reflect the fact that an arrest is, in itself, a type of sanction. Fundamentally, it deprives a person of liberty and the freedom of action. It connotes a stigma that derives from the circumstance that a person's behavior was seen by someone—a police officer—as violating commonly ascribed legal norms. It does not require extended argument to demonstrate that an arrest, analogously to but to a lesser extent than conviction and sentencing, is a negative sanction. Therefore, a concern for the goal of desert in arrest decisions is that the sanction not be applied to the "unworthy"—those whose behavior does not justify the deprivation of liberty and the initiation of the criminal process against the suspect.

The concern with the goal of desert is perhaps most apparent in the legal standards that must be met before an arrest can be made. Thus, "probable cause" and "reasonable grounds to believe" are phrases that seek to justify the sanction of arrest in a specific case on the basis of the behavior of the suspect. To some degree, desert is thus seen as a threshold requirement for an arrest.

Concern about the goal of desert in arrest decisions, however, is not confined to the standards predicating an arrest. This goal is involved also when an arrest is not made, when an officer decides that the consequences of an arrest to the offender would be too severe given the nature of the criminal behavior. Consider again the case of a youth convicted of shoplifting. If it is a first offense and a relatively trivial event, an officer may decide that arrest and possible prosecution is too severe a penalty. Or consider again a domestic assault. In some such events it may be clear that the "victim" may share culpability with the "offender" for the behavior and as a consequence the officer on the scene may decide not to arrest, perhaps for reasons of desert. Thus, nonarrest decisions often may be attempts to serve the aim of just desert.[14]

Our focus on these goals of arrest decisions is intended to raise the requirements of rationality outlined in the first chapter. Certainly it would be an oversimplification to assert a single aim for any such decision or

to claim that goals other than those described may not be critically influential. Moreover, these aims are not easily separable in a given specific
situation. The identification of common decision aims, however, serves
the purpose of raising for discussion and analysis the two other requisites
of rational decision making, alternatives and information.

The decision not to arrest is one major alternative; but "not arresting" has many diverse forms, ranging from doing nothing,[15] to referral
to a private third party (for example, parents), to referral to a public
agency (such as a social service agency), to issuing a citation. Each
alternative may embody a distinct set of goals and, if rationality is desired, requires study to ascertain whether they are achieved.

The range of alternatives available is obviously quite variable, and
some will be discussed subsequently when the need for custody is considered. In many jurisdictions, however, for many of the problems that
arise from their order maintenance functions, police may be faced only
with the alternatives of arrest or doing nothing. One consequence of
this may be, as Goldstein has observed, that "for many of these situations
the system is clearly inappropriate and, even when appropriate, often
awkward in its application. But in the absence of alternatives it is used,
and often perverted in its use, in order to get things done" (1977:21).

The task of deciding whether to arrest becomes a much more complicated one once the legitimacy of discretion, the diversity of goals, and
the range of alternatives are realized. Furthermore, the police officer's
need for information that links the decision alternatives to the decision
goals becomes paramount. Goldstein makes the same point:

> Little skill and talent are required to crudely apply a uniform solution (like
> the criminal justice system) to an array of different problems. Diagnosing a
> situation and selecting an appropriate method for dealing with it are much
> more challenging tasks. (1977:74)

Before we investigate the requirements of rationality further, it is
important that we pause to consider in some detail how arrest decisions
are made. What are the correlates of the decision to take a person into
custody, and what do these correlates tell us about the goals, alternatives, and information requirements of the arrest decision? Abstract considerations of arrest issues may be most helpful when grounded in an
understanding of how the law of arrest is put into practice.

THE DECISION TO ARREST: THE VIEW FROM THE DATA

Social scientists have generated a considerable empirical literature
concerning the correlates of arrest. The range of methods used, variables

considered, and levels of abstraction is vast, and it reflects the diversity of approaches found within the disciplines of political science, sociology, psychology, and criminal justice. As a result, it is extremely difficult to summarize briefly studies that might bear on the issue of the correlates of arrest decisions.[16] This review, therefore, is restricted by two criteria. First, studies of individual arrest decisions (as opposed to aggregate comparisons of agencies with differing political cultures, for example[17]) should be most informative to our focus in this book on decision making. Second, only systematic empirical research in which an assessment of the relative contributions of various factors on the decision to arrest has been attempted will be reviewed. The latter criterion is in keeping with our focus on the rationality requirements for routine case decision making.

It is convenient to classify the research to be discussed into three generic groups according to methods: observational, simulative, and archival. Studies using each method have contributed to our knowledge of the correlates of arrest. Each method has limitations that qualify the inferences that can be made about arrest decisions. Taken together, though, they tell us a great deal about the principal concerns in arrest decisions. Furthermore, there is some consistency of findings that, given the different methods of study used, increases our confidence about how well the correlates of arrest are known. Unfortunately for the present purpose, most of the empirical studies of arrest decisions have focused on the arrest of youth. We will summarize much of that literature, although it must be stressed that factors operating in adult decisions may differ from those pertinent to arrests of juveniles. It seems reasonable to hypothesize that age itself is a major factor influencing the arrest decision. Not only may alternatives to arrest be sought more vigorously for youths, but more alternatives probably are available (e.g., referral to parents, to schools, and to social agencies).

Three major observational studies have generated data about how police decide to make an arrest in police–citizen encounters. One of the earliest was undertaken by Piliavin and Briar (1964). They studied the arrest decisions of thirty officers in a juvenile bureau, riding with them on patrol. They discovered that these specialized police officers encountered young people in one of three ways, in increasing order of frequency: (1) the officers discovered a "wanted" youth; (2) an offense was reported to police headquarters; and (3) the officers directly observed youths committing an offense or in "suspicious circumstances."[18] They noted that the alternatives available to the officers in their study were: (1) outright release; (2) release, but with the submission of a report; (3) release to parents or guardian; (4) citation; or (5) arrest.

Piliavin and Briar found that considerable discretion was exercised by the officers studied. All the alternatives were employed among the sixty-six cases studied. Their general findings may be summarized succinctly: among the serious offenses in their study (about 10% of the encounters)—robbery, homicide, aggravated assault, grand theft, auto theft, rape, and arson—police discretion was affected little by factors other than the offense. For minor offenses, characteristics of the offender, such as prior record and demeanor (coded as cooperative and uncooperative), seemed to influence the decision to a considerable degree.[19]

Although this study is important for its demonstration of the utility of the observational method and the findings that offense behavior, prior record, and personal characteristics of the offender all influence arrest decisions, inferences from it should be drawn carefully. The police studied were in a specialized unit concerned with the prevention of delinquency, a unit whose mandate included making disposition decisions contingent on the character of the youth. Also, the small sample size virtually precludes multivariate analyses of the relative contributions of situational and offender characteristics once the demonstrably relevant variable, gravity of the behavior, is taken into account.

A similar observational study of police arrest decisions has been reported in a series of articles by Black and Reiss (1967).[20] They placed observers with the police in three cities during the summer of 1966 to record a sample of police–citizen encounters. A large variety of data was collected about the encounters, including how they were initiated (for example, by citizens or by the police) and characteristics of the officers, complainants, and suspects. The police observed were regular uniformed patrolmen.

As discussed heretofore, Black and Reiss found that the vast majority of police–citizen encounters were initiated by citizens. For juveniles, for example, 72% of the encounters were initiated by citizens and 28% by policemen on patrol. They comment:

> The mobilization of police control of juveniles is then overwhelmingly a reactive rather than a proactive process. Hence it would seem that the moral standards of the citizenry have more to do with the definition of juvenile deviance than do the standards of policemen on patrol. (1970:67)

In their analysis of 281 encounters between police and youth (suspects under eighteen years of age) Black and Reiss discovered several correlates of arrest decisions. (This is apart from the discovery of the exercise of considerable discretion: of these 281 encounters only 15% resulted in arrest.) First, the legal seriousness of the alleged behavior of the accused youth was correlated strongly with the decision to arrest; "the disposition pattern for juvenile suspects clearly follows the hierarchy of offenses found in the criminal law, the law for adults" (1970:43). Second, they discovered that arrest decisions for nonfelony cases were correlated with the complainant's preference regarding arrest, with the presence of evidence linking the suspect to the crime and with the suspect's degree of respect for the officer (with the very respectful and the very disrespectful more likely to be arrested). The Black and Reiss data show that, within types of crime, black youth were more likely than white youth to be arrested. They attribute this differential not to discriminatory arrest practices by the police but to differences in arrest preferences by complainants. Black complainants tended to prefer arrest more often than white complainants. Black and Reiss commented:

> In not one instance did the police arrest a juvenile when the complainant lobbied for leniency. When a complainant explicitly expresses a preference for an arrest, however, the tendency of the police to comply is also quite strong. (1970:71)

Quite similar findings, based on considerably fewer cases, were reported from this observation study by Black (1971) for adults. Again, the legal seriousness of the alleged behavior was an important correlate of the arrest decision. The preference of the complainant was found again to be correlated with the arrest decision. For felonies in which the police–citizen encounter was initiated by citizens, only 10% resulted in an arrest when the complainant preferred no arrest, compared to 74% when an arrest was preferred. Arrests were also less likely to be made when the victim and offender were known to one another than when they were strangers. For felonies, blacks were more likely to be arrested than were whites, a correlation that appeared attributable to the amount of disrespect shown to the police during the encounter. That is, Black and Reiss concluded that blacks were more likely to show disrespect and the disrespectful were more likely to be arrested.

Friedrich (1977), in a reanalysis of some of these same observational data using multivariate techniques, demonstrated the influence of seriousness on the arrest decision. Furthermore, he found a sizable correlation between arrest and the type of evidence present in the encounter; as the strength of the evidence varied from "none" to "citizen testimony" to "reasonable evidence" to "police witness," the likelihood of arrest generally increased. Friedrich did a multiple regression analysis, treating arrest as the dependent variable and entering as independent variables the seriousness of the alleged behavior, evidence, citizen characteristics (race, class, sex, and age), citizen behavior (for example, preference about arrest), and the number of persons present. By far the strongest correlate when these factors were considered simultaneously was the seriousness of the offense. Friedrich comments that the "coefficient for this factor—greater than that for any other—reveals it to be the primary determinant of whether or not an offender is taken in" (1977:386). Characteristics of the suspects demonstrated virtually no multivariate relation to arrest; the only variable with an appreciable effect other than seriousness was the preference of the complainant.[21]

A third body of systemic observational data was collected and analyzed by Sykes and his colleagues.[22] The basic correlates of the arrest decision found in the Black and Reiss data were in evidence also in the data presented by these investigators.

In a sample of 3,000 police–citizen encounters observed during the course of their research, Sykes, Fox, and Clarke (1976) found that in only 520 nontraffic offenses was an alleged violator present when the police arrived. Again, considerable discretion concerning arrest was found; in less than one-third of the encounters in which an arrest could have been made was an arrest actually made. The influence of seriousness of offense was again demonstrated. When a felony was involved, an arrest almost always was made. Among those cases not involving felonies, Sykes and his colleagues found that several other factors were correlated with the decision to arrest—among which were the suspect's politeness and anger.

In a study with these data that focused only upon drunkenness offenses, Lundman (1974) again found considerable arrest discretion. Of such encounters that could have ended in arrest, only 31% did. The disrespectful, native Americans, and those who were drunk in public places were fund more likely to be arrested. Similar findings have been reported by Petersen (1972).

Lundman, Sykes, and Clarke (1978) reported a replication study of the Black and Reiss study of juvenile arrests. The consistency of the results between the two pieces of research is remarkable: most police encounters with juveniles are in response to citizen initiative; most such encounters are "legally minor"; the probability of such an encounter resulting in arrest is quite low (of the 200 encounters studied, only 16% ended in arrest); legal seriousness is a strong predictor of arrest (for example, all of the felony encounters, but only 5% of the "rowdiness" encounters ended in arrest); the presence of evidence increased the probability of arrest; the preference of the complainant was associated with the probability of arrest; arrest differences by race appeared to be a function of the preference of the complainant; and suspects who are either unusually respectful or unusually disrespectful are more likely to be arrested.

Smith (1984) studied some of the results of a large observational study spanning several cities, numerous forms of crime, and over 1,000 observations. On the basis of multivariate work, he reported:

Results indicate that arrest decisions are independent of the race, sex and age of suspects but significantly more likely in encounters with antagonistic suspects, or when a victim wants a suspect arrested. Arrests occur less often in instances where the complainant requests the police not to arrest and in encounters involving traffic offenses. Finally, if a supervisor is present or if the offense is a violent or property offense, the probability of arrest is significantly increased. Collectively, these effects are consistent with expectations based on previous research [citations omitted]. (Smith, 1984:27)

Similar results seem to obtain from recent studies of domestic assault. For example, Worden and Pollitz (1984) analyzed portions of the data used by Smith but restricted their attention to domestic disturbances. They found that the probability of an arrest's being made increased if: the woman signed a complaint, both parties were present when the police arrived, the man was drinking, or the man's demeanor was disrespectful.

LaFree's (1980) study of 905 forcible sex offenses reported to the police in a large midwestern city suggests that similar conclusions pertain to such cases as well. LaFree examined the relative influence of variables measuring the seriousness of the event and victim and offender characteristics on whether an arrest was made. He concluded that "the two best predictors of arrest were legal variables: the victim's ability to identify a suspect and her willingness to prosecute" (1981:586). Various other measures of the seriousness of the incident were also related to the decision to arrest.

The consistent finding in these observational studies that the seriousness of the alleged behavior is the strongest correlate of the arrest decision may come as no surprise.[23] The gravity of the behavior facing decision makers in the criminal justice system is a factor seen to be relevant to each of the common major aims of these decisions (desert, deterrence, incapacitation, and rehabilitation). As shown in Chapter 2, it largely conditions victims' decisions to report an offense to the police. Subsequent chapters demonstrate that seriousness of offense influences greatly the decisions of each of the other major decision makers in the system as well.

That the complainant's preference appears to have a large effect in arrest decisions underscores the point made earlier that citizens play a major role in decisions about what types of cases will proceed through the criminal justice system. A major reason for this influence here undoubtedly derives from the requirements of subsequent processing; police are aware that successful prosecution of suspects requires the active participation of complaining witnesses. There is little to be gained by an arrest for an offense when the complainant prefers to drop the matter, because prosecution will be futile. This does not deny the importance of this factor, however; citizens may request police service in a variety of situations in which an arrest is possible but not desirable. The complainant may desire only the cessation of the offending behavior, for example, and this is a circumstance that underscores the need for discretion and alternatives.

The role played by suspect characteristics and suspect demeanor, judging by these observational studies, is smaller in its influence on arrest than are the seriousness of behavior and the requirements of subsequent processing. The influence of the extralegal attributes appears to be confined to the less serious events (a finding that parallels what was found about victim decisions to report to the police).[24] Nettler (1978:70) has made a similar observation:

> For those localities in which the matter has been studied, official tallies of arrests do not seem to be strongly biased by extralegal considerations. These studies confirm common sense. They indicate that if you are apprehended committing a minor offense, being respectful to the police officer may get you off. If, on the other hand, you are apprehended for a minor violation and you talk tough to the "cop," the encounter will probably escalate into arrest. However, if you are caught in a more serious crime—if, for example, you are found robbing a bank—being respectful to the police is not likely to keep you from being arrested.

Bittner (1967) has made a similar point: For major crimes, whenever the rule is transgressed, there will be an arrest for that reason alone. For less serious events, however, an arrest might be made but is not determined by the law—these arrests are made within the law but for other reasons.

Despite some consistency with which these observational studies portray the major correlates of the arrest decision, they must be interpreted cautiously. The observational method has well-known limitations, including potential bias associated with the presence of an observer, potential problems of interobserver and intraobserver reliability, the difficulty in achieving very large samples for rare events (such as an arrest), and problems associated with the interpretation of the factors most determinative of the decision and the control of extraneous variance in natural "experiments."

Some of these problems may be overcome by a second type of research study that has examined the correlates of arrest by means of simulation exercises. Simulations can better control some forms of extraneous variance, since all decision makers may be exposed to the same factors, but they may involve other problems, including generalizations beyond the confines of the experiment to natural settings. Unfortunately, very few simulation studies of high quality have been reported. In one such study, however, Sullivan and Siegal (1972) presented twenty-four police officers with data items about the offense and offenders to determine which specific items were most often seen to be relevant to the arrest decision. The items were selected sequentially by specific headings; thus, both the number of items requested and the order in which they were requested could be observed.

They found that the number of individual data items requested by the police officers was small (five, on the average). Furthermore, the type of offense was the single most sought-after item; twenty-three of the twenty-four officers selected it first. Sullivan and Siegal also concluded that the next most important item was the attitude of the offender. These results are certainly compatible with the findings from the observational research cited above and other simulations (Finckenauer, 1976).

A third type of study that bears on the police exercise of discretion uses archival data to track the cases in which an arrest has been made (or in which a complaint has been made) and attempts to discover what happens to them and why.[25] Although several studies of this type have been undertaken that focused exclusively upon youth, data recently have become available for some criminal justice systems as a whole.[26]

Two studies especially pertinent to the problem of rationality in arrest decisions attempted to determine the reasons why some arrests never resulted in prosecution. Forst, Lucianovic, and Cox (1977) used data from the PROMIS system in Washington, D.C., to trace arrests through to conviction. They found a sizable amount of attrition from arrest to prosecution. Of the 17,500 arrests in 1974, only 30% resulted in some conviction. Forst et al. studied the factors associated with arrests that did and did not result in conviction. They discovered that those cases that tended not to result in conviction were supported by less evidence at the time the case was brought to the prosecutor. Arrests were more likely to result in conviction if evidence was obtained by the police, and the evidence obtained by the police tended to be the most critical evidence in terms of conviction. Forst et al. also discovered that convictions were more probable for those arrests in which the police found witnesses to the crime.

Not surprisingly, the Forst data revealed also that the amount of delay between the offense and an arrest was related to subsequent conviction. The shorter the delay, the greater the chance of conviction, a relation that appeared to result from the enhanced ability of the police to recover tangible evidence when the delay was short. But a perhaps unexpected result of their study was the discovery that convictions were more likely to result from offenses occurring between strangers than in similar offenses between nonstrangers. This finding held for both violent crimes and nonviolent property offenses. As we discuss at length in Chapter 10, the victim–offender relationship appears to play a critical and persistent role in decisions across the system. When the victim and offender are strangers, the victim is apparently more likely to report the offense (Chapter 2), the police to arrest, and the arrest to end in conviction.

Forst and colleagues also studied the characteristics of officers whose arrests tended to result in conviction. They discovered considerable variability among officers in the rates at which their arrests led to conviction; that is, 15% of the officers who made arrests accounted for over one-half of all arrests that led to conviction. Although experienced officers tended to have higher rates of conviction for their arrests, these rates were not found to be tied closely to the officers' age or sex but somewhat to their residence and marital status. There are, of course, numerous confounding factors, such as type of assignment, that could condition these results. These are acknowledged and, within the limits of the data, explored by Forst *et al*.

This study by Forst and his colleagues is in a sense prototypical of the kinds of studies that are needed routinely if rationality is to be enhanced in police decisions. That is, a goal must be identified (in this case the goal might be considered to be conviction, although it might more properly be considered to be an objective sought in pursuit of a more general goal or set of goals), and data must be studied that relate decisions in specific cases with the goal.[27] The results of such research can then be "fed back" to decision makers for use in future decisions. Such research, of course, is not likely to resolve all of the questions and issues pertaining to the decision to arrest. For example, conviction is certainly not the only goal involved in these complex decisions. And the Forst data suggest that much remains to be learned about the correlates of even this goal. But consider for a moment the wealth of ideas that are both addressed and stimulated by their research, all of which relate to the concept of rationality in relation to the presumed goal of conviction:

- Should more or less effort be expended by police officers at the scene in gathering evidence and discovering witnesses?
- Are the alternatives to arrest for nonstranger crimes adequate?
- Are residence requirements for police related to an optimization of convictions?
- Should a major effort be expended in follow-up investigations that attempt to secure evidence?

- Can the procedures and techniques used by the small group of officers who seem to make a disproportionate share of the arrests that end in conviction be identified and generalized?

Research such as that done by Forst *et al.* that measures the relation between data items and goals (and hence produces information) is sorely needed to assess and to enhance the rationality of arrest decisions.

A similar study, with some consistent findings, was undertaken by the Vera Institute of Justice (1977). The outcomes of 1,888 felony arrests in New York City in 1971 were studied. The probability that a felony complaint made to the police would result in arrest appeared to be about one in five. Of the 501,941 felonies reported to the police, there were 100,739 felony arrests. (Of course, as these authors note, this probability should not be interpreted too literally. For example, one arrest may clear numerous complaints, and some arrests made in later years may clear some complaints.) As shown in Figure 3, the Vera study found considerable variability in the ratios of reported felonies to arrests according to the type of offense under consideration. Thus, the ratio is relatively small for homicide and relatively large for burglary.

In their examination of the attrition rate of these felony arrests (for example, by police dismissing charges, the prosecutor deciding not to charge, subsequent *nolle proseque* and acquittals) the Vera workers discovered several things comparable to the findings reported by Forst *et al.* (1977) and added some others. The suspect's prior record was found to be a major influence, and the relation between the suspect and the victim was again demonstrated to play an important role. With respect to the latter finding, the Vera study reported that in half the felony arrests for crimes against the person and in a third of the crimes against property, the victim had some prior relationship with the arrestee. These cases tended disproportionately to be shunted from further processing. The authors infer from these results that

> at the root of much of the crime brought to court is anger—simple or complicated anger between two or more people who know each other. Expression of anger results in the commission of technical felonies, yet defense attorneys, judges and prosecutors recognize that in many cases conviction and prison sentences are inappropriate responses. . . . Because our society has not found adequate alternatives to arrest and adjudication for coping with inter-personal anger publicly expressed, we pay a price. The price includes large court caseloads, long delays in processing and, ultimately, high dismissal rates. . . . The congestion and drain on resources caused by an excessive number of such cases in the courts weakens the ability of the criminal justice system to deal quickly and decisively with the "real" felons, who may be getting lost in the shuffle. (1977:XV)

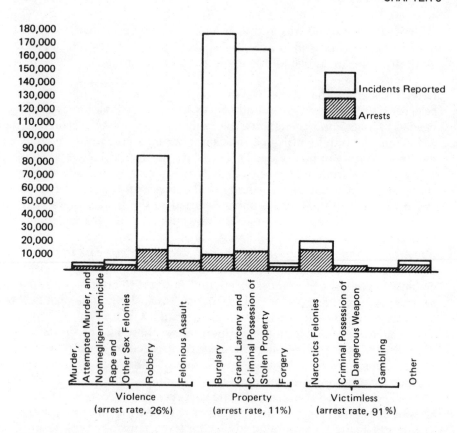

FIGURE 3. Felonies reported to the police and persons arrested for felonies, by type of felony. SOURCE: Vera Institute of Justice (1977). "Other" includes kidnapping, coercion, arson, perjury, bribery, bail jumping, falsifying records, and so forth.

Systematic empirical studies such as these of the Vera Institute and of Forst and his colleagues can suggest where alternatives to arrest are most needed. They can help to discover also the reasons for the outcomes of arrest decisions, and such reasons often can be useful in the design of programs to enhance rationality (see Chapter 10). Clearly they are preferable to bald statements about inherent and irreducible goal conflict among decision makers (for example, between the police and the courts). The potential gains in rationality that may attend such interagency feedback are substantial.

ALTERNATIVES TO ARREST: ASSESSING THE NEED
FOR CUSTODY

One common feature of all arrests is the taking of the suspect into custody. In large part, this is simply a by-product of the way in which the criminal justice process is initiated against an accused person in the typical case. But it is certainly possible to separate, for purposes of analysis, two common features of arrest decisions: the taking of custody and the initiation of the criminal justice process. Then the issue of custody may be used as the subject of an analysis of the requirements of rationality, in which the relation of goals, information, and alternatives may be assessed in some detail. Certainly not every arrest is made with the objective of further criminal justice processing in mind. For a large number of arrests there is no intention of prosecution, but rather the arrest is made to serve some immediate incapacitation objective (e.g., in domestic assaults) or a treatment objective (e.g., for the chronic inebriate). Thus, the distinction is a crude one. A thorough discussion of arrests with no prosecutorial intent is given by LaFave (1965).

The problem of custody has stimulated important work concerning alternatives to arrest decisions. Technically, the standard that guides the decision to arrest is silent with respect to custody concerns. The "reasonable grounds to believe" criterion may reflect a concern for desert (as noted heretofore), but it gives no guidance about the need for custody. How, then, is the decision about custody to be made? On the basis of what criteria?

Raising these questions helps make it clear that decisions about custody in the arrest situation are predictive decisions. As such, the requisites of prediction, particularly with respect to validity, apply. That is, predictive judgments imply a criterion (for example, appearance at later proceedings or the cessation of an ongoing victimization) and a relation between this criterion and elements of the case. The test of validity lies in how well these elements are related to the criterion.

The objectives (criteria) of taking a suspect into custody (apart from initiation of the process) are many. One study that investigated the objectives of custody in the arrest decision identified four generic functions: preventive, demonstrative, administrative and investigative, and social-medical (Asher and Orleans, 1972). Among the preventive objectives are ensuring the presence of the accused at later proceedings and ensuring that future crimes are avoided. The latter objective would include arrests made with the specific aim of stopping an ongoing victimization, as well as the prevention of crimes other than the one for which the police became involved in the first instance. Demonstrative functions of custody involve the use of arrest as a specific deterrent—that is, to impress the arrestee with the seriousness of his behavior and to warn of the consequences if it continues. Administrative and investigative functions of custody may involve the need to gather evidence, search, or conduct lineups. Finally, the social-medical functions involve the taking of custody to provide treatment services or medical attention.

With the possible exception of the administrative and investigative functions, these objectives of custody all imply an estimate of future events. Would the suspect fail to appear later if an arrest were not made? Would the assault between husband and wife continue (or escalate) if one of the parties were not physically removed? If some sanction, if only temporary detention, is not applied now, will the suspect continue to offend? Will the treatment alternative be helpful in diminishing repeated violations? Therefore, the test of the validity of these decisions is whether the predictions are accurate—for example, in the absence of custody, would the suspect appear for trial? Would the victimization stop without physical removal of the suspect?

In practice, of course, much custody is taken without regard to its necessity (in a predictive sense). In most jurisdictions, the police use arrest as the way in which to invoke the process. And there are critical differences between making custody decisions at the scene of the offense, where errors in prediction can have critical implications, and making these decisions dispassionately at a later time (see Chapter 4).[28] Still, it is informative to ask the question, What criteria are used, in practice, to determine whether there is a need for custody? At one level, it may be argued that the custody dimension influences the type of cases in which arrests are even contemplated by the police. That is, some offenses, such as landlord–tenant disputes or shoppers defrauded by a business, are always dealt with by referral of the complainant to the prosecutor. Bittner, for example, argues: "I believe the police tend to avoid involvement with offenses in which it is assumed that the accused or suspected culprits will not try to evade the criminal process by flight" (1974:24). Even granted the validity of this perspective, the predictive aspect of custody decisions at arrest is still present among those for whom arrest is the method of invoking the law. Therefore, the validity of these predictive judgments is an issue. Historically, the distinction Bittner draws may have emerged from the common law practice of arresting (detaining) all felons because they were accused of largely capital crimes. As penalties were reduced over time, detention in fear of flight became less of an issue. At one time arrest was even the normal method by which defendants were brought before the court in civil cases.

Little systematic study has been done to determine either the factors police use when making a custody assessment or, even more critically, the factors that are actually related to the need for custody. On the basis of observations of arrest decisions in three jurisdictions, LaFave (1965) was able to identify criteria that seemed to be used when determining that need. Among the factors thought prominent were the seriousness of the offense (those facing graver punishments were thought to be more likely to flee prior to trial), the nature of the offense (number writers were thought to be good risks), residence in the community, prior criminal history, and likelihood of conviction. Absent a systematic study of how such factors are in fact related to the concerns of custody, however, they must be considered at best as plausible hypotheses that do not constitute information upon which to make such decisions.

A concern that for many arrests there is no legitimate need for custody has stimulated the growth of alternative mechanisms for initiating the criminal justice process, the most widely discussed of which is the use of citations in lieu of arrest. The call for extended use of citations is, of course, not new (it was made, for example, by the Wickersham Commission more than fifty years ago). What is relatively new, however, is studies of innovative use of citation programs that permit the empirical study of the need for custody and some of the correlates of such need.

There is an obvious need for detailed study of the factors that influence custody decisions and the factors that are actually predictive of custody need. We need to know how often persons are arrested solely on the basis of perceived need for custody when no such need exists.[29] To be most informative, studies of the latter issue should be conducted to the extent feasible as experiments, with observations made of both experimental (released) and control (custody) groups randomly assigned, and should include follow-up data. With careful planning and monitoring, such studies could assess the custody need not only with respect to appearance at later proceedings but also in regard to the incapacitative aims of many custody decisions as well. The validity of restricting alternatives to misdemeanors is also in need to study. Properly designed, the results of such studies could add critical information to aid police in this difficult decision if the results of such research were incorporated into policy guidelines designed to enhance the rationality of arrest decisions. We will return to a detailed discussion of the development of systems specifically for such purposes in the final chapter.

ALTERNATIVES TO ARREST: ASSESSING THE NEED TO INITIATE THE CRIMINAL JUSTICE PROCESS

The second common feature of arrest decisions (the component of initiating the criminal justice process) is also of fundamental importance. Thus, we may ask what is known about alternatives to arrest that have as their aim the avoidance of the criminal justice process. Such an inquiry involves a discussion of the police "diversion" literature.

The rationales for diversion from further criminal justice processing are as diverse as the aims of the criminal justice system. Many programs have an explicit crime reduction aim: the implicit theory underlying many diversion programs is that processing through the system is itself criminogenic. Thus, recidivism will be less if this process is avoided. Many juvenile diversion programs adopt this rationale.

For other programs, there is a desire to avoid the costs involved in traditional criminal justice processing: the implicit theory underlying many diversion programs is that an economy of resources may be served if minor cases are not processed by the criminal justice system, leaving the system to deal more efficiently with the most serious cases.

For still other diversion programs, the criminal justice process is thought to be an inappropriate response to the behavior: the implicit theory underlying many of these programs is that a medial or social welfare response is more suited to alleviate the behavioral problem than is the criminal justice response. Many diversion programs aimed at alcoholic or other drug-dependent persons adopt this rationale.

The number of police diversion projects, many of which cannot be sorted neatly into the foregoing classification, is rapidly increasing. Although a detailed review of this literature is beyond our scope here,[30] some common results from this literature may be noted. First, most diversion programs are designed for juveniles, a situation that perhaps demonstrates the dominance of the first rationale for diversion. Second, and unfortunately, the number of diversion projects that provide clear and measurable definitions of purpose, adequate research designs for an assessment of the achievement of purpose, and sufficient data for an evaluation of both intended and unintended consequences of the program are very few. As a consequence, the information that most diversion projects supply the decision maker is meager.[31]

Third, there is some evidence to suggest that many diversion programs become, in practice, extensions of the criminal justice system rather than an alternative to arrest. Klein and associates found, for example, a tendency for those youth in police–citizen encounters who would not be arrested normally (for example, the young, the minor offenders, and those without prior records) to be the persons most likely to be selected for diversion:

> While there is clearly a desire in some police departments to divert juveniles from the system, the more common feeling is that referral should be used as an alternative to simple release. In short, the meaning of diversion has been shifted from "diversion from" to "referral to." Ironically, one of the ramifications of this is that in contrast to such earlier cited rationales for diversion as reducing costs, caseload, and the purview of the justice system, diversion may in fact be extending the costs, caseload and system purview even further than had previously been the case. (Klein *et al.*, 1976:10)

If rationality is desired, the development and availability of alternatives to arrest will not suffice. The simple availability of a choice does not ensure a relation between individual decisions to use the alternative and the goal that is sought. Each of the classifications of common diversion aims described above implies a perceived optimization of some decision goal. The logic underlying the diversion program may seem sound, but the test of soundness that rationality requires is an empirical demonstration that the alternative better serves the purpose of the decision. Thus, whether or not diversion decisions result in less recidivism, fewer costs, or more effective treatment are questions that only data—and not mere implicit theory, plausible hypothesis, or hunch—may answer. And the most convincing data derive from the experimental programs, including a random assignment component and follow-up treatment on both diverted and nondiverted cases. The questions require the empirical identification of factors associated with success in both groups. Quality studies of diversion that permit the assessment of how well these decision alternatives serve common aims of the arrest decision are almost wholly lacking.

One significant exception is the study of the relative effects of arrest, "advice," and "an order to leave" on a sample of domestic assault cases in Minneapolis, undertaken by Sherman and Berk (1984). This study is as important for the demonstration that randomized experiments are both possible and desirable in criminal justice settings as it is for its suggestion that arrest may be the preferable option for the types of cases studied.

Sherman and Berk, with the cooperation of the Minneapolis police, were able to alter the response of the police on a nearly random basis to certain forms of minor domestic assault cases. Although some difficulties arose in the execution of the study, the authors conclude on the basis of the 205 cases studied that of the three alternatives, arrest was preferable to the "diversions" when interest focused on repeated incidents.

The authors caution that their results are tentative and urge replication. They also warn against generalizing to other crimes. But "we do
have findings that swift imposition of a sanction of temporary incarceration may deter male offenders in domestic assault cases. And we have
produced this evidence from an unusually strong research design based
on random assignments to treatments" (Sherman and Berk, 1984:270).
Their evidence, albeit limited, is the strongest in the diversion area.
Their design is to be commended and urged on others.

It should be noted that formal diversion programs are only a small
part of the diversion that is used routinely by the police everyday. Many
of these alternatives have never been studied systematically to ascertain
their utility. Such studies will not be easily designed nor implemented.
They require, at a minimum, the systematic collection of data on arrest
opportunities, both when the decision is to use an alternative (do nothing, warn, refer, etc.) and when the decision is to arrest, as well as
follow-up data on both. As H. Goldstein (1977:71) has noted:

> If the police are to fulfill their responsibilities in a fair and effective manner,
> they must be provided with a set of alternatives, in the form of authority
> and resources, sufficient in a number and variety to enable them to deal
> appropriately with the situations they commonly confront. This means that
> informal alternatives now in use must be evaluated, legitimated and refined
> when necessary, or discarded.

THE ENHANCEMENT OF RATIONALITY IN ARREST DECISIONS

The research reviewed in this chapter suggests that much is known
about arrest decisions generally. The empirical evidence implies that
arrest practices vary by jurisdiction; that the gravity of the infraction
against legal norms is a strong correlate of individual arrest decisions;
that citizens influence arrest decisions both by calling the police in the
first instance and by expressing their preference concerning arrest; that
among the less serious offenses, who the suspect is and how he or she
reacts to the police may influence arrest decisions; that officer characteristics may not strongly influence individual arrest decisions but that
some officers are much more likely than others to produce arrests that
result in conviction; that the victim–offender relationship is an important
factor in arrests and in subsequent dismissals; that for a large proportion
of arrestees the custody need is minimal; and that the quality of evidence
gathered at the scene of an arrest has important implications for later
decisions. Other common findings could be identified.

The police officer does indeed have a decision problem with respect to arrest. Discretion exists and is a proper component to just and effective arrest decisions. Decision goals may be identified, for particular circumstances, as including desert, as well as predictive concerns such as incapacitation, treatment, and deterrence. The alternatives available are many (although their availability varies considerably by jurisdiction). What is lacking with respect to arrest decisions is mainly the third component to rationality—information. A consideration of rationality requires that we ask how the data related to arrest decision outcomes are related to the goals of that decision.

At the aggregate level, plausible arguments could be advanced that the common correlates uncovered in the studies of arrest serve the purposes of desert and the utilitarian aims of the criminal law. We advance some of these arguments in the final chapter. But the requirements of rationality, as we have defined and used that term, focus our attention on specific cases or *types* of specific cases, on the goal(s) of arrest for that particular case, and on the information available to the police in making a decision for that case. Research that can help to answer such questions is only beginning to be done. It involves the systematic tracking of cases beyond the arrest decision (whether or not the decision involves arrest) to see whether goals were accomplished. Was the suspect convicted? Why or why not? Did arrest result in higher than expected recidivism? Was the domestic disturbance resolved by referral to a social agency? Answers to such questions are essential if rationality is to be enhanced. And, quite critically, that enhancement can be accomplished only by feeding back the results of that research to the police officers responsible for arrest decisions.

The value of feedback of this sort cannot be overemphasized. Consider the results of the Forst research and the gains in rationality that policies structured on such research might bring. Improvements in rationality are not the only benefits that a research–feedback cycle afford. Such data have the potential of reducing the apparent conflict among components of the criminal justice system and of diminishing the number of decisions based on faulty assumptions about the decision of the other agencies. For example, evidence cited in subsequent chapters documents considerable consistency in the factors used by various criminal justice decision makers. There is a successive "tightening" along the same criteria as cases move through the system. Police impressions about what prosecutors and judges do might be altered significantly were data-feedback systems in place routinely.

Consider the often aired complaint by police that much of their work is to no avail because the prosecutor or judiciary dismisses so many arrests. The study by Forst et al. (1977:63) did indeed document this: "What happens after arrest, most often, is that the prosecutor drops the case." But then consider their findings further: "The facts suggest that in most of the cases that were dropped it was appropriate both for the police to make an arrest and for the prosecutor either to refuse it at the initial court appearance or dismiss it after initially accepting it" (1977:88). Differences in standards of proof, relative seriousness, and resources may converge to produce apparent conflict where none exists.

Such interagency tracking and feedback systems are essential also for the identification of circumstances where decision alternatives are necessary. The Forst study and the Vera Institute study, both of which employed a case-tracking method, identified the critical role played by nonstranger crimes and the problems associated with processing such cases. Such findings highlight the need for the discovery of decision alternatives (and then their evaluation) at the arrest stage for disputes between nonstrangers. As Forst *et al.* (1977:91) put it:

> An especially challenging research issue consists of determining effective ways for the police to deal with criminal episodes among nonstrangers, without resorting to arrest. These episodes have been found to consume a substantial amount of prosecution and court resources with little apparent benefit.

The mere existence of discretion in such a critical exercise of state power as arrest raises the problem of abuse. When the common alternatives in a decision are not known publicly when taken, there is the added difficulty of controlling discretion in ways that can minimize abuse. This difficulty has plagued police scholars and has led some to conclude that because of inherent difficulties in control, arrest discretion should be wholly eliminated.

In a sense, many problems in discretion control for arrest are analogous to problems at subsequent stages of processing. The identification of rules for decision making that structure choices but do not eliminate the individualization of decisions based on unique circumstances of the case transcends the problem of arrest. But in other respects police discretion to arrest is unique. There are no systematically collected written records that permit the study of decisions not to proceed with full processing (such as exist at all subsequent decisions). And there are profound difficulties even in identifying the pool of potential arrestees about whom such decisions are made. Thus, it is extremely difficult to ascertain whether in decisions not to arrest the decision process operates fairly.

There are, of course, extant mechanisms of control on abuses of arrest discretion. Civil actions brought by the offended citizen against the police, civilian review boards, criminal actions brought against officers who fail to arrest, departmental supervision, and judicial review are all methods that to some extent seek to structure and control arrest discretion. None serves, however, to encompass adequately the range of problems that may arise or to offer specific and public guidance concerning routine arrest decisions. Judicial review by means of the exclusionary rule, for example, serves to constrain only specific behaviors and only for those cases in which prosecution is sought. Civil and criminal actions are costly, make demands on complainants that may be unrealistic, and provide only for *ad hoc* rule making. Civilian review boards undoubtedly are useful for some problems (for example, the use of force) but cannot be expected to provide routine arrest policy.[32]

We outline a general model for the control of discretion in Chapter 10 that we believe has considerable potential if applied to arrest decisions. Here we may briefly describe one major difference between our approach and the approach commonly preferred in the literature.

Many scholars recognize that it is the patrol officer who, by default, is the real policymaker within police departments with respect to when to arrest and when to choose an alternative. The absence of clearly articulated policies for the exercise of arrest discretion that can be monitored, however, raises serious issues of accountability, both with respect to abuses of discretion and concerning the achievement of common decision goals. And, most certainly, inhibitions about acknowledging the legitimate role of discretion in arrest detracts from the development of meaningful arrest guidelines. As Davis (1975:iii–iv) notes:

> The false pretense prevents *open* selective enforcement, prevents top officers
> from making and announcing enforcement policy, prevents special studies
> of enforcement policy, prevents the use of professional staffs for making
> enforcement policy, prevents enlistment of public participation in policy-
> making, and discourages efforts of the police to coordinate their enforcement
> policy with the policy of prosecutors and judges.

Many proposals designed to increase the visibility of the factors influencing arrest practices and to enhance evenhandedness in arrest decisions have centered on administrative rule making by top officers within police departments (American Bar Association, 1973; Davis, 1975; H. Goldstein, 1977; Wilson, 1965). The absence of administrative guidelines to structure discretion turns what for the patrol officer is already a difficult task into a virtual no-win situation. In Goldstein's words:

> The police really suffer the worst of all worlds: they must exercise broad
> discretion behind a facade of performing in a ministerial fashion; and they
> are expected to realize a high level of equality and justice in their discretionary
> determinations though they have not been provided with the means most
> commonly relied upon in government to achieve these ends. (1977:110)

Our own proposal for the enhancement of rationality in these decisions also focuses on the development of administrative guidelines. But it recognizes that it is the patrol officer who is the principal policymaker now. Our model seeks first to discover the implicit policy that these decision makers follow; to make that policy more widely known; then to debate its propriety and effectiveness, to modify it systematically, and to study the effects of modification as a continuous process of development. The day-to-day decision makers in the criminal justice system are the best source to begin such a process of evolutionary policy development. Decision guidelines built in this fashion, when actually used, can both enhance equity and preserve the individualization of justice. Thus, we propose a method of rule making; our method begins with observation of the behavior of the lower-level decision makers rather than the "top officers." To be effective, administrative rule making needs to be predicated on the policies that currently exist, albeit implicitly. And that requires empirical studies (of the types reviewed in this chapter) of how arrest decisions are made, of the available alternatives, of the effectiveness of these alternatives, of the specific goals of the various decisions, and most critically, of the relation between case data and the achievement of these goals. We present these ideas more systematically in the last chapter.

NOTES

1. One bibliography of works only about police decisions listed 138 entries. See Neithercutt and Moseley (1974).
2. Of the many scholarly discussions of police work, the three that should be consulted first are Goldstein (1977), Bittner (1975), and LaFave (1965).
3. The law of arrest is complex and varies, to a limited extent, by jurisdiction. For a discussion of the legal requisites for arrest and the problems inherent in defining arrest for research or analytical purposes, see LaFave (1965: Chapter 1). Our definition here is purposefully restrictive (e.g., excluding citizens' arrests and arrests of witnesses).
4. It clearly would be easy to minimize the impact of the criminal law function of police work on the daily activities and roles of the police. Such an impression, even if generated on the basis of the studies cited above, would be profoundly erroneous. Even though the amount of time police actually spend engaged in criminal law matters such as arrest is small, the impact of this activity on the role of the police is pervasive. See Goldstein (1977).
5. Because of these relations, Reiss (1971) characterizes citizens as "enforcers of the law."
6. Quite obviously, this is something of an overstatement. It applies most convincingly to crimes of common theft and assault and much less so to the so-called victimless crimes—e.g., prostitution and drug offenses—although some evidence indicates that citizen complaints are equally important in bringing drunkenness offenses to the attention of the police. See R. Lundman (1974). There are other types of criminal

behavior for which the police role is extremely limited—e.g., corporate fraud. Here, as in the rest of this book, our discussion pertains principally to the routine common law crimes.

7. The significant exception, of course, is the use of deadly force. The decision to use deadly force is beyond the intended scope of this chapter. We believe that this decision could, however, be analyzed according to the requirements of rationality employed in this book, particularly with respect to agency policy about the use of deadly force. For extended commentary about deadly force policies and their consequences, see Sherman (1980b).

8. This position has striking analogues to other decisions we discuss in this book. At the sentencing decision, for example (see Chapter 6), recent reform proposals that seek more determinacy and greater consistency would have the legislature define explicitly the penalty that must be given for a certain offense. The motive for determinate sentencing is the same as discussed here for arrests—eliminate discretion by legislation in order to control its abuses. We see the same problems in both solutions. The immense variability inherent in criminal acts, persons, and circumstances precludes the elimination of discretion at both decisions. The inequities that such "discretionless" systems would foster would compel resolution by decision makers somewhere in the system. And the problems of low visibility, reviewability, and control would again surface. As we describe in detail in the final chapter, we believe it possible to design systems of decision making that at once both acknowledge the legitimate role of individualized decision making (discretion) and adequately control it.

9. Some may argue that individualized decision making is indeed a value to be pursued by criminal law but that others (prosecutors or judges) who are elected representatives should be empowered to exercise such discretion. Visibility (and hence reviewability) may be enhanced by requiring these latter decision makers to exercise such judgments. Such a position has merit but must be balanced against the impact that arrest decisions *per se* can involve. Thus, if an arrest would aggravate the situation, unfairly stigmatize the suspect, or otherwise be detrimental to important values, the police may be in the best position to employ discretion.

Police discretion involves a good many activities other than deciding, in a given case, whether to arrest. Whether to enforce a law at all, whether to use force, where to patrol, how to patrol, and so forth are all areas of considerable discretion. Although our focus is exclusively on arrest decisions (as defined earlier), these aspects of police discretion are important. See Goldstein (1977:Chapter 5).

10. Decision problems such as these are far from uncommon. See the examples and analysis in Parnas (1967, 1971).

11. Similar positions are advanced by others. Wilson (1965:21) argues, for example, "Discretion exists both because many of the relevant laws are necessarily ambiguous and because under the law of many states governing arrests for certain forms of disorder, the 'victim' must cooperate with the patrolman if the law is to be invoked at all."

Most contemporary standard-setting bodies argue for the acknowledgment of arrest discretion. See American Bar Association (1973), National Advisory Commission on Criminal Justice Standards and Goals (1973), and President's Commission on Law Enforcement and Administration of Justice, Task Force Report: The Police (1967).

12. We describe these aims fully in Chapter 6, where sentencing decisions are discussed. Most of the contemporary discussion about goals of the criminal law has taken place in the context of sentencing. One theme of this book is that these goals transcend a narrow focus on sentencing; they are critically important to the evaluation of victim, police, bail, correction, and parole decisions as well. As we argue in the final chapter

however, any one of these aims is best pursued within the context of specific decision points.

13. The general prevention function of police work has received some evaluation attention (see, e.g., Kelling, Pate, Dieckman, and Brown, 1974). Although a review of this growing literature is beyond the scope of our inquiry here, it is a critical contribution to the information requirements (as we use that term) for rational police decisions. For a review of this and similar issues, see Goldstein (1977) and Sherman (1983).

14. An extensive discussion of reasons for "noninvocation" in arrest decisions is found in LaFave (1965). On the basis of observations in three states, LaFave discovered that some common reasons were: The legislature may not desire full enforcement; there are limited enforcement resources; the victim refuses to prosecute; the victim is involved in the misconduct; the intent is to benefit other aspects of law enforcement (e.g., protect the informant system); the harm caused to the offender or to the victim would outweigh the risk of inaction.

15. It may strike some as strange to consider doing nothing a major alternative in arrest decisions. But we agree with Goldstein that "in trying to develop a rational scheme for handling police business, the option of doing nothing should be recognized as an appropriate alternative in some situations" (1977:40).

16. Sherman (1980a) has provided a classification of research studies concerning police behavior and has reviewed many of their results.

17. See Wilson (1965) and Smith (1984) for studies using this analytical approach. For a study that compares the relative influence of community characteristics and type of police organization, see Swanson (1979) and Talarico and Swanson (1979). For an interesting approach that considers individual rather than organizational policy styles to be influential, see Muir (1977).

    There are considerable difficulties involved in interagency studies of policy correlates of arrest rates, not the least of which involves the definition and subsequent control of extraneous variance. Although such aggregate studies are widely reported, particularly in the sociological literature, we do not find them convincing. For review of many of these studies, and discussion of potential limitations, see Sherman (1980a).

18. The proportion of cases falling into these categories is not given. It should be noted, however, that these data indicate that the juvenile officers in this study may not be characteristic of police on patrol, given the widely reported finding that calls to the police, rather than direct observation, is by far the principal way in which police become involved in such encounters.

19. Piliavin and Briar do not present tabulations of arrest by specific offense type, and therefore the extent of the relation between offense behavior and the arrest decision cannot be determined. They do report that the importance of demeanor appeared to be much less significant for offenders with known prior records.

20. Their data have been analyzed also by Friedrich (1977).

21. Friedrich also examined how well the characteristics of the officers in the study (e.g., race, length of service, and job satisfaction) predicted their arrest decisions in multiple regression analysis. Virtually none of the variance in arrest ($R = .014$) was explained by these factors.

22. A number of papers have been generated by these data: Sykes, Fox, and Clarke (1976); Sykes and Clarke (1975); Lundman, Sykes, and Clarke (1978); and Lundman (1974).

23. At least one body of sociological theory, however, posits no relation between decisions made in the criminal justice system and behavioral differences among the clients of the system (e.g., Black, 1976). For a data-oriented critique of these theories, see Gottfredson and Hindelang (1979b, 1980).

24. A now common practice in the sociological literature is to classify variables into legal and extralegal categories and to assess their relative contributions to explain processing decisions. Some such variables are more easily sorted thus than others (e.g., "amount of evidence" is legal and suspect's race is extralegal). Others are considerably more difficult to classify. The preference of the complainant certainly has implications for evidence, although it is often considered to be an extralegal variable. The demeanor of the suspect (e.g., antagonistic) may be perceived (either rightly or wrongly) by the police to be indicative of the need for custody pending adjudication. It also may be a proxy for racial prejudice and hence, an extralegal consideration.

25. We argue in the final chapter that data systems permitting such studies should be in place and studied routinely by police departments as one step toward the enhancement of rationality.

26. Several excellent reviews of the police referral decision for juveniles are available. See Cohen and Kluegel (1978, 1979), Hirschi (1975), and Nettler (1978). The general findings from this research are compatible with the correlates discussed in the text. In deciding whether to refer arrested juveniles to court, the police seem to rely principally on the seriousness of the alleged behavior and any record of prior illegal conduct. When seriousness of offense is controlled, suspect characteristics (e.g., race and social class) appear to play a role in some places at some times, but not as significant a role as does offense. See Chapter 10 for some implications of these findings, along with the correlates of the other major decisions discussed in this book, for conceptualization about the criminal justice process. Although most police referral studies deal with youth, Pope (1978a) studied police referral decisions for a group of adult burglary arrestees in California. The criterion variable was the postarrest decision (by police) to release suspects or to detain them prior to trial. Although the results are restricted to one type of crime (and hence do not permit inferences about whether the crime itself is related to the decision) the results are informative. The single strongest correlate, among those Pope studied of the release decision, was whether the suspect had a prior record; those without prior records were more likely to be released. Among those with prior records, the young (under eighteen) and those without a history of drug use were less likely to be released. For those without prior records, blacks were more likely to be detained than were whites.

27. Here we are using the term *goal* in a different context than we do usually in this book. Conviction may be better thought of as an objective—that is, as one method of achieving the aims of desert, deterrence, and the like that are associated typically with decision goals in this book.

28. A consideration of errors in predictive judgments is important here, as with most criminal justice decisions. We take up this topic in detail in Chapter 4, where pretrial detention decisions are discussed. Much of what we say there is indeed applicable to predictive custody decisions at the arrest stage. And the omnipresence of predictive judgments throughout the system weighs heavily in our model designed to enhance rationality, presented in Chapter 10.

29. Although not usually discussed in this context, these errors are false positive errors. One important aspect of false positive errors is that they are hidden errors, in the absence of an experiment showing for certain how many exist. Because predictive judgments are made throughout the criminal justice system, these errors are an issue at every major decision. Predictive judgments are discussed more fully in our consideration of bail decision making (Chapter 4), where they have received more scholarly attention.

To some extent the correlates of arrest decisions, identified in the previous section, are indicative of the presumed need for custody. For example, it may be thought that the more serious the offense and the greater the penalties attendant upon conviction, the greater is the custody need at the arrest decision. Such presumptions are in need of empirical testing.

30. Several comprehensive reviews are available: Carter and Klein (1976); Dunford (1977); Klein, Teilman, Styles, Lincoln, and Labin-Rosensweig (1976). For a good study of British practices, see Mott (1983).

31. One review of this literature concludes: "While there seems to be wide-spread agreement about the desirability of diverting youth from the juvenile justice system and a sizeable mobilization of federal, state and local resources for the development of community diversion projects, little has been done to examine how diversion programs have been operationalized or how effectively they function" Dunford (1977:336).

32. For excellent discussions of the problems with and prospects for these various methods of discretion control, see H. Goldstein (1967) and Davis (1975).

Chapter 4

PRETRIAL RELEASE DECISIONS

Once an alleged offender has been taken into custody by arrest, it then must be decided whether he or she will remain in custody pending trial or will be released (and, if so, under what conditions). Traditionally, this decision has been the responsibility of the magistrate at the initial appearance.

Pretrial release decisions illustrate many of the most important issues of concern in this book. They must be made in the face of potentially conflicting goals. At the heart of every pretrial release decision, the goal of preserving the defendant's liberty before conviction (when he or she is presumed to be innocent) must be balanced against the goals of community protection and orderly justice. This difficult juxtaposition of the defendant's interst in liberty with the community's interest in safety was aptly described by the President's Commission on Law Enforcement and Administration of Justice:

> The importance of this decision to any defendant is obvious. A released defendant is one who can live with and support his family, maintain his ties to his community, and busy himself with his own defense by searching for witnesses and evidence and by keeping in close touch with his lawyer. An imprisoned defendant is subjected to the squalor, idleness, and possible criminalizing effect of jail. He may be confined while presumed innocent only to be freed when found guilty; many jailed defendants, after they have been convicted, are placed on probation rather than imprisoned. The community also relies on the magistrate for protection when he makes his decision about releasing a defendant. If a relased defendant fails to appear for trial, the law is flouted. If a released defendant commits crimes, the community is endangered. (1967:131)

The difficult issues that arise concerning the goals of the pretrial release decision are similar to the problems that plague other critical decisions in the criminal justice system. As H. Goldstein (1964:151–160) noted:

> Place this problem within the same context as so many of the other critical issues in the criminal justice system; the need for striking a delicate balance between the concern for the protection of society and the desire to guarantee maximum freedom for the individual; the desire to prevent future crimes vs. the desire to allow the suspect to be free prior to trial.

. The problem of adequacy of information is clearly in evidence at the pretrial release decision. What data are known to be relevant to the achievement of the goals of pretrial release decisions? Is the information useful for achieving the goal of community protection also useful for attaining the goal of maximum pretrial liberty for the accused? What information about the consequences of pretrial release decisions is available to the decision maker?

Pretrial release decision making also serves to illustrate the importance of decision alternatives. For many years, in most American jurisdictions, the principal issue confronting the magistrate at initial appearance was, for those eligible for bail, how much money should be required from the defendant in order that the defendant be released.[1] But the last two decades have witnessed a substantial increase in the decision alternatives available to the magistrate, such that in many areas the judge now may have the option of deciding among outright release on a simple promise to appear in court at the proper time and place (typically referred to as "release on own recognizance" or ROR); release to private third-party custody; supervised release; release to some treatment program; release upon deposit of some portion of the bail amount (for example, 10%); release upon receipt by the court of the full bail amount; or preventive detention. Each of these decision alternatives may have its own information requirements. And each may embody quite different goals and procedural issues. Consider, for example, the likely differences in objectives between releasing to a treatment program and issuing an order for preventive detention.

The variety of decision alternatives at the pretrial release decision serves to illustrate also the nature of the varied consequences of a decision. Some of the research examined in this chapter indicates how criminal justice decisions may have consequences (both to the defendant and to the decision maker) that go far beyond the immediate outcome of the decision. Apart from the choice of detention and the attendant consequences of that confinement, the decision alternatives available to the magistrate at pretrial release may have quite different consequences with respect to later decisions; thus, the decision itself may provide information necessarily considered in rational decision making at a later stage. A concern of researchers in this field has been the ways in which the pretrial decision may influence other important decisions made about the defendant, such as the determination of guilt or innocence and punishment. Indeed, studies of collateral consequences of bail decisions were among the earliest investigations of the interplay among components of the criminal justice system.

Perhaps in no other criminal justice decision is the issue of prediction so centrally involved, so hotly debated, or so difficult to circumvent. Although there is disagreement about the proper goals of the pretrial decision, it generally is agreed that at a minimum the magistrate's task involves a consideration of what conditions (if any) are necessary to assure the defendant's appearance at trial. Many argue that the protection of the community (including witnesses) from additional crimes during the pretrial period is equally important. Because they involve future events, these considerations involve predictions of behavior. As such, they raise all of the issues of reliability, validity, propriety, and consequences that necessarily surface whenever an individual's liberty is conditional on perceptions of measures of what he or she *may* do in the future.

SIGNIFICANCE TO THE DEFENDANT

The most obvious potential outcome of moment from pretrial release decisions is the detention or liberty of accused persons prior to trial.[2] The numbers of persons thus affected by such decisions in the United States are extremely large. Pretrial custody accounts for a greater proportion of those incarcerated each year than does imprisonment following sentencing. In 1982, 57% of the adults in jails were unconvicted (Bureau of Justice Statistics, 1983). On a given day more than 100,000 persons are detained prior to trial in American jails.

These figures take on added significance when read in light of the deplorable conditions found in many American jails. Numerous surveys have characterized jails as the worst aspect of the correctional system, lacking in space, programs, privacy, security, and even cleanliness (Mattick, 1974). Pretrial detainees routinely are housed with convicted persons serving their sentences. Furthermore, the incidence of self-destructive behavior among jail inmates is disturbingly high—higher than that found in prisons (Gibbs, 1978).

An unfortunate irony also exists for many pretrial detainees: they are incarcerated before trial, when they are presumed to be innocent but are freed once convicted. The sentence for many jailed defendants does not include imprisonment. Goldkamp (1979) found, for example, that 72% of the convicted persons in a sample of defendants from Philadelphia were detained prior to trial but were not imprisoned after conviction. Landes (1974), in a study of 858 indigent defendants in New York City, discovered that 34% of the detained defendants did not receive additional detention as part of their sentences.[3]

An even greater irony concerns those persons who are detained prior to trial but who are not then convicted. The evidence suggests that a disquietingly large number of persons—as many as half of those confined before trial—fall into this category. In his study of Philadelphia detainees, Goldkamp (1979) found that of those defendants detained more than twenty-four hours after arrest, 55% were not convicted of anything. And of those defendants detained until their final disposition, 45% were not convicted.

THE CONSEQUENCES OF DETENTION

Apart from the fact of imprisonment itself, it has long been argued that detention before trial has numerous adverse consequences to the defendant (Beeley, 1927; Foote, 1965; Goldkamp, 1979). Pretrial detention may unduly induce some defendants to plead guilty in order to be freed from confinement. This may be particularly true for defendants charged with minor crimes for which the penalty may not include jail. Also, it frequently is argued that, relative to freed defendants, detained defendants are more likely to be convicted and, once convicted, are more likely to be given more onerous punishments (for example, more likely to be imprisoned and more likely to be given longer sentences). There are several hypotheses as to why detention prior to trial may have adverse consequences for the defendant at later stages of the criminal justice process. Detained persons may be less well able to prepare adequately for their defense against the charges because they are less free to consult with counsel, to gather witnesses on their behalf, and to muster the evidence required. There may be, furthermore, psychological consequences of detention affecting decision makers adversely to the defendant, persons confined may be less "presentable" to the court at trial (see Wald, 1964).

Several empirical studies have been undertaken that shed some light on the question of the adverse effects of pretrial detention on subsequent judicial decisions (such as conviction and sentence).

This type of study, perhaps first performed by Morse and Beattie in 1932 (1974), is exemplified by research undertaken by Foote, Markle, and Woolley in Philadelphia in 1954.[4] They studied the dispositions of 946 cases, which were all of the dispositions of the court during a two-month period for selected offenses (rape, robbery, arson, burglary, assault, auto theft, property crimes, sex offenses, and narcotics). In comparisons between jailed and bailed defendants for similar offenses, they found that a much higher number of jailed defendants were convicted than of bailed defendants (72% versus 52%). Furthermore, they discovered that, once convicted, jailed defendants were much more likely than were bailed defendants to be given sentences that included imprisonment (59% versus 22%).

Foote and his coworkers cautiously suggested a number of factors that could have influenced the obtained results. They pointed out that such unmeasured variables as judges' imposing high bail (with resulting detention) on defendants who were more likely to be guilty or setting high bail when there were substantial factors in aggravation could have a bearing on the interpretation of the results. Nevertheless, they concluded that " despite these unmeasurable variables . . . the contrast in comparative dispositions was so striking that it is reasonable to conclude that jail status had a good deal to do with it" (Foote et al., 1965:1054).

There is consistency among studies of this type concerning the influence of pretrial detention on the probability of conviction and the type of sentence. The procedure of simply comparing the dispositions for jailed and bailed defendants, however, leaves substantial room for competing hypotheses. That is, these studies leave us unsure as to whether detention itself is prejudicial or whether the factors that are influential in setting high bail (and hence detention) are the same factors that lead to conviction or more punitive sentences. Examples of the latter could include factors that increase convictability (and perhaps lead a magistrate to believe there is greater risk of flight) or that aggravate the offense (and lead the magistrate to believe the defendant is dangerous).

Unfortunately, in the absence of an experimental design with random allocation to released and detained groups, there can be no entirely satisfactory resolution of these competing hypotheses. Such a study has not been undertaken but studies that attempt to approximate such procedures through the use of statistical controls do exist and are informative.

Four studies have looked at the question of the prejudicial effects of detention with the aid of some form of statistical control (Goldkamp, 1979; Landes, 1974; Rankin, 1964; and Single, 1972).[5] The most thorough study of the question of prejudicial effects of pretrial detention on subsequent judicial decisions was undertaken by Goldkamp (1979). In this study based on an estimated 8,300 defendants in the Philadelphia Municipal Court, he investigated how pretrial status was related to several possible outcomes of the cases: dismissal, acquittal, pretrial diversion, conviction, and sentence. For each of these outcomes, Goldkamp studied the relation to pretrial custody for the group of defendants facing each decision, while statistically controlling for factors other than detention thought relevant to each decision. Thus, he studied a much more exhaustive array of decision outcomes than had earlier studies. His sample was drawn to be representative of the Philadelphia pretrial population, and the number of cases studied was far larger than any previously examined.

When pretrial status was dichotomized to classify those who were released within twenty-four hours of arrest (by release on recognizance, bail, etc.) as opposed to those who were detained longer than twenty-four hours after arrest,[6] he discovered that the persons in the detained group were equally likely to have the charges dropped as were those in the freed group (33% each). The detainees, however, were less likely to be acquitted (8% versus 12%) and were less likely to be diverted (7% versus 39%), but they were more likely (either as a result of a plea or trial) to be found guilty (46% versus 20%).

Goldkamp then used multivariate statistics to see whether these differences were maintained when statistical controls were applied to factors thought to be relevant to both pretrial custody and these later judicial decisions. As controls, he entered variables measuring the seriousness of the charge, whether detainers were present, the number of prior arrests, whether the defendant was currently on parole or probation, the number of open cases, and the number of offenses charged. Both the number and complexity of these statistical controls were greater than those used in earlier studies.

The results may be summarized briefly. Pretrial custody appeared to be unrelated to the dismissal decision, unrelated to the diversion decision, and unrelated to adjudication (acquitted versus convicted) once these statistical controls were exercised. Goldkamp concluded that, for this group of defendants, pretrial custody was not influential in these later judicial decisions. Rather, the observed relations between custody status and these outcomes at the bivariate level were thought to be the result of the common association between custody status and the control variables on the one hand and the control variables and judicial decisions on the other.

The final judicial decision studied by Goldkamp was sentencing. Here he studied the range of sanctions given to the defendants in his sample, from fines and suspended sentences to incarceration for several years. Again, at the bivariate level of analysis, marked differences in dispositions were observed between the freed and detained groups. In general, the freed group was more likely to be given probation whereas the detained group was more likely to be incarcerated.

He then undertook two multivariate analyses of the sentencing decision; one considered the decision as to whether to incarcerate, and the other, for those incarcerated, considered how long a sentence was given. He found that whether or not a convicted defendant received a sentence of incarceration was related to pretrial custody, even after the statistical controls were exercised. Those persons detained prior to trial were more likely to be given sentences to prison, although only a weak relation between pretrial custody and sentence length was uncovered.

Goldkamp's study serves to illustrate the complexity of the question of whether pretrial custody affects later judicial decisions. The complexity of pretrial conditions, the variability in judicial alternatives, and the need to construct statistical controls because of the absence of experimental conditions all serve to complicate the answer to this critical question. The latter problem, requiring that inferences be made only from nonexperimental designs, is especially troublesome and inhibits all but cautious conclusions.

Nevertheless, some conclusions may be reached on the basis of these studies. First, none have been able to reject the hypothesis that pretrial custody influences sentencing decisions to the detriment of those detained. Despite the best statistical controls possible and with the aid of sophisticated statistical models, each of these studies found, in some form, an effect of detention on sentence. Second, the magnitude of this effect, is, from a purely statistical perspective, small. Other factors— principally the offense of conviction and prior record—appear to be much more influential in determining sentence. Third, Goldkamp's study casts some doubt on the existence of a major effect of pretrial custody on whether a defendant is convicted. It may be that judges set bail or other release conditions in part on the basis of factors that are also predictive of conviction.

SIGNIFICANCE TO SOCIETY

On the one hand, freedom from confinement before an impartial adjudication of guilt in which the accused has the opportunity to present a defense symbolically and practically embodies the cherished concept of due process of law. As Dill (1972) has observed, pretrial freedom is

important to society and underlies other basic procedural guarantees—
rights of notice, specific charge, fair hearing, counsel—theoretically granted
to all persons accused of crime.

On the other hand, the pretrial release decision may have an impact
on the security of the community and the ability of the justice system
to operate in an orderly fashion. When a pretrial releasee commits a
crime while on release, members of the community are apt to feel that
the justice system somehow is not working adequately to ensure their
safety. When an accused fails to appear for trial, the justice system is
flouted.

In a survey of rates of failure to appear in seventy-two cities, Wice
(1974) discovered officially reported rates ranging from 4% to 24%, with
nearly 90% reporting rates of less than 10%. Thomas (1976) surveyed
twenty cities for the years 1962 to 1971, finding that the failure to appear
rates for felony defendants ranged from 1% to 15% in 1962 and from
3% to 17% in 1971. The medians were about 6% for 1962 and 11% for
1971. Toborg and Sorin (1980) reported rates ranging from 6% to 21%
with an average of 13% in their eight-city survey. The variability among
the cities surveyed in definitions of "failure to appear" and in the proportions of people released prohibit all but the most cautious interpre-
tions but overall these rates do not appear to be disquieting.

Estimates of the amount of crime committed by pretrial releases are
quite variable. A study of pretrial releases in Washington, D.C., conducted by the National Bureau of Standards, showed that 17% were
rearrested (Locke et al., 1970). In his Los Angeles study, Gottfredson
(1974) found a rearrest rate of 5% for crimes against the person. In a
study of pretrial releasees in the District of Columbia, it was found that
of all those released prior to trial in 1975, 20% were brought before the
court again in 1975 (Welsh and Viets, 1977). And Toborg and Sorin (1980)
found a rearrest rate averaging around 16%.

GOALS OF THE PRETRIAL RELEASE DECISION

With the possible exception of the sentencing decision, perhaps no
decision in the criminal justice system has been the object of more recent
commentary concerning legitimate aims than has the decision to release
or detain defendants prior to trial. The interests at stake in the decision
are profound, complex, sometimes contradictory, and hotly debated.
Unfortunately, all too often the resulting debates are shrouded by spec-
ulation. In most urban courtrooms, the judge, sometimes with the aid
of probation staff, police, prosecutors, public defenders, and pretrial

service agency staff, must weigh these concerns and balance these interests with extreme rapidity. The judge may receive bail recommendations from the police, the prosecutor, or the public defender, each of whom may be responding to different goals. Data about the defendant, alleged offense, prior record, income, residence, family life, and the like may be supplied by probation staff. The judge may have extensive experience in setting bail or may be a novice. Most typically, he or she will be unsure of how the wealth of data presented relates to the task at hand (much data, little information). Almost never will the judge be informed systematically how other judges in the same court—or perhaps even how he or she—has decided similar cases in the past. And almost never will the judge be informed of how well the goals sought to be accomplished were met: Was the defendant able to make the amount of bail set? Did he or she show up for trial? Was a new offense committed during the period of release? Thus, these important decisions are made rapidly, in large numbers, with little information, and generally without feedback on the consequences.

Lack of Feedback!

A discussion of the goals of the pretrial release decision must attend to the confluence of law and social science. The debates about the proper functions of bail are, on the one hand, constitutional in origin and take place as well as in the context of state statutes that outline the criteria to be considered by judges in making release decisions. On the other hand, these debates necessarily concern social scientific knowledge about the ability of decision makers to make predictive judgments and estimates of the costs involved in errors. As with most decisions in the criminal justice system, symbolic goals and system constraints also enter into discussions of the proper aims of the pretrial decision.[7] Moreover, important latent functions may be served by bail decisions—for example, Suffet (1966) has suggested that bail setting often serves to diffuse the responsibility for the defendant's release. Public criticism of a release decision may be muted by the "excuse" that the defendant was released because he made bail—a latent function perhaps seen as more important in jurisdictions in which judges are elected. Similarly, bail may appear to diffuse responsibility for detention. A magistrate may claim that detention was not intended but rather was a consequence of the defendant's inability to post the amount of bail required to assure appearance for trial.

Most of the controversy about the goals of pretrial release decisions centers on the issues of appearance at trial and prevention of new crimes in the interim between arrest and adjudication. The legal arguments address the constitutionality of "preventive detention" and inquire into whether the Eighth Amendment imparts a right to bail.

The most extensive historical and constitutional analysis of the permissible concerns of the bail decision has been undertaken by Foote (1965). He traced the origins of the Eighth Amendment clause, "Excessive bail shall not be required . . . ," through English common law to the framers of the Constitution in order to discover the parameters of the "right to bail" and the constitutionally permissible purposes of bail. His analyses led him to conclude that a right to bail was intended by the framers to be construed broadly, despite certain offenses (capital) that were seen as nonbailable. That the specific language of the Eighth Amendment does not convey this more precisely was the result of a historical accident: "The excessive bail clause was meant to provide a constitutional right to bail and the inadequacy of the form adopted for this purpose was the result of inadvertence" (1965:987). Foote concluded:

> What the precise scope and substance of this right should be under modern conditions neither can nor should be deduced from history. But however such detail may be resolved, the only end which seems consistent with these historical antecedents is that the clause was intended to afford protection against pretrial imprisonment in a broad category of cases. (1965:989)

Furthermore, on Eighth Amendment grounds, on grounds that prediction of dangerousness is inherently impossible without unacceptable error rates, on grounds that it is pretrial punishment, and on grounds that it impairs fair trial, Foote's analyses lead him to reject preventive detention.

Foote's legal analysis of the purposes of pretrial decisions serves well to frame the contemporary debate about pretrial release. First, he raised the question of whether the excessive bail clause imparts a right to bail. He argued that the origins of the clause strongly imply this right.

Second, Foote raised the question of the constitutionality of setting money bail for the poor—regardless of the legitimate aims of the pretrial release decision. Because many defendants cannot afford any bail (hence bail for them is tantamount to pretrial detention), there is the question of whether bail for indigents is unconstitutional because it violates the requirement of equal protection of the laws. As Justice Douglas wrote in *Bandy* v. *United States:*

> To continue to demand a substantial bond which the defendant is uanble to secure raises considerable problems for the equal administration of the law. We have held that an indigent defendant is denied equal protection of the law if he is denied an appeal on equal terms with other defendants, solely because of his indigence. . . . Can an indigent be denied freedom, where a wealthy man would not, because he does not happen to have enough property to pledge for his freedom?

Fourth, Foote's analysis raised numerous issues about mechanisms other than money bail that might achieve the goal of assuring appearance at trial but that would avoid pretrial detention and the discrimination against the poor inherent in money bail. These suggestions, not wholly adopted today, gave rise to two decades of active bail reform.

There appears to be a consensus that assuring the appearance of accused persons is a legitimate goal of the pretrial release decision (whether we know *how* to do this is, of course, a different question). However, other goals of the decision (such as protecting the community from dangerous crimes) are also constitutionally permissible according to the recent Supreme Court decision in *U.S. v. Salerno*.[8]

The arguments advanced by proponents of preventive detention have been summarized succinctly by Wald (1964) in a critique of these views:

> There is no Eighth Amendment right to absolute bail. The mere fact that such an absolute right is not specifically granted in the Judiciary Act of 1789 speaks for itself. There is a long tradition of pretrial detention in England and Europe, and in fact judges have since 1789 used high bail as a way to keep dangerous offenders confined before trial. Capital crimes have always been detainable and many of the crimes for which detention is now sought were in fact capital crimes in 1789. . . . Pretrial defendants can already be jailed not only for want of bail but if the court finds it necessary to protect witnesses. Forty-nine states have excessive bail clauses in their Constitutions and 37 of these also have an absolute right to bail, thereby showing that they are not coextensive.

For others, the controversy about the constitutionally legitimate goals of pretrial release decisions simply cannot be resolved by historical analyses.[9] For example, Dershowitz (1979b:13) notes:

> I do not believe that the framers clearly intended to prohibit denial of bail on grounds of dangerousness . . . because all dangerous crimes were also capital crimes in 1790 the framers simply never had to confront the issue of whether a dangerous offender not facing the death penalty and therefore not likely to flee could be detained solely because of his alleged dangerousness. I suspect the framers simply never thought of the problem.

The controversy about the propriety and feasibility of preventive detention will surely continue. But the Supreme Court's holding in *Salerno* makes clear that there is an "overwhelming" government interest in crime by arrestees, and that pursuit of this interest may involve the *regulatory* (but not *punitive*) use of preventive detention. The use seems limited to serious crimes and some due process must accompany detention hearings.

There is little doubt that an increasing number of jurisdictions (e.g., Michigan, California, the District of Columbia) are modifying their bail laws to incorporate preventive detention (Goldkamp, 1983, 1985).

Apart from the debates surrounding the aims of assuring appearance of defendants at trial and preventing crimes in the interim between the arrest and the trial, several other goals of pretrial release decisions have been suggested. It has been argued that one function of detention before trial may be to protect the integrity of the trial process by inhibiting a defendant's opportunity to tamper with witnesses or other evidence. There can be little doubt that in some situations such protection is necessary, although there may be options short of detention that would be suitable substitutes. Police protection for witnesses or restrictive release conditions are examples used in some jurisdictions.

It has been suggested also that bail or pretrial detention sometimes is used explicitly for punishment. That is, it may be alleged that some magistrates give certain defendants high bail or otherwise detain them in order to inflict suffering for the unproved offense. There is some evidence suggesting that such practices are not uncommon. Landes, for example, interprets the results of his study of bail setting in New York as indicating that pretrial punishment may be a major rationale for these decisions. He argues that his results suggest:

> The possible adaptations of a criminal justice system to a situation where disappearance rates are extremely high and resources for reapprehension are severely limited. In these circumstances the determination of bond becomes the vehicle for effecting punishment because if the accused is released at this time, punishment is a remote possibility. This interpretation is clearly consistent with our empirical evidence. (1974:333)

His interpretation is plausible; it is undoubtedly true that sometimes, in some areas, bail-setting magistrates believe that a "taste of the bars" would be a good thing for some defendants who will not face incarceration if convicted. Unlike the constitutional ambiguity regarding protection of the community as a goal for the pretrial release decision, however, there is no doubt that using the bail decision to inflict preadjudicatory punishment is repugnant to the Fifth Amendment.

BAIL REFORM: A STEP TOWARD RATIONALITY

In 1927, after studying the bail system in Chicago, Beeley (1927) wrote that a large proportion of the defendants in the Cook County Jail were being detained needlessly. He theorized that, using data relating to a defendant's background, family ties, and reputation in the community, it would be possible to rate defendants as "dependable" or "undependable" regarding the probabilities of their appearing in court when required.[10] More than three decades later, the idea that defendants could be evaluated for appearance on the basis of their "community ties" became a major bail reform innovation through the pioneering efforts of staff of the Vera Institute of Justice (Ares, Rankin, and Sturz, 1963).

The Vera strategy was based on a thorough prebail interview with defendants in order to obtain reliable data on their employment, residence, and family ties in the area. According to a weighting scheme devised by Vera, defendants were scored on their ties to the community and either recommended or not for outright release on their own recognizance (ROR) on the basis of their scores. By providing judges with more reliable data on defendants' backgrounds at a very early stage, it was thought that it would be possible to facilitate the release of far greater proportions of defendants than had been the practice previously. Court bail reform projects modeled after the Vera prototype in Manhattan were implemented in many jurisdictions in the United States in the mid-1960s (Freed and Wald, 1964).

Stimulated also by the inadequacies and unfairness of the bail bondsman system,[11] by the concern over the number of defendants needlessly detained prior to trial, by the lack of demonstrated relations between money bail and appearance at trial, and by the discriminatory effect that the bail system has on the poor, many bail projects have developed in recent years. Many of these projects attempt to bring rationality to the pretrial release decision by providing judges with verified background information on defendants that is thought to be related to the likelihood of appearance at trial.

In the first project, the evaluation of flight risk was based upon information in four areas of concern: residential stability, employment history, family contacts, and prior criminal record. A point system was used in order to weight the various factors considered, and if the defendant scored a sufficient number of points (and if he could provide an address at which he could be reached), then verification of the information was attempted. This investigation was confined to references cited in the defendant's signed statement of consent. The project staff then reviewed the case and decided whether to recommend release on recognizance.

In 1964 Freed and Wald reported:

> The Manhattan Bail Project and its progeny have demonstrated that a defendant with roots in the community is not likely to flee irrespective of his lack of prominence or ability to pay a bondsman. To date, these projects have produced remarkable results, with vast numbers of releases, few defaulters, and scarcely any commission of crimes by parolees, in the interim between release and trial. (1964:62)

These authors point out that projects such as these serve two purposes:

1. They free numerous defendants who would otherwise be jailed for the entire period between arraignment and trial.
2. They provide comprehensive statistical data never before obtainable on such vital questions as what criteria are meaningful in deciding to release the defendant, how many defendants paroled on particular criteria will show up for trial, and how much better are a defendant's chances for acquittal or a suspended sentence if he is paroled.

The impact of the Vera program was widespread. Indeed, nearly every subsequent standard-setting body has included the "community ties" idea in bail standards (President's Commission, 1967; Federal Bail Reform Act, 1966; National Advisory Commission, 1973a; National Association of Pretrial Services Agencies, 1978; Attorney General's Task Force, 1981).

Not all jurisdictions have followed the Vera model, however. A significant exception is California, where bail schedules are still used. As summarized by Feeley (1983:59–60):

> Bail reform has developed differently in California. In New York, the ideal among reformers is the eventual elimination of bail bondsmen; in California and elswhere, because of the power of bondsmen, nonmonetary conditions of release have received secondary consideration. The California legislature has mandated that each court develop a bail schedule (in essence, a price list) specifying the amount of bail required for each offense in the criminal code. Arrestees can be released as soon after arrest as practical, thereby avoiding the need to hold someone until arraignment, if they post the specified amount. This procedure does not preclude the possibility of release on recognizance or creation by local courts of special pretrial release units, and several counties, including Alameda (Oakland), San Diego, Los Angeles, and San Francisco, have created such agencies.

One key difference between California programs and those in New York City is that the former intervene after arraignment, after the opportunity for automatic release provided by the bail schedules has been invoked. Thus, to the extent that people who can raise money or who possess enough collateral to satisfy a bondsman are also those with strongest ties to the community, the most likely candidates for release on recognizance are those least likely to use it. Court-sponsored pretrial release units that promote ROR are clearly supplementary programs designed to handle those arrestees not able to secur release by money bail.

By 1978, the bail reform movement, stimulated by the Vera community ties system, had reached over 200 cities (Roth and Wice, 1978). And the results of the reform seem salutory, as summarized by Thomas (1976:78):

> Clearly, the bail reform movement has accomplished much. . . . The obvious correlation which [this] study showed between the development of pretrial release programs and the substantial increase both in the overall percentage of defendants released and the proportions released on own recognizance and other forms of nonfinancial release clearly bespeaks the success these programs have collectively enjoyed in reforming American bail practices.

THE PROBLEM OF PREDICTION

As the bail reform movement makes clear, pretrial release decisions are bound inextricably to the concept of prediction. Whether the concern is with appearance at trial, the prevention of crimes in the interim between arrest and trial, or the protection of witnesses, the judge is faced with the task of forecasting the behavior of defendants. The ability to make such judgments accurately and the consequences of errors are topics that have attracted much social scientific attention in recent years. The results of these studies cast serious doubt on current abilities to predict with great accuracy the statistically rare events of failure to appear at trial and pretrial crime. These studies serve to emphasize again the importance of the concept of rationality in criminal justice decision making. As we have seen, much attention has been given to the legal issues surrounding the legitimate goals of the pretrial release decision, but there is a fundamental difference between the propriety of a decision goal and its feasibility. Regardless of its propriety, if the decision aim cannot be achieved with current knowledge within tolerable costs (both social and economic), then it is difficult to see how the decision may be regarded as rationally made in respect to that goal.

The Vera Foundation criteria developed in the Manhattan Bail Project work in one restricted sense. That is, experience reported thus far supports the view that persons released as a result of recommendations based upon the interview schedule rarely fail to appear for trial. There has been, however, no demonstration that the items used actually are predictive. In order for the items to be useful as predictors, it must be demonstrated that they help to discriminate between the groups of persons who appear for trial and those who do not. A logical case may be made easily for the relevance of items presumably reflecting roots in the community or employment stability. That is, it is reasonable to hypothesize that these items have some predictive relation to appearance for trial or other outcomes of interest in the decision process. Until these items are shown to be related to the various consequences of the decision, however, we must assume that actually they may be unrelated to these consequences. That is, these hypotheses must be tested. What is the degree of validity of the individual items, for example, in terms of correlation with appearance or nonappearance for trial? Are the items equally valid with respect to conviction for new offenses during the period of release? How are the items correlated with one another, and how should they be weighted in order to provide, in some specific sense, an optimal predictive guide to the court?

A study by Gottfredson (1974) demonstrated clearly the need for such investigations. It had two objectives: The first was to assess predictive validity of the Vera Institute's instrument and of its individual items. The second was to improve prediction from a variety of background characteristics of defendants. The design of the study, through a special arrangement with the courts, allowed comparison of subjectively chosen good and bad risks. That is, not only were persons recommended by the ROR project staff and approved by a judge released on their own recognizance, but also 328 defendants not deemed eligible by usual procedures were released. The latter group was compared with a randomly selected 201 defendants released normally. Although there were differences in the rates of failure to appear for trial for the two groups, a striking result was that about 85% of the ROR sample and about 73% of the experimental sample either appeared for trial or returned voluntarily. Similarly, about three-fourths of the ROR sample had no arrests during the ninety days just after release. None of the individual items that made up the Vera instrument was substantially related to the criteria studied (appearance or arrests), and the total score accounted for only 2%–3% of the variance in these criteria. (Although a variety of additional items were studied, the resulting prediction equations, when applied to a validation sample, failed to achieve substantially better prediction than the Vera instrument.)

Thus, although the items included in the Vera instrument seemed plausibly to be related to the goals of the decision, such relations when investigated empirically were found to be slight. This evidence provides a strong argument for the need to test the hypotheses involved in developing screening procedures to determine whether the expected relations indeed are found in practice. Otherwise, decisions may be based on mere data, plausibly related to the decision aims, but in actuality untested hunches providing little or no information.

Other studies of pretrial release decisions confirm the inability to predict either failure to appear or pretrial crime with great efficiency. Feeley and McNaughton (1974) analyzed data on 1,642 cases occurring in a three-month period in New Haven, about which pretrial status decisions are made. The vast majority (86%) of the cases in their sample received some form of pretrial release. Measuring failure to appear by whether a warrant was issued, they tried to predict appearance from data on a number of background factors. These included the seriousness of the charge, prior record, marital status, number of dependents, residency, length of time in the area, and employment status. Thus, the authors incorporated items that measured community ties and the alleged offense. None of the items studied, however, was found to be related substantially, either at the bivariate or the multivariate level of analysis, to failure to appear for trial or to rearrest while on pretrial release.

In a carefully conducted study in Charlotte, North Carolina, Clarke (1974) selected a random sample of about one-third of all criminal defendants arrested (excluding drunkenness, traffic offenses, and fish and game offenses) during the first quarters of 1971, 1972, and 1973. As in the Feeley and McNaughton study, an extremely high proportion of defendants secured some form of release—over 90% in each of the three years. (The program selected defendants according to a point scheme based on the defendant's community ties and gave supervision after release.)

Among all defendants, the factors found most highly associated with failure to appear for trial were the court disposition time, the form of release, and the defendant's criminal history. Data items found not to be strongly related to failure to appear were income, employment, seriousness of the charge, and race. Those items found most highly associated with rearrest while on release were the length of time from arrest to disposition, prior record, and the type of release. Consistent with the usually found results, prediction of either pretrial crime or failure to appear at trial, although improved somewhat over the "base rate,"[12] were not made with a good deal of accuracy. The single variable best able to account for pretrial success was found to be supervision while on release.

Others have examined the ability to predict dangerousness while on pretrial release, with generally poor results. The National Bureau of Standards studied the issue in 1970 with a sample of misdemeanor and felony defendants (Locke et al., 1970). It was found that of those defendants originally charged with crimes of violence, 17% were rearrested during the pretrial period, but only 5% of those originally charged with a violent offense were rearrested for violent offenses. They reported, moreover, little ability to discriminate between the two groups on the basis of background factors. Similar results were reported by Angel and co-workers (1971) in a study of the predictive validity of the criteria in the preventive detention code of the District of Columbia. Reinforcing these results, a study in Washington, D.C., confirmed the generally low degree of predictive validity in the area of pretrial misconduct. In this study of a large sample of persons released at the pretrial stage, neither the seriousness of the charge nor community ties were found to be related to failue to appear at trial. Those who were unemployed and those who were drug users were, however, significantly less likely to appear for trial. This study discovered also that those charged with felonies (especially property crimes), those with lengthy prior records, those unemployed, blacks, and younger defendants were more likely to be rearrested. The general ability to predict pretrial crime accurately again proved to be poor (Roth and Wice, 1978).

It would be inaccurate to claim on the basis of these studies that it is impossible to predict failure to appear at trial or pretrial crime. Most studies that have examined the issue have found that such predictions could be made, based on background factors, that improve on chance. Predictive validity is, after all, a matter of degree. At issue when such fundamental issues as liberty and safety are at stake, however, is the accuracy of those predictions and whether the costs of the errors associated with them can be tolerated.

The prediction problem posed by pretrial release decisions is made difficult by the relative rarity of the undesired behavior of concern. For example, in the Clarke study, the overall failure to appear rate was only 10% in 1973 (the highest of all the years studied). The rearrest rate was the same. In the Feeley and McNaughton study only 7% were rearrested while on release. In the Gottfredson sample, only 5% were rearrested for crimes against persons while on release. On statistical grounds, with such a small number of failures, it is extremely difficult to find predictors that can discriminate adequately between successes and failures. As has been discussed repeatedly in the literature, the unfortunate consequence of predictions resulting from low failure rates is the extremely high number of false positives—cases in which the prediction is made that the individual will fail when in fact he will succeed. In the Gottfredson study, 73% of the sample of defendants not normally released were false positives according to the major classification of failure to appear at trial. When it is recalled that some empirical evidence suggests there are negative consequences that failure to secure release from confinement pending trial can have for defendants (in addition to the consequences of incarceration *per se*), the false positive issues take on paramount importance. Further complexity in these predictive aspects of pretrial release arises from the issue of requiring conditions on the release of defendants. Not only is it difficult to establish predictors of either failure to appear or future criminality—that is, to find factors associated with these behaviors—but it is necessary to know which defendants can be released only with specified conditions. This involves the conditional probabilities of the criterion categories (failure to appear or future criminality) given classifications of both defendants and required treatments or modes of supervision. There is also the question of the effectiveness of requirements for specific kinds of defendants, about which little is known.

After an elaborate statistical analysis of failure to appear and pretrial crime in the District of Columbia, including study of a wide variety of factors, Roth and Wice (1978:iv–6) were led to conclude:

> The power of our model to predict the outcome of individual cases is extremely limited. Low values of R^2 (. . . .05 in the nonappearance equation, and .10 in the rearrest equation) indicate a high degree of randomness in individual equations. . . . Based on an analysis of our sample, the model was "wrong" in predicting misconduct only about half as often as random guesses made with appropriate frequencies; however, it was "wrong" about as often as a guess that every defendant would appear when required and that no released defendant would be arrested before disposition of his original case.

A recent study of the correlates of pretrial misconduct was undertaken on a very large sample of defendants in Philadelphia by Goldkamp and Gottfredson (1985) in conjunction with their development of policy guidelines for the Philadelphia judiciary (discussed later in this chapter). In all, they studied more than 4,000 defendants released before trial, following each for 90 days after release. Both willful failures to appear at court hearings and rearrest during the pretrial period were studied (in fact, several types of rearrest were studied). Their results are complicated and not easily summarized, but several noteworthy conclusions emerged:

1. They demonstrated that although predictions of pretrial misconduct are difficult, statistical methods can greatly improve upon subjective judicial judgments.

2. The correlates of pretrial crime (arrests) and failure to appear are largely similar, suggesting that *empirically*, to predict one is to predict the other.
3. The vast majority of releases have no pretrial misconduct during the 90-day interval.
4. The amount of financial bond was not related to pretrial misconduct, once the risk of the defendant was taken into account.

One finding that emerges consistently in these prediction studies is that the length of time elapsing between arrest and trial is associated substantially with pretrial misconduct. Gottfredson reported a correlation of .53 between length of pretrial release and arrest while in that status. Clarke reported a similar relation. The research thus suggests strongly that the most adequate way to diminish the rates of failure to appear and of pretrial crime may be to shorten considerably the time between arrest and trial. As Feeley (1983) has shown, however, it is one thing to desire speedy trials but quite another thing to achieve them given the diverse interests served by delay.

In any event, the available studies demonstrate the difficulty of achievement of either of the predominantly expressed goals of the pretrial release decision, both of which require predictions—failure to appear for trial and pretrial crime. It should be emphasized that this does not imply that such predictions cannot be made more accurately than chance; reliable correlates of both failure to appear and pretrial crimes have been shown to exist. What it does imply is that the errors involved in such predictions are very large: both failure to appear and pretrial crime may be expected to be substantially overpredicted from the information now available (Dershowitz, 1970a; von Hirsch, 1972).

One aspect of the difficult prediction problem faced by magistrates that has not received adequate attention is the differential consequences of decision errors. Not all decision errors have the same costs. A decision error that permits release of a child molester who repeats his offense has gravely different consequences than a similar release error involving a check forger. Similarly, the release of certain defendants, regardless of their risk of failure to appear, might be impractical from the point of view of the bail judge—for example, if it were clear that they would threaten victims or witnesses or if the feeling in the community against a defendant were strong.

Some data are known to provide information about release risks, but much remains to be learned if rationality is to be enhanced. We know, for example, that for many, perhaps most, defendants, financial conditions are not necessary to ensure their appearance at trial. We know that many more defendants can be released safely before trial than was thought prior to the bail reform movement of the 1960s and early 1970s. We know that it is possible to discriminate statistically between defendants who will appear for trial and those who will not. Similarly, those who will be rearrested and those who will not can be distinguished at better than chance levels. We know also, however, that our ability to make such predictions currently is weak—that is, predictions are of low validity. When such predictions are used to define decision rules, they therefore involve substantial overpredictions that would result in the erroneous detention of very large numbers of defendants. Significantly, these false positives or errors in prediction would be hidden errors. They would be hidden in the sense that it never would be known to the decision maker that persons confined on the bases of predictions about their conduct would, if set free, not engage in misconduct. The person kept in jail cannot demonstrate the invalidity of the prediction made for him or her.

The legal debates over the legitimate goals of pretrial release must be read in the light of this social scientific research. Propriety and feasibility are not necessarily synonymous in the realm of criminal justice decision making. Propriety (as, for example, of detention for dangerousness) may have to be conditioned substantially by feasibility.

CORRELATES OF THE DECISION TO RELEASE

As with all discretionary decisions in the criminal justice system, it is possible to infer, from the avowed goals of pretrial release decisions, too much about how these decisions are made. Such an assessment must rely as well on research that examines the bail-setting behavior of judges as it takes place in the courtroom.[13]

Many have suggested that, whatever the legal or social scientific problems associated with the goal of community protection, it is given priority by judges in practice. Furthermore, it has been suggested often that judges seek to accomplish this aim by attending especially to the gravity of the charges facing the defendant. For example, Vorenberg has argued that

> what is usually on the minds of magistrates and prosecutors [on whose recommendation magistrates often rely] is whether the defendant will commit another crime while awaiting trial . . . almost always the issue for the magistrate is not how much bail will make the released defendant reappear, but how high it must be set in order to prevent release. (1976:651)

Thomas explained the connection between the gravity of the charge and setting of bail as follows:

> Reasoning that the likelihood of a defendant failing to appear increases with the severity of the charge and the consequent sentence which can be imposed upon conviction, judges generally increase the amount of bail in relation to the seriousness of the alleged charges. The single most important factor in the setting of bail is therefore the alleged present offense. (1976:12)

The disjunction between setting bail principally on the basis of seriousness of charge and the aims of the bail reform movement, which sought to encourage magistrates to set bail according to the defendant's community ties, is large. Several researchers have studied the factors that seem to influence bail setting in practice and have confirmed the preeminence of the charge criterion.

Bock and Frazier (1977) studied the criteria used in bail decisions in one Florida judicial district. The amount of bail given (including none or own recognizance release) was analyzed in relation to the defendant's community ties, prior record, seriousness of the charge, and demeanor at the bail hearing (respectful versus disrespectful). They found that the seriousness of the charge was the factor most highly correlated with bond; demographic characteristics, community ties, employment, and family ties were not found to be significantly related to bond. (The disrespectful, however, were given higher bonds, all other factors in the study held constant.)

Bynum (1976) studied the influence of community ties, demographic characteristics, prior record, and charge on whether defendants in three release programs were released on their own recognizance. The study sample included only those eligible for release in the three programs. Of all the variables studied, only prior record was consistently related to the probability of a defendant's being granted release; both demographic characteristics and community ties were found to have little impact.

Roth and Wice (1978) in their study of 11,000 pretrial releasees in Washington, D.C., found, at the bivariate level of analysis, considerable evidence that the seriousness of the charge had an impact on the pretrial release decisions of the judges in their study. So also did the extent of the defendant's prior record. Race, sex, age, employment status, and residence were unrelated at the bivariate level.

In multivariate analyses of these same data, they found that when the criterion of interest was release on nonfinancial conditions versus financial conditions, the type of charge, prior record, judge, and the capacity of the District of Columbia jail were consistently related to the decision.

Of interest to the question of rationality in pretrial release decision making was their comparative analysis of the factors found influential in setting bond with those they found to be related to failure to appear at trial and pretrial rearrest. Table 4, from their report, shows these comparisons. As summarized by Roth and Wice:

TABLE 4. Comparison of Variables Explaining Financial Conditions, Failure to Appear, and Pretrial Rearrest

	Behavior being explained		
Explanatory attribute	Use of financial bond	Failure to appear	Pretrial rearrest
Current charge			
Homicide	+	0	0
Assault	−	−	0
Drug violation	−	0	0
Bail violation	+	0	0
Sexual assault	0	−	0
Weapon violation	0	−	0
Robbery	0	0	+
Burglary	0	0	+
Larceny	0	0	+
Arson or property destruction	0	0	+
Crime severity			
No weapon used	−	0	+
Defendant history			
Nonappearance in pending case	+	0	0
Parole or probation when arrested	+	0	0
Number of pending cases	+	0	+
Number of prior arrests or all crimes	+	0	0
Number of prior arrests or crimes against person	0	0	+
Arrested in last 5 years?	+	0	0
Number of arrests in preceding 12 months	0	0	+
Defendant descriptors			
Local residence	−	0	0
Employed	−	−	−
Low income	−	0	0
Drug user	0	+	+
Caucasian	+	0	−
Older	0	0	−

SOURCE: Roth and Wice (1978).

The exhibit illustrates that, with few exceptions, variables that seem to predict misconduct do not influence the financial-nonfinancial decision; moreover, variables that seem to affect the decision do not predict misconduct. For one example, holding other variables constant, a history of drug use is associated with greater risk of both nonappearance and rearrest, yet known drug users were found no more likely than others to receive financial conditions, and accused drug violaters were actually less likely to receive such conditions. (1978:iv–4)

Goldkamp (1979) examined the bail-setting process for a large sample of defendants in Philadelphia. At the bivariate level of analysis, he found that bail decisions were related to age, race, sex, employment, income, prior record, and criminal charge. Older persons, whites, females, employed persons, those without prior convictions, and those with the least serious charges alleged were more likely to be given release on their own recognizance than were their counterparts. After exercising statistical controls by means of multiple regression, however, the single variable that remained substantially correlated with the own recognizance release decision was seriousness of charge. Goldkamp concluded:

Perhaps the most interesting of these results is the finding that bail decision making, in its various facets, seems to operate almost exclusively on the basis of the seriousness of the charge. That is, the ROR decision option appears to screen "out" defendants who are not charged with serious crimes. . . . Community-ties indicators, such as family ties and residence in the community, appear in the face of charge and prior-record concerns to have had almost no impact at all on the granting of ROR or on the setting of cash bail. This finding may suggest that Philadelphia bail judges do not deem community ties reliable indexes for assessing defendants' propensities toward flight. But it may also demonstrate a lesser concern for the evaluation of flight risk, pointing instead to the dominance of other bail decision concerns that may be intuitively linked to charge seriousness and past criminal history criteria—such as a concern for potential defendant dangerousness or a tendency to prejudge or even prepunish defendants at their first appearance. (1979:157–58)

A study of the bail process was conducted by Fleming (1982), who studied bail setting in Detroit and Baltimore in the 1970s. Besides documenting the diversity of approaches to the pretrial process around the nation, Fleming found that in many ways the themes driving bail decisions in the two court systems were the same. Thus, he reports (1982:10): "For both cities, then, the defendant's formal charge functioned as a major cue in the initial decision regarding the type of bail or release option." Fleming goes on to document how the policies of the two courts greatly affect release rates and conditions of release prior to trial, what Fleming calls "punishment before trial."

The dominant influence of the criminal charge in bail setting is confirmed again and again in empirical research (Frazier, Block, and Hensetta, 1980; Goldkamp and Gottfredson, 1985) as is the role of prior criminal record. When the charge is not serious and the defendant does not have a recent or extensive prior record, the defendant receives a less restrictive release condition. Other factors matter to some degree, but these two dominate according to the research evidence (Goldkamp and Gottfredson, 1985).[14]

IMPLICATIONS FOR RATIONALITY

The research reviewed in this chapter might be viewed as the first steps that must be taken on the road toward increased rationality in pretrial release decision making. Much has been learned about the ways in which magistrates make pretrial release decisions, about the consequences of these decisions to defendants and to society, about the goals of the decisions and current abilities to meet those goals, and about the effectiveness of various decision alternatives. The implications of these studies for the next steps that must be taken if pretrial release discretion can fairly be said to be exercised rationally should be discussed next.

Pretrial release decisions in which an accused person is either set free pending trial or held in custody are a direct consequence of two features of our system of justice. First, recall that the principal way in which the law is invoked is by arrest—that is, the taking of the suspect into physical custody. Second, note that there is a period of time between arrest and adjudication that permits the accused some time to prepare a defense. The latter feature is central to the American notion of due process of law. The state may not make decisions affecting liberty without the accused having a fair chance to rebut the charges with the aid of counsel. In the absence of summary adjudication, which would be repugnant to the concept of fairness, there always will be a period of time between custody decisions (made on the basis of suspicion) and adjudication (made on the basis of an impartial hearing). The first ingredient of pretrial release decisions, however—that of arrest as a principal method of invoking the law—is a matter that merits reflection. We know, from the studies reviewed in this chapter, that the vast majority of defendants pose no risk of failing to appear for trial or of committing crimes before trial. We know also that we have very little information— in the sense in which we use that term in this book—about defendants to aid in distinguishing those who will appear and those who will not. It might be, therefore, that the most profitable enhancement of rationality in these decisions rests not with the magistrate but with the police. This unusual claim merits more discussion.

As Thomas (1976:200) has stressed, most arrestees are jailed "not because someone has decided that there is a need for their incarceration, but because the traditional method of beginning criminal cases is by arrest, the taking of the person into physical custody." As we noted in Chapter 3, in deciding whether to arrest a person suspected of committing a crime, the police officer may operate primarily on the basis of perceived guilt. Certainly this is an oversimplification of that complex decision; however, in the routine case the decision may not include an assessment of whether there is a need for custody. The rationality of taking persons into physical custody on the basis of perceived guilt certainly is questionable. Surely the evidence available about flight risk does not support the contention that absconding is significantly related to convictability (Roth and Wice, 1978).

It may be, then, as LaFave, Foote, Thomas, and others have suggested, that the most significant inroads into the problems posed by pretrial release decisions may be made by reforming the immediately prior decision—that is, the more critical decision to be addressed may be that of arrest. Projects modeled after the Vera Institute's point system, designed to increase the use of summons instead of arrest, have been found to be effective in increasing the use of summonses for misdemeanants (Feeney, 1972). Research designed to assess the custody need for arrest decisions and to study the information needs of such decision goals is clearly indicated. It should be noted, however, that current evidence suggests that custody taken because of perceived flight risk probably is taken too routinely and that large numbers of detainees could be freed by the police pending trial.

The evidence concerning both ROR and bail release encourages the belief that requiring money bail generally is illogical, unnecessary, and discriminatory. There still is no valid empirical demonstration that money bail serves any purpose of deterring flight. Thus, the requirement of rationality suggests that the use of bail should continue to decline in prominence as a principal mechanism justifying pretrial release decisions.

Despite the inroads that decision alternatives such as ROR and citation in lieu of arrest should make in the bail system, the difficult problem of prediction will continue to haunt those who must make pretrial release decisions. If it has no other purpose, money bail undoubtedly will continue to serve a preventive detention function. There are people whom magistrates will refuse to set free prior to trial because, perhaps subjectively, they are perceived as posing a danger to the community or seem very likely to flee. To ensure their detention, magistrates will fix very high bail. The central question that faces further reform with respect to rationality in bail practices is whether such preventive detention should continue to be accomplished *sub rosa* through money bail or whether it should be openly acknowledged, guided by explicit criteria, and regulated by guarantees of due process. At least one standard-setting body has selected the latter choice (National Association of Pretrial Service Agencies, 1978).[15] Certainly, it does not seem too much to ask of a justice system that the goals of such a significant decision be stated openly, explicitly, and honestly (cf. Feeley, 1983).

Both roads, in any case, are fraught with hazards. Ignoring the significant constitutional questions that surround preventive detention, it may be asked what criteria are thought to serve the required predictive purpose. The evidence reviewed in this chapter suggests that none now perform that function adequately. Given the apparent negative influence of detention on later decisions, how should that information be used? Would an explicit provision for pretrial detention result in needless increases in detention simply because it would be a practical expedient for magistrates?

On the other hand, it hardly can be denied, from the studies reviewed here, that much preventive detention currently takes place. It might be, as Vorenberg (1976:672) has suggested, that at least as much overprediction of dangerousness goes on under the guise of setting bail to "ensure appearance" as would take place under a system of explicit criteria and procedural safeguards. Explicit criteria and an evidentiary hearing would have at least the merits of visibility. The prediction problem, of course, remains.

Improved rationality of the pretrial release decision need not rest solely on the outcome of this debate, which is dependent eventually upon more definitive guidance from the Supreme Court of the United States. Much has been learned about the value of decision alternatives and about information that can enhance rationality.

BAIL GUIDELINES

Perhaps the most important future requirement is the design and implementation of systems of feedback to the magistrates about the consequences of their decisions. A recent research project by Goldkamp and Gottfredson (1985) developed a set of policy guidelines with a feedback system for use by the Philadelphia judiciary. The research program resulted in the adoption, by the Philadelphia judges, of a set of guidelines used to make bail decisions. Because those guidelines are of the type we advocate in this book (see Chapter 1, and elsewhere; Gottfredson and Gottfredson, 1984), and because we believe the model for their construction to be applicable to nearly all the decisions discussed in this book, it may be useful to describe the Philadelphia research and its findings here.

The study was designed in two parts, both undertaken in full collaboration with the judiciary and the Philadelphia Pretrial Services Agency, through a steering and policy committee comprised of six judges and the director of the Pretrial Services Division. The committee consulted on major policy issues throughout the study. The first phase involved empirical analyses of approximately 4,800 bail and release-on-recognizance decisions Philadelphia judges had made, as well as analyses of the pretrial performance of defendants in terms of appearance at required court proceedings and pretrial arrests. The goal of this phase of the study was to describe the practices of the judiciary as accurately as possible, to identify those factors that seem most heavily to influence their decisions, and to provide a platform for constructing a set of guidelines for future use. Also, the predictive concerns of the judiciary were modeled with the background data available for each defendant.

On the basis of these analyses and extended discussions and debates within the Steering and Policy Committee, three separate guidelines models were constructed for judicial consideration. Each model was fitted against the data developed to assess the possible consequences of its adoption. After considerable discussion and modification, the Steering and Policy Committee chose to implement one of the models on an experimental basis. The model, shown in Figure 4, had a two-dimensional matrix form similar to the sentencing and paroling guidelines discussed in subsequent chapters of this book. On one dimension is arrayed the principal charge along a continuum of seriousness. Along the other dimension is arranged a point scale, developed empirically to establish risk differences among defendants appearing before the bail judge according to the probability of either failure to appear or rearrest.

The guidelines are intended to operate in the following manner. Before the hearing by the judge, the staff of the Pretrial Services Agency investigates the background of a defendant and develops the information required for the guidelines. The staff determines both the category of risk and that of appropriate severity of charge. This information is given to the judge along with the background file on the defendant for the bail hearing. The confluence of the appropriate risk dimension and the charge dimension thus produce a presumptive bail decision: release on recognizance, release on recognizance or a low cash bail range, or a cash bail range. Judges are expected to reach decisions with these presumed decision outcomes for presumably typical cases. They do, however, retain the option of departing from these presumptive decisions to make decisions outside the guidelines. If the judges do so, they are expected

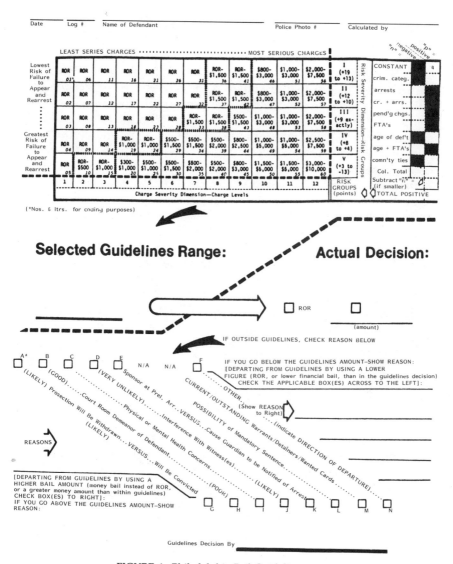

FIGURE 4. Philadelphia Bail Guidelines.

to note the reason for departure. Reasons that the Steering and Policy Committee thought would appear with some regularity and would be correct from this policy perspective are indicated on the guidelines form.

The Philadelphia Bail Guidelines were meant to improve four aspects of bail: rationality, equity, visibility, and evolutionary decision rules. Rational decision making requires a knowledge of the probable consequence of decision alternatives. More specifically, rational decision making presupposes, at the least, a set of agreed-upon decision goals and a body of information (e.g., descriptive of the persons about whom decisions are made) that is known to be relevant to the desired goals and that therefore aids in their accomplishment. In the absence of either component of rational decision making (that is, in the absence of either agreed-upon decision goals or a body of relevant information useful in achieving these goals), decisions in the field of justice are unsatisfactory because there is no way of knowing whether they are reasonably undertaken or effectively transacted. Specifically, if appearance for trial is seen as a valid aim of the bail decision, and if decision makers typically employ the prior record of defendants as a measure of the likelihood of flight, then this is a rational decision only if there is a relation between appearance at trial and the defendant's prior record. Because the guidelines provided such information, they were meant to improve rationality.

A second important concern about the bail decision within the guidelines framework is equity. Just as equitable decisions are sought at the sentencing stage of the criminal process, fairness in bail decision making dictates that similarly situated persons be treated similarly. The equal justice problem for judges at bail is analogous to the problem of disparity at the sentencing stage. There are a number of possible outcomes at bail, ranging from release on recognizance or cash bail to outright detention, and because these decision options can be viewed as less or more drastic in the hardships they impose on defendants, equity requires that persons in similar circumstances receive similar treatment.

Two principal obstacles to equity in bail decision making present themselves, however. The first is rather basic: there appears to be little agreement concerning the appropriate application of the "similarly situated" concept to the bail decision. Should "similarly situated" in bail decision making be understood to be based upon the seriousness of the alleged offense, for example? Or should it be defined using defendant's community ties, or even financial resources? It is difficult to respond to these questions principally because the purpose of the bail decision is not usually unambiguously articulated. Moreover, whenever multiple decision goals are acknowledged, the equity question is further confounded because what at first may be viewed as dissimilar treatment for similar cases may simply be evidence of use of alternative kinds of information to achieve different decision goals. Another question related to equity is: What outcome should be the basis for comparison—bail or detention? If two defendants receive the same bail, but one is detained and the other is not, has equity been achieved?

The second major obstacle to effecting equity in bail decision making is the lack of information available to decision makers about their decisions. Inconsistent treatment of given categories of defendants at first appearance by (a) "within-judges" variability—that is, decision makers compared to themselves over time; or by (b) "between-judges" variability—that is, decision makers compared to each other, would contribute to inequitable bail decisions. Without some mechanism that can provide sytematic feedback of bail dispositions in previous cases to the decision makers responsible for them (both as individuals and as a group), consistency will be difficult to attain and equitable practices will be elusive.

Several studies indicate that equity, in the sense of similar treatment for similar persons, is problematic in the realm of the pretrial release decision. In one Chicago court Sperlak (1974) found a great deal of variability among judges in the proportion of cases given release on personal recognizance. In the Roth and Wice (1978) study already discussed it was discovered that the judge deciding the case strongly affected the release conditions. Variability in release conditions was associated with judges preferring release on recognizance versus those with a preference for supervised release. And the feasibility study for the Philadelphia guidelines project found substantial variability among the twenty judges studied in setting bail, even after relevant case characteristics were considered (Goldkamp and Gottfredson, 1985).

A third major goal of the Philadelphia project was to increase visibility. The bail decision and the determination of pretrial custody are low-visibility occurrences for at least two reasons. First, to the extent that money bail is relied on as a bail decision option, the determination of pretrial custody is only an indirect outcome of the bail decision. For example, once cash bail is set, a defendant's prospects for pretrial release may be determined more by his or her ability to afford bail or to raise the cash than by direct decree of the decision maker. Because the cash bail option does not directly determine pretrial custody, though it may heavily influence the prospects, little that is explicit can be said about the resulting release or detention of defendants. The common criticism that judges abuse their discretion in effectuating preventive detention of defendants *sub rosa* by setting unaffordably high cash bail is, among other considerations, a visibility problem. Yet, even if the bail decision did directly determine the release or detention of all defendants, it would still be difficult to feel confident about the criteria relied upon by judges in reaching their decision.

Visibility in a decision-making process in which such paramount individual and community interests are at stake is desirable, for one reason, because without it equity cannot be assured. For another, without visibility in the decision as to *how* (the criteria employed) and *why* (the goals pursued) decisions are made, it is impossible either to make sense of decisions in individual cases or knowledgeably to conduct the policy debates that should surround such crucial decision points in criminal justice (Gottfredson, Wilkins, and Hoffman, 1978). Clearly, there are policy decisions that must be made about the conduct of the bail decision (e.g., is the principal goal to prevent flight?), as there are individual case decisions to be made within the context of that policy (e.g., to maximize the probability of achieving the policy goal, should this individual be detained?).

The guidelines developed in the Philadelphia study were tested in an experiment, with random allocation of judges into two groups, those who used the newly developed guidelines to set bail and those who conformed with the traditional procedure. The results are somewhat complicated to describe briefly, but overall it may be said on the basis of the experimental results (which need replication):

1. Judges will voluntarily comply with policy guidelines and will give reasons when they depart, thus increasing visibility.
2. Policy guidelines greatly increase equity in decision making.
3. It is difficult to improve on the predictive capability of bail by judges, given conflicting goals.
4. Evolutionary systems that permit decision makers to change policy as they learn from feedback are feasible—that is, change can be institutionalized with guidelines.

CONCLUSION

A recent study by the Comptroller General's office (1978) concluded that marked disparities exist in bail practices in the federal courts. Inconsistent use of money bail, widely varying detention rates, and differential weighting of the criteria of the Bail Reform Act were found to characterize federal bail practices. The principal recommendation of the report to reduce these inequities squares precisely with the major theme of this book. A system should be established:

> To provide judicial officers feedback on the results of their bail decisions in relation to the decisions of other judicial officers and to monitor and evaluate the bail process. Such a system is needed to enable judicial officers and the judiciary to identify and correct problem areas and promote more consistent bail decisions.

The research reviewed in this chapter suggests strongly that such systems can be built and that they work. When such systems are routinely in place in criminal justice agencies, we will have moved a long way toward enhanced rationality.

The days in jail are long for the innocent as well as for the guilty. If the traditional presumption of innocence is valued and if every citizen is entitled to liberty unless deprived of it by due process of law, then the goals, information needs, and alternatives consistent with ensuring those values are deserving of much more attention than has thus far been given them. Today, magistrates make pretrial release decisions in virtual ignorance of their consequences. Only through feedback can such ignorance be reduced. Only with a reduction of present ignorance can rational decision making in pretrial release decisions be claimed with any assurance.

[handwritten annotation: ? How can decisions in setting bail or in custody/noncustody be more rational when the evidence presented in this chapter clearly shows that predictive categories other than seriousness of charge work at a significant level?]

NOTES

1. Certainly this is a simplification of the operation of bail in the past. For discussions of the history and purposes of bail, see Foote (1965), Dill (1972), Goldkamp (1979), Thomas (1976), and Feeley (1983).
2. In some cases, somewhat analogous issues are raised by considerations of detention or liberty after conviction by a trial court during the course of appeals from conviction.
3. Note that if it were not for the period of detention prior to trial, some of these persons released after conviction may have been required to serve some time in prison—that is, the judge, in passing sentence, may consider the pretrial detention in setting the penalty. There is some reason to believe this. See Landes (1974), Goldkamp (1979), and McCarthy and Wohl (1965).
4. Several studies using similar methods report essentially the same results; see Alexander et al. (1958); Ares, Rankin, and Sturz (1963); and Angel, Green, Kaufman, and Van Loon (1971).
5. For critiques of the methods of these studies see Hindelang (1972) and Goldkamp (1979).
6. Goldkamp used several measures of pretrial custody in his analyses, but for simplicity only this méausre is discussed here. Generally, his results maintained regardless of the measure used.
7. An example of a "symbolic" goal might be a case in which a magistrate set very high bail for a notorious white-collar crime defendant, even though the risk of flight and the potential danger to the community were perceived to be low. An example of a system constraint might be an impetus to set low bail or ROR for a time because the detention facilities are full. To the extent that detention induces guilty pleas, it may have "system advantages."
8. The best discussions of these issues are found in Goldkamp (1979, 1985).
9. Compare *Stack* v. *Boyle* 342 U.S. 1 (1951) with *Carlson* v. *Landon* 342 U.S. 524 (1952). For critical discussions, see Foote (1978); Goldkamp (1979, 1985).

10. Portions of this discussion draw upon Goldkamp and Gottfredson (1979).

11. For thorough discussion and critique of the bail bond system see Goldfarb (1965), Thomas (1976), and Flemming (1982). One study examined the effectiveness of bondsmen in preventing defaults in comparison to an alternative of having defendants post 5% of the bail with the court and sign a bond to pay the rest upon default. The 5% was returned to the defendant when he or she showed up for trial. A before-and-after design was used that indicated that the default rates for all defendants released on bail were about the same under the professional bondsmen system and under the deposit system. See Conklin and Meagher (1973).

12. The base rate is defined as the relative frequency of occurrence of an event in the population of interest. Thus, improvement over the base rate in this case requires greater accuracy in prediction than that achieved by predicting that all defendants will be "successes."

13. The criteria that are intended to influence the bail decision have been surveyed widely in recent years. In addition to the several standard-setting bodies, many states and specific courts outline the criteria to be relied on, in theory. In all, the major influence of the Vera Institute's community ties criteria is obvious. For a review, see Goldkamp (1985).

14. Other researchers who have studied bail-setting behavior include Landes (1974) and Ebbesen and Konecni (1975). The Landes sample, however, was restricted to only those cases handled by the Legal Aid Society of New York, and thus generalization of his results to bail-setting behavior in general is hazardous. Ebbesen and Konecni undertook a simulation study with eighteen judges and found that community ties, prior record, and the district attorney's recommendation were related to bail.

15. Preventive detention statutes that coexist with the money bail system have been found to be little used, in part because the procedural requirements and the time involved in invoking preventive detention may be circumvented simply by setting high bail (Roth and Wice 1978).

Chapter 5

THE DECISION TO CHARGE

After a suspect has been arrested, and in the absence of a dismissal by the police or a magistrate at first appearance, it must be decided whether to initiate prosecution and, if so, for what crime or crimes. In most American jurisdictions this decision rests with the district attorney.[1] In this chapter we will review selected empirical studies bearing on this important decision; investigate the goals, information, and alternatives pertaining to the decision; and assess how what is learned bears on the requirements of rationality.

The discretionary power to initiate formal criminal charges against a suspect places the prosecutor in a position of influence perhaps unmatched in the entire system of criminal justice. This power and control has long been recognized by students of prosecutorial discretion. In 1940 Jackson (1940:18) wrote: "The prosecutor has more control over life, liberty and reputations than any other person in America." Similarly, Mills has argued:

> A State's attorney potentially has more control over the liberty and future of an individual than any other public official or public body. His discretion and authority are vast and vest him with powers which are unparalleled by those of any other single person. (1966:511)

Prosecutorial influence on the system of justice has many aspects. It includes, in addition to the charging decision, negotiating guilty pleas, trying contested cases, and investigating proactively to discover crimes. The focus of this chapter on the decision to charge is based on the belief that such decisions, perhaps more than any others made by the prosecutor, affect critically the lives of suspects and victims and the flow of cases through the criminal justice system. At the same time, we must consider decisions about plea bargaining, given the preeminence of guilty pleas in the process. These decisions embody all of the significant issues of goals, information, and alternatives that also characterize other aspects of prosecutorial decisions. Even though throughout this chapter we speak of "the decision to charge," the reader must bear in mind that we intend to cover the several decisions that go into the decision to charge.[2]

The discretion granted the prosecutor in making charging decisions is indeed vast. The principal decision alternatives, of course, are to charge a suspect with a crime or not. In addition, the prosecutor, in some jurisdictions, may decide to refer the suspect elsewhere; diversion programs, mental hospitals, community agencies, and misdemeanor courts are examples. Also, the prosecutor may charge a suspect initially and decide later to drop the charges. The power of *nolle prosequi* enables a prosecutor to decide not to pursue a case despite enough evidence to do so.[3]

The breadth of this discretion is not matched, however, with extensive formal controls over its exercise. Certainly, subsequent review by the courts, in the nature of the potential for adjudication of guilt, is a major control of overextensive prosecution. But the decision whether or not to charge is the single most unreviewed exercise of the power of the criminal law available to an individual in the American system of justice. Wide discretion both to abstain from prosecution and to prosecute selectively generally is recognized in case law.[4] Although, as will be seen in this chapter, the charging decision is influenced by other decision makers in the criminal justice system (such as victims, police, and judges), it generally does not involve the suspect or the suspect's counsel in an adversarial way.

The necessity and the propriety of prosecutorial discretion in pressing charges is accepted by most commentators. That not all arrests do or should result in prosecution is clear. Some victims may not be interested in prosecution. There may be insufficient evidence to convict "beyond a reasonable doubt."[5] The suspect may be innocent of any wrongdoing. Appropriate noncriminal alternatives may exist, and full charging may be unrealistic given available resources. According to the President's Commission on Law Enforcement and Administration of Justice:

> Among the types of cases in which thoughtful prosecutors commonly appear disinclined to seek criminal penalties are domestic disturbances; assaults and petty thefts in which victim and offender are in a family or social relationship; statutory rape when both boy and girl are young; first offense car thefts that involve teenagers taking a car for a short joyride; checks that are drawn upon insufficient funds; shoplifting by first offenders, particularly when restitution

is made; and criminal acts that involve offenders suffering from emotional disorders short of legal insanity. (1967:5)

Despite agreement on the existence and propriety of prosecutorial charging discretion *per se*, the form that its exercise should take and the purposes that it is thought to serve are unclear. Typically, virtually no guidance is available from penal statutes, and charging decisions are almost never supervised judicially. At this stage in the process the prosecutor has few facts about the suspect, the offense, or the alternatives available. As a result, the prosecutor may rely on intuition, beliefs about the value of various sanctions, or personal assessment of the purposes of the criminal law. Rarely does he or she have systematic knowledge of past decisions in similar cases. Almost never is information about the consequences of his or her decisions routinely conveyed back to the prosecutor. Seldom are the goals articulated clearly in a way that facilitates individual case decisions. The absence of these requirements of rationality produces low visibility, and assessments of fairness and justice are thereby made especially difficult.

[handwritten margin notes: no guidelines / no information / no feedback]

The importance of studying the ways in which prosecutors decide whether to charge a suspect with a crime is conveyed vividly in Figure 5. This graphic, taken from a study by Forst and his colleagues (1977) of felony processing in Washington, D.C., portrays the major influence of the charging decision. In fully half of the felony arrests brought by the police, the prosecutor decided not to charge, either at initial screening or later (by *nolle prosequi*). Obviously, the procedures by which such dramatic selection occurs can influence greatly the rationality of the entire process. Boland (1983) has shown that similar diagrams characterize many prosecutors' offices, with some variability in *when* prosecutors drop charges.

The central significance of the decision to charge is that it radically changes the status of the alleged offender. It transforms the accused from a suspect to a defendant. The decision to charge is the consequence of the prosecutor's belief that the accused should either bear the economic and social costs of a defense or plead guilty and suffer the attendant legal and social consequences. The charging decision itself may irreparably damage the defendant's reputation. It requires that the defendant provide money bail (or other surety) or remain incarcerated pending further action by the court. Charged defendants who are subsequently acquitted suffer these consequences needlessly. Guilty persons who are not charged cannot be subject to the penalties of the criminal law.

Apart from the profound consequences for the defendant, charging

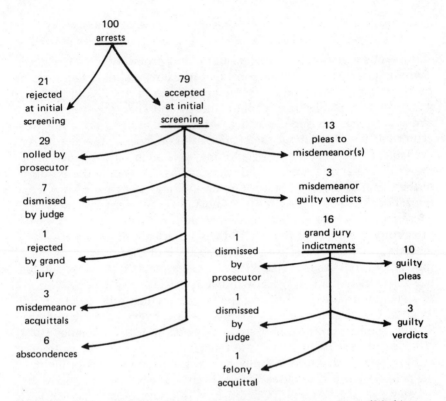

FIGURE 5. Outcomes of 100 "typical" arrests brought to the Superior Court of Washington, D.C., in 1974. SOURCE: Based on actual flow of 17,534 arrests recorded in the Prosecutor's Management Information System (PROMIS). B. Forst, J. Lucianovic, and S. Cox, *What Happens After Arrest?* Institute for Law and Social Research, Publication Number 4 (Washington, D.C.: U.S. Government Printing Office, 1977): 17. *Note.* Total does not agree due to rounding error.

decisions by prosecutors can greatly influence other significant actors in the criminal justice process. Repeated refusals to prosecute certain types of arrests may lead to a decline in such arrests. Evidence standards adhered to by prosecutors may lead to changes in evidence-gathering practices by the police. The charging decision largely circumscribes the adjudicatory and dispositional functions of trial judges. Use of such extended penalty provisions as prior record or weapon possession aggravations or of habitual criminal statutes influences the parole board's release decisions.

The critical function served by the charging decisions of the prosecutor in the American system of justice is quite clearly difficult to overestimate. We begin our assessment of rationality by an examination of the goals of this complex decision.

GOALS OF THE CHARGING DECISION

The purposes to be served by charging a suspect with a crime may, without some reflection, seem straightforward and noncontroversial: those persons against whom sufficient evidence exists to sustain a finding of guilt by a court should be charged, whereas cases lacking the requisite evidence should not. Charging only the guilty, and all of the guilty, serves to maximize the proportion of charged persons who eventually are convicted. Some argue that conviction is itself the primary goal of the charging decision. Forst et al. (1977:65) suggest "that the principal objective of the prosecutor is to convict offenders is well beyond dispute."

Consideration of the prosecutor's place in the system of justice, however, indicates strongly that aims other than the maximization of conviction rates play a prominent role in this complex decision. Mr. Justice Sutherland suggested in *Berger* v. *United States* (294 U.S. 78, 88) what some of these other aims might be:

> The United States Attorney is the representative not of an ordinary party to a controversy, but of a sovereignty whose obligation to govern impartially is as compelling as its obligation to govern at all; and whose interest, therefore, in a criminal prosecution is not that it shall win a case, but that justice shall be done. As such, he is in a peculiar and very definite sense the servant of the law, the twofold aim of which is that guilt shall not escape or innocence suffer. He may prosecute with earnestness and vigor—indeed, he should do so. But, while he may strike hard blows, he is not at liberty to strike foul ones. It is as much his duty to refrain from improper methods calculated to produce a wrongful conviction as it is to use every legitimate means to bring about a just one.

Thus, in addition to assessing the odds of conviction in deciding whether or not to bring charges, the prosecutor is rightly concerned as well with determining the desirability of charging. The idea that the prosecutor should assess impartially the justice of prosecution is consistent with the historical antecedents of the office. Miller suggests that the prosecutorial role developed as a distinctively American institution, to prevent overzealous charging by partisan victims of crime. The theory was that a person in a position of public trust could make more impartial decisions than could victims (Miller, 1970).

Apart from notions of convictability and justice (both of which present obviously difficult operational problems for prosecutors), it is commonly asserted that charging decisions should attend also to crime reduction. Such a concern is expressed in numerous ways. It might find expression in an emphasis, in terms of resources, on repeat offenders or in the invocation of habitual offender statutes. For example, Forst *et al.* (1977:63) argue: "The prosecutor might reject or dismiss a convictable arrest in favor of another somewhat less highly convictable one when the latter case involves an arrestee who has revealed a high propensity for the repeated commission of serious criminal acts." The thought is that a greater reduction in future crime will attend the incarceration of those who have committed the most offenses. Thus, the issue of prediction again surfaces as an important component of criminal justice decision making. As we will discuss later in this chapter, the consequent issues of validity and of prediction errors then must also arise (the charging decision is fundamentally predictive in another important sense: the forecast by the prosecutor of convictability by the court).

Other major goals of charging decisions might be identified similarly. Certainly, the best utilization of scarce resources is an important pragmatic aim with significant implications. In many jurisdictions there simply are not enough resources to permit prosecution of every case desired. The rehabilitation of the suspect also might be a frequent goal of the decision to charge, as recommended by the President's Commission on Law Enforcement and Administration of Justice (1967). Although seldom acknowledged, there may be political and personal goals. Satisfaction of the political aims of publicly elected prosecutors doubtless directs the charging decision, perhaps principally shown in the desire to maintain a "winning record." Finally (although not exhaustively), certain system constraints impinge on the goals of the charging decision. Thus, the decision not to charge a chargeable suspect may stem from the desire to support the police informant network or to accommodate the prosecution of more significant "higher ups" in a criminal conspiracy (Miller, 1970; Newman, 1966).

Besides the problem of articulating goals associated with selective prosecution, there is a problem of specifying those classes of cases that the prosecutor decides not to prosecute at all. That is, there may be a "policy of nonprosecution" (Abrams, 1975). In such situations, rarely studied by social scientists, prosecutors decide not to enforce a particular statute. Several commentators have outlined criteria that might properly influence the prosecutor to refuse to prosecute a specific class of offenders. Abrams suggests four criteria: opposition by the community, difficulties in enforcing a statute in a legal manner, existence of an effective alternative, and the ability to prosecute for another offense. The requirements of rationality, however, mandate the articulation of the aims of nonprosecution decisions, just as for selective prosecutions, so that the degree of their achievement can be assessed.

Crime reduction, efficiency, equity, just desert, politics, and both interagency and intraagency relations are all to some extent identifiable aims of the decision to charge. Several may be present in any one charging decision; often they will conflict quite obviously.

The complexity of the goals of charging decisions is reflected in the criteria urged upon prosecutors by such standard-setting bodies as the American Bar Association (1971). In addition to "the weight of evidence," the ABA suggests that in deciding whether to bring charges the following criteria be considered: the prosecutor's assessment of guilt; the extent of harm caused by the offense; the disproportion of the punishment to the offense; possible improper motives for a complaint; prolonged non-enforcement of a statute, with community acquiescence; reluctance of the victim to testify; cooperation of the accused in the apprehension or conviction of others; and the availability and likelihood of prosecution by another jurisdiction.

Criteria such as these are important starting points for the development of a rational charging policy, but they do not go far enough. The application of such criteria requires that they be ranked in priority and weighted in some fashion. Most are broad and only loosely defined (for example, "the extent of the harm caused by the offense"). As written, such criteria could be construed very differently by different prosecutors in relation to identical cases. Thus, they are not likely to enhance consistency (and, thus, equity) in charging decisions.

The complexity of concerns that may legitimately influence the decision to charge and the innumerable vagaries of individual cases may lead some to argue that explicit criteria for the achievement of rationality or even equity are unattainable (McIntyre and Lippman, 1970). Such an assessment should, perhaps, await at least a survey of what the research literature implies about the principal influences on the decision to charge.

SOME CORRELATES OF THE DECISION TO CHARGE

Studies of charging decisions are not extensive. The widely acknowledged importance of this topic has not yet begun to be matched by systematic study. The research that has been done, however, tells a good deal about how prosecutors make charging decisions.

One early report about how prosecutors decide to charge is Kaplan's

(1965) discussion of personal experiences as an assistant United States attorney. According to Kaplan, the first and most important factor influencing the decision to charge was the assistant United States attorney's view of the guilt of the accused. Even if there was more than enough evidence to sustain a charge, Kaplan reports that the assistant United States attorneys themselves needed to be convinced of guilt before they would file charges. Second, the question of whether the case could result in conviction was considered. Both resource pressure and the attorney's conviction record were important factors in this assessment, according to Kaplan. He also reports that there were lower conviction standards for serious cases, which was an attempt to give some weight in the charging decision to the likelihood of future crimes by the accused. Kaplan notes that some defendants were seen to be more valuable as witnesses than as defendants and therefore were not prosecuted in order to preserve their testimony for use against others. Finally, Kaplan stressed that a major factor in charging decisions was the assistant United States attorney's assessment of proportionality: Was the sanction associated with the charge considered to be too severe given the nature and circumstances of the offense?

The significant influence of many of these factors was reaffirmed by the single most important observational study of the charging decision. This was Miller's (1970) multijurisdictional study for the American Bar Foundation. Studying charging decisions in Kansas, Michigan, and Wisconsin, he amply demonstrated the complexity of this important decision and documented the many influences upon it. The detail of his study makes its summary difficult, but the major correlates he identified may be discussed.

Besides the minimum requirement that the prosecutor believe in the guilt of the accused, Miller suggested several factors important in determining that a person would not be charged: the attitude of the victim, the cost to the system, attendant undue harm to the suspect, the availability of alternative procedures, and the suspect's willingness to cooperate in the achievement of other enforcement goals. Thus, for example, if the victim refuses to testify, if extradition is possible, if the penalty is too severe, if revocation of parole or an insanity commitment is preferable, or if the suspect agrees to be a witness against more significant defendants, the prosecutor may decide not to charge even though there is enough evidence to do so.

Similarly, Miller enumerated and illustrated some factors that influence the decision to charge when otherwise the prosecutor would not. In the jurisdictions studied, pressure from the public or the press, the perceived ability to perform a social service for the suspect, the facilitation of other investigations, the anticipation of new developments in the case (for example, more evidence), and the desire to be rid of a particular suspect all could induce a prosecutor to charge an accused when regular enforcement procedures would indicate nonprosecution.[6]

McIntyre stresses that public acquiescence to, or toleration of, certain crimes also may play an important role in the decision to charge:

> The public does not demand rigid enforcement of certain laws, and this is an important consideration in the decision not to prosecute. When the prosecutor feels that the community no longer considers criminal a pattern of behavior prohibited by statute, he either refuses to prosecute or strives to convince the complainant to drop charges. (1967:111)

Such observational studies are valuable. They can identify the multitude of factors bearing on the decision to charge and underscore its complexity. If systems are to be designed to enhance rationality, however, it is important also to know what factors are the primary influences in most cases. This requires systematic empirical study based upon representative samples and quantifiable data. Several such studies have been done.

Bernstein, Kelly, and Doyle (1977) studied all males arraigned for felonies in New York City during a five-month period in 1975. Their aim was to determine the factors most influential in the decision to prosecute fully (rather than terminate by dismissal). Of the 1,213 cases in their study, 40% were dismissed. The independent variables studied included the suspect's race, age, education, marital status, prior record, cooperation during the arrest, and type of offense, as well as a measure of the seriousness of the charge. Their analysis indicated that the likelihood of any given suspect's being dismissed increased if the most serious charge was a burglary or an assault, if the number of charges was low, and if the suspect was not subjected to pretrial detention. They interpreted these major correlates as indicating the primary influence of the weight of the evidence on the decision. Burglaries rarely involve witnesses and therefore lack this important type of evidence, and a large number of charges may be an early indication that a strong case can be made. The demographic variables studied had little apparent impact on charging decisions.

In another study, Bernstein, Kick, Leung, and Schultz (1977) studied the issue of charge reduction. Again, the aim was to assess the major influences of this aspect of the charging decision. They studied 1,435 persons convicted of burglary, robbery, assault, and larceny charges in a New York court. Independent variables were similar to those of the previous study. Charge reduction was defined in terms of the magnitude of reduction relative to the absolute reduction possible. They discovered that the higher the original charge, the greater the reduction. No race or sex effects were found, but older defendants received larger reductions. The greater the defendant's prior record, the greater was the reduction in charges, suggesting to Bernstein and her co-workers that more experienced defendants fare better in this aspect of the criminal process.

Forst *et al.* (1977) used data from the Prosecutor's Management Information System (PROMIS)[7] in Washington, D.C., to study the interaction between the police and prosecutors and to assess influences in the charging decision. The PROMIS system permitted Forst and his colleagues to track cases from arrest through charge, discovering where and why cases fell out along the way. Besides defendant criminal history and case data, the PROMIS system included data on the reasons given by prosecutors for their charging decisions.

As we saw in Chapter 3, the study confirmed the significant role that the evidence-gathering ability of arresting officers can play in subsequent prosecutorial decisions. Table 5 shows the reasons given by the prosecutor for refusing prosecution at initial screening. In 21% of the arrests the prosecutor decided at initial screening not to charge. Witness and evidence problems were the reasons given by the prosecutors for not charging in more than half the cases. Witness problems included failure to appear, refusal to testify, and lack of credibility; evidence problems included the unavailability of physical evidence. Witness prob-

TABLE 5. Arrest Rejections at Initial Screening: Reasons Given by Prosecutor, by Major Offense Group (1974)

Reason for rejection	Crime group					
	Robbery	Other violent	Nonviolent property	Victimless	Other	All crimes
Witness problem	43%	51%	25%	2%	5%	25%
Insufficiency of evidence	35%	18%	37%	40%	41%	34%
Due process problem	0%	0%	2%	20%	3%	5%
No reason given	0%	0%	1%	0%	1%	1%
Other	22%	30%	36%	38%	50%	36%
Total rejections	100%	100%	100%	100%	100%	100%
Number of rejections	242	876	1,257	654	621	3,650
Number of arrests	1,955	3,176	6,562	3,659	2,182	17,534
Rejection rate	12%	28%	19%	18%	29%	21%

Source: Forst *et al.* (1977).

lems appeared to be especially important in property crimes. Arrest problems associated with police violations of due process rights of suspects appeared to be a major problem only with victimless crimes, a factor probably associated with the lack of complaining witnesses for these events.

Forst and associates also studied the reasons given by prosecutors for dismissing cases accepted initially for prosecution. Of the 8,766 arrests made in 1974 which the prosecutor decided not to charge, 58% were dismissed (*nolle prosequi*) after having been accepted initially. A substantial portion of these later dismissals (28%) were the result of the successful completion of diversion programs. Again, witness problems accounted for a sizable share of the dismissals (13%), but evidence and due process problems were cited very infrequently at this stage. Boland's (1983) study of seven jurisdictions revealed that problems with witnesses and evidence account for the vast majority of rejections and dismissals, although "office policy" also plays a role for minor crimes.

The ways in which victims' characteristics may influence the prosecutor's decision to charge a suspect were studied by Williams (1978), also using Washington, D.C., PROMIS data. Examining homicide, assault, sexual assault, and robbery arrests, she discovered that attributes of the victim did indeed play a significant role in such decisions. Cases in which victim provocation seemed to be a factor and cases involving victims with known histories of alcohol abuse were refused prosecution twice as often as cases lacking these factors. She found no effect on the charging decision of the victim's arrest record or age, but cases with female victims were rejected more frequently. The relationship of the victim and the accused was found to vary in its effect on the charging decision depending on the type of crime. In aggravated assault, cases involving spouses or friends were more likely to be dropped than others, as were cases involving friends in sexual assault cases. When the victim and accused were ex-spouses, cohabiting, or in a girlfriend–boyfriend relationship, cases of simple assault tended not to be prosecuted.

A third study using the same data set examined whether prosecutors gave priority to cases involving recidivists. Examining data for the years 1971 through 1975, Forst and Brosi (1977) discovered that of the 37,840 persons prosecuted, persons who were prosecuted twice accounted for 28% of all prosecutions, and persons who were prosecuted three times accounted for 12%. Of all prosecutions, persons prosecuted two times accounted for 53%, and persons prosecuted three times accounted for 32%. The authors conclude: "The apparent conclusion is that a small number of individuals represent a significant proportion of the prosecutor's and court's work load" (1977:4). They argued that goals of both crime reduction and minimization of workload might be better served if these cases received special prosecutorial attention:

> Given the disproportionately large share of crime committed by repeat of-
> fenders, prosecutors seem more than justified in structuring their discretion
> so that an appropriate percentage of time and staff is focused on recidivists,
> even though this might mean that other cases with as much or more evidence
> and involving less frequent or less serious offenders would have to be rejected
> or pursued with less-than-normal intensity.
>
> A great reduction in future crime rates and future workloads . . . is likely
> to follow the incarceration of those whose criminal histories reflect their
> relatively high potential for future criminality. (1977:12)

The relative importance that the prosecutor attached to the seriousness of the current case, the defendant's criminal history, and the probability of conviction was assessed by Forst and Brosi by a multivariate analysis of 6,000 felony cases. The probability of winning (that is, of conviction) was measured by empirical relations of various factors to conviction. These factors included assessments of witnesses, of tangible evidence, of the number of days between the offense and arrest, and of the victim–offender relationship. Their aim was to discover the extent to which the prosecutors employed the strategy of priority to repeat offenders. Prosecutorial effort was measured by the number of days the prosecutor carried the case.

They discovered that, *ceteris paribus*, prosecutors attached the most importance to the strength of the evidence and, to a lesser degree, to the seriousness of the case. Their findings were thus consistent with both the observational and the systematic empirical studies already discussed. They discovered also, however, that virtually none of the prosecutorial effort could be accounted for by the criminal history of the defendant. They concluded that their data "provide no empirical support to the hypothesis that the prosecutor attempts to give more attention to cases involving defendants with extensive arrest records" (1977:191).

This study by Forst and Brosi calls attention to the predictive element of many prosecutorial charging decisions. To the extent that prosecutors select out some defendants from a larger group of otherwise chargeable defendants for a crime control purpose (for example, to incapacitate them so that their future crimes will be delayed if not avoided), their selection decisions are predictive ones. Similarly, if prosecutors select cases with a view to the probability of conviction, this selection, too, involves prediction. It is appropriate, though, to assess the predictive validity of the basis for such selections. Forst and Brosi cite the large number of persons who are prosecuted for the second and third time as evidence of the need for a crime reduction aim for charging decisions, and they suggest that prior record be given a priority in the charging process. Such a rationale undergirds the many career criminal programs that have sprung up in prosecutors' offices throughout the country.

It should be realized, however, that the large number of recidivists who are subject to new prosecution is not convincing evidence of the predictive utility of prior record in such a crime reduction program. The questions that must be asked are, What proportion of those prosecuted once are again prosecuted for a new offense? And what proportion of those prosecuted a second time are again prosecuted for a new offense? Although prior record is found consistently to be a predictor of subsequent offending, the association typically is a very modest one. Considering prior criminal history only, a very substantial number of errors are likely to be made in predicting future offending. It is likely that less attention will be generated by these false positives than by those that attend predictive decisions at the bail, sentencing, and parole decisions since all of the cases from which the selections are made theoretically are chargeable. Assigning priorities in charging decisions on the basis of unverified predictive criteria may nonetheless be questioned.[8] To the extent that crime reduction is regarded as a proper prosecutorial charging aim, there is a clear need for empirically demonstrated predictive criteria.

A similar study undertaken in the federal courts (Northern District of Illinois) has been reported by Frase (1980) studying the factors used in prosecution decisions in a sample of 800 "matters" between 1973 and 1974. He confirmed the considerable degree of discretion among prosecutions; only about 20% of the defendants were prosecuted for anything. Also confirmed was the role of seriousness of charge in the decision to prosecute. Frase reports that many declinations were based on evidentiary obstacles to prosecution, but that triviality was the major factor.

Besides these studies of the decision to charge in a single jurisdiction, there have been some informative systematic-empirical studies of comparative practices. Greenwood and his colleagues (1973) examined charging practices among various counties in California and within offices in Los Angeles County. They discovered substantial variation in the charging practices among counties in the proportions of felony arrests that actually resulted in the district attorney's filing felony charges. Much of this variation appeared to be attributable to the proportion of arrests that initially were classified by the police as felonies. Within Los Angeles County (where 78,000 felony complaints were studied), they also discovered substantial interoffice variability in charging. Overall, the district attorney refused to file felony charges against more than half of the defendants arrested by the police, although there was considerable variation in felony charging according to the type of offense. The highest rates of prosecution rejection were associated with wife and child beating (85% rejected), assault with a deadly weapon (87%), and rape (63%). The lowest rejection rates were found for bookmaking (7% rejected), attempted robbery (10%), and the sale of dangerous drugs (7%). Most of the rejected felony arrests were based on a lack of evidence and the district attorney's belief that the case was not serious enough to warrant felony processing.

Greenwood and his colleagues interpreted these results (particularly those pertaining to interoffice variability) as demonstrating a lack of equity in the charging decision. Their evidence suggests that many defendants may be overcharged by the police (that is, charged with an offense more serious than is warranted) and, therefore, "many citizens who are subsequently found not guilty of behavior deserving felony punishment are subjected to the anxiety, costs and loss of freedom associated with a felony arrest, as opposed to the much more limited costs and inconveniences associated with a misdemeanor arrest" (1973:vii). Such findings emphasize the need for clear, specific, and carefully articulated criteria upon which to base charging decisions. They suggest also an important need for routine feedback to the decision makers so that they may determine the decision patterns of their colleagues. Without knowledge of how similar decisions are made by other decision makers within the same jurisdiction, inequity must continue to be expected.

In another interjurisdictional analysis of felony-charging decisions, Brosi (1979) studied the attrition of felony cases in several large cities (using PROMIS data). Although overall about half of the cases dropped out of the system after arrest and before disposition, there was considerable variability in the ways these arrests fell out. Figure 6 demonstrates these interjurisdictional differences in the proportions of arrests rejected at screening (that is, with no charge by the prosecutor), *nolle prosequi*, referred, and adjudicated. These comparisons must be judged in light of the procedural differences among these jurisdictions. In Washington, D.C., for example, almost all arrests are taken to the prosecutor. In others (for example, Los Angeles), the police book suspects with a charge and suggest the charge to the prosecutor, who can accept, modify, or drop the charge. Regardless of the jurisdictional variation in how cases are brought to the prosecutor, however, Brosi (1979) found significant rates of rejection at intake (that is, decisions by prosecutors not to charge); these ranged from 18% in Cobb County, Georgia, to 40% in New Orleans.

Different types of crimes were found to have different rates of re-

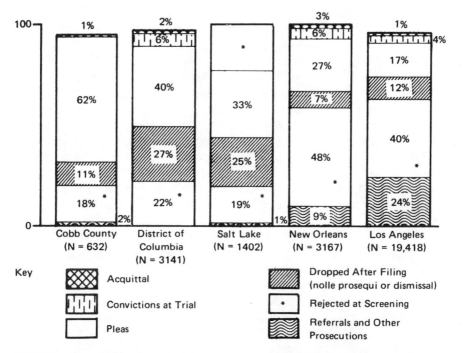

FIGURE 6. Dispositions of criminal cases from arrest, PROMIS data, January to June, 1977, felonies. SOURCE: K. Brosi, *A Cross-City Comparison of Felony Case Processing* (Washington, D.C.: Institute for Law and Social Research, 1979): 7. *Note.* Totals do not always add up to 100; open cases and administrative and "Other" disposition are not included. Asterisk (*) indicates data not available.

jection. Accusations of assault and of rape consistently were more often rejected at screening by the prosecutor than were other felony allegations. Those involving property (for example, robbery) were less often rejected. Brosi suggests that the victim–offender relationship is critical in this initial charging decision. Some victims who desire prosecution initially later reconcile with the defendant. She also suggests that a major factor in some of these decisions not to prosecute is the quality of the arrest; in others, the initial arrest was intended principally as a technique to stop an ongoing victimization.

In many arrests in each jurisdiction studied, the prosecutor filed charges initially but later dropped them (*nolle prosequi* or dismissal). Seven percent of the arrests in New Orleans and 27% in the District of Columbia were dropped in this fashion. Thus, the total proportion of cases in which the prosecutor decided not to prosecute (including those rejected at screening, referred elsewhere, and dropped after filing) ranged from about a third in Cobb County to about half in the District of Columbia to about three-fourths in Los Angeles. These data demonstrate quite clearly that the prosecutor's decision whether to charge plays a major role in the criminal justice process.

Brosi also studied the reasons given by prosecutors in these jurisdictions for deciding not to charge the suspect in these felony arrests. Consistent with the studies cited earlier in this chapter, both evidence problems and witness problems accounted for the greatest share of rejections (among those cases in which reasons were given). Overall, these two reasons accounted for over half of the arrests that were rejected. Witnesses appeared to present special problems in accusations of felonious assault. She reported data showing that about a fourth of the "noncooperative" witnesses were people who could not be located because their names, addresses, or phone numbers were recorded incorrectly at the crime scene. Half of the rest of the "noncooperative" witnesses did not receive adequate information about the court appearances. The majority of the arrests rejected at screening because of evidence problems involved insufficient testimonial evidence to corroborate the offense or to establish a necessary element of it. Such problems were most prevalent in burglary and larceny arrests.

Consistently with previous studies, Brosi discovered that due process problems played only a minor role in decisions not to charge at screening. From 1% to 9% of the rejected arrests were rejected for this reason. She concludes, "While it may be that the police do not arrest some suspects because of search and seizure limitations, these percentages seem to counter the conventional wisdom that Supreme Court decisions cause many arrests to fail because of technicalities" (199:17). Most of the decisions not to charge related to due process occurred with drug arrests.

The complexity of goals in prosecutorial charging decisions perhaps is reflected further in Brosi's finding that a sizable proportion (from 3% to 22%) of the rejections at screening were attributed to the reason that the case "lacks prosecutive merit." Although interpretation of this reason is difficult because of its ambiguous phrasing, she inferred that this category is the "fairness valve" in the exercise of prosecutorial discretion—used for cases that violate the letter but not the spirit of the law.[9]

PLEA BARGAINING

Closely bound up with decisions to charge is the practice of plea bargaining. Defined as "the process by which the defendant relinquishes his right to go to trial in exchange for a reduction in charge and/or sentence" (Heumann, 1975:515), plea bargaining is generally regarded as a pervasive practice around the country, and the literature on the topic is vast (Alschuler, 1968; Casper, 1972, 1979; Eisenstein and Jacob, 1977; Feeley, 1983, 1984; Heumann, 1978; Mather, 1979; McDonald and Cramer, 1980; Rosett and Cressey, 1976). Certainly the plea-bargaining decision is often part of the decision whether to charge at all and, if so, what to charge. It is also a topic that has aroused considerable controversy and debate, including recommendations to make it impermissible (National Advisory Commission on Criminal Justice Standards and Goals, 1973) and several attempts actually to abolish it (Daudistel, 1980; Rubinstein and White, 1980). Although we cannot explore the important literature about plea-bargaining decisions in detail here and must refer the reader to the sources cited, we can highlight some of the issues of concern to the theme of this book.

Interest in plea bargaining usually surfaces by virtue of the fact that the vast majority of persons adjudicated guilty are guilty as a result of a plea rather than as a result of trial. Certainly not all guilty pleas result from negotiations and concessions, but the high proportion of cases with pleas of guilty focuses attention on the process by which the pleas are obtained. Estimates differ, but a survey by the Bureau of Justice Statistics (1984) reported that in urban jurisdictions, guilty pleas outnumber trials by about ten to one. There is, however, considerable variation among jurisdictions in guilty plea rates. The BJS study found that whereas the median ratio of pleas to trials among the jurisdictions studied was eleven to one, in some it was as high as twenty to one and in others as low as four to one. Those jurisdictions with a high proportion of trials appeared to be more selective in the early stages of prosecution.

It does not appear to be the case that a reliance on guilty pleas is a modern phenomenon (Friedman, 1979). Heumann (1975) has shown that guilty pleas have predominated (at least in the jurisdiction he studied) since 1880, a circumstance he attributes to the fact that a very large majority of the defendants in the criminal justice system are now and always have been both factually and legally guilty, standing nothing to gain by trial (cf. Casper, 1979).

An important body of empirical research is beginning to appear concerning plea bargaining, especially in the last ten years. As a result, much of the conventional wisdom about the causes and effects of plea bargaining is coming under scrutiny.

Among the common justifications for the practice is that it is a necessary consequence of heavy caseloads; there simply is not enough time or resource to bring every case to trial. If a jurisdiction attempted a full adjudication of every case the system would quickly become overloaded and grind to a halt. However, Heumann's (1975) and Friedman's (1979) suggestions that plea bargaining may not be a consequence of modern urban congestion and the considerable variability among modern jurisdictions in the rate of guilty pleas (BJS, 1984) suggest that forces other than simple caseload pressures spawn the practice (cf. Nardulli, 1979).

Whether or not extremely heavy caseload pressures the courts to accept plea bargaining, it has been believed widely that persons who plead guilty get lighter sentences than do those who exercise their right to a trial. The most frequent explanation is that leniency is given by the court to those who do not waste the court's time with "frivolous" trials. Such a practice is obviously controversial (see, generally, Brereton and Casper, 1981–1982). Recent systematic empirical work has suggested that such concessions may be more a matter of perception than of reality and that other factors, notably the seriousness of the charge and the nature of the offender's prior record, are much more important in setting the penalty (Eisenstein and Jacob, 1977). Still, sentencing differentials continue to be reported favoring those who plead guilty (Brereton and Casper, 1981–1982).

Other benefits of plea bargaining have been noted from time to time. It is sometimes said that in addition to relieving caseload pressure, plea bargaining permits individualizing of penalities by circumventing mandatory penalties, allows the defendant to avoid some publicity attendant to a trial, and even allows for the first step toward rehabilitation by permitting the defendant to admit his or her guilt (see, generally, Casper, 1972, 1979; Heumann, 1978).

Certainly, plea bargaining has its critics (Alschuler, 1968). Common complaints include the circumstance that some innocent (either morally or, more likely, legally) persons may be induced to plead guilty by promises of leniency, that plea bargaining does in fact result in excessive leniency, is impossible to control, shifts sentencing policy from the judge and legislature to the prosecutor, and mixes up two distinct features of the criminal process, the determination of guilt and proper punishment (Brereton and Casper, 1981–1982; Casper, 1972, 1979).

Dissatisfaction with the practice has led to attempts to abolish plea bargaining, several of which have been systematically evaluated. Heumann and Loftin (1979) studied the impact of a recent change in Michigan's gun law (prohibiting plea bargaining) and discovered that trial rates stayed low, because, they argue, of the use of alternative methods discovered to offer concessions to those who plead guilty. Rubinstein and White (1980) studied the effects of a ban placed on plea bargaining by the attorney general of Alaska. They discovered that the court processes did not seem to become overwhelmed, that defendants seemed to plead guilty at the same rate after the ban as before it, and that little change was detected in conviction rates. Brereton and Casper (1981–1982) suggest that even with the ban defendants in Alaska perceive an advantage to pleading guilty, hoping to receive a lighter sentence even though none is promised.

While some social scientists have wrestled with the troublesome issues involved in the evaluation of bans on plea bargaining (see also Daudistel, 1980), others have sought to study the determinants of plea negotiations. Although this is a difficult area of study, given the low visibility of most plea-bargaining practices, some interesting research has been done.

Figueira-McDonough (1985) has categorized the common hypotheses about the determinants of plea bargaining for her study in Washington, D.C. The hypotheses include:

1. *The lesser offense hypothesis.* The argument that more seriously charged cases will tend to go through full trial, whereas less serious cases will usually be plea-bargained.
2. *The calculated risk hypothesis.* This position assumes that the less serious cases will more readily plead guilty because the anticipated consequences of conviction are less severe.
3. *The sure guilt hypothesis.* This position argues that the stronger the evidence on a charge, the greater the likelihood that conviction will result through plea bargaining.
4. *The weak case hypothesis.* The opposite of the sure guilt hypothesis, this position is that the weaker the evidence, the greater the likelihood of plea bargaining.
5. *The defense hypothesis.* This position holds that the stronger the defense response, the greater the probability of plea bargaining.

These hypotheses, which Figueira-McDonough has culled from the plea-bargaining literature, clearly are not consistent but rather often lead to opposite predictions. Certainly they may all be true to a limited extent or in some circumstances, but the need for empirical research testing is clear and, given the contradictory claims of proponents and opponents, of high priority. In her own research, Figueira-McDonough studied nearly 4,000 cases and undertook some clever operationalization of the concepts implicit in these hypotheses. The findings are complicated but include: (1) defendants charged with the more serious crimes tended to plead guilty less often and to bargain or plead innocent more often than those charged with less serious offenses; (2) when strong evidence was available simple pleas of guilt increased; and (3) a strong defense was associated with charge bargaining.

Rossman, McDonald, and Cramer (1980) studied the determinants of plea negotiations with simulation techniques with 136 prosecutors and 104 defense attorneys. They sought to test the relative importance of seriousness of offense, prior record, and strength of the case on decisions to plea-bargain. Subjects were shown a folder containing index cards with case information on them; the researchers recorded what cards the decision makers selected to view and in what order. They found some differences between prosecutors and defense attorneys, but overall they chose most often to look at the charge, prior record, and evidence factors. They found a greater willingness among prosecutors than among defense attorneys to enter plea negotiations.

A novel and important study of plea bargaining from the defendant's perspective was reported by Casper (1972). It is intriguing to discover, as Casper did, that most of the defendants represented by public defenders thought that their major adversary in the process was neither the judge nor the prosecutor, but rather their own attorney. Because it was usually the public defender who presented the "deal" to the defendant, defendants tended to view the public defender as a surrogate of the prosecutor. Casper's insights from these interviews—including a sense of the moral lessons that plea bargaining does or does not teach defendants—suggests that much could be gained by a more visible and open system of adjudication.

TOWARD RATIONALITY

The results of empirical study of prosecution decisions and their implications for rational systems of decision making is summarized well by Forst (1983:170–171):

> In fact, for many (if not most) cases, the decision whether to prosecute is virtually automatic—cases in which the evidence is either extremely weak or strong and cases involving either trivial or very serious offenses. Numerous studies agree that prosecutors' case-screening and handling decisions have been influenced primarily by the strength of the evidence and the seriousness of the offense. More recently, prosecutors in many jurisdictions have instituted programs to "target" their resources on cases involving repeat offenders. Prosecutors' decisions on these questions are assuredly not random.
>
> Within these boundaries, however, there is substantial discretion. In deciding whether to accept cases, in selecting charges to file with the court, in negotiating pleas with defense counsel, in preparing cases more or less extensively for trial, and in recommending sentences to judges, prosecutors have a good deal of room to maneuver. Written policies used even in the most rule-conscious offices do not provide unambiguous instructions about how to handle every type of case. Because of this discretion, even the best

statistical models of prosecutors' decision making are incapable of accurately
predicting screening, charging, or plea-bargaining decisions in particular cases.

The results of these studies are at once encouraging and discouraging. They are encouraging because they show that the charging decision is not beyond the province of social science methods. Many of the goals and influences pertaining to this complex decision are capable of measurement and systematic study. These studies indicate, as is found throughout the criminal justice system, that a small number of factors have most salience in the decision. In this case, evidence sufficiency, witness problems, the victim–offender relationship, and the seriousness of the alleged behavior have critical influence on the charging decision. They are discouraging because they report such variability—not only among prosecutors' offices but within them as well—in the goals, information, and alternatives used in the charging process.

We noted at the beginning of this chapter the very large grant of discretion given to prosecutors in making charging decisions. In a sense, the studies reviewed provide some indications of the consequences of this discretion. In pursuit of individualizing case decisions, and in the absence of well-defined criteria and goals, similar cases often are not treated similarly, and this, of course, raises fundamental issues of fairness. The need for discretion in this decision is clear. In order to accommodate the variety of offenses, offenders, and alternatives with the many goals of prosecution, rigid and mechanical policy standards in sufficient detail to deal with this complexity are inappropriate. No doubt they simply would be circumvented if they existed.

The existence of discretion, however, need not mean that inconsistency must exist as well. The problem, as with the other decisions discussed in this book, is the creation of standards that structure the discretion in such a way as to enhance equity of treatment simultaneously with maximizing the achievement of the other important goals. The creation of such flexible standards requires, however, an undergirding. The base needed is relevant knowledge upon which the prosecutor can draw that relates empirically the data available to the alternative goals sought. Moreover, a systematic process is essential to permit judging the consistency with which these standards are applied. It also is required that the goals be given a clear priority ordering, with some degree of consensus.

As Abrams has indicated:

There is a competing tension between the need in prosecutorial decision making for certainty, consistency, and an absence of arbitrariness on the one hand, and the need for flexibility, sensitivity, and adaptability on the other.

> The problem is to design the system so as to reach an acceptable balance
> between the two sets of values. (1971:3–4)

In later chapters we discuss in some detail what we believe to be such
a system. Here, we can describe the significant advances toward such
methods that have been made in the area of charging decisions.

One such important advance has been the PROMIS system for the
development, testing, and implementation of computerized case evaluation systems in many prosecutors' offices.[10] The aim of the system is
to indicate priorities for prosecution from the cases available for it. Priorities are assigned to cases on the basis of computer-generated scores
that evaluate the gravity of the alleged crime and the criminal history
of the suspect. The scores are tallied on the basis of two scales. The
first, developed by Sellin and Wolfgang (1964), provides an assessment
of the seriousness of the alleged criminal behavior by assigned weights
of various elements of the offense and the sum of these values. The
factors used typically pertain to physical injury, property loss or damage,
and intimidation. Thus, for example, if a particular crime involves the
loss of property worth less than $10 and no injury or intimidation, it
might receive a value of 1, whereas a crime involving death to the victim
might receive a value of 26. The assumption underlying this use of this
scale is that the greater the seriousness of the offense, the higher should
be the prosecutorial priority. This assumption, then, appears to be consistent with some commonly stated prosecution goals reviewed earlier
in this chapter and with some of the empirical data on charging decisions.
The second scale is used to measure the gravity of the criminal history
of the defendant, or perhaps the risk of new offenses. Developed originally by Gottfredson and Bonds (1961) as a parole prediction device,
this scale weights, *inter alia*, the extent of the defendant's prior record
and its characteristics. The assumption underlying the use of this scale
is that defendants with more serious prior records should be prosecuted
with priority. Because the scale was developed to measure the probability of recidivism on parole, its use perhaps also reflects a crime control
purpose.

Each case entering the system is scored according to these dimensions. In some jurisdictions another dimension is added, the evidentiary
strength of the case. Figure 7, from Jacoby's (1977) discussion of the case
evaluation system instituted in the Bronx District Attorney's Office, indicates how these scores are derived. (The "nature of defendant" score
here is based on prior record and legal status.) The sum of the weighted
items determines the priority score for the case. There could be several
uses of such a scoring procedure. Cases with the highest scores might

Pre-Trial Screening Evaluation

(Office Name) _____

(Address) _____

_____ (phone) _____

Name of Defendant

_____

Address

| Prosecutor Action: | Accepted | Refused | Other |

Reason (if not accepted)

Police Arrest Charge(s)

Prosecutors Charge(s)

Charging Assistant Name: _____ **Date:** _____

Evaluation Received Date

Coder _____

Verifier _____

| Sex | Race | DOB |

| Date Offense | Date Arrest |

Coding only

Coding only

000-00-000

(Serial Number preprinted)

Complaint Number

Defendant I.D. No.

Court Case Number

A. NATURE OF CASE

	check if applicable	pts
Victim		
one or more persons	☐	2 0
Victim Injury		
received minor injury	☐	2 4
treated and released	☐	3 0
hospitalized	☐	4 2
Intimidation		
one or more persons	☐	1 3
Weapon		
defendant armed	☐	7 4
defendant fired shot or carried gun, or carried explosives	☐	15 7
Stolen Property		
any value	☐	7 5
Prior Relationship		
victim and defendant—same family	☐	- 2 8
Arrest		
at scene	☐	4 6
within 24 hours	☐	2 9
Evidence		
admission or statement	☐	1 4
additional witnesses	☐	3 1
Identification		
line-up	☐	3 3

B. NATURE OF DEFENDANT

		pts
Felony Convictions		
one	☐	9 7
more than one	☐	18 7
Misdemeanor Convictions		
one	☐	3 6
more than one	☐	8 3
Prior Arrests—Same Charge		
one	☐	4 5
more than	☐	7.2
Prior Arrests		
one	☐	2 2
more than one	☐	4 2
Prior Arrest—Weapons Top Charge		
more than one	☐	6 4
Status When Arrested		
state parole	☐	7 1
wanted	☐	4 2

DISTRICT ATTORNEY'S EVALUATION _____

TOTAL SCORE _____

RANKING CLERK _____

FOR EACH CHARGE RECORD: (1) Disposition, (2) Reason, (3) Process Step, (4) Date _____

FIGURE 7. Model form for evaluation of an individual local pretrial screening project. Source: Jacoby (1977): 42.

be subject to special prosecutorial effort, and score values might be useful in determining whether or not to charge in the first instance.

Some of the potential advantages of such systems have been proposed. For example, Jacoby (1977:47) notes that "since each case presented for prosecution review is scored on the basis of the same factors, the evaluation is uniform and consistent. Objectivity is achieved also because the factors used for the evaluation are statistically derived (quantifiable) and require only minimal subjective interpretation." In addition, visibility is enhanced when such systems are used routinely, since the policy (for example, one indicating that seriousness and offender record deserve emphasis) is explicit, as are the criteria to be used (for example, the Sellin–Wolfgang weights). This then permits informed debate about the propriety of both. (For example, should a measure of the probability of recidivism determine who is to be prosecuted?)

Additional advantages of the PROMIS method of prosecutorial priorities have been suggested (Institute for Law and Social Research, 1976). Legal nomenclature may mask underlying differences among cases—for example, not all aggravated assaults are alike—whereas this system permits the assessment of cases on the basis of specific elements of the offense. Also, once the similarities of cases are taken into consideration on the basis of consistent criteria, then major differences that require different handling may be more readily apparent. By emphasizing the major differences among defendants, moreover, such systems may increase the motivation to seek alternatives suitable to the individual case.

Perhaps the most important advantage to a computerized evaluation system, however, is that it facilitates the acquisition of *information* as the term is used in this book. Thus, the development and application of explicit criteria permit the study of how those criteria relate to the goals of the charging decision. In the absence of a relation they may be modified. Perhaps the most salient example would relate to factors predictive of future offending.

Such systems permit the acquisition of another type of information: how consistently cases are handled by the prosecutors making charging decisions. That is, cases with similar scores may be followed to see whether they receive similar treatment at each of the major charging decisions (such as charge or no charge, or plea bargaining). Relevant to the equity goal, information about inconsistent treatment may be reported back to the decision makers with the aim of enhancing uniformity of treatment. Only when explicit criteria exist, such as those in the PROMIS system that identify what is meant by "similar offenders," can such information be available. In order to have consistency, each prosecutor in a jurisdiction must know what the others are doing. In order to know this well, systematic, reliable procedures keeping track of representative cases are essential.

If the systems implemented are truly designed as evolutionary ones, in the sense that they are to be judged repeatedly in the light of evidence and, when they do not fit, are adapted accordingly, it should be possible to "fine tune" the case evaluations. Some of the apparent disparity in case processing, for example, may be the result of application of criteria in individual cases that, although they may be both proper and rational, are not included among the case evaluation criteria. A significant challenge at all of the decision points discussed in this book is to identify, articulate, and structure the influence of nonapparent, difficult to weigh, and uncommon criteria (Abrams, 1971). If prosecutors were required to give specific reasons for their belief that a particular case should deviate from "consistent" treatment, then, if appropriate, these reasons could serve as the fuel for adapting future case evaluation procedures. Equity should be sought in charging decisions, but with cognizance of the danger of treating unequal cases alike. The development of explicit standards with uniform application should facilitate the identification of significant differences among cases that permit alternative decisions within a rational, flexible decision policy.

The development of decision aids such as PROMIS go a long way toward increased rationality. Research of the type reviewed in this chapter permits additional steps to be taken. Some of the fundamental correlates of the decision to charge are becoming known. What needs now to be known is how these correlates of the decision relate or fail to relate to the goals that also have been identified and to the various decision alternatives. As we repeatedly stress, only when confidence can be held that these correlates of the decision are adequately informative about the goals of the decision can it be claimed that charging decisions are made rationally.

NOTES

1. For discussion of practices in different jurisdictions, see Miller (1970), McIntyre (1967), and President's Commission on Law Enforcement and Administration of Justice (1967). In some jurisdictions the police may file charges directly with the court without prior screening by a prosecutor.
2. As Newman points out, and as will be demonstrated in this chapter, the decision to charge consists of two components, one qualitative and one quantitative:

> Qualitatively, the question is whether, in the judgment of the district attorney, the accused ought to be charged with a crime at all, or if in the interest of equity, individualization of justice, or mitigating circumstance, it would

be fairer, more just, or sufficient for the purposes of law and the objectives of his office to refrain from prosecuting at all. The quantitative facet relates to the vigor of prosecution once it is determined to be possible and desirable. In some cases the prosecutor may charge a crime as serious as the evidence permits, may multiply charges to their fullest, or may even level "extra-Maximum" charges by invoking habitual-criminal statutes or similar provisions. (1974:608)

3. Although sometimes provided by statute, this power originates in common law. See Newman (1974). For discussions of informal charging alternatives, see Remington *et al.* (1969, esp. pp. 417–419; President's Commission, 1967).

4. For citations and discussions, LaFave (1970), and Comment (1969).

5. Although the formal evidence standard to charge is the same as to arrest—"probable cause"—for the prosecutor this standard must be forward looking to the conviction standard of "beyond a reasonable doubt." See Newman (1966). Miller's (1970) observations of prosecutorial charging lead him to conclude that "it is not inaccurate to assert that an affirmative initial charging decision usually requires a belief on the part of the prosecutor that the suspect is guilty beyond a reasonable doubt." Both limitations on resources and the belief that it is unfair to charge a suspect who cannot be convicted result in this standard. Miller found no evidence in his study to indicate that prosecutors charge suspects who would be unconvictable so as to coerce a guilty plea. On the other hand, McIntyre (1967) reports that unconvictables are sometimes charged— for example, when the police promise that additional evidence will be forthcoming.

6. The influence of outside agencies in the decision to charge is documented amply by Miller. He shows that to some extent the police may control the charging decision by their decision not to arrest. That is, if the police decide that prosecution is not warranted, they do not arrest the suspect, effectively negating the prosecutor's influence. Judicial dismissals serve an analogous function at the other end.

     Other observational studies report similar interagency influences on charging decisions. Cole (1970) reports that in Seattle the decision whether to charge often is made with other criminal justice agencies in mind, particularly the police.

7. The PROMIS system will be discussed more fully in a subsequent section.

8. Because the vast majority of persons charged with an offense who subsequently are found guilty are found guilty by virtue of a plea to the charge, and because in most jurisdictions the charge largely circumscribes the available sanctions, the charging decision also can be considered (for some purposes) as a sentencing decision. So conceived, the predictive aim of charging to reduce crime may give many contemporary sentencing theorists considerable pause. See the discussions in Chapter 6.

9. As with rejections at screening, Brosi found that the major reasons for postfiling dismissals and *nolles* were evidence- and witness-related. Plea bargaining was an important factor in some of these later decisions not to charge, whereas again due process problems rarely occurred. For a qualitative comparative study of these decisions, see Mellon *et al.* (1981).

10. For discussions of these systems and their purposes, see Hamilton and Work (1973), Jacoby (1977), and Institute for Law and Social Research (1976).

Chapter 6

SENTENCING DECISIONS

Once convicted, the offender must be sentenced. This human decision lies at the hub of current controversies about the basic purposes of the entire criminal justice system. Indeed, recent trends in the philosophy of sentencing address issues so fundamental to criminal justice that they must be expected to have a profound impact on the entire system in the next few years.[1] These tendencies toward changed conceptions of the purposes of sentencing also involve debates about the extent of discretion that ought to be allowed judges in choosing alternative sentences. In this chapter we seek to summarize these trends, to speculate about their potential implications for rationality in decision making, and to identify some of the research challenges that they present.

In fixing the sentence, the judge occupies a central role capable of markedly influencing all other parts of the system. Sentencing decisions can and do have an impact on the roles and behaviors of police, prosecutors, and correctional authorities. Thus, changes in sentencing law or practice may have very important implications for the entire law enforcement, court, and correctional enterprise (Ohlin and Remington, 1958).

The purposes of sentencing, however, are by no means agreed upon. Not only is there disagreement about the proper goals of the sentencing decision but also much current debate about appropriate alternatives. It is in the context of these arguments that the trends to be discussed in this chapter have emerged. Before discussing them, however, it may be useful to define the disputes by outlining briefly the most commonly held theories of sentencing and their philosophical underpinnings.

SENTENCING GOALS

The bifurcation of American criminal trials (between determinations of criminal liability and of the sentence) is such that one important sanction already has been imposed before sentencing. This is the conviction itself, which, as described by Weiler (1974), publicly, authoritatively, decisively, and enduringly certifies that the defendant is guilty of blameworthy conduct causing harm to an innocent victim. Although, as Weiler (1978:107) notes, it often is overlooked in discussions of sentencing, this stigmatization of a person as an offender inflicts "not only a damaging, but also one out of the most enduring, sanctions which the state can mete out."

Rarely, however, is the conviction alone considered to be a sufficient sanction, and a variety of justifications for additional ones have been argued. The controversies have endured for thousands of years, and the disputes of today continue to be lively.

Weiler points out that two basic moral conflicts lie at the root of this complex of theories of sentencing. The first distinction is found between utilitarian and desert perspectives.[2] The former is committed to maximizing the general good; the latter is addressed to principles of justice, fairness, and equity. A second, related distinction poses the conflict between reductionism and retributionism. This fundamental difference has profound implications not only for the basis of sentencing in the criminal law but also for the judge as sentencing decision maker. It is a critical distinction as well in respect to debates about the justifiable role of prediction in sentencing decisions. As summarized by Weiler (1974:121):

> The one view holds that criminal penalties can be justified if, but only if, they will reduce the level of crime within the community. The other responds that sanctions are justified if, but only if, the defendant has done something for which he merits their infliction. It is clear then that the arguments within the first perspective are focused forward in time, toward the future beneficial consequences of punishment; within the second the arguments look backward, to events which have already occurred, as the source of moral support.

The literature on sentencing goals is vast,[3] but the major currently debated perspectives may be identified in order to examine the implications for rationality in sentencing. Accordingly, we shall discuss four sentencing aims widely advocated and argued about: deterrence, incapacitation, treatment, and desert.[4] Each has a long history in philosophy, literature, and criminology.

DETERRENCE

The concept of deterrence refers to the prevention of criminal acts in the population at large by means of the imposition of punishment on persons convicted of crime. This concept often is called *general deterrence* in order to distinguish it from *special* or *specific* deterrence, the latter referring to the inhibition of criminal activity of the person being punished as a result of the imposition of that punishment. (The term *deterrence* is used here to refer only to general deterrence, since special deterrence may be subsumed under the general term *treatment.*)

In this theory, the punishment given to an individual or class of individuals is explicitly designed to decrease the probability that others will engage in unlawful behavior. Hence, the validity of deterrence as a sentencing goal is determined by the efect that a given punishment applied to a particular offender has on the future criminality of those not punished.

Thus, the deterrent aim is future-oriented, and its objective is to persuade or warn others not to commit criminal acts. The goal is clearly the prevention of crime; the term *general prevention* is sometimes used for the same concept (especially in Europe).

The aim of reducing the probability of crime in the population at large has long been held to provide a justification for punishment. Publius Syrus wrote: "Qui culpae ignoscit uni, suadet pluribus" (Pardon one offense and you encourage many).[5] Herbert Spencer claimed that "failure of justice tempts men to injustices" and that "every unpunished delinquency has a family of delinquencies." And Daniel Webster in a similar vein argued, "Every unpunished murder takes away something from the security of every man's life."[6] Not merely crime but, by implication, sinful behavior is to be controlled by punishment. According to Shakespeare: "Nothing emboldens sin so much as mercy." The concept of prediction is fundamental to this perspective, since it is expected that the punishment of offenders will decrease the likelihood of crime by others.

INCAPACITATION

Incapacitation (sometimes called *neutralization* or *isolation*) refers to the sentencing aim of restraining the person being punished from committing further criminal acts. To the extent that the intent of the sentence is purely incapacitative, attention is not focused on the reduction of the offender's *propensity* for future criminal acts; rather, the offender is controlled so as to preclude his *opportunity* for such behavior, at least while under the authority of the state. Clearly, this aim, too, is future-oriented. An essential component of the incapacitative purpose is prediction; that is, an assessment is made of the probability of future criminal conduct by the offender and the imposition of penalties for the offense reflects that assessment. Thus, incapacitative dispositions are meant to be preventive.

The incapacitative perspective is similar in this way to that of deterrence; but whereas the latter focuses on prevention of crime by others, the incapacitative frame of reference seeks prevention of crime by the convicted offender. Its justification must be that restraints are necessary for what the offender may do, rather for what he or she has done.

Incapacitation has recently captured the imagination of some researchers and policymakers. Today it is common to distinguish two forms of incapacitation: collective incapacitation and selective incapacitation (Blumstein, 1984; Cohen, 1984). As defined by Blumstein (1984:134):

> A collective incapacitation effect occurs under any sentencing policy . . . as long as any of the offenders sentenced under the policy would have committed crimes on the street during their period of confinement and those crimes would not be replaced on the street by others (as, for example, the drug sales of a sentenced drug dealer would be replaced by other dealers still on the street).

Selective incapacitation, on the other hand, seeks to find high-risk offenders and sentence them to prison terms because of their disproportionate risk. Proponents of selective incapacitation (Forst, 1984; Greenwood, 1982) see it as a method whereby crime rates could be cut and imprisonment levels reduced, simply by increasing the selectivity of incarceration decisions.

Others have disputed the claims made for incapacitation on both moral and empirical grounds (Cohen, 1984; von Hirsch, 1985; von Hirsch and Gottfredson, 1984). Because of the inherent problems of predicting criminal behavior with high accuracy (see Chapter 4), those who question incapacitation argue that overpredictions of criminality will be frequent and will result in unfair imprisonment. Such critics also point to the inadequate empirical justification for the prediction instruments developed up to this point (Cohen, 1984).

TREATMENT

Treatment aims in sentencing are future-oriented, preventive in design, and focused on the individual offender. The goal is to lessen the propensity of those convicted of crime to commit further crimes. The term *treatment* is used here in its broadest sense to include anything done to, with, or for the offender for the purpose of reducing the probability of new criminal acts. Thus, potential vehicles for achieving this aim include all programs designed for rehabilitation, restoration, or reintegration of the offender into the community, the punishment of the offender with the aim of specific deterrence, and variations in place of confinement or length of sentence when designed to change the offender's behavior. In short, it includes all means intended to reduce the offender's proclivity toward future criminal acts. (It must be recognized that the term *treatment* is widely used with other meanings, for example, to refer to procedures intended to modify some state of the person in ways not necessarily related to crime reduction.) As with the other utilitarian purposes of deterrence and incapacitation, the prediction of future events is inextricably involved with a treatment purpose.

Plato combined a treatment aim (special deterrence) with that of general deterrence; he explained the purpose of punishment as at once a means of correction and a warning to others:

> Not that he is punished because he did wrong, for that which is done can never be undone, but in order that in future times, he, and those who see him corrected, may utterly hate injustice, or at any rate abate much of their evil-doing.[7]

Hobbes would limit the use of punishment to these same two aims:

> In revenges or punishments men ought not to look at the greatness of evil past, but at the greatness of the good to follow, whereby we are forbidden to inflict punishment with any other design than for the correction of the offender and the admonition of others.[8]

In 1764 Beccaria named various criteria for the justification of punishment that continue to provide bases for current debates. In addition to his widely cited arguments for general deterrence, to be acceptable for Beccaria, punishment had to be public and prompt, it had to be "necessary," and moreover (besides being lawful), it had to be proportional in severity to the seriousness of the offense. At the same time, it had to be the least severe sanction possible in the circumstances.

The goals of deterrence, incapacitation, and treatment thus each have a probabilistic nature. Although the element of prediction is perhaps most obviously necessary for the incapacitative and rehabilitative rationales, it is inherent equally in the concept of deterrence. That concept requires the assumption that there is an expected relation (prediction) between the punishment of individuals or classes of individuals and the future behavior of other individuals and groups. All three of these major goals are aimed at reducing the probability of crime.

DESERT

In the desert theory of sentencing, the only question answered is, What sanction is deserved in this case? The desert rationale has no explicit crime control aim; its purpose is to express disapprobation or to exact retribution. Desert thus differs from the other three major purposes in that it focuses exclusively on the past criminal behavior of the offender and punishment is given solely to express condemnation of that behavior.[9]

The concept of desert may be, of course, a component of various other perspectives on the purposes of punishment. It may be used with a utilitarian aim, for example, for the prevention of anomie. Or it may refer to retribution, to an affirmation of moral values, or to reprobation. But the hallmark of this position is that as a result of his or her offense, the offender deserves a certain amount of punishment, and the severity of punishment ought to be in proportion to the gravity of the criminal conduct, taking into account the culpability of the offender. Thus, the concept contains neither utilitarian nor predictive components, distinguishing it in principle from deterrence, incapacitation, and treatment purposes.

Like the utilitarian aims of deterrence, incapacitation, and treatment, the concept of desert as a purpose of the sentence is as old as philosophy and is found repeatedly in literature. Aristotle used the term: "Justice is that virtue of the soul that is distributive according to desert."[10] Similarly, Justician defined justice: "Justitia est constans et perpetua voluntas jus suum cuique tribuendi" (Justice is the firm and continuous desire to render to everyone that which is his due).[11] The principles of desert and proportionality (to the gravity of harm done) is implicit in a psalm of David (28:4), who prayed, "Give them according to their deeds, and according to the wickedness of their endeavors: give them after the work of their hands; render to them their desert." If Shakespeare was a utilitarian, believing in general deterrence as implied by the quotation above, he must be regarded also as recognizing the principle of just desert: "Where the offense is, let the great axe fall." The term *justice* often is equated with *desert,* as in Fielding's Tom Jones: "Thwackum was for doing justice, and leaving mercy to Heaven."[12]

The concept that desert alone provides a legitimate basis for punishment was quite acceptable to Kant, as illustrated by his famous example:

> Even if a civil society resolved to dissolve itself with the consent of all its members—as might be supposed in the case of a people inhabiting an island resolving to separate and scatter themselves throughout the whole world— the last murderer lying in prison ought to be executed before the resolution was carried out. This ought to be done in order that everyone may realize the desert of his deeds.[13]

Indeed, Kant spoke of the penal law as a categorical imperative and cautioned "woe to him who creeps through the serpent-windings of utilitarianism."[14]

It is clear that the principle of desert has nothing whatever to do with the utilitarian purposes of crime control, with prevention, with deterrence, with the ideas of incapacitation or rehabilitation, or with any other aim of crime reduction. This is not to say that the application of the concept of commensurate desert may not have such effects; that is a different question. The aim is satisfaction of a moral imperative. Rewards and punishments provide means to the end of desert.

INDIVIDUALIZATION OF PURPOSE IN SENTENCING: A LOOK AT SOME DATA

If purposes conflict, the possibility exists that the individual judge, in selecting among sentencing alternatives, may also select among purposes. That is, in the individual case the judge may emphasize one or another purpose in the process of decision making, and this emphasis may vary among cases. Some evidence that this is so is derived from a study by Gottfredson and Stecher (1979) of sentencing in one court in a large eastern metropolitan county.

In this study, eighteen judges completed forms documenting their judgments on various factors at the time of sentencing, including (for 982 cases) identification of the sentencing purposes that they defined as appropriate to each case. Purposes listed were retribution, incapacitation, special deterrence, rehabilitation, and "other" (including general deterrence). (The list was devised in collaboration with the judges at the start of the study.) The judges were asked to distribute 100 points among these items or to assign this value to any one item, provided only that sums would be 100 points.

The judges usually did not select any one aim as the single purpose of the sentence. Rather, it was typical to distribute the 100 points among the alternative purposes listed (of course, the nature of the question may have suggested such distribution). When the purpose given the highest weighting was classified as the "principal purpose," the most commonly identified main purpose was that of rehabilitation. That is, rehabilitation most often was given the most weight. That was the case in 36% of the sentences. When, as suggested earlier, special deterrence was regarded as a variety of rehabilitation (that is, treatment), then 45% of the sentences were classified as having a treatment aim according to the judge who imposed the sentence.

When all utilitarian aims were combined (forward-looking goals with a predictive element), then 83% of these sentences were included. The aim of retribution was cited relatively infrequently as the main reason for the sentence, although it was selected 17% of the time. (Note that the term *desert* was not used in the question, since it was not suggested by any judge when the item was formulated.) Incapacitation was cited as the aim given the greatest weight in only 4% of the cases. The proportions of sentences for which these aims were given the largest weightings by these judges are shown in Figure 8.

A further analysis of differences between offenders sentenced with a primary retributive purpose and those sentenced mainly with a re-

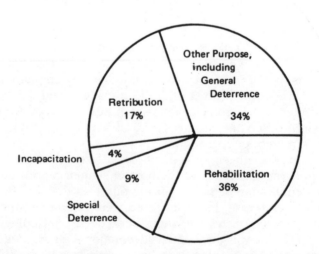

FIGURE 8. Main purposes cited by 17 judges in sentencing 982 adult offenders. Source: Adapted from D. Gottfredson and B. Stecker, "Sentencing Policy Models" (Newark, N.J.: School of Criminal Justice, Rutgers University, 1979), manuscript.

habilitative intent was done (using the discriminant function). The results suggested that

> generally, these judges were more inclined to sentence offenders retributively when the conviction offense was more serious, when the offender had a record of prior prison incarceration, when the judge expected recidivism (and particularly when a new offense against persons was predicted) and when social stability was questioned. When the converse was true, the judges tended to see rehabilitation as an appropriate sentencing aim. (Gottfredson and Stecher, 1979:30)

The one item that appeared from the discriminate analysis to have the strongest association with the choice of primary aim (in the context of all the items included) was the judge's prediction of recidivism by an offense against persons. This suggests that the relatively infrequent selection of incapacitation as a principal goal may be misleading and that judges may employ this concept without necessarily labeling it as such. Alternatively, it may suggest that, for those judges, utilitarian purposes may provide a partial justification for retributive aims.

In a major study of sentencing in Canada, Hogarth (1971) did a factor analysis of 107 attitude item scores. A result was that the first factor found, accounting for more than 70% of the explained variance (42% of total variance), appeared to the author easy to interpret as measuring "the degree to which an individual wishes to see offenders punished severely" (at 126). High loadings were found on items agreeing with capital and corporal punishment, that prisons should be places of punishment, and "the most important single consideration in determining the sentence to impose should be the nature and gravity of the offense" (at 126). Hogarth called this factor *justice* and related it to the concept of just deserts. After rotation, he found factors labeled "punishment corrects," "intolerance," "social defense" (apparently related to general deterrence), and "modernism" (" 'new world' puritanism") (at 128–129).

In any case, these data support the contention that all the main purposes of sentencing play a role in the choice of alternative sanctions. The specific purposes related to judgments are rarely specified explicitly, however, and such identification is required if it is desired to learn how the rationality of such decisions can be improved.

SENTENCING DISPOSITIONS

Sir Francis Galton noted a peculiarity of the distributions of punishments when he studied the sentences of all males imprisoned in

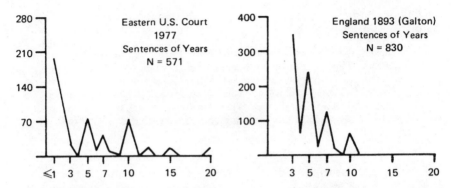

FIGURE 9. Number chosen in sentencing to years, Eastern United States Court and England (1893). SOURCE: Adapted from Banks (1964): 74.

England in 1893 without the option of a fine. The frequencies of sentences of years (rounded up to the nearest tenth) are shown in Figure 9, adapted from a presentation of his work by Banks (1964:75), who cited Galton as follows:

> It would be expected that the various terms of imprisonment . . . should fall in a continuous series. Such, however, is not the case. . . . The extreme irregularity of the frequency of the different terms of imprisonment forces itself on the attention . . . [and] it is impossible to believe that a judicial system is fair which allots only 20 sentences to 6 years, allots as many as 240 to 5 years, as few as 60 to 4 years and as many as 360 to 3 years.

As may be seen in the figure, sentences of 3, 5, 7, and 10 years appear to be preferred to the values between, resulting in an irregular polygram with a series of spikes.

Galton noted a similar phenomenon when sentences to months were plotted. Thus, although there were some 300 sentences to 18 months, there were none to 17 and only 20 to 19. Moreover, he noted a rhythmical series of 3, 6, 9, 15, and 18 or greater years, "a round figure which must commend itself to the judges by its simplicity." Beyond this rhythm, however, Galton accounted for his results "by the undoubted fact that almost all persons have a disposition to dwell on certain numbers, and an indisposition to use others," and he remarked, "These trifles determine the choice of such widely different sentences as imprisonment for 3 or 5 years, 5 or 7, and of 7 or 10 for crimes whose penal deserts would otherwise be rated at 4, 6 and 8 or 9 years respectively," (Banks, 1964:75–76).

The sentences of the court in the eastern United States discussed in the previous section of this chapter are also shown in Figure 8. Sentences of 6, 12, and 18 months were common, so the figure is not comparable with that derived from Galton at the lower range, but the tendency to use sentences of 5, 7, 10 (12, 15, 20) is apparent.

CORRELATES OF SENTENCING DECISIONS

Before we begin a discussion of recent trends in sentencing, we should pause to examine how sentencing decisions appear to be made in practice. As with the other decisions discussed herein, we think it is imperative that the correlates of actual practice be understood so far as existing research permits.

Galton apparently was among the earliest to suggest comparison of different courts or judges who might, for the same kind of person, assign very different penalties (Banks, 1964). There have been many studies since that show, or at least suggest strongly, that variation among courts and among individual judges even in the same court contributes substantially to sentence variations. In an early study, Gaudet, Harris, and St. John (1933) found, for example, from a study of more than 7,000 persons sentenced in a New Jersey court by six judges, a percentage variation in imprisonment ranging among judges from 34% to 58%. Although cases were assigned on a rotational basis, so that it is plausible that types of cases were distributed evenly, this was not demonstrated, and the variation in sentences might have been due to differences in that distribution. Sutton (1978) studied variability in sentences imposed in federal district courts, using multiple regression procedures. He discovered that the factors that appeared to determine whether an offender was sentenced to prison, as well as the factors that appeared to influence the length of imprisonment, varied considerably among the district courts.

A sizable body of research literature focuses on the issue of what factors are most determinative of sentencing dispositions. A major theme of much of this research, apart from the issues of variability discussed heretofore, is whether *legal* or *extralegal* factors are more influential in sentencing. Unfortunately, much of the existing research is quite limited in the extent to which inferences about the relative importance of these factors can be determined. Problems in design and analytical methods have been numerous.[15] Common problems include the failure to control statistically for legal variables when assessing the relevance of extralegal variables, failure to compute measures of association for the factors with significant effects, and the use of very crude proxy measures.

Some research on sentencing of adult offenders has atempted to overcome some of the problems of earlier studies. Tiffany, Avichai, and

Peters (1975) studied sentencing practices in the federal district courts for the four crimes of bank robbery, auto theft, interstate transportation of forged securities, and forgery for the years 1967 and 1968. The dependent variable in their multiple regression analyses was a scale of possible sentences that ranged from zero (suspended sentence) to fifty (over 120 months imprisonment). Their independent variables included the type of crime committed, prior record, age, type of counsel, race, and the type of trial (bench versus jury). They discovered that the seriousness of the crime committed had the greatest impact on sentencing and that prior record and type of conviction also were related significantly to disposition, although less strongly. Prior record appeared to have its greatest effect on the least serious crimes, and type of conviction appeared to be more influential than did prior record. Persons convicted by jury trials tended to receive more severe dispositions than did persons convicted by judge trials. Overall, age, race, and type of counsel did not appear to be related to disposition.

Sutton (1978) used multivariate methods to analyze incarceration and sentence length decisions in the federal district courts. His analyses are complicated; separate analyses were undertaken for different offenses under consideration. A variety of factors were used to try to predict sentencing dispositions, including offense, prior record, method of conviction, sex, race, and so forth. Overall, the best predictors of both the decision to incarcerate and the decision about the length of sentence were the legal variables in the study. Demographic characteristics of the offenders appeared to play a relatively small role in these decisions.

Sutton also found differences in the factors that appeared to be used in the decision to incarcerate compared to the factors used in the decision as to sentence length. In determining the length of prison term, the conviction offense and whether the conviction was by a jury trial or not were the strongest correlates in multivariate analyses. On the other hand, the strongest correlate of the decision to incarcerate was the offender's prior criminal record, with method of conviction and type of offense less strongly related.

In a series of papers, Pope (1975, 1976, 1978b) analyzed sentencing correlates in several California counties using offender-based transaction statistics. A considerable variety of independent variables was included, and the data permitted study of sentencing differences according to lower and superior courts and according to whether the court was in an urban or a rural area. As with Sutton's study, Pope's research is complicated and difficult to summarize fairly in relation to the intricacies of the results. The factors correlated with sentencing dispositions did vary between urban and rural courts and between lower and superior courts. Overall, Pope discovered that two legal variables were relatively strong predictors of sentencing for burglary and assault offenders: the seriousness of the prior record and whether the offender was on some form of supervised release at the time of arrest.[16]

Pope's study is valuable, not just for the substantive results it produced, but also for its demonstration of the value of transaction data— data that have as their base the individual offender (or suspect) and that trace the individual through various steps in the criminal justice process. As we have seen, many criminal justice decisions are predicated upon decisions made earlier in the process, and prior decisions may greatly influence subsequent decisions. Transaction data can play a major role in the evaluation of these decisions because, if a lengthy enough follow-up on the individuals is made, they can reveal to decision makers some of the consequences of their decisions (in addition to permitting evaluations of fairness, such as those undertaken by Pope). We argue in the last chapter that such data systems are a requisite for the enhancement of rationality in criminal justice decision making.

Studies of sentencing correlates using transaction data are rare. One additional study of the sentences received by a cohort of felony arrestees in New York City has been reported by the Vera Institute (1977). The Vera researchers tracked these persons through to disposition, and although the number of independent variables studied was not large and multivariate statistical methods were not used, their results generally confirm what prior research had found:

> The more serious the offense charged at arrest . . . , the stiffer is the sentence likely to be following conviction, whether the conviction was for the felony originally charged, a lesser felony or a misdemeanor. . . . Defendants with heavier criminal histories were more likely to be convicted and, if convicted, more likely to receive heavier sentences than those with lighter or clean records. Seventy-seven percent of the convicted defendants with no prior record avoided jail or prison; only 16% of convicted defendants who had previously been sentenced to prison were as fortunate. (1977:13–20)

These results also clearly indicate the value of transaction data in the study of decisions in the criminal process: subsequent decisions may "accommodate" earlier decisions in ways that heavily influence the final outcome. In Chapter 9 we report similar results with respect to the ways in which parole decisions may "supersede" earlier decisions by prosecutors and judges.

Some research attention has also been devoted to the ways in which judicial attitudes may influence sentencing decisions. Green (1961), in a study of 1,437 cases sentenced in Philadelphia in 1956–1957 by eighteen judges, concluded that legal factors such as the type of crime, the number of indictments, prior criminal record, and recommendations to the court accounted for most of the disparity apparent from a simple comparison. Using a prediction measure combining these factors to classify the convicted as to expected sentences, Green concluded, however, that as cases move from the extremes of gravity or mildness judicial standards tend to become less stable and sentencing increasingly reflects the individuality of the judge. Related studies of sentencing variation among courts or among judges tend to emphasize either differences in the sentencing policies of courts (as between smaller, rural courts or larger, urban ones), or a rather vague reference to the attitudes, habits, or individuality of judges.

In his study of sentencing of 71 judges in Ontario, Canada, Hogarth (1971) found substantial correlations between various attitudinal measures and a variety of sentencing behaviors. Although he was appropriately cautious in interpretations concerning the impact of judicial attitudes on sentencing behavior, his results are persuasive that such attitudes can indeed be quite influential.

In the study of sentencing by Gottfredson and Stecher (1979) discussed in the preceding section, data items from case files and various ratings made by the judges at the time of sentencing were analyzed to determine their association with various sentencing alternatives. Since the judge makes not one but a variety of decisions in sentencing, this is a complex matter; but the results may be illustrated by summarizing the findings mainly with respect to one aspect, namely, the decision whether to require the offender's incarceration. These analyses were based on 976 of the sentences by seventeen judges.

The offenders sentenced to confinement tended to be those with more serious offenses, by two measures of that concept. The average scores for the legal offense class were higher (more serious) for those sentenced to incarceration, and the judges' ratings of seriousness were on the average higher as well. On other variables there were significant differences between the groups in the variability of the scores on the items. Generally, it appeared from the analyses that judges tended to incarcerate the offenders who were convicted of crimes with stronger legislatively set sanctions and perceived as having committed more serious offenses. In the context of all the items included, the judges' prognoses for any recidivism, his or her ratings of the seriousness of the offense, and the legal class of the offense were the best indicants of the sentencing outcome as to incarceration.

Wheeler, Weisburd, and Bode (1982) undertook an important study of the factors determining sentences for white-collar offenders in federal courts. Defining white-collar offenses as economic offenses committed by fraud, deception, or collusion (e.g., antitrust, bank embezzlement),

Wheeler and his colleagues gathered data on over 1,000 crimes sentenced from 1976 to 1978. They collected a vast array of data about each case (how much was stolen, who the victims were) and about the offender (prior record, social class). The findings are remarkably consistent with the research discussed previously for ordinary "street crimes" that are sentenced in state courts. The variables with the greatest role in the decision whether to imprison were the seriousness variables—the statutory penalties possible, amount of loss, and type of victim—and the criminal history variables. They found that the higher the offender's social status, the more likely was a sentence to imprisonment. There was no discernible effect of race, but men were more likely than women to be sent to prison, as were those sentenced from particular jurisdictions (i.e., the chances of imprisonment were dependent somewhat on where the offense took place).

Overall, these studies of sentencing decisions yield some important and consistent findings. It appears that a major correlate of incarceration versus nonincarceration, or of the length of maximum sentence to imprisonment, is some measure of the seriousness of the offense. The concept has been defined differently in various studies, but the type of behavior for which the offender has been convicted (or, in some cases, the behavior charged) exerts a powerful, and not unexpected, influence on sentencing decisions.

So, too, does the nature and gravity of the offender's prior record. Again, different measures have been studied, and not all of the research reports an effect. But in the aggregate these studies support the claim that the prior criminal history of the offender is influential, although not so influential as seriousness of offense, in determining sentence. There is also evidence that a critical concern in sentencing is the judge's prognosis for the recidivism of the offender.

A recent, thorough review of sentencing research undertaken by a panel established by the National Academy of Sciences agrees with our conclusion:

> Using a variety of different indicators, offense seriousness and offender's prior record emerge consistently as the key determinants of sentences. The more serious the offense and the worse the offender's prior record, the more severe the sentence. The strength of this conclusion persists despite the potentially severe problems of pervasive biases arising from the difficulty of measuring—or even precisely defining—either of these complex variables. This finding is supported by a wide variety of studies using data of varying quality in different jurisdictions and with a diversity of measures of offense seriousness and prior record. (Blumstein, Cohen, Martin, and Tonry, 1983:11)

Most of the existing research also indicates that there is considerable unexplained sentencing variation, both between and within courts (e.g.,

Roberts, 1983). There is some evidence that some of this variation is due to individual differences among judges—that is, to variations in particular attitudes or beliefs about the purposes of sentencing. And there is some evidence that sugests that a portion of the unexplained variation may be due to extralegal decision-making criteria, although the legal factors appear to be, in the recent past anyway, considerably more predictive of sentencing.

SENTENCING FOR EFFICIENCY

One potentially important yet typically neglected purpose of sentencing is to control the flow of cases through the system in an efficient manner. Thus, it is often suggested that those defendants who choose to have their cases tried by a jury will, if found guilty, be given a sentence harsher than the one they would have received if they had pled guilty. The point of such an often alleged yet rarely articulated policy is to discourage the expensive and time-consuming jury trial by guilty defendants. Or, in the language of the court, "If you take some of my time, I'll take some of yours."

Although the propriety of a penalty for the exercise of a constitutional guarantee can certainly be questioned, the existence of such accommodations to the workload of the courts has long been understood. An empirical study by Uhlman and Walker (1980) has demonstrated that the cost of pursuing a jury trial can be very high, with considerably harsher sentences for those found guilty than they would have received if they simply pled guilty. They examined the sentences for nearly 30,000 felons in an eastern city. Those convicted by a jury had average sentences over twice as long as those convicted by plea or by bench trial. These differences held subsequent to multivariate controls for offense severity and prior record. They conclude:

> The cost of a jury trial for convicted defendants in Metro City is high: sentences are substantially more severe than for other defendants. Jail sentences are much more likely to be given to jury defendants, and the sentences meted out are uniformly more severe. It is ironic that the element of the legal system expected to individualize and moderate justice is transformed into the vehicle by which the most severe criminal sanctions are applied. (1980:337)

Such practices are undoubtedly widespread in the criminal justice system. The harsher expected sentence following a jury conviction would be expected to assist the prosecutor in efforts to obtain plea bargains. Certainly such coercion weighs heavily on the innocent as well as the guilty, thus giving rise to the fear that some innocent defendants will agree to plead guilty to avoid the potentially stiffer penalty should they be convicted by a jury. On the other hand, as discussed in Chapter 5, the system in many places would have great difficulty in allocating sufficient resources to grant everyone a jury trial. In the Uhlman and Walker study, only 2% of the guilty verdicts were the result of a jury trial. To increase this substantially would be very difficult.

It is not unreasonable to expect that judicial sentences sometimes also seek to accommodate the other end of the system, corrections. In an era of overcrowded prisons, there is considerable implicit pressure on the judiciary to use incarceration very selectively. And in one system—Minnesota—the sentencing statute permits the guidelines structure in use there to be modified to accommodate overcrowded faculties (Minnesota Sentencing Guidelines Commission, 1984). We believe such explicit statements of policy are preferable to the implicit, unstructured and *sub rosa* policies surrounding penalties for jury trials, a topic to which we turn our attention in the last section of this chapter.

SENTENCING TRENDS

Until recently, sentencing and correctional structures in the United States have been guided mainly by utilitarian principles. Consistent with the treatment ideal, the indeterminate sentence has been the general rule, adopted increasingly since the early 1900s. Usually, the actual determination of the specific sentence has been deferred (when incarceration was used) until late in the term of confinement, when it has been decided by a parole board. The premise at the origin of this common model was that the offender could be diagnosed and treated and should be released when ready to assume a law-abiding life. Thus, the treatment goal of sentencing—future-oriented, preventive in design, and focused on the individual offender—was paramount.

Now this is being changed. One reason, but perhaps not the most important, is a widespread disenchantment with the effectiveness of the design. Increasingly it has been argued that we do not have enough knowledge of diagnosis and treatment to implement this model—in short, it is argued that it does not work.[17] Thus, this utilitarian regime is criticized on utilitarian grounds, often by those arguing from a desert perspective. Such criticism may be in order from the utilitarian orientation or a pragmatic one, if justified, but it is hardly consistent with a position that already has rejected these perspectives. The fundamental challenge, however, rests on moral arguments about justice and fairness, and its basis is the desert perspective. The shift, which is readily apparent and pronounced, is to determinate sentencing and to an emphasis on desert.

Determinate Sentencing

Arguments against the indeterminate sentence have been many and varied. Besides the criticism of ineffectiveness, they have addressed two areas of perceived basic weaknesses. First, there has been a set of criticisms of procedures on grounds of unfairness. Both sentencing and paroling decisions have been widely faulted as arbitrary, capricious, and leading to unwarranted disparity (Harris, 1975). Second, the uncertainty felt by the convicted offender has been said to be unfair. (Alternatively, the utilitarian argument that such uncertainty is counterproductive to rehabilitative aims also has been made.) These assertions, combined with the decline of support for the rehabilitative model, have been persuasive to many, and recent legislation in a number of states as well as the federal jurisdiction has moved in the direction of greater determinancy. As of January, 1983, nine states (California, Colorado, Connecticut, Illinois, Indiana, Maine, Minnesota, New Mexico, and North Carolina) had determinate sentencing with no parole board release function (Bureau of Justice Statistics, 1983).

Loftin, Heumann, and McDowall (1983) studied the effects of a determinate sentence law for gun offenses. In the Michigan law, a mandatory two-year prior sentence was added to the ordinary sentence for those convicted of possession of a firearm in the commission of a felony. The gun law went into effect on January 1, 1977, and mandated a two-year "flat-time" sentence. They evaluated the impact of the law in Detroit, in part because the prosecutor adopted the policy that the law would be charged whenever the facts warranted it. This meant that the data "are not affected by a common response to mandatory sentences, namely, a shift in discretionary decision-making from the court to the prosecutor" (1983:289). They discovered, however, virtually no effect on dispositions or on violent crime that could be attributed to the new law during the two years subsequent to its implementation. Rather, they believe that sentences for the felony that involved gun use were systematically lowered to maintain the "going rate" for these crimes that existed prior to the implementation of the law.

Perhaps the most sweeping determinate sentencing law that has been evaluated systematically is California's 1977 abolition of the indeterminate term. Under the Determinate Sentence Law (DSL), the judge who sets a prison term is required to select that term from a limited set of possibilities specified by the legislature, the release discretion of the parole board was eliminated, "good time" rules were changed, and parole supervision was essentially eliminated (Casper, Brereton, and Neal, 1982).

The new law has many purposes, some of which depend upon the point of view of those discussing it. Many seek greater consistency in sentences and more definiteness in prison terms both for the offender and for society. Others desire that a greater proportion of offenders be sent to prison and expect a lower crime rate as a result of tougher terms.

Critics of the law assumed that the greater determinacy and consistency would not be forthcoming. Rather, they pointed to the myriad "enhancements" to sentence that are matters of discretion for prosecutors and judges. They believed also that the guilty plea process would mean that any discretion removed from judges would surface in the hands of the prosecutor.

Two studies of the impact of the DSL are particularly noteworthy. Casper and colleagues (1982) studied three counties before and after the implementation of DSL and Utz (1983) studied two. Both studies permitted analyses of various case factors and processing variability among the sentencing jurisdictions. Their research is complex, but the findings of general interest may be summarized briefly:

1. Considerable discretion was exercised by prosecutors in charging enhancements, although less variability was noted in their imposition by judges once they were proven.
2. Little effect was discovered for the DSL in terms of the number of charges filed.
3. Plea bargaining was widespread after passage of DSL and varied widely among the counties.
4. There were no changes in the rate of guilty pleas.
5. Little impact on prison commitments was discovered.
6. Some reduction of disparity seemed attributable to DSL.

Many, however, have been dissatisfied with the general results of legislatively based determinate sentencing schemes. Some of the more common criticisms have been aptly summarized by von Hirsch (1982):

> When called upon to write specific punishments for crimes, a legislative body has two major vulnerabilities. First, it has little time available: it cannot devote much effort and thought to developing a coherent rationale, comparing proposed penalties with one another for consistency and proportionality; projecting the new penalties' impact on sentencing practice and on the limited resources of the correctional system; and, once the penalties have gone into effect, reviewing the manner in which they have actually been administered. Second, legislatures are exposed to particularly strong and disruptive political pressures in the sentencing field. There are many voters who fear crime and

criminals, and few convicted offenders who do (or even may) vote, making
it tempting for legislators to adopt posturing stances of toughness. Under
the traditional indeterminate sentence, such posturing did not make much
difference: legislators inflated maximum sentences during election years, but
those did not determine the times actually served by prisoners. However,
the politics of legislative sentencing do matter when a legislature undertakes
to prescribe actual durations of confinement.

Indeed, recent experience seems to suggest that, under legislatively set
determinate sentencing, revisions are almost continuous, typically in an
upward direction, with little regard to the impact of revisions on corrections or even the crime rate.

The Fair Sentencing Act (FSA) enacted by the North Carolina legislature in 1979 set presumptive standards for felonies, established aggravating and mitigating factors, required that judges either impose the
presumptive term or give written reasons why not (with some exceptions), and abolished most discretionary parole release (Clarke, 1984).
Clarke evaluated the FSA and was critical of the discretion still possible
even with the act. As one example, judges still decided, with few constraints, whom to send to prison and whom to assign to probation.
Nevertheless, on the basis of a systematic study of about 2,500 felony
defendants and their dispositions, Clarke discovered some important
effects for the determinate sentence law. There appeared to be an increase in the proportion of convicted felons who received a prison sentence, but the length of sentences became both less severe and less
variable. Although the study was only a prepost test with one year of
post-FSA data, Clarke cautiously concluded that the effects were generally positive.

Desert Trend

Combined with this trend toward more determinate sentences has
been an increased acceptance of desert as the fundamental purpose of
sentencing and justification of punishment. That is, there has been increased support for the view that not only should the sentence be specified more precisely, at the time of sentencing or soon after, but that it
should provide penalties commensurate with the gravity of the offense
of conviction—that is, with the harm done by the conduct, considering
the culpability of the offender. These assertions have been made on
ethical rather than scientific grounds, but the present lack of firm empirical support for treatment effectiveness often has been cited for good
measure. The central argument has been that it is a fundamental requirement of justice, including fairness, that offenders with similar crimes
be punished similarly and that the severity of the penalty be proportional

to the seriousness of the offense. The basic concepts of the theory, therefore, are closely related to the idea of equity and hence are intertwined with issues of sentence disparity, about which there also has been widespread concern.

Discretion, Disparity, and Guidelines

Criticisms of sentencing and parole structures in the United States have focused on the problem of disparity, or unwarranted variation, in penalties imposed on offenders convicted of similar crimes. Three types of structural changes have been proposed as remedies, and each has been adopted in various jurisdictions. First, there are advocates of mandatory sentencing, with specific, unvarying penalties for specific crimes (Fogel, 1975). Second, there are proposals for "presumptive sentencing," according to which punishments would be set for the "normal" case within much narrower bounds than has been customary under the previously prevailing philosophy of indeterminacy (Dershowitz, 1976). (Some deviation ordinarily would be allowed for unusual cases involving aggravating or mitigating circumstances). Third, systems of guidelines have been developed, with sentences determined according to an explicit policy intended to structure and control, but not eliminate, the exercise of discretion (Gottfredson, Cosgrove, Wilkins, Wallerstein, and Rauh, 1978; Gottfredson and Gottfredson, 1984). Specific ranges of penalties are provided for combinations of offense and offender characteristics, with some discretion permitted within the prescribed range and also with provision for further deviation for specified reasons. Each of these models (including the latter, although to a lesser extent) reduces the discretion of the sentencing judge.

The sentencing trends now in progress thus may be summarized as tending toward more definite sentences, according to desert principles, with markedly reduced discretion by the relevant authorities. The word *discretion* has interesting ambiguities. It may mean either being discrete (making distinctions) or being discreet (being prudent or careful). It may also mean the "liberty or power of deciding or acting without other control than one's own judgment" (McKechnie, 1975). Current debates focus, of course, on issues of the judge's discretion in the latter meaning of the word. Although the making of careful distinctions seems desirable in a judge, the proper degree or amount of uncontrolled freedom in judicial decision making is a subject of considerable controversy.

But discretion in sentencing, in the sense of freedom to exercise judgment, may be justified on the grounds that it allows for individual handling of each offender. Thus, if each person is unique (as must be agreed) or if each criminal act is in some way different from all others (as must certainly be the case), then it may be expected that sentences will be disparate (that is, variable). The word *disparity* in sentencing, however, has acquired a surplus meaning. It has come to be a pejorative referring to variation in sentences that is perceived as inequitable and hence unfair and unjust. If some discretion is justified on grounds of individual differences and it is not assumed that all variation in sentencing outcomes for ostensibly similar "cases" (offenders and criminal events) is based on invidious factors, then some disparity (that is, variation) may be warranted. (Therefore, it is undoubtedly preferable to refer not to the problem of disparity but to that of *unwarranted* disparity.)

Almost no methodological work has been done in measuring disparity, a curious state of affairs given the importance most attach to the concept. An important exception is the work of Barry and Greer (1981), who developed a scheme for statistical treatment of disparity that emphasizes the importance of classification of factors that may legitimately influence sentences in the first instance.

The current shift toward greater determinacy in sentencing would, if carried to its logical extreme, mean that a fixed penalty would be required for every offender–offense combination. The penalty would be specified in advance, and no room for variation in the discretion of the judge would be allowed. Thus, discretion in sentencing would be removed entirely. At the other extreme, a completely indeterminate system of sentencing would allow complete freedom in selecting the appropriate penalty (or treatment). Actually, few persons argue that the judge should have no discretion in sentencing, and similarly few now argue that it should be unlimited. The concept of establishing an explicit sentencing policy in which the idea of guidelines plays a critical part has been proposed as a practical solution that begins by rejecting both extremes of determinacy and indeterminacy.

Scholars and practitioners have long wrestled with the problem of differences in the decisions rendered in similar cases, especially in the areas of parole and sentencing. Explanations for the apparent inequities have centered on the lack of clear and explicit decision goals and criteria, on the idiosyncrasies of individual decision makers, and on the absence of systematic feedback concerning the manner in which similar past cases have been decided. A common response to the problem of unequal treatment of like cases has been to call for greater constraints on criminal justice decision makers, to limit choice in selection of decision options, or to specify more precisely the criteria upon which decisions properly may be made. Determinate and mandatory sentencing laws, prohibitions against plea bargaining, and death penalty statutes are examples that come quickly to mind.

The debate concerning the competing demands of individualized versus systematic justice is not new. Criminal justice practitioners argue that attention to individual factors or special circumstances is a major component of "doing justice." Measures designed to increase consistency in decisions take a larger view of the nature of cases processed through the system. Determinate and mandatory sentencing schemes, for example, clearly depart from the "each case is unique" rationale in criminal justice decision making. Proponents of the individualized approach to justice contend that rigid rules designed to foster equity remove necessary flexibility and make decisions appear more equal, but at the expense of treating unequal cases alike.

The task of coping with discretionary decision making to arrive at more evenhanded justice may be complex and frustrating. Too much discretion without explicit goals or criteria produces decisions that are chaotic and, by definition, inequitable. Yet, strict rules that do not incorporate some flexibility for individual circumstances may foster decisions that are equal along some measurable dimension but unequal along others. The challenge, of course, is to arrive at an appropriate balance between the demand for consistency and the demand for consideration of the uniqueness of individual cases. Remington *et al.* (1969:889) may have aptly summarized this problem for present research:

> For every government decision there is an optimal point on the scale between the rule-of-law at one end and total discretion at the other end. The task . . . is to find that optimum point and to confine discretion to the degree which is feasible.

Decision guidelines are one tool for discovering and describing, through policy formulation and review, the "optimum point." They are meant by design to provide explicit rules for deciding cases (or, more precisely, to establish a limited range of decision choices) and, at the same time, to provide the flexibility necessary for individualized decision making.

DEFINING GUIDELINES[18]

In the introductory chapter we explicitly stated our definition of guidelines and need not repeat it here. The term *guidelines* however, has become increasingly common in criminal justice jargon. Two meanings, one broad, the other narrow and specific, are current. Some statutes, for example, mention few or no criteria, whereas others list so many as to be meaningless. When criteria are specified, no weights are given to emphasize their relative importance. Thus, such broad guidelines may have little impact on judges' decision processes and, certainly, would not permit accurate prediction of case decisions. Our meaning of the term refers to rules that are specific and precise, though not overly complex, and that are responsive, in a more direct fashion, to the concerns of the decision makers. These guidelines set forth appropriate decision options for similarly situated defendants but, at the same time, permit and even encourage noncompliance when special circumstances are present. Thus, guidelines, as defined here, are narrow enough to promote consistency in decisions, yet do not lose sight of the individual defendant.

This concept of guidelines was first used by Gottfredson, Wilkins, and Hoffman (1978) in their study of parole decision making. The concept was developed as a mechanism for structuring the discretion of decision makers with several aims in mind: to increase the equitableness of decisions, to bring greater visibility to the decision process, to enhance the rationality of the decisions, and to provide a vehicle for modifying decision practices and policy when this is desirable. Over the years, reformers have found these goals to be quite elusive.

Collaboration

In a very real sense, the construction of decision guidelines, following the model established by Gottfredson, Wilkins, and Hoffman (1978), is predicated upon a theory of change. The threshold requirement of this type of guidelines research is that it be *collaborative*. Meaningful change is seen as most likely to occur and to be effective when the principal decision makers whose behavior is the subject of the change effort are themselves involved in the process of study and change. The collaborative model is important for several reasons: First, it is assumed that the goals of change are more likely to be accepted by the decision makers in question if the decision makers themselves have participated in formulation of the issues and the plans for change. Second, impediments to realization of the goals are more likely to be anticipated and resolved by those most familiar with the decisions under study. In short, efforts to structure discretion in criminal justice are most likely to be successful, according to this view, when the change comes from within rather than being imposed externally.

The Method: Description and Prescription

Guidelines development of the most common variety proceeds in two stages: the descriptive and the prescriptive. The objective of the first phase of guidelines research is to describe as well as possible current practices in the jurisdiction under study. If current practices do not conform to desired policy, guidelines research may move into the second, prescriptive phase, wherein guidelines governing future decision practices may be formulated. The descriptive stage of the research is important because it may provide the point of departure for prescriptive guidelines, depending on the degree to which decision makers may wish to anchor future practices on the foundation of what is desirable in current practices. Commonly, much debate will be generated about the desirability of current practices and about the goals of the decisions. It is not inconceivable, however, that findings generated during descriptive analyses may persuade decision makers that current practices reflect their desired policy quite well, thus obviating a perceived need for a prescriptive phase.

The Descriptive Component

A common objection to the guidelines development process is based on the notion of the uniqueness of cases that move through the criminal process. It has been argued that cases are so diverse that attempts to describe them systematically either will be doomed to failure or will produce overly simplistic inferences about decision policy. In the original guidelines research (Gottfredson, Wilkins, and Hoffman, 1978), this issue was addressed empirically, through study of a body of recent decisions. With that method, it is assumed that if patterns and regularities can be found that "explain" decisions for a large proportion of the cases, then these factors may indeed be seen to constitute an operating policy. Describing what these major influences on decision making appear to be and identifying how they operate is what Gottfredson and associates have referred to as "making implicit policy explicit." Experience has now shown in a variety of settings that it is possible to surface policy themes on the basis of such empirical study (Goldkamp and Gottfredson, 1985; Gottfredson, Cosgrove, Wilkins, Wallerstein, and Rauh, 1978; Gottfredson, Wilkins, and Hoffman, 1978).

The Prescriptive Component: Policy Review

The development of policy guidelines does not stop with the description of current practice. Description is only the first step in the development of explicit rules for case decision making—a step conditioned on adequate previous conceptualization of the decision by a collaborative research team and on the belief that data and analytic procedures are sound. Now rooted firmly in experience, the decision makers themselves are capable of addressing the significant policy issues that lie at the heart of their decisions. How are descriptive findings to be interpreted in terms of policy? Is the policy reflected by empirical study to be preferred? Can it be improved? Are the decision criteria general enough to identify the themes guiding case decision making and narrow enough to foster evenness in decisions? Is the provision for consideration of special aspects of individual cases adequate?

The summary of experience provided by data analysis is fed back to the decision makers for their criticism and possible modification into policy guidelines. Clearly, with the feedback provided by the empirical study of past decisions, the decision makers are in a better position to chart their future course. They may ask for further analyses concerning certain points (as have judges and paroling authorities in the studies cited) or ask how past practices might be modified better to pursue agreed-upon decision goals. When care has been taken beforehand to design a sample capable of addressing not only past decisions but also their ultimate consequences, this may be possible.

In short, the product of description and review is the formulation of prescriptive guidelines for use in future decisions. In developing guidelines, the research staff supplies the judiciary, parole board, or other decision-making body with a tool for reviewing and reshaping operating policy. Specific criteria needed to inform discretionary decision making are made visible, are subject to scrutiny and debate, and, when necessary or desirable, are modified. The guidelines that emerge from the collaboration between judges and researchers do not consist of fixed, rigid rules that preordain decisions for every given case. On the contrary, guidelines are conceived as ranges or "ballpark" boundaries within which the body responsible for decisions has agreed that decisions ought to fall. The ranges produced through the guidelines construction process are meant to enhance the consistency of decisions within the jurisdiction by specifying the normative decision for defendants who are defined, based on carefully weighted criteria, as "similarly situated."

Exceptions

Although guidelines are designed to provide decision ranges to cover a majority of the cases processed, guidelines are not intended to apply perfectly or automatically to the endless variety of complex decisions that confront judges. Nor is this guidelines decision tool meant to routinize decision making or rigidify procedures to the point of abolishing the decision maker's discretion. In fact, a principal feature of the approach is its provision for the unusual or unique case—that is, for *individualized* decision making. Quite simply, if a judge (or other decision maker) decides that a case departs from the norm, he or she will choose to go outside of the decision range suggested by the guidelines. Because guidelines have been constructed with an eye to guiding decisions in the majority of cases, it is expected that exceptions will occur infrequently. Under guidelines, the decision maker makes the unusual decision and merely notes explicitly the reason for the exception.

Studying reasons for exceptions permits evaluation of the utility of the guidelines as a policy tool and suggests areas wherein modifications are needed. If it is determined that current practices are at odds with the guidelines as originally proposed, the court may take one of two actions: (1) encourage greater compliance with the guidelines on the part of the judges or (2) modify the guidelines to reflect current practices by raising or lowering the decision ranges, adding or deleting criteria, or changing the weighting scheme.

Periodic feedback to judges about the use of the guidelines and their associated effects comprises an important feature of the guidelines tool. Guidelines are intended to be revised and updated in an effort to maintain their relevance as a current policy instrument. In a sense, when adequately institutionalized, guidelines are never in final form, because the need for feedback and revision in the light of changing realities will be ongoing. Through periodic review, guidelines may be "fine-tuned" to reflect various decision concerns.

In most guidelines the offender is classified on the two dimensions of offense and offender. That is, scores are assigned first to the seriousness of the offense and second to the offender (on the basis of prior record and other items). Thus, a grid is provided such that the intersection of the seriousness of offense and offender scores provides the location of the guideline sentence. The guidelines provide, in this fashion, a part of an explicit statement of sentencing policy.

An example of decision guidelines applied to sentencing comes from sentencing guidelines now operating in Minnesota, shown in Figure 10. The Minnesota legislature set up a Sentencing Guidelines Commission to create a new set of guidelines that would then be subject to legislative review and approval. Rather than undertaking an empirical review of current decision-making practices, the commission chose a process of theoretical guidelines development. The result, which is basically similar to all established sentencing and paroling guidelines, is a two-dimensional matrix, the cell values of which are presumptive sentences. As stated by Knapp (1984:185):

The vertical dimension of the grid indicates the level of severity for the offense. The offenses listed in each category are the most frequently occurring offense(s) at each severity level. A measure of an offender's criminal history is provided with the horizontal dimension of the grid. The line running across the grid is the dispositional line—all cases that fall in cells below the dispositional line receive presumptive imprisonment sentences, and cases that fall in cells above the dispositional line receive presumptive non-imprisonment, unless a mandatory minimum sentence applies. The single number at the top of each cell is the presumptive duration of the sentence, in months, that should be stayed or executed.

Any sentence within the ranges shown in cells below the dispositional line can be imposed without deeming the sentence a departure from the sentence guidelines. A sentence outside of the range can be imposed if the judge provides written reasons as to the substantial and compelling circumstances of the case that warrant departure. The judge can also depart from the presumptive disposition (that is, imprisonment or nonimprisonment) if he or she provides written reasons. A short nonexclusive list of aggravating and mitigating factors is contained in the sentencing guidelines. The adequacy of reasons for departure as applied to an individual case is judged by appellate court review if the case is appealed by either the defendant or the state. In application, therefore, the Minnesota Sentencing Guidelines are conceptually identical with the Philadelphia Bail Guidelines described in Chapter 4. All the essential aspects of a sentencing policy and guidelines system that we advocate are included in the conceptualization and practice of the Minnesota program.

A special relevance, however, to control of prison population stems from an additional central feature of the legislation that established the commission. In its enabling statute, the legislature required the commission, when formulating the guidelines, "to take correctional resources, including prison capacities, into consideration." Although this might not have been considered to set a definitive constraint on the guidelines to be developed, the commission decided that the guidelines were to be written so as not to cause the then current rated capacity of Minnesota's state prisons to be exceeded. This decision by the commission has resulted in a linkage of the concept of guidelines and that of the control of prison crowding; and that is the central, innovative idea of the Minnesota Sentencing Guidelines Commission.

Moreover, the use of guidelines for sentencing in Minnesota, as in other examples discussed in this book, apparently has resulted in a greater degree of fundamental fairness. An initial assessment of the impact of the initiation of the new policy using guidelines included these

risk
prior record
incapacitation
also
Special deterence
general deterence

In-Out Decision

seriousness

reserts

CRIMINAL HISTORY SCORE

SEVERITY LEVELS OF CONVICTION OFFENSE		0	1	2	3	4	5	6 or more
Unauthorized Use of Motor Vehicle Possession of Marijuana	I	12•	12•	12•	15	18	21	24 23-25
Theft Related Crimes ($150-$2500) Sale of Marijuana	II	12•	12•	14	17	20	23	27 25-29
Theft Crimes ($150-$2500)	III	12•	13	16	19	22 21-23	27 25-29	32 30-34
Burglary - Felony Intent Receiving Stolen Goods ($150-$2500)	IV	12•	15	18	21	25 24-26	32 30-34	41 37-45
Simple Robbery	V	18	23	27	30 29-31	38 36-40	46 43-49	54 50-58
Assault, 2nd Degree	VI	21	26	30	34 33-35	44 42-46	54 50-58	65 60-70
Aggravated Robbery	VII	24 23-25	32 30-34	41 38-44	49 45-53	65 60-70	81 75-87	97 90-104
Assault, 1st Degree Criminal Sexual Conduct, 1st Degree	VIII	43 41-45	54 50-58	65 60-70	76 71-81	95 89-101	113 106-120	132 124-140
Murder, 3rd Degree	IX	97 94-100	119 116-122	127 124-130	149 143-155	176 168-184	205 192-215	230 218-242
Murder, 2nd Degree	X	116 111-121	140 133-147	162 153-171	203 192-214	243 231-255	284 270-298	324 309-339

FIGURE 10. Minnesota Sentencing Guidelines Grid. *Note.* Cells below heavy line receive a presumptive prison sentence; those cells above the heavy line receive a presumptive nonprison sentence (and the numbers in those cells refer only to duration of confinement if probation is revoked). Closed circle (•) indicates one year and one day. First degree murder is excluded from guidelines by law and continues to have a mandatory life sentence.

reports from the commission (Minnesota Sentencing Guidelines Commission, 1984):

1. A significant change occurred in the types of offenders imprisoned—more person offenders and fewer property offenders were imprisoned.

2. Disparity in sentencing was reduced, as indicated by increased uniformity in sentences for persons similarly categorized in accordance with the sentencing guidelines (with the same level of offense seriousness and criminal history score).
3. An increase in proportionality occurred, such that persons convicted of more serious offenses received more serious sanctions. This was interpreted as a further indicant of disparity reduction.

A major objective of the development of judicial policy through devising guidelines has been the articulation of the basis for decisions in more explicit terms in order that sentencing may be more open, more public, and hence more readily subject to review and criticism. If this can be achieved, then sentencing rationales may be more open to debate in more specific terms. Similarly, the empirical issues may be more easily tested, and the moral issues may be examined with a sharper focus.

In a general sense, this is precisely what the guidelines concept has been supposed to provide—a more open system for evolution of sentencing policy. If sentencing can be rehabilitated, the concept of sentencing guidelines may help. And there is some evidence that sentencing guidelines are a major trend around the country. As of January, 1983, as we have already mentioned, nine states had adopted some form of sentencing guidelines, and fifteen had some form of parole guidelines (Bureau of Justice Statistics, 1983). Also, the federal jurisdiction is now organized to develop and to adopt sentencing guidelines in 1988. To date the results of sentencing guidelines have been salutory: they have made policy explicit and reduced inequity. More testing of these models is, however, surely required.

NOTES

1. Portions of this section are adapted from Gottfredson (1975a). The literature on sentencing is vast and is growing rapidly. Perhaps the best account of the many issues and complexities of sentencing is Dawson (1969). A good annotated bibliography of current sentencing controversies is Ferry and Kravitz (1978).
2. This is an oversimplified distinction. Mueller (1977:38–58) distinguishes between "utilitarian" and "nonutilitarian" aims. By the latter he means "those aims or methods for achieving crime prevention of which it is usually said that they are not designed at all to achieve prevention—in fact, that it would amount to a perversion of high ideals to use them in a utilitarian manner" (at 38). As nonutilitarian aims he includes vindication, retribution, and penitence. Some, however, would use the concepts of desert or of punishment in a clearly utilitarian sense—for example, to prevent anomie or to affirm moral values. Weiler divides sentencing perspectives as utilitarian or neo-Kantian, including in the latter category those who locate morality "in adherence to principles of right, justice or fairness" (at 122).

3. See, for example, Hart (1968), Weiler (1974), Rawls (1971), and Feinberg (1970).
4. This section summarizing common sentencing draws heavily on O'Leary, Gottfredson, and Gelman, (1975). As these authors point out, various other sentencing goals not easily classified into these categories could be cited, such as penitence or control of vigilantes or personal vendettas.
5. Publilius Syrus, *Sentential*, No. 578, as cited in Stevenson (1967:1031).
6. D. Webster, *Argument*, Salem, Massachusetts, August 3, 1830, The Murder of Capt. Joseph White. Cited in Stevenson, *supra* note 5 at 1036.
7. Plato, *Laws II* 934, as cited in G. Newman (1978:201).
8. *Idem.*
9. See, for example, von Hirsch (1976).
10. Aristotle, *Metaphysics: On the Virtues and Vices—Justice*, as cited in Stevenson, (1967:1027).
11. Justician, *Institutions*, Book I, section 1, as cited in Stevenson (1967:1027).
12. H. Fielding, *The History of Tom Jones, Book III*, ch. X (Garden City, New York: International Collector's Library): 76, n.d.
13. I. Kant, *The Philosophy of Law*, trans. W. Hastic (Edinburgh: T.T. Clar, 1887), as cited by Weiler (1974).
14. *Idem.*
15. Because several comprehensive reviews of this literature exist, including methodological critiques, a thorough review of the early research will not be undertaken here. Hagan (1974) reviewed twenty studies of sentencing to assess the contribution of socioeconomic status, race, age, and sex in disposition. He concluded: "Review of the data indicates that, while there may be evidence of differential sentencing, knowledge of extra-legal offender characteristics contributes relatively little to our ability to predict judicial dispositions" (at 379).

    Our focus in this book is on the adult criminal justice system, but it should be noted that a substantial body of research on the correlates of sentencing for juveniles also exists. For a review and an interesting empirical study, see Cohen and Kluegel (1978). A recent general review of this research indicates that the legal factors (seriousness of the offense and prior record) are the most powerful predictors of disposition; see Hirschi (1975).
16. A study of sentencing practices in some southern states has also found that legal variables account for a greater proportion of the variation in sentencing than do extralegal variables (in particular, socioeconomic status); see Chiricos and Waldo (1975).
17. See, for example, Martinson (1974); Bailey (1966); Kassebaum, Ward and Wilner (1971); Robison and Smith (1971). *Contra,* see Palmer (1974 and 1975). For a more recent analysis, see Sechrest, White, and Brown (1979).
18. Portions of this section are adapted from Goldkamp, Gottfredson, and Mitchel-Herzfeld (1981).

Chapter 7

CORRECTIONAL DECISIONS IN THE COMMUNITY

Decisions about convicted offenders do not end with the sentence of the judge. Indeed, a new series of decisions is only beginning—whether the offender is to be placed on probation (usually with suspension of a more severe sanction), whether he or she is to be sent to jail (or these sanctions are to be used in combination), whether another alternative is to be selected, or whether the person is to be sent to prison. All these decisions that are now required may be called *correctional*, not because they necessarily are corrective of the person's behavior, but because the term *corrections* has come into common use to designate the complex of activities, programs, and systems such as probation, jail, prison, and parole that have been designed to deal with adjudicated persons in state custody. Setting aside issues of paroling decisions for Chapter 9, we seek in this chapter and the next to outline the general nature of some common decision problems in areas of corrections.

The term *corrections* suggests the dominance, during the last half century, of utilitarian aims (particularly treatment) rather than of retribution or desert as a principal *raison d'etre* for these systems. (As discussed in Chapter 6, desert recently has been more widely argued and debated as placed more properly in this role.) In any case, even a cursory review of the kinds of decisions made daily by corrections staff will show that rehabilitation is not now, and never has been, a sole concern.

Immediately upon arrival in jail or prison, for example, some screening ordinarily is seen as necessary, whether done systematically or informally and haphazardly. The concerns addressed require decisions aimed at preventing low-probability but high-risk events. Especially notable are three classes of events that appropriate screening (classification) might help avoid; suicide (or self-injury), escape, and victimization (for example, homosexual rape).

In large correctional systems, the first weeks after institutional commitment or placement in programs of community supervision will see a great variety of procedures aimed at assessment of the offender for the purpose of program assignment. Much data concerning the individual's personal and social history, present offense of conviction, prior record, and aspirations often will be collected. Educational and psychological tests may be administered, and vocational counseling may be provided. Following this assessment, when the offender has been incarcerated, decisions such as these must be made:

- What level of custody must be assigned initially?
- In what geographical region should the offender be housed?
- In what institution should the offender be placed initially?
- Should the offender be placed in an academic program?
- At what level?
- A vocational program?
- Should the person be assigned to any program of counseling or psychotherapy?
- Group or individual?
- Therapeutic community program?
- Behavior modification program?
- What work assignments should be recommended?

If the convicted offender is not sent to prison but, alternatively, placed in a community program such as probation, a similar variety of decisions may be required:

- Should the person be placed in a regular caseload or is more intensive (or more minimal) supervision called for?
- Should the person be placed in a specialized caseload? What kind?
- Are referrals to treatment or other social service agencies to be made?

For these and other decisions, the correctional agency staff will have much data but little information. Large sums of money will have been spent and a great deal of concerned, even dedicated, effort will have been made collecting data on individual offenders. Much effort and more financial resource often will have been expended to record these data in individual folders, to prepare detailed personal and social histories, and to record recommendations of the clinical and custodial staff or of probation officers. Further large expenditures of time, energy, and funds will be made later in efforts to restudy the person, to reassign him or her, or to implement those recommendations already made. Little will have been spent in assessing the relevance of these data to the goals the agency wishes to achieve, either for the individual offender or for the agency's general mission. In short, there may be much data, but there is little information, and relatively meager resources are expended to improve the quality of information on which the decisions rely.

The term *corrections* has, as already noted, come to include a wide range of criminal justice programs. These include probation services (usually, but not always, provided as "an arm of the court," usually within county but sometimes state structures), jail programs (usually operated by counties through sheriff's departments, sometimes called prisons or correctional centers, usually confining sentenced persons for a year or less plus persons awaiting trial), prison programs (usually operated by state corrections departments and handling persons whose maximum sentence is more than a year), and parole programs (usually operated by state departments of corrections or parole boards). In view of this complexity, programs of probation will be discussed in this chapter, since they are the most common forms of community corrections. Then, in Chapter 8, institutional corrections programs will be examined, followed in Chapter 9 by a discussion of parole.

It must be noted that distinctions between community and institutional corrections programs are somewhat arbitrary and have become increasingly so in recent years. That is, distinctions between programs of confinement and of community supervision have become increasingly blurred. A brief look at the history of corrections in the United States, in terms of predominant emphases on differing correctional goals, will show why this is the case.

Early in the development of correctional systems in the United States, when imprisonment began to replace punishments used previously such as mutilation, whipping, or public humiliation, stress began to be placed on the reformation of the convicted person. Whether reform was to be achieved through isolation, deprivation, and penitence (in the penitentiary) or through work (and development of good work habits) was debated; but that the reform of the person who had behaved badly was a principal aim seems clear.

With the advent of social science development and its increased impact on social thought, and particularly with psychoanalysis and its offspring in psychiatry and in social work, this stance tended to change. Less often was the offender perceived as "bad" and in need of reform through penitence or work; more often he or she was regarded as sick, disturbed, or disordered. Hence, the goals of confinement tended to shift toward increased emphasis on treatment that would be rehabilitative. In recent decades, the term *reintegration* has been used increasingly to denote a concept that includes rehabilitative aims but gives stress to the role of the community environment (and to interactions of person and community) in achieving the status of productive, or at least law-abiding, citizen behavior on the part of the convicted offender. If lesser emphasis in correctional programs were to be given to reform, or rehabilitation, or reintegration, and more to the incapacitation of the offender (to prevent further crimes), then the restraint perspective would dominate.

One commonly held conception among correctional workers is that if the offender is imprisoned, the degree of custodial control required may perhaps be reduced gradually, as depicted in Figure 11. Thus, there may be incremental decreases in custody classification within the institution (for example, from maximum, through close, medium, and minimum, with increasing freedom for the convicted person). There could be similar decreases periodically in the level of parole supervision assigned (such as high or intensive supervision, medium or average-level

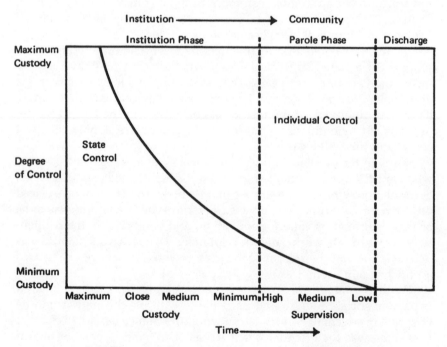

FIGURE 11. Degree of control as a function of time served.

supervision, and low or minimal supervision). It should be noted that within correctional structures characterized by a degree of indeterminacy in sentencing, both institutional confinement and parole supervision traditionally have been regarded as part of the sentence, one portion to be served in the institution and the other on parole.

In practice, various placement decisions (made by institutional or parole staff as well as the critical parole decision) may be made that affect whether the convicted offender is housed in the institution or in the community. Thus, in various jurisdictions there are programs of work or study release, various community corrections programs such as "halfway houses," or programs allowing for short-term return to confinement for rules violations by a parolee. There may be programs of weekend or overnight jail confinement or use of probation conditions requiring such short-term periodic institutionalization. All these provide examples of the blurred, often arbitrary distinction between institutional and community correctional programs.

Even the distinction between probation and parole may be more a matter of the location of responsibility for supervision, within government structures, than of substantive difference in underlying concepts. The term *probation* usually implies community supervision in lieu of incarceration (such sentences usually having been imposed but suspended conditional upon following orders of the court regarding the conditions of probation), whereas *parole* usually refers to community supervision after a period of confinement. "Split" sentences often are used, however, negating even that distinction. This refers to the circumstance that the convicted offender is required by the sentence to serve a portion, first, in jail, then a further term on probation. Thus, Figure 10 could, for split sentences, refer as well to a notion of decreasing control by levels of custody in jail followed by increasing freedom during probation supervision. Despite these ambiguities, it is convenient to divide the discussion of correctional decisions between concerns of traditional community corrections (probation and parole) and institutional corrections (jails and prisons).

GOALS AND ALTERNATIVES IN COMMUNITY CORRECTIONS DECISIONS

In the past, the importance of community corrections decisions has been given by the sheer numbers of offenders involved. At the end of 1983 there were more than 1.5 million persons on probation in this country (including 50,00 on probation in the federal jurisdiction). An additional 250,000 were on parole. For most states these numbers have been increasing in recent times; between 1979 and 1983 the probation population grew by more than 38%, and the parole population grew by 15%. When prison, jail, probation and parole populations are combined, 1.4% of the adult population is under correctional supervision (about 2/ 3 of a million adults are incarcerated either in jail or in prison).

Both probation and parole are subjects of considerable controversy at present, widely heralded by some as the best hope of effective, humane, and efficient corrections and marked by others as systems that should be abolished.[1] The report on corrections of the National Advisory Commission (1973:311) asserted that "probation is viewed as the brightest hope of corrections." Some leading scholars are more skeptical. Wilson (1975:202) suggests that probation be "virtually abolished." Another (Morris, 1974:48) offers an exquisite ambivalence when he remarks that an important latent function of probation is "to allow a judge to give the appearance of doing something while in fact doing nothing." There is similar debate about parole. In the National Advisory Commission report, one proposed standard would require legislation in each state "authorizing parole for all committed offenders," while von Hirsch and Hanrahan (1978:iii) propose that "instead of routinely imposing supervision on ex-prisoners, supervision should be eliminated entirely, or if retained, should be reduced substantially in scope" and suggest further that other substantial changes are needed. The objective of this chapter, however, is not to enter these debates except insofar as an examination of goals, alternatives, and information for decision making in community corrections may be found relevant to them.

The aims sought in community corrections programs are, like those of sentencing discussed in Chapter 6, diverse and often apparently in conflict. The placement of the convicted offender on probation (by the judge) may reflect any of the broad goals of sentencing (general deterrence, incapacitation, treatment, or desert). Once those actions have been taken, however, a somewhat different question may be raised: What are the goals of probation or parole supervision? Generally, it may be assumed that three main goals are paramount: treatment, control, and organization maintenance.

The treatment aim—that, is the rehabilitative-reintegrative goal—has been reflected in writings on both probation and parole since their invention. Probation, as is widely cited, began in concept with the volunteer efforts of a Boston shoemaker, John Augustus, who in 1841 apparently persuaded the court to release some offenders to him. This led to the first formal establishment, by legislation, of probation (in 1878 in

Massachusetts). The basis was a crime reduction aim: the objective was to decrease the likelihood that the convicted person would engage in further criminal behavior. The system of treatment or supervision, however, was not to be trusted completely; there was also a control function of supervision.

This control function may be perceived in the attention given not only to remedial, rehabilitative, or reintegrative efforts of assistance but also to surveillance. Thus, if rules violations can be demonstrated, the suspended sentence may be imposed (by the court), usually meaning the incarceration of the violator. The purpose generally is held to be the prevention of further crime (rather than desert). This function, too, is thus aimed at crime reduction. As with other social agencies, it is reasonable to assume as well that probation decisions include objectives of continuing or enhancing the organization or making it more efficient and effective.

The two principal purposes of probation and parole are thus apparently utilitarian, reductionist goals (see Chapter 6 for a discussion in the context of sentencing; compare with Chapter 9 concerning purposes of paroling decisions). Given the crime reduction, prevention, or control aims of these two types of community corrections systems, a principal question to be answered empirically is how well these aims are achieved.[2] In relation to sentencing goals, the treatment aim is paramount: incapacitation may be a perceived goal when the control function is exercised and culminates in confinement of the offender; the aims of general deterrence and desert appear to receive much less emphasis.

Given the broad array of differences in administrative structure, government subdivision, geography, economics, and legal frameworks that characterize probation and parole supervision programs, it must be expected that the resources available to administrators of these programs will be highly varied. Nevertheless, there are certain program issues concerning the classification of probationers or parolees and their assignment (that is, with program placement decisions) that have been of wide interest.

A topic closely related to issues of differential classification and assignment is that of caseload size. These concerns have to do both with the question of optimal case load size for probation or parole supervision programs generally and with the question of whether differing levels of intensity of supervision are appropriate with differing classifications of probationer or parolee populations. This issue, which involves the hypothesis that differential assignment to levels according to risk will be more effective than random assignment, involves also the problem of classification of offenders according to predicted success or failure on probation or parole. Thus, an examination of alternatives available to probation or parole administrators should include a brief overview of the current status of research on probation and parole prediction, on the caseload size question, and on certain troublesome problems related to criteria for judging success as required by the crime reduction and control aims of these services. Each of these issues is complex. For each, there is substantial literature.

PROBATION AND PAROLE PREDICTION

Most studies of probation and parole prediction have been done in the areas of parole, beginning more than a half century ago (Bruce, Burgess, and Harno, 1928; Bruce, Harno, Burgess, and Landesco, 1928), although probation studies date at least to 1932. Since thorough reviews of the large literature on parole and probation prediction are available,[3] our focus here will be on certain methodological and management issues thought to be most pertinent to the decision problems related to program placement of the offender (Albanese, 1977). These issues, of course, are interrelated.

In any discussion of prediction methods in criminology (or other areas of human affairs), the issue of the relative efficiency and effectiveness of clinical (that is, global judgmental) predictions and statistical (numerical or objective classification) predictions soon arises. The continuing debate may be due, as suggested by Mannheim and Wilkins, to the circumstance that "people seem . . . to be more inclined to accept the judgment of other people than to trust numerical procedures which appear abstract and impersonal," a conjecture that led them to assume that "if this prejudice is to be overcome we require the experience table procedures to be more accurate than other systems of making assessments." And they reported that in their study it seemed that "the statistical procedures were at least three times as efficient as the subjective judgments of Governors of the Institutions, and far more accurate than a psychologist's prognosis" (1955:140–141).

The classic work on the topic is that by Meehl (1954), who found, after reviewing studies that compared clinical and actuarial (that is, statistical, methods), that in all but one study the predictions made actuarially were either approximately equal or superior to those made by a clinician. A further review, with a generally similar result, was done by Gough (1962). Thus, when empirically derived statistical prediction devices are pitted against clinical judgment and the accuracy of prediction compared, the statistical prediction instrument generally has fared better in the comparison.

One study that pitted clinical prediction against statistical prediction for parole success can serve as an example of the general finding. Gottfredson (1961) compared, for the same 283 parolees, the validity of prediction scores obtained by subjective ratings made by a prison associate superintendent (after prerelease interviews) and ratings of clinical staff (psychiatric) reports with ratings based on a statistical device. The two subjective prediction ratings and the statistical prediction method all were related to parole outcomes, in the expected direction. The clerks using the prediction method were much better predictors, however, than were the administrators or the clinical team. Furthermore, the clinical ratings did not improve the prediction beyond that demonstrable using the prediction device alone.

When a statistical prediction device is available to the decision maker, the decision policy may include the provision for discretion as to relying on it or revising the attempted prognosis on the basis of specified reasons for the decision maker's judgment. Two current examples of the use of such individualized decision making is given by the use of a "salient factor" prediction device as one dimension in the guidelines policy of the United States Parole Commission (see Chapter 9) and the risk scale of the Philadelphia Bail Guidelines (see Chapter 4). Given the "advice" of the statistical prediction method, the decision maker may "override" it, giving specific reasons that, in his or her judgment, the prediction may be in error. If these instances of subjective impressions supplementing the statistical prediction device are recorded and later tested for their potential contribution to prediction, then they may be incorporated in the prediction method, whereas those found useless may be discarded. Thus, a systematic procedure for the improvement of predictions can be provided.

A variety of methodological problems that arise frequently in prediction studies tend to affect the usefulness of the resulting devices for probation or parole decision problems. Issues of representativeness of the samples studied, of sample size, of improvement over the base rate, and of the methods used to combine predictor items provide examples.[4] Some of these are discussed later in this chapter. The point to be made now, however, is that such devices may have direct utility for probation and parole decision making in several ways. These potential uses include applications in program evaluation studies, in program planning, in classification for program assignment, and in other decision problems. Thus, prediction methods may be useful tools for decisions of both individual cases and institutional policy.

In program evaluation studies, probation or parole prediction measures can provide a measure of control for demonstrable selection bias when comparisons are desired in the absence of experimental designs (for example, with control groups randomly assigned). Various writers have discussed this use or offered examples. Such measures have been called "expectancy tables" by (Bruce, Burgess, and Harno, 1928) or "experience tables" (Ohlin, 1951) or "prediction tables" (Mannheim and Wilkins, 1955) or "base expectancies" (Gottfredson, 1963). All these designations are apt: on the basis of experience, they provide a ground for further research by quantifying expectations (in terms of probabilities of success or failure) before the intervention of interest.

Although experimental designs provide more rigorous means to test hypotheses about treatment or supervision effects, such designs are difficult to implement in practice. In addition, it is rare that the opportunity obtains for a comparison of a treatment with the absence of any treatment (Gottfredson, 1965). Furthermore, even with prediction methods based on information known only before treatment, the circumstances of derivation of the method ordinarily are such that it must be considered to reflect an average expectancy from a variety of treatments (rather than a treatment-free expectancy; Simon, 1971). Nonetheless, a search for treatment or supervision contingencies that invalidate previously validated expectations may be useful in eliminating some plausible but incorrect hypotheses and in directing research toward fruitful areas.

In program planning, prediction methods may be found useful in classifying offenders as an aid to administrative policy decisions that in turn affect individual case decisions. Examples are given by applications in California that sought to alleviate problems of prison overcrowding and increased confinement costs. These were based on use of the base expectancy scale devised by Gottfredson. The prison administration, through its research division, screened the entire confined population of California's prisons (more than 20,000 persons), first by base expectancy (parole prediction) scores, then by further clinical criteria (Dunbar, 1961). The result, with both male and female prisoners, was that some persons were referred for parole consideration at a date earlier than originally scheduled. Some of these were then released on parole by decisions of the parole board.

In an application of a base expectancy measure more directly relevant to assignment to supervision, minimal supervision caseloads of male and female parolees were established. Persons assigned to classifications having a high probability of successful parole completion received minimal supervision. Experience demonstrated that these cases may be given less supervision with no increase in the parole violation rate (Havel, 1963). This enabled parole workers to deploy their forces from areas where help was demonstrably less necessary to those where it was perceived as likely to be more helpful.

These two applications resulted in reported substantial monetary savings with (demonstrably) no increase in parole violations. It was claimed that with use of the female offender classification program the institutional population had been reduced; and it was the opinion of correctional administrators that this program had obviated the necessity of building a new women's prison.

In 1961, the California legislature approved a program based on screening of inmates by base expectancy scores combined with programs for more intensive institutional and parole services. The goal was reduction of institutional costs for nonviolent cases by release slightly ahead of the expected time. By 1963 the Department of Corrections reported to the legislature that this program had reduced the institution population by more than 840 men and women, that support savings were at least $840,000, and that $8.5 million in capital outlay had been deferred. These savings were attributed to the new program and to initial efforts by the paroling authorities to base decisions partly on base expectancy measures (Burdman, 1963).

By 1969, the California Department of Corrections reported an assignment system for parolees with three classes of supervision. The program objectives were to increase community protection, improve performance by parolees, and save institutional costs. The base expectancy measure provided a basis for the assignment procedures. The agency reported to the legislature that total prison returns for new crimes and violation of parole rules had been reduced by 25% since the beginning of the program in 1965. They concluded (from analysis of base expectancy scores and actual outcomes, illustrating a research use of these measures) that 1,543 additional men had succeeded on parole who, on the basis of past experience, would have been expected to fail. The saving from men kept in the community rather than in prison was estimated as the equivalent of the entire population of an average-sized major prison. Savings in operating expenses were estimated at $4.5 million yearly and in construction savings at $20 million (Parole and Community Services Division, 1969).

Subsequent to these explorations of differential supervision for various risk classifications using the base expectancy scale in California, a number of authors have proposed using prediction scales as an aid in supervision assignment. The suggestions for use have been varied—for example, as an administrative tool to equalize high-risk offenders among various caseloads or to focus services and attention on the probationers who need the most help, or to assist case managers in making decisions about how much time and effort to devote to working with certain groups of persons.

CASELOAD SIZE

A large body of correctional literature addresses the general question of how the size of caseloads of probation or parole officers affects the subsequent success or failure of the offenders who are supervised. Various reviews are available, including a number that provide detailed discussions of the methodological issues involved in evaluations of programs manipulating caseload size (Adams, 1967; Neithercutt and Gottfredson, 1973; Vetter and Adams, 1971). These issues are much more complex than may seem at first glance; the results of the studies are mixed, and the methods used are criticized frequently as flawed. It may be said with assurance, however, that (1) no optimal caseload size has been demonstrated and (2) no clear evidence of reduced recidivism, simply by reduced caseload size, has been found.[5] The importance of this general negative result to the concerns of this chapter may be seen by a brief examination of the history of public policy on a presumably proper caseload size—policy that has been unrelated to any empirical evidence whatever.

The earliest assurance on proper caseload size known to us is that of Chute, who asserted in 1922 that no probation officer should have more than fifty cases. By twelve years later, Sutherland (1934) stated that fifty probationers was generally regarded as the maximum number for one officer. By 1946, the American Prison Association described "sound practice" as no more than fifty cases under continuous supervision, and the 1954 Manual of Correctional Standards also included this standard.

Similarly, the National Council on Crime and Delinquency (1962) argued that fifty cases seemed an appropriate maximum. The President's Commission on Law Enforcement and Administration of Justice (1967) reduced this value to an average of thirty-five.

Such pronouncements, devoid as they are of empirical support, may serve political purposes or humanitarian ones—for example, by assisting managers to obtain resources for what seem to be more reasonable caseload levels than those with which they currently struggle. They cannot, however, be justified as demonstrably rational, leading to more efficient or effective practice toward correctional objectives. What is needed for more rational planning and program development is the assessment, through experimentation or, at least, quasi-experimental systematic study, of this and related issues. Such repeated assessments should be a part of a general program of study and evolutionary development of the agency. We will return to this proposed method for solution of such complex issues in later sections of this book, including the final chapter.

THE CRITERION PROBLEM

Uncritical pronouncements about recidivism or recidivism rates are too common in discussions of correctional effectiveness. There is little agreement on any preferred operational definition of the term; and this clearly makes comparisons of outcome studies in probation and parole exceedingly difficult and complex. Some relevant issues concerning parole are discussed in Chapter 9; to illustrate the variance in probation recidivism definitions that are used, we cite as examples (from a recent review by Powell, 1977) several studies of adult probation conducted since 1951. In order to analyze various criteria used in these studies, she noted that it is useful to distinguish between "on probation" and "postprobation" periods. For example, in an "on probation" study, a failure rate may refer to the ratio of the number of failures while on probation to the total number on probation. A "probation termination" study may, on the other hand, define failure as the ratio of failures upon termination to the total number terminated. Or in a "postprobation" study, where interest is focused on postprobation outcome, a failure rate may be defined as the ratio of failures of probationers who have been terminated to all those terminated. Combinations of these also have been used. Adding to the complexity, cohort studies provide yet another means of defining rates of success and failure. An example cited by Powell is given by Davis's "cohort/probation termination" study.

Problems in comparisons of studies using such varied definitions of probation success or failure are well known. These are similar when, rather than single project studies, annual reports by probation systems are examined. Rector (1958; 1962), in a comment still apt although written nearly thirty years ago, after reviewing 146 such reports received in one year, stated that "any thought of compiling recidivism data from annual reports for comparative purposes had to be abandoned early because of wide differences in definitions, in methods of computing, and in factors of measurement."

Problems of comparison, of course, are compounded also by differing follow-up periods and samples of offenders. These vary widely on factors known from many studies to be related to outcomes, such as offense, age, and prior record of criminal offenses.

Is this diversity of definitions of *recidivism* a problem? In a sense, of course, it is; it certainly provides a source of frustration for those who seek comparisons while rendering useless the heretofore mentioned uncritical claims or allegations concerning probation recidivism rates without further definition. Seeking a standardization, the National Advisory Commission on Criminal Justice Standards and Goals (1973:528) provided (for system reviews) their recommended definition:

> Recidivism is measured by (1) criminal acts that resulted in conviction by a court, when committed by individuals who are under correctional supervision within the previous three years, and by (2) technical violations of probation or parole in which a sentencing or paroling authority took action that resulted in an adverse change in the offender's legal status.

In another sense, however, the variability in definition is not a problem. Each investigator may have his or her reasons for preferring a different definition, and it is the same with program administrators. Notably, the National Advisory Commission, in enunciating the definition just quoted, listed differing criteria for program reviews. And it may be noted that the comptroller general, soon after the National Advisory Commission report, used a different definition. The utility of various definitions of outcome, for differing purposes, has been discussed well by Glaser (1973). After considering the multiple manifest and latent goals characteristic of corrections and hierarchies of goals and types of success, he discussed criteria under the headings "most objective," "most attainable," "most continuous," and "most support-relevant." Arguing that more rational choices in fund allocation (for programs) requires cost–benefit analyses, he also provided a helpful discussion of criteria in relation to these.

It is also of considerable interest to note that despite the tremendous variation in recidivism rates used by various probation studies there is a remarkable consistency in findings with respect to factors associated with failure. One study that compared the correlates of failure in ten studies published since 1951 found considerable stability in correlates despite widely differing criteria (Powell, 1977). In ten studies reviewed, Powell found that, generally, factors associated with failure were previous criminal history, youthfulness, status other than married, unemployment, low income, low education, alcohol or drug abuse, and property offense.

INFORMATION

Any discussion of data available for probation or parole decision making, whether individual or program decisions are at issue, must, it appears, begin with some discussion of the presentence report. For most probation services, this is a basic document intended not only to serve the court (in the disposition of the case) but also to guide the initiation of supervision. If the offender is jailed, it may provide nearly the only resource for classification and assignment purposes, including the issue of custody and security assignments. It would provide, in most instances, the only basis for allocation to counseling, training, education, or work assignment. If the offender is imprisoned, this document provides the basis from which any study of the offender and written reports therefrom are derived. Thus, it may have impact on the institutional program placements of the prison inmate as well, and data from the presentence investigation find their way also into the materials on which paroling decisions may be based. Given this importance, it is perhaps surprising that so little attention has yet been given to assessing the relevance of the data of presentence reports to the objectives of the myriad decisions made on its basis. If that is surprising, it must be said to be astounding that for great numbers of cases, the report is not prepared at all.

A first need of many if not most probation and parole systems, if more effective decisions are to be made and if learning from experience is to occur in a more systematic manner, must be to improve the quality of data collected on each offender at the time of the presentence investigation. Extensively discursive social histories with opinions and judgments of the writer will not serve, no matter how excellent in literary style. A core set of the same data for each person, collected with attention to reliability concerns, is needed. Such data then can be examined to determine the relevance of individual items, or combinations of them, to a wide array of significant decision problems. These include, it must be stressed, not only the sentencing decision, but decisions such as those at issue earlier in this chapter. Without such careful, systematic data collection, the probation or parole administrator is in the familiar correctional situation—much data, collected unsystematically, variably, and subjectively for individual case studies, but no information demonstrably relevant to either program or individual decisions.

The needs for information are similar when jails are considered; and although it is a digression in this chapter, the relevance of the presentence reports to management in jails must be stressed. If the offender is jailed, whether by sentence of the court or while awaiting trial, first concerns are for security, custody, and safety. The jailer must be concerned with the security of the institution, while maintaining custody of the person, and with the offender's and others' personal safety. Usually he or she has not much more than the presentence report—and often not even that.

As an example of the kinds of information that may prove to be valuable to the jail administrator, Figure 12 presents a classification form developed by the sheriff's department in Pima County, Arizona. The form, filled out immediately upon reception at the jail, provides the kinds of systematic information necessary for a rational placement decision structure.

The essentially predictive purpose of these decisions, and the requirements that such a purpose raises, must be stressed. Maintaining the security of the institution, for example, may imply a need for identifying persons prone to assault. Keeping the person in custody may imply that predictions are made about the likelihood of attempted escape. Ensuring the offender's personal safety may require identification of persons with a high risk of suicide attempts, those with a high probability of becoming a target of abuse by other inmates, or those in need of emergency physical or psychiatric care. Each of these prediction problems is especially difficult in part because of the relatively low prevalence of the undesired event. With the data collected by Pima County, research to determine the appropriateness of placement decisions is possible.

The data collected for preparation of the presentence investigation report, traditionally intended primarily as an aid to the court in choosing among sentencing alternatives, do not serve well the additionally needed functions of analyses aimed at improving these correctional decisions. (The same shortcomings militate also against useful analyses for improving the court's selections among available alternatives.) The inadequacies of presentence reports for these analytical functions, including variability in content, lack of attention to explicit definitions, absence of reliability assessments, and a high degree of subjective judgment, stem understandably from the individualized case analysis perspective that was central to the historic development of these documents.

The diversity of data included typically in presentence investigation reports is well illustrated by some results of a survey by Carter (1978). His findings serve also to depict the types of data collected. Concerning the "cover sheet," Carter identified 118 data elements (tabulated from 105 cover sheets analyzed). His analysis of the content of these reports led to the conclusions that individual officers have considerable discre-

PIMA COUNTY ADULT DETENTION CENTER
INITIAL CLASSIFICATION INTERVIEW

Name _____ Initial Security Level _____

I. GENERAL CLASSIFICATION DATA

Special Needs and Considerations

Medical Problems

YES NO Is inmate known to have any major medical problems?
         Nature of the problem(s) _____
YES NO Does inmate appear to be in drug or alcohol withdrawal?
YES NO Does inmate appear to have any serious physical handicaps?
YES NO Should Medical Department be notified?

Emotional Problems

YES NO Previous admission to a psychiatric facility?
YES NO Does inmate appear to have any major mental health problems at this time? If
         yes:
              ————Hallucinations: Private sensory experiences?
              ————Delusions: Obviously exaggerated beliefs.
              ————Orientation: Doesn't know name, location, date.
YES NO Do you believe inmate may be suicidal?
              ————Is there current suicidal ideation?
              ————Is there suicidal intent?
YES NO Do you believe inmate needs immediate follow-up counseling to assist with
         adaptation to incarceration?

Sexuality

YES NO Do you believe inmate's sexuality or sexual perference would pose any potential
         security problems?
YES NO Are there any current or previous charges regarding sexual conduct with a minor?

Additional Security Concerns

         To the best of your knowledge is this inmate:
YES NO An informant or witness?
YES NO Involved with any criminal organizations, prison gangs, etc.?
YES NO Have any enemies within the facility?
YES NO Have any codefendants within the facility?
YES NO A current or previous law enforcement employee or a relative of a current or
         previous law enforcement employee or a relative of a current employee?
YES NO Have any previous escape attempts?
YES NO Have a history of institutional misconduct?
YES NO Have any other potential security problems?

FIGURE 12. Jail classification form. SOURCE: Pima County Sheriff's Department.

Criminal and Correctional History

Inmate has been charged with or convicted of:
———Misdemeanor charges only
———Nonserious, nonviolent felonies
———Some serious, violent felonies
———Mostly serious, violent felonies

Inmate has been incarcerated:
———Less than 6 months
———6 months to a year
———1 to 5 years
———Over 5 years
———Most of adult life*
———Frequently, and has a history of serious institutional misconduct*

*Constitutes 5 points on custody level assignment

Behavior and Personality Characteristics

Circle one word in each line which most closely describes your experience with this inmate:

Quiet	Responsive	Talkative	Verbose
Fearful	Anxious	Confident	Arrogant
Passive	Assertive	Aggressive	Dominating
Obedient	Cooperative	Argumentative	Defiant
Naive	Alert	Perceptive	Sophisticated
(1 Point)	(2 Points)	(3 Points)	(4 Points)

Total points assigned: ———

II. INITIAL CLASSIFICATION ASSESSMENT

Custody Level Assignment

A. Severity of charges   B. Previous experince
C. Behavior and personality characteristics

A.	Misdeameanors only	Nonserious Nonviolent Felonies	Some serious Violent Felonies	Mostly serious Violent Felonies
B.	Less than 6 months	6 mos. to a year	1 to 5 years	Over 5 years
C.	1–6 pts. (1 point)	7–9 pts. (2 points)	10–12 pts. (3 points)	13–20 pts. (4/5 points)

Custody Level Assignment Score———
———Low Medium Custody (3+)   ———Low Close Custody (9+)
———High Medium Custody (6+)   ———High Close Custody (12+)

YES   NO   Do you believe it is necessary to override this custody level assignment?
            If yes, fully document rationale.

FIGURE 12. (*continued*)

tion as to the details of presentence report narrative content and that the content of the presentence report is the concern almost solely of the probation organization and its officers.

Our purpose here is not to argue against diversity. As Carter asserts, there may be a need for both standardization and localization—for example, for adapting a common model, with some constant set of standards, in individual jurisdictions. But if ever a consistent set of data elements suitable for the classification studies needed (and for an assessment of the relevance of information to decisions) is to be available for analyses, these obvious shortcoming cannot be ignored.

The argument that there is a need to improve the consistency and reliability of data collected about offenders in presentence investigations may seem rather far afield from the central thesis of this book, that rational decision making requires the selection among alternatives in the light of information demonstrably relevant to specified objectives. But it is information in this sense, not merely data, that is required. Thus, an analysis of the available data, to determine its information content, is needed; and this in turn requires a consistently and systematically acquired data set. Stated another way, it is necessary to have information about the information if its utility is to be assessed (Wilkins, 1976).

There is little evidence from systematic study of how the data now included typically in presentence investigation reports is used in decision making, either by the courts or by probation or parole administrators. There is some evidence that (1) only a small number of data elements tend to be used in decision making in individual cases and that (2) the recommendation of the probation officer as to granting probation, when made, tends to be consistent with that made later by the judge (Carter, 1978; Carter and Wilkins, 1967; Wilkins and Chandler, 1965).

Data items used by probation officers in arriving at presentence recommendations were investigated in a small study by Wilkins and Chandler (1965). Using an "information board," they asked probation officers to select items in order of their importance. Items were arranged on cards, with a heading at the top and content below extracted from a case file; only the heading was visible until an item was selected. After choosing four items and examining the content of each in turn, a decision was requested (as well as ratings of confidence and difficulty in the decision) after each subsequent selection. Wilkins found no persistent pattern used by the seventeen officers studied (in this one case) and considered that the way information was sought and used was perhaps more characteristic of the officers than of the information.

In the study by Carter and Wilkins (1967), using a similar method, fourteen United States probation officers in California with five hypothetical cases were used and twenty-four data items were studied. Of these, an average of only seven or eight per case were used. Carter and Wilkins reported a considerable consistency, or "style," in selection by the individual officers, but noted that the final recommendations made by these officers were considerably divergent. Gottfredson, Wilkins, and Hoffman (1978), in a related study of parole decisions, reported that different decisions may be reached on the basis of the same information. Of the twenty-four data items available to the decision makers, only eight were selected more than half the time. Offense and prior record were examined invariably. Eighty percent of the time the psychological-psychiatric data were examined, and 70% of the time the defendant's statement was chosen. Attitude (62%), employment history (61%), age (54%), and family history (52%) were fairly popular items for examination.

Carter and Wilkins (1967) also studied the relation between probation officers' recommendations and judges' decisions as to probation. They found that when probation was recommended it was granted in most of the cases studied. Of course, it may be that the probation officer and judge are arriving at a similar decision on the basis of the same or similar data. There was, however, a considerable variation in the proportions of persons granted probation by different courts, and this appeared to be associated with variation among the probation officers.

THE EFFECTIVENESS OF PROBATION

Probation programs currently are both heralded as the best hope of corrections and regarded as relatively useless. Positions on community corrections may be derived from a review of the state of the art in this field; they may reflect mere opinion, wish, or hope; or they may be based upon a careful analysis of systematic empirical knowledge about the success or failure of efforts to rehabilitate offenders in the community. There is, however, little conclusive evidence from the latter source. An often cited study by Lipton, Martinson, and Wilks (1975) analyzed and summarized 231 studies of correctional rehabilitation. But what can be learned from this review of adult probation services in the United States is quite limited. Only five pertinent adult probation studies were included. Four of them assessed probation in respect to recidivism, and one evaluated also the effect of probation on vocational adjustment. One study assessed personality and attitude changes associated with intensive probation services and supervision.

Gottfredson, Finckenauer, and Rauh (1977) sought to define and discuss some critical issues about adult probation in the United States and to seek out and review the evidence since 1950 bearing on these issues.[6] About 130 available studies concerning probation client caseload characteristics, probation prediction, probation revocation and recidivism, and probation treatment modalities were reviewed. An attempt was made to find and obtain reports from all relevant studies conducted since 1950.

In correctional research there are many opportunities along the path from the research design to a conclusion for a study to veer off course, a deviation that can limit the confidence that may be placed in the findings. Some of these pitfalls, noted in the Gottfredson *et al.* review, may be examined briefly to illustrate these problems. Research done in action settings is criticized easily after the fact, in the manner of the traditional "Monday morning quarterback." This is not our purpose, and we are aware that many of the faults identified may have been a function of the circumstances of time and place that precluded the use of what we (and perhaps the research workers involved) perceive as better methods. The problems we wish to cite, however, set limits to the conclusions that can be drawn.

An obvious essential first element is the careful formulation of the research design prior to implementation of a study. A carefully planned research design is important to keep the study on course. A lack of careful, detailed planning was apparent in many of the studies reviewed.

The selection of an appropriate sample (or samples) for study is, of course, another critical element. It is a fundamental point that if a sample is selected for study that is not representative of the population of interest, the findings may not appropriately be generalized to that population. There are techniques available, such as probability sampling, that can ensure that a sample may be considered representative. Unfortunately, this requirement is sometimes not understood. *Random* is equated with *haphazard*, or samples are drawn on some basis of convenience, with a consequent introduction of possible bias.

The use of a classical research design generally provides a useful procedure in evaluation of program effectiveness, but numerous difficulties often are encountered in attempts to use such designs. This type of plan requires the selection of samples such that an experimental group (treated) and control group (untreated) are created. Subjects are randomly allocated to both. Typically, "before" measures are made of each group to determine a base line against which change can be measured. The experimental group is then exposed to treatment, controlling or restricting the interference of unwanted outside factors. After treatment, an "after" measure is taken in both groups to determine the changes that have occurred. Because of difficulties in implementing and adhering to this type of research design in probation work, compromises frequently are made in order to conduct the evaluations. Gottfredson and his associates found that a commonly used compromise design in probation studies is the "after only" design. In such a study, a group receives treatment and then a measurement is made, ostensibly to determine what changes have occurred. No control group is used for comparison, and there is no measurement of the prior state of affairs and no basis for estimating expected outcomes. It is therefore not possible to determine the extent to which treatment may be considered responsible for any change.

Another compromise design frequently encountered in the probation literature is the "before–after" design. It may provide some evidence, although a control group is still lacking. A measure of the dependent variable is taken both before and after treatment. Various potential sources of error are inherent in this design, particularly the possibility of selection bias, such that attributing any observed change to treatment is hazardous at best.

If one asks about the effectiveness of probation or of specialized probation services, one must ask, Compared with what? The importance of comparisons in probation evaluation research is apparent; yet many of the studies reviewed by Gottfredson and colleagues lacked this vital element. Various studies are reported that lack either a control group in the sense of a classic experimental design, comparison groups considered to serve this purpose, or any statistical correction for known bias entering into the comparison.

A frequent problem encountered in the review of those probation studies was a lack of clear definition of critical terms. Therefore, the operational meanings of critical variables or concepts often were unclear. An important variable not defined in any of the studies reviewed, for example, was the concept of individual counseling. Despite the wide variety of behaviors that may reasonably be considered to fall within this general concept, studies were found that purported to study individual counseling without specifying what such treatment entailed.

Although it is often recognized that the sampling of probationers is important to generalizations about persons on probation, little if any attention is given to the problem of sampling of treatments of a given type. Since, for example, individual counseling is not all alike and indeed may proceed from a wide variety of theoretical frames of reference, the simple, unelaborated characterization of the treatment variable as "individual counseling" clearly will give little if any information about individual counseling in general, no matter how the study comes out. Problems of representative sampling of treatments of a given type are extremely complex, but in any treatment study there at least should be a careful description of the treatment used.

Thus, inadequate operational definitions of the treatment provided, and inadequate descriptions of the treatment afforded comparison groups, were commonly encountered in this review. From the study reports, it often appeared that each staff member was left to interpret individually the treatment to be delivered. Lack of consistency in the delivery of treatment may affect the results and certainly would preclude the rigorous examination of consistent application of the treatment technique. Minimally, three dimensions of concern must be clear from the description of treatments. The first is that of intent, or of the theory underlying the treatment. The second is some measure of intensity, or, to choose a medical analogy, of the dosage administered (not in the plan only but also in the practice); and the third is some evidence of the consistency with which the treatment actually was administered.

It is well known that the quality of information obtained is a critical element in all correctional research and that the most sophisticated analytical techniques cannot compensate for data of poor quality. It is well known, too, that care must be taken during data collection to ensure its reliability. It is surprising, then, that the reliability of data used in evaluations is so rarely assessed and reported.

The issue of reliability should be, but often is not, considered when subjective ratings about probationers (for example, by probation officers) form the data base for determining risk levels or the need for treatment and services. Since the use of such subjective ratings results in different interpretations by different raters, leaves room for personal bias, and is notoriously unreliable, the need for reliability measurement is apparent.

Thus, there are many opportunities at each step of a research plan for a study to go astray, and some of the probation studies reviewed did so to a greater or lesser degree. Each detour from the prescribed path can have serious consequences for appropriate and warranted conclusions and generalizations.

Methods are available for the careful formulation of research designs, for ensuring careful and adequate sample selections, for statistical control of the "nuisance variables" of selection factors biasing comparisons, for measurement of reliability, and for statistical tests of significance appropriate to the level of measurement possible with the data obtainable. The issues involved in improving the quality of information about probation and its results are critical to the general problem of making decisions with increased rationality in probation program placement.

It is a tenet of faith in corrections that persons on probation are less likely to recidivate than those in prison. There is some evidence that this is true. The comparison may be biased, of course, because judges have deliberately placed the best risks on probation in the first place. There is evidence that this is also true. As a result, comparisons of probation versus prison outcomes typically have been akin to comparisons of apples and oranges. Probationers have different characteristics than prisoners, and these differences are related to success or failure, however defined.

The Gottfredson, Finckenauer, and Rauh (1977) review of adult probation studies disclosed what is known about the profiles of the types of offenders who receive probation and the types who are incarcerated. Some evidence is provided by a Missouri Division of Probation and Parole (1976) study covering the fiscal years 1968 to 1970 which compared individuals committed to the Missouri Department of Corrections (3,197) to those placed on probation (5,083). The probationers were mostly young first offenders without significant alcohol or drug problems. The prison commitments were older than the probationers (averaging twenty-six years versus twenty-one), and the prison commitments were more likely to be divorced (15% versus 6%). There were significant differences in educational level, and there were no differences in ethnic classifications of the two groups. The authors found some differences in the types of offenses committed by probationers and prisoners. Offenders against the person—particularly persons convicted of robbery—constituted a greater proportion of the prison population than of the probation population. On the other hand, those convicted of auto theft and drug offenses were more frequently placed on probation.

A study by Babst and Mannering (1965) compared male offenders who were imprisoned with similar types of offenders who were placed on probation. The population sampled included all adult males released from a state correctional institution or placed on probation from 1954 to 1959. Three items were found to be most predictive of violation rates for both probationers and parolees: number of prior felony convictions, type of offense, and marital status at the time of commitment (these three items were found also to have been related to the initial judicial decision as to placement).

Certain personal characteristics repeatedly have been found to be positively correlated with successful probation outcomes. Kusuda (1966) found that 97% of the probationers who were employed at least 75% of the time, lived with their spouse, and had "nondisreputable" associates successfully completed probation. Hopkinson and Adams (1964), in their study of a specialized alcoholic caseload project, found prior arrest history, mandatory attendance at Alcoholics Anonymous, and marital status (married) to be associated with a "favorable response" to probation. Irish (1976) found that an offender's adjustment on probation was related to the type of crime committed—that is, persons convicted of crimes against persons, drug offenses, or other offenses were more likely to make a successful adjustment on probation than those convicted of property offenses.

Some studies relevant to the issue of program placement decisions for probationers report positive results, and others report no difference. It should be noted that both types of results, if the quality of the analysis can be accepted, provide information useful in making decisions. A drug unit caseload evaluation (Kaput and Santese, 1972) found that nearly five contacts (half in person) per month did appear to have an effect on probation outcomes (recidivism, welfare, and educational program involvement). Similarly, Clarkson (1974) reported that reducing caseload size improved the probability of successful probation completion. Sheppard's (1975) evaluation of an intensive supervision project reported lower one-year rearrest and reconviction rates for intensive samples compared with regular caseloads.

Other studies report different results. In a preliminary evaluation of the San Francisco project (Lohman, Wahl, and Carter, 1966:37) the authors concluded:

> The findings in our preliminary evaluation of intensive, ideal, and minimum supervision caseloads raise some serious questions about the nature and efficiency of the prevailing models of supervision. We have observed that the probationers, parolees, and mandatory releasees routinely assigned to these various caseloads, despite substantial differences in the supervision effort, exhibit violation rates which are not significantly different from one another.

Furthermore, they observed that in the intensive caseloads, despite fourteen times as much attention as provided the minimum supervision cases, the violation rate not only failed to decline significantly but increased with respect to technical violations.

Even when rigorous experimental designs have been utilized in studies of client and caseload characteristics (and that has been unusual), the time perspective has been generally no longer than the project duration. Without more detailed research, including more extensive follow-up study, it is impossible to know what it is about intensive supervision or reduced loads that is or is not working.

Recently an evaluation of some aspects of probation was completed on a sample of California probationers by Petersilia, Turner, Kahan, and Peterson (1985:vi–vii). The conclusions of their report were widely announced and immediately controversial:

In our opinion, felons granted probation present a serious threat to public
safety. During the 40-month follow-up period of our study, 65 percent of the
probationers in our subsample were rearrested, 51 percent were reconvicted,
18 percent were reconvicted of serious violent crimes, and 34 percent were
reincarcerated.

Portions of the Petersilia *et al.* findings are shown as Figure 13. Given
the importance of probation generally as a disposition and the importance of the conclusions reached by Petersilia and her colleagues, the
study requires further discussion.

Some Inferences from the Data on Probation

The researchers studied 1,672 felony probationers sentenced in Los
Angeles and Alameda counties (California) and about 16,500 sentencing

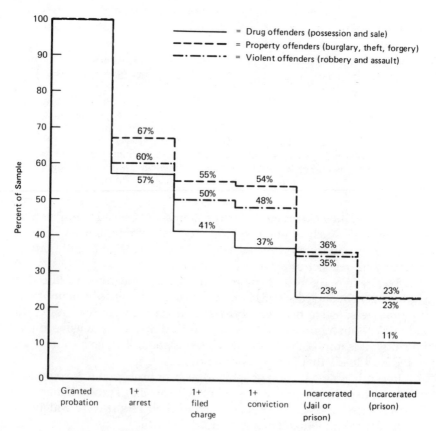

FIGURE 13. Probation recidivism rates. SOURCE: Petersilia *et al.* (1985:23).

decisions for male offenders whose sentences could involve either prison or probation. The Rand researchers selected a sample of persons convicted of robbery, assault, burglary, theft, forgery, and drug offenses. Although the Rand researchers refer to their study as a study of felony probation, we must keep in mind that not all felony probationers and, of course, not all probationers are represented in their sample. As the researchers note (Petersilia et al., 1985:16), in addition to studying two nonrepresentative counties (counties with larger caseloads, court congestion, and jail crowding):

> We are not assessing probation's overall effectiveness. We are studying only adult males convicted of six felony crime types, a population that represents only about 35 percent of the adult probationers in California in 1983. The characteristics of felony probationers are not necessarily those of probationers in general.

It is also critical to note that most (88%) of the probationers in the Rand study also spent time in jail prior to the probation. And the average length of stay was about eight months. Thus, the probationers in the Rand study may more fairly be characterized as split-sentence offenders, and any conclusions about the effectiveness of probation drawn from this study necessarily includes the effects of imprisonment. (And inferences about public danger must recognize the fact that some incapacitation was administered to the group.)

The Rand study thus illustrates a problem all too common in criminal justice evaluation: treatments are rarely pure and therefore their evaluations are necessarily complicated. This circumstance does not argue against such evaluations, but it provides a warning of caution that it is necessary to guard against unqualified assertions about results. The authors' caution, cited above, must be borne in mind when making generalizations about "felons granted probation."

Other facts of crime complicate the Petersilia evaluation further. Younger offenders tend to recidivate more often than do older offenders. They also tend to receive probation more frequently than do older offenders, for reasons quite apart from their recidivism potential. Rightly or wrongly, the criminal justice system is prepared to take greater risks with the young, a stance that shows up in recidivism statistics for probationers.

The meaning of recidivism as it relates to probation must also be considered, particularly if the public danger concern of Petersilia and her colleagues is itself to be evaluated. Generally, probation officers believe that they serve the two highly interrelated functions of treatment and supervision in the community. That is, not only are these officers working to integrate offenders back into the community, but they also must seek to detect offenders who pose a threat to public safety and seek to remove them from the streets. Both jobs are obviously complicated by huge caseloads (the Rand researchers estimate many to be between 150 and 300 per officer) and few resources. Clearly, bringing about offenders' classification as recidivists (arresting them) might correspond to what probation officers try to do when circumstances warrant it.

Now consider the recidivism rates, shown in Figure 13 in light of these dual functions and in light of the resources (and also in light of the incarceration experiences of the offenders). Complicate the problem by adding the fact that the Rand researchers used no control group in their study, that is, no group of offenders who had received a different treatment and whose recidivism rates also had been followed. Are the rates for comparable offenders higher or lower if they go to prison or if they get no probation supervision? It is apparent that glib assertions about how well probation works are not warranted.

The probation studies we have discussed in this chapter and elsewhere do permit some limited inferences that are useful starting points for rational decisions in this area. For example, these studies collectively provide some evidence as to which probationers succeed. Probationers who have no previous record of arrests and who are convicted of property crimes have the greatest probability of successfully completing their probation terms. These same offenders, having been released from probation as "improved," have also the greatest probability of postprobation success. On the other hand, variables most often significantly associated with failure are measures of previous criminal history, youthfulness, unemployment, and the classification "not married."

But the inferences possible from the research in probation are not limited to statements about classifications of probationers who are probable successes. We believe that several questions are addressed by these studies collectively; some questions remain unanswered, and yet other questions are raised.

If we ask who is placed on probation, some observed differences with selected imprisoned offenders may be cited (they tend to be younger, to be convicted of less serious offenses, and to have shorter prior records, see, e.g., Petersilia et al., 1985), but a detailed profile of such differences, generalizable to probationers and prisoners in general, cannot be given. The necessary research has not been done.

If we ask whether probation is more effective as a rehabilitative treatment than is imprisonment, we must respond again that the necessary research has not been done.

If we ask whether the personal characteristics of offenders are more important than the form of treatment in determining future recidivism, we must answer that evidence tends to support this conjecture.

If we ask whether the size of the caseload makes any difference to results in terms of recidivism, we must answer that the evidence is mixed. From limited evidence, it appears that intensive supervision may result in more technical violations known and acted upon and also to fewer new offense convictions.

If we ask who succeeds and who fails on probation supervision, we may reply that a useful technology for development and validation of prediction instruments is available, that there is some information on the question (for some jurisdictions), that attempts to develop such instruments for probationers have been rare, and that these attempts have been put to relatively little use.

If we ask what works, out of interest in discovering what forms of treatment and supervision provide more effective results when applied to probationers generally or to any particular classification of offenders, we must reply that there is limited evidence and that it is mixed.

If these issues are indeed critical to adult probation decisions, pointing as they do to inadequacies of the information on which placement decisions currently are based, then the most obvious conclusion to be reached is that too few resources have thus far been applied to providing adequate evidence on the questions raised. Trite as it may be to plea that further research is needed, this is inescapable.

This is not to say that nothing has been learned, but rather that there have been too few studies of these probationer issues, many of which—because of the nature of the studies or because of faulty research designs or implementations—cannot give the definitive, general answers that are sought. And although space prohibits an analogous review of relevant parole studies here, we are familiar enough with that literature to draw a similar conclusion. As a result, these studies cannot give planners, judges, or parole or probation managers the guidance that could provide a systematic program for increased rationality in probation decision making. In the final chapter we outline in some detail a general model that we believe is applicable to making decisions on probation and parole. Some brief notes in that direction can be given here in the context of probation decisions.

In any probation or parole agency, a management information system is needed. Smaller agencies might have to collaborate or join larger agencies in order to develop and use this system. The management information system must be designed to provide feedback on such critical issues as are discussed in this book. This requires the reliable collection of standardized and comprehensive information on the characteristics of probationers or parolees at the time of sentence. Also needed is a system of follow-up, with carefully defined and agreed-upon measures of outcomes. Prediction measures, based upon relevant information about offenders, must be developed and tested to assure their validity. Such measures can provide, for any classification of probationers or parolees, the expected outcomes (such as recidivism rates) through the follow-up system. Differences between the expected and observed outcomes can then be assessed, to provide some information on the programs that appear to be useful and those that do not, for what kinds of offenders, with respect to various definitions of success and failure. Those treatment programs identified as apparently effective can then be investigated by the use of more rigorous research designs. Such a system can provide a continuous assessment of probation or parole programs, making use of presently available technology and guiding the development of programs much more rationally than the hit-or-miss basis that has thus far characterized program development in this field.

Probation and parole are on trial, but the evidence is not yet in. Much of the presentation of both the "prosecution" and the "defense" must be regarded as scientifically inadmissible. Methods are available to provide the needed evidence in a systematic management information program. Those who judge probation and parole can then be better informed, and more rational decisions in the administration of community corrections may be expected.

NOTES

1. Portions of this section are adapted from Gottfredson, Finckenauer, and Rauh (1977).
2. Not all criticism of these systems is based on negative or questionable evidence of effectiveness in reducing crime. For example, von Hirsch and Hanrahan (1979) argue concerning parole supervision that lower standards of proof and differing standards of disposition (from those affecting other offenders) lead to undesirable consequences to fairness or the imposition of justice.
3. For reviews, see the following sources: Mannheim and Wilkins (1955; Chapter I provides a historical survey of American and European prediction studies in criminology. The book also provides a review of pertinent methodological issues up to the time of its publication and, so far as we know, the first use in criminological research of prediction as a control tool in quasi-experimental designs. See, for example, Chapter IX, "A Note on the Future of Criminological Research," at 211–224, especially at 211); Simon (1971; Chapter 3 is titled by the author "A Review of Some Selected Prediction Studies" but she seems conservative; the review provides a quite thorough analysis of many important studies); Gottfredson (1967:171–87); Albanese (1977); Gottfredson, Wilkins, and Hoffman (1978); Gottfredson and Gottfredson (1984).
4. For discussion of these methodological issues, see Simon (1971), Geason and Hangren (1958), Ford and Johnson (1976), Meehl and Rosen (1955), Cureton (1957), Hanley (1961), Walters (1956), Gottfredson (1967), and Gottfredson and Gottfredson (1985).

5. This is not to say that no positive results have been reported but that differences generalizable to other jurisdictions or otherwise having sufficient generalizability for formulation of general public policy are not available. Perhaps, however, this is too much to expect from single project evaluations and the questions have not been asked in the right way. The development of information systems for individual corrections agencies, as outlined later in this chapter, can guide policy decisions in that particular agency without the requirement of such jurisdiction-wide generalizability.
6. This section is adapted from Gottfredson, Finckenauer, and Rauh (1977).

Chapter 8

CORRECTIONAL DECISIONS IN INSTITUTIONS

Decisions made in correctional institutions may be classed as program decisions (on program planning or resource allocation) or as individual decisions (affecting the placement of persons in differing institutions, custody levels, degrees of supervision, or treatment programs). As with correctional decisions in the community, these decisions are subject to a complexity of goals, alternatives, and information. Goals are diverse, and again they may be apparently conflicting—a criminal justice problem not unique to correctional management. Alternatives, too, are found to have a great variety of forms; moreover, they are subject to wide variation in both resources and imagination. Information demonstrably relevant to correctional objectives, as in other areas of criminal justice decision making, often is lacking, or evidence is conflicting, or questions of the reliability of potentially useful information must be weighed.

Yet, as with the police officer, the prosecutor, the judge, or the probation administrator, decisions must be made daily. The complaint that "the data are not yet all in" hardly will be found satisfying to the jail or prison manager who is apt to be beset with difficult decisions demanding prompt resolution.

In this chapter, the goals involved and some examples of alternatives and of information resources and needs will be examined. This is a large topic indeed: there is a wealth of relevant literature related to it, and only selected examples may be given. Our general aim is to develop a general strategy for improving information for correctional decisions.

The broad goals of correctional institutions have already been discussed in Chapter 7: reform, rehabilitation, reintegration, or restraint. GOALS

With somewhat more specificity (but still at a very general level), we may identify goals at least of security, treatment, incapacitation, and organizational maintenance.

These broad goals are related closely to sentencing aims and to those of community corrections, but here the context of decision making differs substantially. The decisions are constrained in complex ways, a very large number of decisions per person is at issue, and, generally, more data about the individual offender typically are available to the decision makers. Burnham (1975: 93–94) has described this context of special features of correctional decision making as follows:

> First . . . there is the very strong effect of system constraints and requirements. All prisons are, in several senses, run by their inmates, and a regular supply of these to essential jobs, such as kitchen and the laundry, must be maintained. Thus there are two types of decision usually collapsed into one. (1) "What is the appropriate disposition for that particular inmate?" (in terms of which institution, which work assignment, which training program, etc., is the most suitable for him), and (2) "Which inmates are to be used to provide the manpower for the following essential tasks?" The problem emerges in the collapsed form as (3) "Is this inmate suitable for what he requests, and does it suit system requirements for him to be so allocated?" or more simply (4) "Can we allow him to do what he wants?" In version (4), the factors involved in "allowing" refer to both the personal qualities of the inmate (e.g., offense, violence record, intelligence, aptitude test scores) and vacancies, either open to be filled or which must filled.
>
> Second, the sheer number of decisions is different. For each passage through the system, each inmate usually is arrested once, tried once, sentenced once, paroled once, and so on. In the correctional stage, he is subject to frequent decisions which affect where he lives, what he does, and other issues which matter deeply to him. Thus, in one respect correctional decisionmaking impinges more on an inmate's life. But in a more important way, it matters less—for most of these decisions are reversed with relative ease; and thus, as well as having less far-reaching implications for the subsequent system career path of the individual, they are not so final.
>
> The third main difference is in the amount and type of information available to the decisionmaker. The arresting police officer, the district attorney or whoever brings the charge, the court which tries, and the judge or jury who sentence will often have, or probably feel they have, a shortage of data upon which to base their decision. But what they do have is significant. Once an individual is in the correctional system, however, data about him are accumulated very rapidly, so that a great deal is known, but much of it seemingly trivial and uninformative with regard to the particular decisions required.

The security aim, in prisons as in jails, involves both institutional security (and this is related closely to the objective of institutional maintenance) and the personal security of individuals. In neither prisons nor jails has their been much research aimed at the classification of offenders for either purpose. This area has been a neglected one in which classification and prediction studies could provide needed assistance in decision making (Megargee, 1978).

There are some major exceptions to the generalization that there is a lack of research aimed at improved classification of inmates in ways compatible with the goals of correctional decision making. Toch (1977) has investigated the relation between inmate concerns and aspects of the prison environment, developing a "Prison Preference Inventory" to aid the classification task. This instrument, derived on the basis of profile analysis of interviews with inmates, describes concerns that inmates may have with respect to such aspects of the environment as safety, privacy, and freedom. The aims of the research were to develop classification tools to match inmates with institutional programs and to develop an instrument allowing the identification of persons in need of special attention. (See also Gibbs, 1978; Moos, 1974.)

The treatment aim has been emphasized in a great deal of research, with conflicting results and the familiar questions of uncertainty about information concerning the information. There is an extraordinary diversity of "treatments" offered in some, though not all, prisons, for example, varieties of academic education, vocational education, individual or group counseling, physical therapy, behavior modification programs, work assignments, or on-the-job training, to name only some of the most common.

In recent years it has become popular to express a complete disenchantment with the rehabilitative ideal that undergirded correctional reform in the earlier part of this century (based though it was on philosophical underpinnings of several thousand years). This abandonment of hope was based in large part on a series of widely cited reviews of correctional treatment evaluations (Bailey, 1966; Kassebaum et al., 1971; Lipton et al., 1975; Martinson, 1974; McCord, 1978).

These documented generally negative evidence on the effects of treatment and a rarity of promising leads that, when found, usually were based on small samples and on flawed research methods and, furthermore, were unreplicated.

Nevertheless, the evidence does not require or even support a policy of abandoning the goals of treatment. A panel from the National Research Council for the National Academy of Sciences (Sechrest et al., 1979:34) in the most recent thorough review of the evaluation research literature concluded: "There is not now in the scientific literature any basis for any policy or recommendations regarding rehabilitation of criminal offenders. The data available do not present any consistent evidence of efficacy that would lead to such recommendations."

This conclusion does not state that nothing works, but neither does it state that anything does work. The emphasis is upon the lack of consistent evidence that could provide policy guidance. The National Research Council panel also concluded, noting flaws in both the treatment interventions and the evaluation research methods, that "the quality of the work that has been done and the narrow range of options explored militate against any policy reflecting a final pessimism. The magnitude of the task of reforming criminal offenders has been consistently underestimated" (1979:34).

One of the panel members noted separately:

> In short, because there is so little evidence that credible treatments have been implemented with fidelity, and because much of the evaluation research done to date has been inefficient or defective in other ways, we have no compelling experimental evidence for the contention that powerful, theoretically defensible, and faithfully executed interventions hold no promise. (Gottfredson, 1979)

Indeed, with respect to the effectiveness of treatment, the panel concluded: "The strongest recommendation that the Panel can make at this time is that the research on offender rehabilitation should be pursued more vigorously, more systematically, more imaginatively, and more rigorously" (p. 34).

It is not our aim to undertake a thorough review of the literature on effectiveness of treatment. Several reviews, including the NAS study, are widely available. Instead, we devote our space in this chapter to some ideas about how making decisions within institutions can be made more rational. We start with a discussion of a specific example of the method we propose and then describe in some detail how data available to correctional decision makers can be structured to provide an evolutionary model for policy control. Both of these discussions carry us deeply into the research data and hence also reveal some important patterns of much interest to correctional decision making. Our example concerns estimating the relation between time served in prison and parole success.

TIME SERVED IN PRISON AND PAROLE OUTCOMES

In a sense, commitment to prison itself is a treatment, and arguments abound simply around the issue of whether the length of sentence (that is, time served in prison) is related to outcomes after the treatment. The time actually served in prison as a result of conviction is an end result of a complex of decisions by legislators, judges, correctional administrators, and others, as well as by the paroling authority (the latter are discussed in Chapter 9). Setting this complexity aside, it may be noted that debate is common about the relative merits of long or short terms of confinement not only in relation to desert but in regard to effectiveness in recidivism reduction. That is, unsupported claims are often heard that longer or shorter terms will reduce the likelihood of recidivism. Arguments for shorter terms, for example, often invoke the notion that prisons are schools of crime in which "prisonization" and increased commitment to criminal behavior may be enhanced by long terms. On the other hand, it may be argued that a harsher punishment may enhance specific deterrence; or it may be suggested that since age is inversely related to recidivism, keeping the offender longer will decrease the chance of new offenses or recommitments.

A study bearing on these issues used data collected from paroling authorities across the United States in the Uniform Parole Reports Program (Gottfredson, Neithercutt, Nuffield, and O'Leary, 1973). The purposes of this study were to describe, for a large number of selected offenders, the lengths of time served in prison and to assess the relation of time served to parole outcomes (all offenders included for study in this program were parolees). The study is unusual in that a very large number of parolees was studied (more than 100,000) from a substantial number of jurisdictions (data from all adult parole boards in the United States are included in the data set used, though not with representative sampling) and with an attempt to control statistically for offense, age, and prior record variation (items found repeatedly to be related to parole violation).

Prior research had indicated that there was little or no effect of time served on recidivism rates. A committee of the California Assembly reviewed data on time served and recidivism in California and concluded that "no evidence can be found to support extended incarceration as a determinate element in the deterrence of crime. Recidivism rates for offenders who had served comparatively long terms (compared to others of the same offense class) were higher than those who served comparatively short terms, if narcotics history and prior record are ignored" (Kolodney, 1970). Mueller (1965) studied 800 men paroled three months earlier than the usual parole date and found little difference. In general, it has not been demonstrated that specific deterrence is enhanced by increasing the duration of imprisonment, nor has it been shown that recidivism increases with increased time served.

In the study of Uniform Parole Reports data, 104,182 male felons paroled for the first time from prison sentences were included. All were paroled between 1965 and 1970. (It should be noted that persons released by means other than parole, including discharge or mandatory conditional release, were not included. In 1970, about 70% of all those released from prison were paroled.) The criterion of "favorable outcome" used in this study was that within a one-year follow-up period the parolee was reported as having had "no difficulty or a sentence of less than 60 days" and had not absconded and that no adverse action had been taken by the paroling authority. All others, including those who absconded or were returned to prison with or without a new conviction, were classified as having "unfavorable" outcomes. Only offenders whose commitment offense could be classified into fourteen major offense categories were included (see Table 6).

Each offender was classified further in terms of the time-served pentile, for his offense category, into which he fell. That is, the distributions of time served for each offense were divided into five approximately equal parts: the 20% of cases in each offense category that served the shortest time before parole were classed in the first pentile, and so on.

Each offender was classified also according to age (at last admission to prison) and prior record. The indicant of prior record used was "one or more known prior sentences other than prison" (this attribute was found to be more closely related to the outcome criterion than the item "prior prison record"). The relations of offense classification and of prior record to the parole violation criterion used are shown, for the parolees of this study in Table 6.

These associations are similar to those found in many prior studies. Typically, as in this sample, the property offenses such as theft, burglary, check fraud, and vehicle theft have been found to be associated with higher violation rates; and person offenses such as homicide, assault, and sex offenses have been found to be associated with lower rates. Similarly, indicants of prior criminal record have been found consistently to be associated with parole violation criteria. In this sample, persons without any prior record other than prison had higher favorable rates in each offense classification. A similar result has been found when other indicants (for example, any prior arrest or sentence or conviction or confinement) are used; generally, the proportions that violate parole conditions or are returned to prison with new convictions increase with increased history of such prior records.

Age has been found to be associated with parole violation criteria also, such that older offenders are more likely, in general, to be found in the favorable outcome category. Age and offense are themselves associated, however. Often, older offenders are found to have been convicted of person offenses such as homicide, manslaughter, or sex offen-

TABLE 6. Percentage of Favorable Parole Performance for Various Offense Groups by Prior Record

Offense	Percentage favorable			Number of cases		
	Priors	No priors	Combined	Priors	No priors	Total
Homicide	88	93	90	4,738	3,311	8,049
Manslaughter	85	94	89	1,030	863	1,893
Other sex offenses	84	92	87	1,908	1,150	3,058
Statutory rape	82	89	84	572	306	878
Forcible rape	81	88	84	1,480	886	2,366
Aggravated assault	78	86	80	4,487	1,812	6,299
Narcotics offenses	76	86	78	3,916	1,051	4,967
Other fraud	75	84	78	673	335	1,008
Armed robbery	74	84	77	8,851	3,450	12,301
Unarmed robbery	72	83	75	3,050	1,119	4,169
Theft or larceny	71	80	74	7,448	2,755	10,203
Burglary	69	78	72	23,790	8,487	32,277
Check fraud	64	72	66	8,493	2,482	10,975
Vehicle theft	63	71	65	4,285	1,454	5,739
Total number				74,721	29,461	104,182

Source: Adapted from Gottfredson *et al.* (1973:10).

ses that are associated with relative high rates of favorable outcome. An exception is check frauds, for which prison inmates tend to be older at prison admission and for which parole violation rates tend to be relatively high. Younger offenders in prison often have been convicted of burglary, theft, or auto theft, for which violation rates tend to be comparatively high.

In view of these commonly found associations, and in order to exercise some degree of control for offense, prior record, and age, the analyses of the association of time-served pentile categories and parole outcome were done separately for offense classes and (within those) for the prior record classification.

The question of the relation of time served in prison to recidivism often is expressed in a quite simplistic fashion: Do persons who serve more time in prison do better or worse in terms of some criterion of performance after release? A somewhat more sophisticated version (since it does not assume a linear or any monotonic relation) asks what is the optimal time for release for lower recidivism or parole violation rates. It is known from much prior work that any comparisons (of differences in groups according to time served or of other differences in treatment) must take account of differences in the kinds of offenders who are paroled. Parole violation rates among or between different treatment groups cannot be compared with confidence unless relevant differences in parolees (in the treatment groups involved) are considered. That is, if different types of offenders are released following different periods of imprisonment and if some are better "risks" than others, this must be taken into account in any comparison of violations associated with the time served treatment groups. Thus, a simple comparison of violation rates associated with differing periods of incarceration does not necessarily indicate that parole violation rates are or are not due in whole or in part to variation in the length of incarceration.

The three variables believed, from much prior study, to be most important for inclusion in such analyses were offense, prior record, and age. In order to take account of these variables—that is, to remove their influence upon variation in parole violation—the analyses were performed separately for subgroups defined by offense and prior record, and, in addition, a statistical correction was made for the effect of age.

Patterns of parole performance rates differed somewhat when offense classes were analyzed separately. Similarly, patterns from different jurisdictions were found to differ. In general, however, it may be said that (1) observed differences in parole outcomes associated with the differing time-served classifications were relatively small, but (2) with some exceptions, offenders who served the longest terms in prison before their first parole, relative to others with similar offenses, tended to be classed more often as parole violators during the first year after release. When the entire sample was considered, which in effect collapsed the analyses over offense groups, the results of Table 7 were obtained.

Of course, if the poorer risks are selected to serve longer terms in relation to others of their offense classification and better risks are selected to serve shorter terms, and if this selection is based on information in addition to age and prior record (and in the offense-specific data to

TABLE 7. Parole Performance Rates for All Offenses (104,182 Subjects) across Time-served Pentiles: Age-adjusted, One-year Follow-up[a]

Percentage of favorable outcomes adjusted for age	Percentage of favorable outcome by time-served pentile					Percentage differences 1st–5th pentile
	First	Second	Third	Fourth	Fifth	
No priors	84.2	83.2	83.1	81.6	79.2	−5.0
Prior record	74.0	72.2	72.7	71.4	70.8	−3.2
Combined	77.7	75.7	75.3	73.7	73.1	−4.6

Source: Adapted from Gottfredson et al. (1973:10).
[a]Results reported in this table were obtained by combining subjects from each offense category on the basis of their time-served pentile assignment for their respective offenses.

be described subsequently), then the comparison may test the risk classification rather than effects of time served. In any case, the differences are not large. Perhaps the main policy implication is found not in the slight trend shown but in the result that time served does not appear to have a substantial impact on parole violation rates. In the context of unsubstantiated arguments that increasing or decreasing time served will markedly affect recidivism, this finding of no substantial difference has a substantial practical significance.

Further caution in generalizing from the results of Table 7 is given, however, by examination of the similar analyses conducted separately for offense groups and for the prior record classification. These results can be summarized briefly. In general, there was a tendency, although by no means a consistent one, for persons who served the most time, in relation to others with similar offenses, to be found more often in the parole violator group. Considering offenders against persons, the trend was slight at best, and there were several reversals of it. For property offenders the trend seemed usually apparent and somewhat more pronounced in both the "prior record" and "no prior record" classifications. But when a narcotics offender group was considered alone the trend was opposite: those who served the most time, compared to others in their offense classification, tended to have the more favorable outcomes.

Speculative interpretations of these data are easily contrived but not easily tested. Considering the general trend, for example, various hypotheses may be advanced. It may result from parole board retention of poor risks in pursuit of incapacitative aims. The relatively small differences in outcomes associated with time served may result from constraints on parole decision making; that is, it might be argued that a paroling authority unencumbered by legislatively or judicially set minima and maxima might then exercise a stronger incapacitative role. Alternatively, it could be argued that the fairly small differences observed may mask more pronounced differences to be observed when different jurisdictions are considered separately. Other hypotheses might call attention to the diversity of behaviors encompassed by such general offense classifications as used in this study. Paroling authority "sanctioning," for example (see Chapter 9), may result in more severe penalties for professional car theft as a business than for "joy riding"; or in generally more time for burglary of a home at night than of a business during daylight; or for "unarmed robbery" by a person actually, perhaps admittedly, armed who plea-bargained down from armed robbery. An alternative hypothesis about the general trend, of course, is that the prison experience is damaging, in general, to rehabilitative aims. Such hypotheses may be formulated in testable terms, and that will be needed to support speculations that raise issues that cannot be settled by these data. The results described do suggest strongly that the arguments of those who perceive increasing (or decreasing) prison time as a ready panacea to reduction of recidivism should be viewed with a healthy dose of skepticism.

Results of a similar study of one jurisdiction (Ohio) were, in general, consistent with these (Gottfredson *et al.*, 1977). Since the offenders serving different periods of time may not be comparable parole risks, all offenders in the study first were classified according to risk. Persons studied were a 10% random sample of all parolees in Ohio released between 1965 and 1972 (5,349 men and 238 women). From study of a random half of the males in this sample (2,726 persons), predictive classifications were developed on the basis of the method of predictive attribute analysis. (A similar procedure was used to study the female sample, but the limited numbers of cases did not permit confident statements of relations.) Nine risk categories were defined thereby, with proportions of favorable outcome (with one-year follow-up) varying in the construction sample from a low of 63% to a high of 99%. When the other half of the sample was used for validation ($N = 2,623$), there was substantial agreement in the success percentages for each category in both samples. (The overall success rate was, in each sample, 84%.)

Attributes taken into account in the risk classification included such items as type of offense, type of sentence, prior sentences, history of drug use or alcohol involvement, types of admission to prison, and age. Generally, with men not differentiated according to risk categories (that is, not controlling for attributes such as those just listed), the success rates decreased with increasing time served up to fifty months but increased somewhat thereafter. When the risk groups were studied, however, in order to control for the known associations of offender attributes and parole outcomes, a different picture was apparent. Either no relation was found (between time served and parole outcomes), as was the case in four groups, or no single pattern obtained (five groups). The study demonstrated that for men paroled in Ohio between 1965 and 1972 (1) for some specific classifications of offenders, time served is not related to parole outcome; (2) for some groups of offenders there are complex patterns of association between time served and parole outcomes; and (3) there clearly is no consistent pattern of increasing parole success with increased time served; rather, in general, success rates decrease or remain fairly constant with increased time served in prison. More generally, although pointing to the complexity of the question of the relation of time served to parole outcome and suggesting that such relations, if they exist, may differ in important ways according to differences in inmate characteristics, the results mainly support the contention that there is no large positive relation between time served in prison and favorable parole outcome.

INFORMATION FOR CORRECTIONAL DECISIONS: A POLICY CONTROL MODEL

If more rational decision making in corrections is to be achieved, data concerning offenders, treatments, and outcomes must be more systematically and reliably collected and analyzed than heretofore. In the remainder of this chapter, an outline for a general strategy of correctional study is proposed. An important feature of the system we advocate as a means toward an evolutionary correctional policy control model is that prediction issues occupy a central role. Therefore, some results of a parole prediction study (for the base expectancy scale devised by Gottfredson and described briefly in Chapter 7) from one jurisdiction (California) will be presented in some detail. It is believed also that the technology involved has relevance to what is perhaps the greatest problem currently affecting correctional decision makers.

That problem is the overcrowding crisis in prisons. Nearly every jurisdiction is confronting record high levels of incarceration and is struggling to find ways of dealing with the problem. As just one indication of the magnitude of the problem, the number of inmates in state and federal correctional facilities at the end of 1984 was 463,866. Since 1980 there has been a 40% increase in the number of inmates. This growth has been accompanied, not surprisingly, by a major growth in spending: expenditures by state correctional authorities in 1984 increased by $1.2 billion over the previous year and reached an all-time high of 7.2 billion dollars. At year's end state prisons were estimated to be operating at an average of 10% over capacity (with an estimated 11,500 offenders also kept in local jails because of prison overcrowding) and federal prisons 24% over capacity (Bureau of Justice Statistics, 1985).

In our view, guidelines systems of the type discussed generally in Chapter 1, described in relation to bail in Chapter 4, and reviewed in regard to sentencing in Chapter 6 are well suited to bring some rationality to the correctional response to the crowding problem (Gottfredson and Gottfredson, 1984).

"Emergency Release" Provisions

As of January, 1983, seven states had adopted some form of emergency release provisions in response to prison overcrowding. Michigan's Prison Overcrowding Emergency Powers Act, adopted in 1980, is illustrative. Under the act, if the prison population exceeds the rated capacity for thirty days the commissioner of corrections files a report with the governor and certifies that all administrative remedies have been exhausted. The governor is then required to declare an emergency. This results in a ninety-day reduction of the sentence of those prisoners who are serving the minimum statutory term, creating a new pool of persons eligible for parole. If enough paroles are not granted to reduce the population to 95% capacity within ninety days, another ninety-day reduction of minimum terms is granted. The emergency is lifted whenever the 95% capacity population level is reached.

A related mechanism has been used in Illinois. Beginning in June, 1980, the Department of Corrections used a forced release policy to achieve population reductions by awarding additional "good time" to certain categories of offenders. When the population exceeded capacity, the commission could grant thirty, sixty, or ninety days of administrative good time, such that persons approaching mandatory release dates who had convictions for class 2, 3, or 4 felonies and who had no disciplinary infractions for six months were released earlier. A later modification involved additional screening criteria (and a limitation of a ninety-day shortening for any one inmate). The potential generality of this concept is suggested by the circumstance that the federal system, the District of Columbia, and all but four states have some provision for administrative reduction of time served in prison. The existing rules are highly variable among jurisdictions, but perhaps they provide a basis for similar emergency release planning.

One common feature of emergency release planning involves some screening method to help decide which inmates might be expected to pose the least risk to the community if released. A description of the development and validation of the parole prediction instrument that played a part in earlier release programs in California (see Chapter 7) may be useful since it is generally applicable (that is, this technology may be applied to similar guidelines problems).

The Base Expectancy Scale

The motivation for the development of the parole prediction device (called a base expectancy scale) was to provide a method to aid in program evaluation research and in prison and parole management decisions. The prediction device was developed from study of the records of 873 men. They were selected by a procedure assumed to approximate random selection, from all men who were released from prison to California parole supervision in 1956. Items found related to parole outcomes were combined and weighted by a multiple regression analysis. The calculation of base expectancy raw scores is shown in Figure 14. The initial validation study of this prediction scale consisted in its ap-

To Obtain Raw Scores:

If		*Add*	
A. Arrest free five or more years		16	_____
No history of any opiate use		13	_____
No family criminal record		8	_____
Not checks or burglary		13	_____
B. Age at commitment times 0.6			_____
21 is added for all persons			___21___
C. Subtotal: A + B			
D. Aliases: − 3 times number		−	_____
E. Prior incarcerations: − 5 times number		−	_____
F. Subtotal: D + E		−	
G. Score: Subtract F from C			

FIGURE 14. Base expectancy form 61B score calculation.

plication to a sample of 937 men, all of whom were (like the study-sampled subjects) released from prison on parole in 1956. The validity of the method, judging from that test sample, was reasonably good.

Then the offenders were followed for eight years after parole to obtain evidence of the validity of the scale over a longer time after parole. Data were extracted for each person from arrest records covering an eight-year period after parole. The only source of follow-up data used was the arrest records of these parolees. (A major shortcoming of these data is that the court dispositions of arrests is not always known. It may be noted also that deaths occurring after discharge from parole may not be expected to be identified from this source.)

The performance criterion was defined by eight categories. The three representing the least difficulty in adjustment were:

No difficulty: the subject has no convictions (except that convictions resulting in maximum sentences of less than sixty days of confinement were ignored), and none of the remaining classifications were applicable.

Continued on parole after minor convictions: the parolee had been continued on parole after one or more convictions (for one or more offenses after his parole) resulting in maximum sentences of at least sixty days of confinement but less than one year.

Returned to prison, no violation: the parolee had been returned to prison for medical reasons or for other reasons not reflecting on his performance, or the parolee had been returned to prison on a new commitment but the crime had taken place before his parole.

The above three classifications were not considered to constitute "major difficulty." Similarly excluded from the major difficulty criterion, and from the "minor difficulty" classification as well, were behavioral problems not resulting either in court convictions or paroling authority actions identified with the categories below. (Such problems would not be known from the arrest records.) Examples of other exclusions were arrests not resulting in convictions, convictions resulting only in fines, and certain categories of detention. The latter included detention awaiting trial or execution of sentence, or confinement for suspicion or for investigation, or detention because of nonpayment of a fine.

If any of the following five classifications was applicable, then the subject was classified into the "major difficulty" (or "unfavorable") category:

Absconders: the whereabouts of the parolee was unknown and a warrant had been issued for his arrest.

Returned to prison as a technical violator with no convictions: the parolee had been adjudged by the paroling authority to be in violation of parole and returned to prison; however, no criminal convictions were related to the reason for his return to prison.

Returned to prison as a technical violator with minor or lesser conviction or in lieu of prosecution on a minor or lesser offense: the parolee had been adjudged by the paroling authority to be in violation of his parole and had been returned to prison after committing an offense punishable by confinement with a maximum sentence of greater than sixty days and less than one year.

Returned to prison as a technical violator on a "major offense" charge, punishable by a maximum sentence of one year or more, and returned to prison in lieu of prosecution: the parolee had been declared a parole violator by the paroling authority and had been returned to prison on the basis of a clear admission of guilt by the parolee of the commission of a crime that, if successfully prosecuted, would have resulted in a maximum sentence of one year or more.

Convicted and committed to prison with a new major conviction: the subject had been convicted, sentenced, and committed to prison in the same or any other jurisdiction for an offense committed since he was paroled with a new sentence of one year or more maximum.

It is clear that the arrest records do not provide, in every case, adequate information for correct classification of offenders into the above categories. The main interest in this study, however, was in the dichotomous classification provided by the "major difficulty" designation; and it was assumed to be safe to consider that those counted in the major difficulty category have absconded from parole or have been returned to prison either as a technical violator or with a new prison commitment.

Before examining the relations of the prediction method classifications to later performance, this performance itself should be described in some detail. How many were again in trouble, of what kind, and when, during the eight years after parole? Thirty percent of the 1,810 men were classified as having no difficulty, meaning for each of these men that he was neither an absconder, nor convicted of offenses resulting in a maximum sentence of sixty days or more, nor returned to prison. Seventy percent, however, fell into the remaining categories, as shown in Table 8.

Fifty-eight percent were classified into the major difficulty category. Only twenty-two men were classed as absconders not returned to prison, and 56.5% of the sample were returned to prison either as parole violators or for new offenses. Forty percent of the parole sample committed new major offenses (in California or other states) and were again imprisoned before the eight years had elapsed.

One-fourth of all new major offenses were forgery or check frauds. Second most frequent were convictions and recommitments for burglary (one-fifth of all new major offenses), and one-third were violations of

TABLE 8. Performance of Men with Minor
Convictions, Absconding, or Prison Return before Eight
Years after Parole

Performance	Number of men	Percentage of all paroled sample (1,810)
Minor conviction	225	12.43
Absconding	22	1.22
Parole violator returned (no convictions)	214	11.82
Parole violator returned (minor convictions)	82	4.53
Major offense (California)	626	34.59
Major offense (elsewhere)	103	5.69
Total	1,272	70.28

narcotics laws. New assaultive offenses against persons (not counting armed robbery) were found in 2.5% of all paroled. Armed robbery convictions were found in less than 4% of all paroled. Thirty-five percent of all with minor or major difficulty during the eighty-year period were so classified during the first year after parole. Sixty-one percent of these men had committed a new major offense, and about 10% had minor convictions or had absconded. The eighth year contributed only 2.5% of all with minor or major difficulty; of these, furthermore, 84% were those with minor convictions or absconding records, while about 16% were men with new major convictions. No "technical" parole violators were found after the fifth year following parole (when, of course, most had been discharged).

What proportions of parolees may be classified into the "no difficulty" category, bearing in mind that this includes all those with no record of absconding from parole, of sentences to confinement for sixty days or more, or of return to prison? The answer depends very much on the length of the follow-up study, as is shown clearly in Figure 15. The proportion with no difficulty ranges from 75% if a one-year criterion is used to 30% if the men paroled are followed for eight years.

It often is assumed that parole violations, if they occur, tend to occur soon after parole. A corollary is the belief that the longer a man goes without difficulty after parole, the greater is the likelihood that he will not be in further difficulty. Both contentions are supported by the data, although perhaps not so markedly as some would have expected.

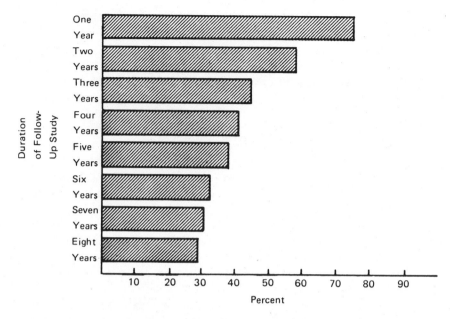

FIGURE 15. Percent of parolees with no minor or major difficulty according to various lengths of follow-up study after parole.

When the percentage of successful parolees is calculated with only surviving parolees in the denominator, (that is, the percentage is that of men in difficulty among those who were still exposed to the risk of difficulty) the proportions with no difficulty increase, for a given year, with increasing time after parole. This is not true for all categories of difficulty; that is, the rates of minor convictions are nearly constant, whereas rates of major offenses decrease.

If a parolee has survived the first year after parole without difficulty, is he less likely to be in difficulty during the next year? The data give little support to this contention, since the percentage with no difficulty in the second year (among those exposed to the risk of difficulty) is little different from the percentage with no difficulty during the first year. Seventy-five percent were so classified during the first year and 76% in the second. Thereafter, however, the proportions with no difficulty tend to increase, so that in general (after two years without difficulty), there is less likelihood of difficulty the longer the man has been in the community without difficulty (minor convictions excepted). The number of men surviving without difficulty decreases quite rapidly in the first few years and continues to decrease more slowly up to eight years after parole. The percentage of men with no difficulty in a given year after parole increases with the number of years after parole.

The accumulation of men with difficulties in three categories—minor convictions or absconding from parole, technical parole violation or minor convictions and prison return, and new major offenses with prison return—may be seen in Figure 16. The minor conviction (or absconding) category includes a fairly constant increment of men with these difficulties; the cumulative proportions of parolees in this category appear to be (after the first two and a half years) a linear function of the number of months since parole. The slightly more rapid accumulation in this category during the first thirty months is associated with absconding, a difficulty that is not found later because many have been discharged.

The category that includes men with technical parole violations or minor convictions and prison return accumulates men at a slightly decreasing rate until about thirty months after parole. After thirty-six months few are added, and after sixty-six months, none.

The category that includes men convicted of major new offenses and men returned to prison accumulates men at a decreasing rate until ninety-six months, that is, until the end of the follow-up study. It is a linear function of the logarithm of time since release. While the typical new offense and prison return (judging from the median) occurs before eighteen months after release, the average (judging by the mean) occurs more than two years after parole.

The shapes of these distributions are shown in Figure 17. All are quite skewed to the right. They show that although the majority of difficulties occur during the first three or four years after parole, some are found up to eight years. There is in these distributions little support for limitation of follow-up study to two years (or less) as in much current research in this field. Judging from this sample, a one-year follow-up study can be expected to identify fewer than half the men in difficulty during eight years in any of the three categories included in Figure 17. Not until four or five years after parole can we expect to identify correctly the bulk of the parole sample that is classified into the unfavorable performance category.

An indicant of validity of this prediction instrument is the point biserial correlation coefficient describing the relation of the scores to the performance criterion in the validation sample of 937 men. This relation (.32) is about the same as that found in the sample with the slightly different criterion and a two-year follow-up study. Figure 18 shows that for both a two-year and eight-year follow-up, the proportions of men in the favorable performance category increase with higher base expectancy scores.

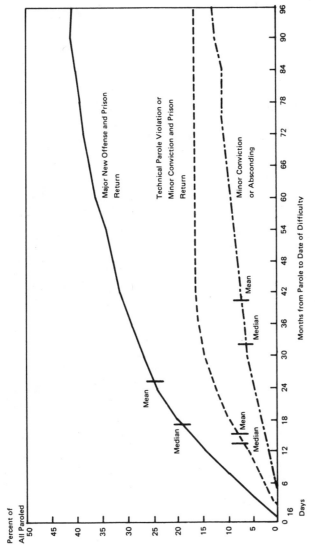

FIGURE 16. Cumulative percents of parolees with various types of difficulty from month of parole to ninety-six months after parole, based on 1810 men paroled in 1956.

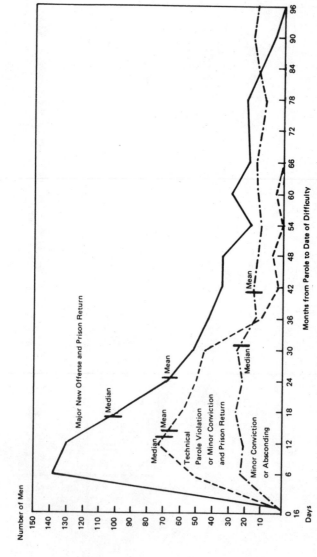

FIGURE 17. Number of men with various types of difficulty from month of parole to ninety-six months after parole, based on 1810 men paroled in 1956.

Much correctional folklore concerns the question of the proportions of parolees who are found later to be in difficulty, variously defined. This study demonstrates at least that the controversy regarding this issue, which cannot be resolved by debate, can be settled by systematic record keeping in order to account for later performance by persons paroled. The data of this study suggest further that the answer to such a question is closely dependent upon the length of the follow-up study.

Two widely held beliefs are not supported by the results presented here. One is the frequently heard contention that most parole violation behavior occurs soon after parole. The data presented here do indicate that parolee difficulty tends to occur early; however, 65% of the difficulties found in this study occurred after the first year, and 40% were found after the second. Difficulties occurred, though with decreasing rates, up to the end of the eight-year study period. The second belief that may be questioned is that a two-year follow-up study after parole is adequate for program evaluation studies. This may be a useful expedient, and it may provide useful information; but a substantial share of offenders back in trouble again with the law may be expected later than two years after release.

Use of a two-year follow-up criterion was, however, supported in the case of the prediction method, in that the measure devised from a two-year follow-up was found equally valid with an eight-year study.

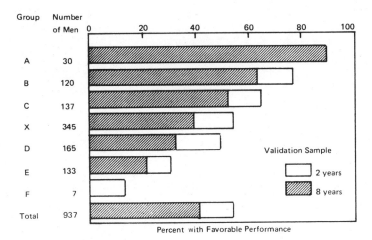

FIGURE 18. Base expectancy from 61B scores and percent with favorable performance when validation sample subjects were followed two and eight years after parole.

The base expectancy measure is predictive of major difficulty as defined for this study and predictive of new property crimes. It was not predictive, however, of new crimes against persons, new sex offenses, or new violations of narcotics laws. This result points to the need for development of methods for prediction of these more specific outcomes.

Classifications of offenders for a predictive purpose, as with the methods described, may, of course, have no relevance to the problem of classification for the purpose of assignments to differing treatments. On this problem, the whole literature concerning offender classifications with this purpose in view is relevant. But the general need, within any correctional agency, for an information system undergirding a continuous search for information related to correctional goals is apparent. The development and evaluation of programs aimed at reduction of recidivism, however defined, as well as improved individual assignment decisions, can be expected only when a reliable system of record keeping, analysis, and feedback has been established. The required classification studies and necessary assessments of relations of offender treatment or of environmental variables to the outcomes that define correctional objectives can be performed only after an adequate base of data on these variables has been established. Only in such a context can data now presumed pertinent to decisions be transformed into information demonstrably useful in efforts to make such decisions more rational.

Utilities in Relation to Crowding

To return to the issue of overcrowded prisons: how can such prediction studies be useful? As early as 1961 one of us collaborated in California with the director of corrections, the Adult Authority (the parole board), and the Women's Board of Prison Terms and paroles in the effort (described in Chapter 7) to reduce an expected need for prison construction. The correctional administration credited these and related efforts with obviating the need to build two new prisons, one for men and one for women.

Emergency release provisions, whether operating by rolling back parole dates already set, selecting categories of offenders for earlier parole consideration, or selectively granting administrative good time, offer the potential of at least temporary reductions in prison crowding. Under crowding-alleviation programs of this type, there is a need to articulate a policy for decisions as to selective early release that is clear, based on explicitly defined criteria, consistently applied, and related to considered judgments as to the purposes of imprisonment. This policy should allow some discretion for decisions in unusual cases, require reasons for atypical decisions, and include a system for monitoring. It should include provision for examination and revision as needed. If these features are needed, then the guidelines policy models we advocate are needed. Furthermore, if emergency release mechanisms are implemented, they should be administered with equity; similarly classified persons should be treated similarly. And, as demonstrated, guidelines policy models can help to achieve at least that result.

Another example of the application of guidelines in decision making for correctional management of prison crowding is given by a New Jersey program created by the legislature in response to prison overcrowding. The program is intended to establish "an intermediate form of punishment between incarceration and probation." Persons already serving time in prison may apply for release to an intensive community program of supervision and community service. Both the selection process and the program are complex, and only some features most relevant to the use of guidelines in the selection process will be mentioned here. Inmates must apply between the thirtieth and sixtieth day after imprisonment. Persons sentenced for homicide, robbery, or sex offenses are excluded, as are persons with mandatory minimum terms. Decisions are taken first by a screening board, and later by a resentencing panel of three judges.

The screening board uses a matrix guidelines screening policy model. On one dimension, there are nine categories of crime seriousness. On the other, there are seven categories of prior criminal record. There is a dispositional line (continue the process or reject the application) analogous to the Minnesota Sentencing Guidelines "in–out" dispositional line (see Chapter 6). An allowance for discretionary decisions by the screening panel, however, is made by a band of one or two cells adjacent to the dispositional line, within which the panel may continue the decision process or reject the application as a discretionary decision. Decisions outside the decision suggested by the guidelines may be made when specific aggravating or mitigating factors are cited from a nonexclusive list. If the decision is to continue, then judgments are made regarding the adequacy of specific factors of the inmate's plan. When these are generally favorable, the person's application is referred to the resentencing panel of judges with reasons for the decision and comments. The project has been started only recently, but experience with a small number of cases has been that most prisoners whose cases were referred to the judicial resentencing panel after this process have been released to the community under the intensive supervision program.

This application illustrates the idea that guidelines may be used at a variety of points in criminal justice processing systems and in innovative programs designed explicitly to reduce prison crowding. The bases for decisions for this release option are reasonably clear and explicit. These include seriousness of offense and prior record classifications as well as ratings of specific features of the inmate-developed program plan, plus some judicial discretion. It also illustrates that the general guidelines model may be used in combination with clinical judgments.

GUIDELINES: A STRATEGY FOR IMPROVING INFORMATION FOR CORRECTIONAL DECISIONS

The establishment of a data base of the character suggested by the illustrations of the previous sections is a requisite for the evolutionary system toward increased rationality and effectiveness of prison management. Such a data base can undergird a systematic study both by experimentation and by careful analyses of natural variation in the system. Problems of improved predictive classification, of more useful treatment-relevant classifications, and of program evaluations are distinctly different but are nevertheless closely related problems that can be addressed together in a systematic search for information to improve decisions.

This search requires, first, the collection of reliable data with potential predictive utility at each critical decision point in the processing of offenders in the correctional system. Studies of the relations of hypothesized indicants of probable outcomes are then required, and those found useful can be combined by various means to provide prediction methods. Repeated validation of such methods is needed. When the validity of such methods has been established, these then may be used in order to control statistically for known biases in treatment groups to be compared; and the comparisons of expected and observed outcomes may at least give valuable clues as to the improvement of practice. Such clues may be followed and more rigorously tested by experimental designs.

A continuous cycle of data collection; information search; program development; program evaluation; and of decision guidelines development, implementation, and revision is required. This is a large task, but if we are to learn from experience rather than merely repeat it, data that truly constitute information useful in decision making must be identified and incorporated in policy models. An evolutionary system of analysis, guidelines, policy modification, testing, feedback, and repetition of the cycle is the principal means available, using current knowledge, to increase the rationality of correctional decision making. Some additional features of the model proposed will be described in the last chapter.

Chapter 9

PAROLE DECISIONS

In 1870, at the organizational meeting of what is now the American Correctional Association, Sir Walter Crofton, who had been in charge of the Irish prison system, was a featured speaker. Crofton believed that the intent of the law was to make prisons "more than places of safe-keeping" and that there should be programs of reform in prison with "tickets of leave" given only to those who evidenced a change in attitude (Newman, 1963:29). Tickets of leave had been used in England, along with quasi-indeterminate sentences (within a fixed range) since 1853; and they had been used first in 1840 in the program of transporting prisoners from England to America in accordance with an English law of 1597 (Newman, 1963). The ticket of leave, as originated by Alexander Macanochie (who was in charge of the English penal colony at Norfolk Island in 1840), was part of a plan for passing convicts through several steps: first, strict imprisonment; second, chain gangs; then, freedom within a limited area; and finally, a ticket of leave resulting in a conditional pardon pending the full restoration of liberty (Rubin, Weihofen, Edwards, and Rosenzweig, 1963). The concept, therefore, rested upon a system of progressive classification and assignment to increasingly lesser levels of supervision and custodial control, as discussed in Chapter 7, with increasing freedom while still under sentence.

The ticket of leave evolved into the concept of parole, gradually adopted over the next half century or so by all states and the federal government. In relation to the sentencing aims discussed in Chapter 6, the utilitarian goals of treatment and incapacitation both were clearly involved at the outset, and so were the concepts of classification and prediction. These clearly are not the only goals that have provided the motivation for developing parole systems or that have given the basis for parole decision making. All the goals of sentencing, however, may be seen to be involved as well in decisions as to whether the prisoner will be paroled from prison.

The paroling decision thus provides another point at which critical decisions about the offender are made. In this chapter we seek to examine further the goals and objectives of these decisions, to discuss the diverse and often conflicting points of view that decision makers bring to bear on these decisions, to describe alternatives related to these goals and attitudes, to discuss the information needs of paroling authorities, to indicate potential avenues for improvement of the process, and to identify some prominent needs for research.

To set the following discussion in context, recent data concerning the sheer numbers of people dealt with by paroling systems can be noted. At year's end, 1983, there were in excess of a quarter of a million adults on parole under state or federal jurisdiction (Bureau of Justice Statistics, 1984). Among the states, the use of parole varies tremendously, from 104 parolees in Alaska in 1983 to over 32,000 in Texas. Despite some movement to abolish parole, or to reduce considerably the discretionary authority of parole boards, the numbers of adults on parole continues to increase (15% between 1979 and 1983).

There is considerable variability among the states in the structure of parole decision making. Thus, in some states (41 as of 1983) offenders enter onto parole as the result of discretionary decisions by a parole board. In others, (nine states as of 1983) offenders are released to parole once they have served a determinate sentence of imprisonment, less the amount of "good time" their behavior in prison has earned (Bureau of Justice Statistics, 1983). The vast majority of offenders, at least through 1983, enter parole in the first way (62%). Those states that use discretionary release vary markedly in the proportion of releasees who are paroled, from less than 10% (Colorado) to over 90% (Michigan, Pennsylvania).

The importance of these data is, first, to indicate the magnitude of the paroling function and, second, to demonstrate the inappropriateness of simple conclusions about the effectiveness of parole on the basis of simple recidivism statistics. We will return to this problem later.

GOALS AND OBJECTIVES

The goals of paroling authorities in making parole decisions involve the sentencing aims heretofore discussed: treatment, incapacitation, deterrence, and desert. They may also involve aims related to the control of the prison and parole system, and they may reflect concerns for fairness and equity in treatment. Thus, for example, the four primary reasons for parole denial listed in the 1962 Model Penal Code of the American Law Institute (1962) bear upon most of these, if not all:

1. There is a substantial risk that he will not conform to the conditions of parole.
2. His/her release at the time would depreciate the seriousness of the crime or promote disrespect for law.
3. His/her release would have a substantially adverse effect on institutional discipline.
4. His/her continued correctional treatment, medical care, or vocational or other training in the institution will substantially enhance the capacity to lead a law-abiding life when released at a later date.

The first goal, which requires prediction, is related to incapacitation and crime reduction. The second involves, if not desert, the reductionist purpose of deterrence. The third is an institutional control purpose, apparently also involving deterrence (that of unwanted behavior by other prisoners in confinement). The fourth clearly reflects a treatment purpose.

That paroling and sentencing aims are similar is not surprising, since in many jurisdictions the parole decision is actually more a deferred sentencing decision than a dichotomous decision as to whether or not to parole. That is, the question often is when to parole, rather than whether to do so, although this varies among jurisdictions, as does the use of parole as one mode of release from prison (Gottfredson, Wilkins, and Hoffman, 1978). Further insight into the goals of paroling authorities, and their complexity, is given, however, by the conceptual development and discussion by O'Leary and Hall (1976) of six "frames of reference" or value systems commonly providing orientations to parole decision makers in their task. Each may be discussed in relation to the sentencing goals outlined in Chapter 6.

FRAMES OF REFERENCE IN PAROLING

Over a period of years, O'Leary and his colleagues developed, as part of a continuing program of National Parole Institutes for parole board members, a conceptual model and measuring instrument concerning general categories of concerns important in paroling decisions. Six general areas of concern have been included in the instrument. Although each frame of reference has been given a short word title, the authors suggest caution in ascribing common meanings to them. The meanings indicated below are adapted from their short summaries, except that we have tried to relate the frames of reference to the aims of sentencing as discussed previously.

The *jurist* value system "reflects an attitude that the parole process is part of the main stream of American criminal justice. It is sensitive to concepts such as due process, appeal, rules of evidence, impartiality, and the protection of individual rights" (1976:2). In relation to sentencing, this orientation for the parole decision maker is related to concerns of fairness and equity.

The *sanctioner* value system also emphasizes exacting equitable penalties for criminal offenses. From this orientation, however, "the amount of time an offender serves should be linked closely to the relative seriousness of the offense committed. He should pay the penalty deserved, no more, no less" (1976:3). The relation to the desert perspective in sentencing theories is apparent: penalties are to be assigned such that their severity is commensurate with the seriousness of the offense.

The remaining four frames of reference of paroling authorities outlined by O'Leary reflect utilitarian aims. In each case they are directed ultimately at the reduction of crime. They are concerned with offender treatment, risk, maintenance of the social order, and maintenance of the prison and parole system.

The *treater* value system is a point of view that tends to emphasize "dealing with the offender in such a way as to lessen his propensity toward crime" (1976:3). This is identical with the treatment aim of sentencing. The *controller* value system names an orientation for which "the risk posed by the offender is the major concern" (1976:3). From this frame of reference the emphasis in decision making is on maintaining external controls on the offender to prevent further criminal acts. It is apparent that this set is akin (or identical) to the sentencing aim of incapacitation or containment. The *citizen* value system "reflects itself in concern for the maintenance of community harmony and the preservation of social order" and in "a special sensitivity to the desires of citizens and officials and to their expectations regarding the appropriate handling of convicted persons" (1976:3). This frame of reference appears to be related to the sentencing aim of deterrence. The *regulator* value system "reflects a concern about the effect of the parole board's decision on the prison and parole supervision system" and is "sensitive to the powerful influence of its decision on the treatment of inmates and the reaction of inmates to those decisions" (1976:3).

The paroling objectives implied by these frames of reference may conflict, just as the purposes of sentencing may be in opposition. Particularly, the treatment orientation suggests aims that may lead to quite different decisions than do the sanctioner, controller, citizen, or regulator perspectives.

Different objectives of the decision maker may be associated with different decisions, but it is also the case that different objectives may lead to the same decision. Different information may be used by different people to arrive at the same conclusion. Thus, the sanctioner may deny parole (or extend time in prison) after concluding that not enough time has been served to provide a commensurate desert for the seriousness of the crime; the controller may do the same from an opinion that there is a need for incapacitation; and the citizen may come to the same conclusion as a result of a belief that preservation of the social order requires this decision in order to support general deterrence or to assure the citizenry that crime is punished appropriately. The treater may believe that a denial of parole may be detrimental or counterproductive to rehabilitative aims in the particular case; and the regulator may conclude that a failure to parole will be detrimental to prison treatment programs in which the offender has been participating.

O'Leary and his colleagues do not assert that paroling authorities tend to be classified readily as to these orientations. On the contrary, they argue that paroling authorities generally share these concerns, although there are individual differences in the emphasis given to the various perspectives. It is clear that there is much room for conflict among parole board members, but there is also a likelihood of internal conflict for individual members as they struggle to reconcile the conflicting demands perceived to be placed on them by their roles.

EVALUATION CRITERIA

How is the performance of a parole board to be evaluated? At first glance, the answer may seem obvious and straightforward: persons paroled who subsequently commit new crimes or are returned to prison for violations of parole rules may be counted as "failures," and the more successful paroling authorities will have fewer cases in this category. Indeed, frequent criticisms of parole boards are seen in the press when such failures occur, especially when particularly heinous crimes are involved. The problem, however, is not that simple.

Recall that in some jurisdictions nearly all persons who leave prison do so as a result of placement on parole, whereas in others parole is the mode of release for a relatively small proportion. Although nearly all who are sent to prison are released at some point, they may be released by discharge when the sentence has expired or, in some jurisdictions, mandatorily released to supervision when certain criteria have been met. (In 1980, about 74% of prison releases were parolees; the range in the use of parole as a mode of release was vast.) Since the parole decision often involves a decision not as to whether to release but as to when to release and in what circumstances, it is apparent that recidivism measures may provide little information on the effective decision making of a parole board.

The problem is complicated by the diversity of legal structures in various jurisdictions and by myriad influences other than the paroling authorities' decisions on the length of time that offenders serve in prison. Legislative, judicial, and administrative decisions all interact as a complex system to determine the time finally served in prison by inmates (Glaser, Cohen, and O'Leary, 1966). Moreover, as implied by the diversity of objectives associated with the various frames of reference already discussed, the assessment of risk for incapacitative purposes is only one of the aims of parole boards.

Consider, moreover, the shortcomings of a recidivism criterion even for evaluation of effectiveness from the incapacitation standpoint. Decisions to parole are not merely decisions to release from prison, nor are they concerned only with the timesetting function. Rather, they are placement decisions: parole release is linked to supervision in the community that otherwise may not be provided. In this circumstance, the parole board member, even from the controller perspective, may wish to release poor risks to supervision if a denial of parole will mean that the inmate otherwise will be released without such supervision and added control. Indeed, if the maximum sentence date is approaching, then discharge, rather than parole, may be imminent. It often has been assumed that a function of the parole supervision process is to permit return to prison if parole rules are violated such that the parolee is judged to be in danger of committing new offenses. That is, there is presumed to be a crime prevention function of parole supervision. From this perspective, the return of a technical parole violator may—if new crimes were prevented—be viewed as a success of the parole decision–parole supervision system. (The demonstration that new crimes were prevented is of course another, different matter; so are the problems of fairness that arise in the circumstance, which always must be expected, of imperfect prediction.)

How are sanctioning aims to be assessed? As shown later in this chapter, there is no doubt that, in general, paroling decisions (as decisions elsewhere in the criminal justice system) operate to require more severe sanctions (if time served in prison is the measure) for offenses perceived generally as more serious or harmful. Again, however, the criteria are a result not only of parole board actions, but of myriad legislative, judicial, and administrative decisions.

How are the treater, citizen, jurist, or regulator aims to be assessed? Simply raising the question in this manner, pointing as it does to the complexity of the problem of parole decision evaluation, is instructive as to the inadequacy of a simple recidivism criterion as a measure for evaluation. The decisions of parole board members, like those of judges, involve the aims of the whole of the criminal justice system.

Generally, the broad, unspecified question, How effective are parole boards? is meaningless. When specific objectives of the paroling authority may be stated in advance, some evaluation tasks may be more straightforward. But nearly any statement concerning parole in general is in danger of being shown to be a false generalization. The goals and objectives of parole boards are as diverse as the criminal justice system, the different state systems, the federal system, and the legal structures, procedures, and attitudes that obtain.

For similar reasons, the general question, How effective is parole? is likely to be meaningless. This is not to say, of course, that the crime reduction purposes of parole supervision and treatment should not be rigorously addressed through empirical study. But such study is complicated; it involves the assessment of the two analytically distinct, yet difficult to separate, aims of incapacitation (supervision) and treatment. And answers to this question also must attend to variations in paroling policies, in offenders and parole officers, in forms of treatment, in levels of supervision, and the like.

ALTERNATIVES

The alternatives available in parole decision making also are so varied that the study of individual jurisdictions to identify decision options and constraints is needed before analyses very useful to individual boards can be accomplished. Factors affecting them, for example, commonly include the location of discretion concerning minimum and maximum terms (that is, in the legislature, the judiciary, or the parole board), systems for awarding "good time" credits or time off for "good behavior," the nature and degree of discretion for amending earlier decisions, and administrative rules adopted by the board itself.

Commonly, the legislature sets a maximum limit on sentence length for a given offense (or combination of offense and prior record). It is usual also, but not invariable, that judges may set a lesser maximum than that statutorily permitted. A prescribed maximum or a judicially fixed maximum will place a constraint on the board's decision, but in most instances some amount of "good time" may be deducted from the maximum. In some jurisdictions, a "minimum maximum" concept is used: the court may set a maximum sentence lower than that prescribed as an upper limit but not lower than a fixed amount (varied by crime class). Thus, in most but not all jurisdictions, minimum terms are also set, either by the legislature or by the courts. This constrains the boards' decisions as well, except that ordinarily prison and parole time both have been considered parts of the total sentence. Thus, if the prisoner is paroled, this constraint will apply not only to the term in prison but also to the total term, including the length of parole supervision required by the board's decision. In a number of jurisdictions, the legislature has fixed a minimum term that may not be changed judicially or by the board; this usually is a fraction of the maximum term, commonly a third or a fourth. In at least one jurisdiction (the state of Washington) the court may set a minimum term, but this may be waived by the parole board. Another frequent model allows the judge to set a minimum but requires that this not exceed some fraction of the maximum term. In other jurisdictions, however, the judge may set the minimum and maximum terms at about the same length, leaving little discretion to the parole board. A still different common model has been one in which no minimum term is set by either the legislature or the judge. In these instances, the paroling authority commonly sets a date for first parole consideration, and this often is the decision outcome for initial hearings. In still other jurisdictions, the judge may have the authority but may waive the setting of a minimum term, thus passing discretion to the parole board (O'Leary and Hanrahan, 1976).

The alternatives available to parole boards are thus exceedingly complex and varied. The decision outcomes may include such results as fixing the date for first parole consideration; fixing the date for subsequent hearings; fixing minimum terms; waiving minimum terms; modifying earlier decisions; fixing parole dates; denying further parole consideration; awarding "good time" credits; fixing the length of sentence to be served in prison and/or parole; or setting special conditions of parole, including requirements of supervision or treatment programs.

In order to understand better how parole decisions are made in practice, it is useful to consider in some detail the frames of reference identified by O'Leary and Hall. This classification can be used to structure our review of the research bearing on parole decisions and to help highlight gaps in our knowledge. As we shall see, O'Leary's classification also is useful for the explication of research models that tie together the concepts of goals, alternatives, and information that are the focus of this book.

SANCTIONER FUNCTIONS

The time served in prison by offenders who have reached the stage of parole is not a function solely of parole board decision making. Rather, it may reflect legislative, judicial, and correctional decisions as well. Nevertheless, there can be little doubt that one influence on the severity of the sanctions imposed by the criminal justice system operating as a whole—and including those legislative, judicial, and paroling decisions—is the sanctioner frame of reference or desert perspective. Consistently, persons convicted and sentenced for violent crimes serve, on the average, longer terms in prison before parole than do others sentenced for crimes not involving violence. The example given by Table 9 shows the average time served in prison before first parole for various offense classifications for 104,182 persons paroled between 1965 and 1970. Offenses involving violence (or the threat of violence) result generally in longer periods of incarceration (the only exception in the table is the case of aggravated assault).

Although the data of Table 9 include only paroled offenders, a similar ranking of crimes against persons versus property was obtained when the time served by persons discharged from prison, rather than paroled, was studied. In Table 10, the median number of months served in prison for four offense classifications was compared according to data

TABLE 9. Average Time Served in Months before First Parole for Offense Groups, 1965–1970

Offense	Number of persons	Median months	Mean months	Standard deviations
Homicide	8,049	58.6	79.3	72.3
Forcible rape	2,366	49.5	68.7	63.9
Armed robbery	12,301	33.1	44.4	40.2
Other sex offenses	3,058	25.4	34.4	32.6
Unarmed robbery	4,169	24.8	32.1	29.3
Statutory rape	878	22.6	34.9	36.0
Manslaughter	1,893	20.8	29.3	27.2
Narcotics offense	4,967	19.9	27.3	23.3
Burglary	32,277	16.2	22.3	23.0
Aggravated assault	6,299	15.4	22.7	24.4
Check fraud	10,975	14.7	18.9	15.4
Vehicle theft	5,739	13.8	18.0	16.2
Other theft, larceny	10,203	12.8	17.3	16.9
Other fraud	1,008	12.2	16.0	13.6

SOURCE: Adapted from Gottfredson (1973).

TABLE 10. Median Time Served in Months, Comparing Data
from 1964 *National Prisoner Statistics (NPS)* and from
Uniform Parole Reports, 1965–1970 Surveys

Offense category	National Prisoner Statistics (1964) first releases to parole and discharge[a]		Uniform Parole Reports (1965–1970) first releases to parole only	
	Number	Median in months	Number	Median in months
Homicide	3,686	48.5	9,942[b]	47.4
Robbery	7,318	36.1	16,470[c]	30.5
Burglary	19,760	20.1	32,277	16.2
Vehicle theft	3,077	17.9	5,739	13.8

SOURCE: Adapted from Gottfredson (1973).
[a] State prisoners: Admission and Releases, 1964, *National Prisoner Statistics,* Washington, D.C., 1967.
[b] Includes both manslaughter and homicide, for comparability with the homicide category of *NPS.*
[c] Includes both armed and unarmed robbery, for comparability with the robbery category of *NPS.*

on first paroles (from the National Uniform Parole Reports program) and on first paroles and discharges from a different data source (the National Prisoner Statistics Program). The offense rankings according to length of time served were quite similar, although the national prisoner survey data include about 40% discharged, rather than paroled, offenders.

Offenders with a prior record generally may be expected to serve longer periods of confinement than those without. In Table 11 the median times served, in months, are shown for the same cases from the Uniform Parole Reports data as included in Table 9. The generalization just made is supported in each instance except two: homicide and statutory rape. In any case, there is little doubt that the criminal justice system as a whole operates in such a way that more severe sanctions generally are imposed when the offender has a prior criminal record. (It should be noted that in Table 11 "prior record" means "one or more known sentences other than prison.")

Similar findings to these have been reported repeatedly on the basis of systematic empirical study of paroling decisions. For example, Heinz, Heinz, Senderowitz, and Vance (1976), in a study of parole decisions in Illinois using multiple regression procedures and treating the parole decision as the dependent variable, found that the seriousness of the

TABLE 11. Median Time Served by Offense and
Prior Record

Number	Offense	Record	Median time served (months)
3,311	Homicide	No priors	60.5
4,738		Prior record	56.9
886	Forcible rape	No priors	44.0
1,480		Prior record	52.5
3,450	Armed robbery	No priors	29.2
8,851		Prior record	34.8
1,150	Other sex	No priors	23.9
1,908	offenses	Prior record	26.3
1,119	Unarmed	No priors	20.4
3,050	robbery	Prior record	26.1
306	Statutory rape	No priors	24.0
572		Prior record	22.3
863	Manslaughter	No priors	19.8
1,030		Prior record	22.3
1,051	Narcotics	No priors	15.1
3,916		Prior record	21.1
8,487	Burglary	No priors	13.8
23,790		Prior record	17.0
1,812	Aggravated	No priors	14.3
4,487	assault	Prior record	15.7
2,482	Check fraud	No priors	12.5
8,493		Prior record	15.3
1,454	Vehicle theft	No priors	12.9
4,285		Prior record	14.2
2,755	Other theft,	No priors	11.7
7,448	larceny	Prior record	13.5
335	Other fraud	No priors	11.3
673		Prior record	12.5

SOURCE: Adapted from Gottfredson (1973).

inmate's commitment offense and the number of prior offenses were predictive of the decision. And Scott (1974) studied parole release decisions in one midwestern state for 1968 and found that the seriousness of the crime (measured as the minimum sentence length) was the strongest correlate of the decision.[1]

If the desert perspective (sanctioner function) is accepted, then one must ask whether the severity of the sanctions is commensurate with the seriousness of the offense. These data, of course, cannot answer such broad questions adequately, but they raise other important ones that must be dealt with if we are to make progress toward such assessments. First, these data and the general question of commensurate desert call attention to the need for more adequate measurement of both se-

riousness of offense and severity of penalty, obvious requisites to studying the question. Second, these data call attention to a critical issue from
the perspective of just desert: is the penalty that is deserved to be based
on the present offense alone, or are more severe penalties to be required
when there is a record of prior criminality? We return to both of these
issues in the final chapter.

JURIST FUNCTIONS

The first discussed frame of reference in O'Leary's conceptualization
(the jurist perspective) dealt not with the severity of the sanction but
with issues of procedure, fairness, and equity. Concern for these issues
has accounted for much recent criticism of parole board decision making.

In her review, Harris (1975:326) sorted the increasing criticism of
parole systems into three categories:

> Many critics focus on procedural failings, contending that present parole
> procedures lack the safeguards necessary for fair and accurate decisionmak-
> ing. Other critics believe that the present parole system creates a level of
> anxiety and frustration among confined populations that is counterproduc-
> tive in terms of institutional management and the correctional process. A
> smaller, but growing, number of critics are questioning the wisdom of having
> a parole system at all, contending that the system is not, and perhaps cannot
> be, effective in achieving its stated goals.

The first concern focuses on issues of procedural due process and
on concerns for equity. It includes arguments that paroling decisions
are arbitrary or capricious or reflect the exercise of unfettered discretion
without due care. The second criticism, that the parole process is counterproductive, asserts that it arouses a high level of tension and frustration in prisoners and "epitomizes for most inmates a system of whim,
caprice, inequity, and nerve-wracking uncertainty" (Kastenmeir and Eglit,
1975). The third criticism addresses the problem of effectiveness of treatment. In this section we consider the first two criticisms (of unfairness
and uncertainty). In a subsequent section we will consider the third.

The concept of *fairness* is not the same as the concept of *justice*. There
may be, however, reasonable agreement that justice requires fairness or
that "justice includes fairness, but is more demanding" (Wilkins, 1975b).
Similarly, it appears that fairness includes the concept *equity*, which may
be taken to mean that similar persons are dealt with in similar ways in
similar situations.

It is trite, but nevertheless true, that equal injustice is no better than
unequal justice; but if models of parole decision making can provide
increased equity—hence, fairness—at the same time providing explicit
statements of policy and reducing uncertainty as to sentence length,

these models would appear to be pertinent to the first two measures of criticism directed at parole.

The concept of paroling models calls attention to the two general classes of decisions made about parole by paroling authorities, individual case decisions and policy decisions. The latter, which may be assured to set the framework within which the former are made, generally are not stated explicitly.

As noted in our discussion of sentencing (Chapter 6), recent attention has been directed toward a guidelines model for articulating decision policy, aimed at providing a flexible and feasible method to structure discretion in several criminal justice contexts. The development of such models began in the field of parole (Gottfredson, Wilkins, and Hoffman (1978). At the time the studies leading to paroling guidelines began, there was considerable criticism of the United States Parole Commission (then the United States Board of Parole), including arguments that its decision-making practices were arbitrary, capricious, and disparate. The board began a pilot project in 1972 that included hearings by panels of hearing examiners, the provision of written reasons in cases of parole denial, an administrative review process, and the use of guidelines for decision making. Previously, the board had had no written general policy providing a framework within which its individual case decisions could be made. The decision making procedures developed were expanded in October, 1974, to all federal parole decisions.

The guidelines developed by study of the decisions of the board in the prior years were designed to structure and control—but not to eliminate—the board's discretion. They were developed in close collaboration with the board in a larger study of parole decision making. These guidelines were based on the research finding that prominent considerations of the board were for the seriousness of the offense, the risk of recidivism if parole was granted, and the inmate's institutional behavior.

Matrix Models

The guidelines used by the parole commission are in the form of a two-dimensional chart, grid, or matrix, as illustrated in Table 12. On one dimension, the seriousness of the offender's commitment offense is considered. Six categories of offense seriousness are designated, and for each the commission has listed examples of common offense behaviors for that category, arrived at by consensus judgments of the commission members. On the other dimension, four categories of parole prognosis or "risk" (of parole violation) are defined. These classifications of offenders were established by an empirically developed parole pre-

TABLE 12. Parole Guidelines Model of the Matrix Type Similar to That Used by the United States Parole Commission

| | Prognosis | | | |
Seriousness of offense	Very favorable[a] (11–9)	Favorable (8–6)	Fair (5–4)	Poor (3–0)
Low serious e.g., minor theft	6–10	8–12	10–14	12–16
Low to moderate seriousness e.g., forgery, frauds (less than $1,000)	8–12	12–16	16–20	20–25
Moderate seriousness e.g., theft, forgery, fraud ($1,000–$19,999)	12–16	16–20	20–24	24–30
High seriousness e.g., theft, forgery, fraud ($20,000–$100,000)	16–20	20–26	26–32	32–38
Very high seriousness e.g., robbery, weapon or threat	26–36	36–45	45–55	55–65
Highest seriousness e.g., willful homicide	(greater than above, but not specified becaue of limited number of cases for establishment of ranges)			

SOURCE: Adapted from Gottfredson, Wilkins, and Hoffman (1978:24–26).
[a]Categories of prognosis based on "salient factor score." See Hoffman, Stone-Meierhofer, and Beck (1978).

diction device, called a "salient factor score," used as an aid in making prognosis assessments (Hoffman, Stone-Meierhofer, and Beck, 1978).

At each intersection a decision range in indicated. This decision range specifies the customary paroling policy in terms of the number of months to be served before release (subject to the limitations of the judicially imposed sentence) assuming that the prisoner has demonstrated good institutional behavior. After the offender is classified according to both seriousness of offense and risk of parole violation if released, the parole board member or hearing examiner checks the grid to determine the expected decision. The guidelines define the usual policy. A range of months is used in order to allow for some variation (discretion) within broad seriousness and risk categories. Should the decision maker wish to make the decision outside the expected range, then he or she is required to specify the factors that made that particular case unusual (such as particular aggravating or mitigating circumstances, unusually good or poor institutional adjustment, or credit for time spent in a sentence of another jurisdiction). Decisions outside the specified guideline ranges are not only permitted but expected, and they are taken in about 20% of the cases, with specific reasons given.

Since it was thought that use of the guidelines could induce rigidity, just as the absence of guidelines could produce disparity, the commission adopted two procedures for examining, modifying, and updating them. First the commission may modify any guideline category at any time. Second, at six-month intervals the board is given feedback from the decision making of the previous six months and examines each category to see whether the average time served has changed substantially. At these policy meetings, the board is also provided with feedback concerning the decisions that fall outside each guideline category and the reasons given for these decisions. This serves two purposes: the reasons for deviations from the guidelines may be examined to consider their appropriateness, and the percentages of decisions within and outside the guidelines for each category can be evaluated to determine whether the discretion range for the category is considered appropriate. That is, too high a percentage of decisions outside the guideline range without adequate explanation may indicate either that a wider range is thought necessary or that the hearing panels are exceeding inappropriately their discretionary limits. On the other hand, a very high percentage of decisions within the guidelines may indicate a mechanical, rigid application. The guidelines themselves cannot provide answers to these questions of policy. But by articulating the weights given to the major criteria considered, explicit decision guidelines permit assessment of the rationality and appropriateness of parole board policy. In individual cases they structure and control discretion, thus, it is hoped, increasing equity without eliminating that degree of discretion thought necessary.

A major advantage of this system is that its development requires the explicit statement of paroling policy. Hence, it is open and available for public review and criticism. Indeed, a central feature of the system is its provision for repeated review and revision. This allows for, and indeed invites, rigorous scrutiny of parole decision-making criteria now in use with respect to questions of both morality and effectiveness. The moral issues may be debated more readily; matters of effectiveness can be tested.

As of 1983, fourteen states, the District of Columbia, and the federal system operated under explicit parole guidelines (Bureau of Justice Statistics, 1983). Does the use of such guidelines result in reduction in unwarranted disparity? Numerous authorities have argued that one latent function of parole boards is to reduce unwarranted disparity; and the originators of the guidelines system posed that as one principal objective. According to the National Advisory Commission on Criminal Justice Standards and Goals (1973):

> Though it is seldom stated openly, parole boards are concerned with supporting a system of appropriate and equitable sanctions. This concern is reflected in several ways, depending upon a jurisdiction's sentencing system. One of the most common is through decisions seeking to equalize penalties for offenders who have similar backgrounds and have committed the same offense but who have received different sentences.

Similarly, Foote (1978) has argued that, despite their shortcomings, parole boards "are able to mitigate some of the abuses of discretionary sentencing." His observational studies in California led him to believe that the parole board reduced some of the intercounty disparities in sentencing and plea bargaining.

Not all scholars are in agreement. A number doubt the existence of empirically demonstrated disparity reduction by the parole board. For example, although Dawson (1969:221) recognized the potential influence of parole decisions on disparity in sentencing, his observational studies found that this goal typically was not deliberately or consciously undertaken in making release decisions.

In the context of debate on the abolition of discretionary parole release decision making, the question of the existence of a disparity reduction function for parole is one of a series of questions that must be raised and answered if the expected full effects of abolition are to be appreciated. It is, within the context of our discussion here, a question raised by the jurist function. The data strongly suggest that guidelines do serve such a function. As Cohen and Tonry (1983:438) summarize the evidence: "All of the studies reviewed that assessed the impact of parole guidelines on disparity found evidence that the guidelines reduced sentencing disparity. Thus, it appears that well-managed parole guideline systems can operate to reduce sentence disparity among persons imprisoned." That parole release decision making can serve such a function does not, however, in itself argue against abolition, for once the empirical question has been addressed, the question must be asked whether it is desirable for the parole board to serve a jurist function or whether alternative mechanisms (for example, rigid constraints on judicial sentencing discretion) are preferable.

On the assumption that with explicit decision guidelines the parole board can exert a substantial and consistent disparity reduction influence without lengthy indeterminacy, some benefits of such a sentencing system over the alternatives merit attention. The flexibility required to take note of individual variability is preserved both for the judiciary and for the parole board. The impracticality of the statutory precision required by some legislatively fixed determinate sentencing proposals is avoided, as is, perhaps, much of the unavoidable shift in discretion and power to the prosecutor inherent in such proposals.

Although these findings must be regarded as tentative due to the limitations heretofore outlined, they do suggest that when the task of disparity reduction is raised to a central correctional objective, parole boards may play a major role in the fairness of the criminal justice process. In a time when new proposals are profoundly altering the correctional role in the sentencing process, the extent to which this and other latent roles of the parole process are achieved needs empirical study, so that the full impact of the suggested reforms may be better understood.

TREATER FUNCTIONS

Because parole seemingly serves so many diverse and often contradictory functions, the broad question of whether parole "works" is neither meaningful nor heuristically useful.[2] And, as we have said earlier, in addition to the complexity of the putative functions of parole, tremendous variation exists in the paroling processes of the many jurisdictions that employ it and these processes are constantly changing. Furthermore, the search for facts about parole must contend with the world of values within which parole is embedded and with a limited opportunity to engage in the kinds of experimentation that engender scientific confidence.

It is true that many statements about the functions of parole are essentially empirical assertions and are, at least in principle, objects of test. Such tests must of course acknowledge the limited set of possible functions that can be examined at any one time and must acknowledge as well the peculiar features of the system under examination.

Little of the existing research on the effectiveness of parole supervision meets all the minimum standards for scientific confidence. One response to this situation could be to dismiss the extant research and make statements and recommendations about parole release on other than empirical grounds. The ambiguity inhering in the available research therefore permits the question of effectiveness to be subordinate to other considerations or, if desired, to be predominant until refuted. Consider the comment by von Hirsch and Hanrahan: "[the] research is too scanty and its results are too equivocal to warrant the inference that supervision succeeds (1979:63)." Quite obviously the opposite inference could be drawn, depending upon where the burden of proof lay, as von Hirsch and Hanrahan also point out.

Although the existing research is far from definitive and common limitations of the research prohibit unqualified inferences, there does exist a small body of recent, good research on the question of the effectiveness of parole supervision.

Five of these studies are especially pertinent because of the similarity of their design and substantive approach. Although none was a true experiment in the sense of random allocation to supervised and unsupervised groups, each used reasonable statistical controls, adequate sample sizes, and defensible outcome measures.

One of the most important studies of parole effectiveness was reported by Sacks and Logan (1979,1980). These researchers took advantage of natural variation that occurred in the paroling experience in Connecticut as a result of a decision by the state's supreme court. When a number of minor (Class D) felons who otherwise would have been released to parole supervision were released by court order without supervision, Sacks and Logan were able to make comparisons with a group of similar class felons released one year earlier but to parole supervision. One- and three-year follow-up periods were studied with a variety of outcome criteria ranging from subsequent convictions and seriousness of offenses to the time of parole failure. Statistical controls for differences in risk of failure between the two groups were constructed and applied in the analysis of the results. And a number of hypotheses to account for the results were systematically explored against the data.

Although the results of Sacks and Logan's research are not easily summarized, it can be said that the study indicated that (1) the eight-month period of parole supervision studied appeared to delay the recidivism of the parolees studied; (2) once the period of supervision was over, the parolees studied achieved a recidivism rate comparable to the unsupervised group (by the end of the three-year period); (3) the reduction was a modest one (Sacks and Logan, 1980:20). The data appeared to indicate that the parole supervision, rather than rehabilitative effects, accounted for the delay.

Lerner (1977) undertook a study of misdemeanant jail parole in New York. Using an arrest criterion, a two-year follow-up period, and a sample that included 195 persons released either to parole or at the expiration of sentence, Lerner examined the success of the postprison experience for these persons, controlling statistically for differences in the risk of recidivism between the two groups. Lerner concluded that "the data from this study indicate that parole supervision reduces criminal behavior of persons released from local correctional institutions" (Lerner, 1977:220). He noted that this seemed to be the case even though the parolees were at somewhat greater risk of arrest because of the greater degree of supervision to which they were subject.

Gottfredson (1975b) reported the results of a study of federal releasees, in which comparisons were made in conviction experience between those released on parole and those discharged without parole supervision. After the application of statistical controls for risk, it was found that parolees did somewhat better during the two-year follow-up period.

Two studies undertaken outside of the United States also are important contributions to the literature of the effectiveness of parole supervision. As with the other studies summarized, the designs included statistical controls for risk classifications.

Waller (1974) studied a sample of men released from federal penitentiaries in Canada and concluded, subsequent to the application of controls for risk, that parole may have a delaying effect on recidivism. The criterion of failure used for the two-year follow-up study was arrest for an indictable offense and/or revocation of parole.

Nuttall and colleagues (1977) studied the effectiveness of parole supervision in England by making comparisons between paroled and nonparoled groups on the basis of a two year follow-up period. Two sets of data were studied, a sample of 381 parolees released in 1968 and a comparison group of 431 men selected randomly from those who had been eligible for parole and who were released but not paroled during the same period; a second group was selected according to similar procedures but consisted of persons released in 1969 and 1970. The criterion for the study was any conviction recorded by the Criminal Record Office during a period of two years from the date of release. Subsequent to the application of controls for predicted risk of recidivism, neither sample produced evidence that parole reduced the number reconvicted in the two-year period. However, when the data were analyzed according to a six-month-long criterion (the average period of time spent by the sampled men on parole) the data indicated that parolees did better than predicted. Since the nonparolees also did worse than predicted, the data are also consistent with the hypothesis that selection effects accounted for the observed differences during the six-month follow-up period.

There have been many other studies of the effectiveness of parole supervision, such as studies of caseload size variations (for a review, see Neithercutt and Gottfredson, 1975) and studies that simply compare the recidivism statistics for paroled and nonparoled groups without a consideration of selection bias. (More general reviews of the parole effectiveness literature may be found in Sacks and Logan, 1979; Stanley, 1976; and Waller, 1974). But if the research reviewed above is regarded as permitting the strongest inferences about the question of supervision versus no supervision following imprisonment, some consistency appears to emerge from the research. First, none of the studies have indicated a lasting effect of parole supervision beyond the period of supervision itself. Second, the research appears to indicate an effect of parole supervision on recidivism during the course of the supervision, particularly in the initial period of release. Third, the effects indicated by the research do not appear to be very large.

THE CONTROLLER FUNCTION

The orientation of the controller frame of reference, which is related to the sentencing aim of incapacitation, is a concern for the risk posed by the potential parole of the prison inmate. Such concern has been, as already noted, a part of the concept of parole since its inception as the ticket of leave. There can be little doubt that although emphases vary, most parole board members perceive this function, in greater or lesser degree, to be one of the main functions of their role. The controller frame of reference refers to some weighing of the assets and liabilities of the person or his or her history and life situation. This consideration has a purpose: the aim is prediction of that person's future behavior or future status in the criminal justice system.

Specific outcomes that the parole board member wishes to predict may vary among parole board members and differ also when different offenders are considered. The decision maker may be interested in predicting outcomes of a quite general nature, such as parole violation, or return to prison, or conviction of new crimes. He or she might, however, wish to predict more specific behavior such as assault, sexual aggressiveness, drug use, alcohol abuse, or stealing. The decision maker may be more concerned with some of these outcomes than with others, some being considered in some sense more damaging or costly. If so, chances are that greater confidence in the accuracy of prediction would be required before deciding on release for these cases. That is, the board member may be more willing to take a chance with a relatively innocuous offender, more cautious when the potential harm is perceived to be greater. The parole board members's predictions may be still more complicated. They often have a sequential nature: if the person returns to his previous environment (or to his family, or gets a certain job, or has close parole supervision, or receives outpatient psychotherapy), then . . . .

Thus, the prediction made often is conditional upon the offender's expected life situation after release.

It must be remembered that these complex predictions are made within a more general context of the parole decision problem, with its conflicting demands from the other frames of reference. These demands may affect the perceived relevance of the risk assessment in arriving ultimately at a decision.

For example, consider these three aspects of decision problems: scarcity of resources, alternatives, and a desire to optimize (it may be agreed that if none of these is present, there is no decision problem). Usually, the paroling authority is confronted with a scarcity of resources. Although such scarcity—for example, of prison beds, of treatments of a given kind, or of parole supervision—may relate mainly to the regulator frame of reference, it may be relevant also to the controller perspective, since the extent of resources available may help determine the risks that must be taken. Similarly, a perceived good risk may not be paroled if it is judged that not enough time has been served to satisfy the sanctioner function. On the other hand, a perceived poor risk may be paroled if it is judged that parole to supervision is preferable to a longer stay in prison followed by outright discharge without the surveillance of parole.

The decision maker may grant or deny parole. Or often the decision maker may continue the case—that is, postpone the decision—for a later consideration. (A decision not to decide is, of course, a decision, and in this case it constitutes a denial of parole at that time.) Each of these decisions may, of course, be regarded also as a decision as to the length of time the offender must remain in prison. The decision problem may be complicated, moreover, by the availability of alternatives within one or another of the major choices. It may therefore be more appropriate to consider the parole decision not as a problem of selection (which may be the usual naive view) but as one of placement. If this analysis is correct, then the appropriate question may not be, How can offenders best be selected for parole? but, How can offenders best be placed in order optimally to achieve the goals of the agency? The former question usually would be associated with the idea that the parole board members' task is limited to (or consists principally in) selecting the best risks, the other, with the desire to optimize that and other competing ends.

What, then, is it desirable to optimize? The answer can be given only by the parole board member, by the board as a whole, or in statements of policy somehow derived within the legal framework. In general, however, it is safe to assert that parole boards generally are interested in optimizing successful parole outcomes (although debate about the operational definition of this term may be expected), in societal protection, in equity, and in releasing offenders at the optimal time with respect to both desert and probable success on parole. At the same time, they may be interested in reducing costs and adverse reactions within prisons and in furthering general aims of sentencing such as deterrence.

It is clear that the nature of the parole decision problem may differ markedly among parole boards; so too, the roles that prediction methods might appropriately play may be expected to vary. Among parole boards legal constraints vary. So do resources. The latter help determine available alternatives. The choices available, together with goals and the information on hand, will determine the optimal decision.

A vast array of methods have been proposed to aid in the evaluation of risk. These range from interviews and subjective impressions through structured tests and statistical parole prediction devices. All these methods, however, may be regarded generally as of two types, each with special advantages but also with certain limitations. These kinds of methods, which have been called "broad-band" and "narrow-band," both have strengths and weaknesses for the risk evaluation task (Cronbach and Gleser, 1957).

Procedures such as interviews and written evaluations prepared by institutional staff (the most frequently used basic data for parole decision making) provide a wide variety of data that may or may not constitute information. All such broad-band procedures are entirely unsatisfactory by the usual, widely accepted standards of reliability and validity for prediction of parole behavior. This does not mean that these procedures are useless for other purposes. The special virtue of the interview is that because it has the potential for covering a broad range of data, it may provide information useful for many different decisions. It does not bear only on the issue of parole risk. Thus, the broad-band methods are capable of covering a wide range of concerns, but they are undependable. Any specific predictions from this wide array of data are notoriously unreliable (different observers are not apt to agree), and they cannot be depended upon to be valid.

The narrow-band procedures can provide more reliable and valid information in respect to specific outcomes, but they may give no information at all concerning other outcomes. Among such methods, which would include objective psychological tests with demonstrable validity for predicting specific behavior, the parole prediction devices such as those described in this chapter and in Chapter 8 are perhaps most directly relevant to paroling authority objectives. Their virtue is generally more dependability than the interviews or other broad-band methods in parole violation prediction. The main limitation (besides exhibiting only modest validity) of these devices is that such prediction covers only one aspect of the complex objectives of the decisions. That is, it is relevant only to that part of the decision process that is addressed to the specific question of the likelihood of parole violation. In arriving at a decision, the parole board member may be more concerned with predicting much more specific outcomes, such as assaultive behavior; and unless the method has been shown to be valid in prediction of such discrete behaviors, it provides no information for that purpose.

Predictive decisions related to the controller function raise important issues about the accuracy of those predictions and the propriety of making time-served decisions on the basis of estimates of future illegal conduct (the so-called false positive issue). We have discussed those issues throughout this book (see especially Chapter 4 and 6) and will return to them again in our final chapter.[3]

Prison Behavior and Parole

One issue relating to the controller function is the degree to which the parole board is able to forecast illegal behavior on the basis of behavior within the institution. This issue is of current importance because the abolition of discretionary release by parole boards is being widely debated: such abolition is, of course, often urged for a variety of reasons (as noted earlier in this chapter). But many have argued that because no factors that are not known at the time of sentencing are predictive of postrelease behavior, there is no need for a body such as a parole board to consider postsentencing behavior in decisions about length of custody (Gottfredson and Adams, 1982). For example, Morris (1974:35) has argued that

> protracted empirical analysis has demonstrated . . . *that predictions of avoidance of conviction after release are no more likely to be accurate on the date of release than early in the prison term* [citations]. Neither the prisoner's avoidance of prison disciplinary programs nor his involvement in prison training programs is correlated with later successful completion of parole or with later avoidance of a criminal conviction. (Emphasis in the original.)

Similarly, von Hirsch and Hanrahan write:

> Some studies have measured how prisoners' behavior during confinement correlates with recidivism [citations]. These studies generally find little correlation. This is not surprising, given that living conditions in the institution are so different from those outside. (1979:32)

Despite the claims that institutional misconduct is not predictive of postinstitutional success, few studies have examined the relation. The available research may be classified broadly for purposes of discussion into two categories. The first consists of assessments of the predictive value of institutional variables. These studies have as their central aim the development of equations that optimize the predictability of parole success. The value of institutional misconduct for such a purpose is judged by whether it weighs heavily in such equations. The second category consists of studies of the bivariate association between some measure of institutional misconduct and parole success. Less frequent than the first kind of research, these studies generally seek an association between the number of rule infractions while in the institution and some measure of recidivism.

There is considerable question as to whether either class of study is capable of directly determining the extent to which institutional misconduct is prognostic of future illegal involvement. With respect to the first class of studies, the extensive research on parole prediction does suggest that the most discriminating indicators of recidivism are known prior to incarceration: age, previous convictions, type of current offenses, and age at first conviction. The fact that such equations as have been developed do not contain items relating to institutional behavior, however, does not validate the assumption that it is unrelated to parole success. To begin with, institutional misconduct items may not have been studied as predictor items. Many of the equations that have been developed were designed to study the effects of treatment during incarceration, and, as a logical consequence, the investigators explicitly ignored data not known at the time of institutionalization. Furthermore, when institutional misconduct items have been studied, they may have been substantially correlated with other more powerful predictors. As these other predictors are selected for inclusion in prediction equations, a large portion of the information value of institutional behavior becomes redundant. In addition, the relative infrequency of serious institutional misconduct when correlated with the also relatively infrequent variable of parole failure may yield low correlation statistics. Therefore, such items may not distinguish themselves in the commonly used multiple correlation methods of prediction, and the extent to which they are related or could, with other methods, bring about a gain in predictive efficiency is unknown.

The second class of studies looks at the bivariate association between institutional misconduct and parole performance. O'Leary and Glaser (1972) present information of this type. Drawing upon data from the federal system, they found a slight relation between the seriousness of an inmate's disciplinary record and the postrelease reimprisonment rate. In a second analysis of these federal data O'Leary and Glaser made a distinction between first-time incarcerated offenders and those who had been incarcerated previously. This analysis revealed that the relation between prison conduct and recidivism was not significant for first-time incarcerated offenders. But for those with a record of prior confinement, inmates with unsatisfactory prison conduct had a 58% reimprisonment rate, whereas those with satisfactory prison conduct has a 38% rate.

The principal impediment to the use of such research findings to determine whether institutional misconduct is predictive of subsequent parole performance is the failure to control for a priori risk. That is, any association discovered between misconduct in prison and subsequent behavior may be accounted for by preprison factors that predict both. This, of course, would then have implications for the issue of delayed penalty setting by parole boards; if a priori risk accounts for the relation, the rationale for a delay in setting the prison term until after some period of observation in the institution loses credibility.

In a study designed to try to overcome some of these shortcomings, Gottfredson and Adams (1982) studied the relation of prison misconduct to release performance for a sample of federal releasees. Three measures of institutional misconduct were studied (assaultive infractions, escape history, and prison punishments) in relation to release performance during a two-year follow-up (follow-up data were collected from both the parole commission and the Federal Bureau of Investigation). They discovered that at the bivariate level, each of the misconduct variables was related to performance in the follow-up period. But, more importantly, they also studied the relation between misconduct and release performance, controlling statistically for a priori risk. Using the U. S. Parole Commission's salient factor score as the measure of risk, they discovered that even "holding risk constant" prison misconduct was often significantly related to release performance. For example, among "poor risks" they found that 68% of those with no prison punishments were successful, whereas 47% of those with one or more prison punishments were successful. Among "fair risks" the difference was 78% versus 60%; and among "good risks," 89% versus 66%. Among the "very good" risks there was no significant difference. Similar patterns were found for the other misconduct variables in the study.

Findings such as these certainly run against the conventional wisdom that postsentencing information is not predictive of postrelease performance. There are certainly limitations to the research, and considerably more study is needed. Further, it is not clear that the ability better to forecast future illegal behavior by observation of institutional behavior should determine where the locus of sentencing authority should lie. But rational decision making about sentencing policy must attend to the empirical answers to what are essentially empirical questions. Mere repetition of the conventional wisdom may help advance a point of view, but it may also simply obscure complex issues and difficult policy choices.

THE CITIZEN FUNCTION

The citizen orientation of the parole decision maker, concerned with the preservation of the social order, is most closely related to the sentencing aim of general deterrence. Therefore, little relevant information to guide decisions may be expected to come from analyses within the correctional system itself. Since the aim of imposing sanctions is, in this case, the prevention of crime by others, the empirical questions to be answered must have to do with the behavior of persons not convicted, sentenced to prison, and considered for parole. In order to understand general deterrence, it will be necessary to study those who are deterred, not only those who are not. A review of this evidence is beyond our scope here; interested readers may consult the National Academy of Sciences report on this subject (Blumstein, Cohen, and Nagin, 1978).

THE REGULATOR FUNCTION

Although it is widely believed that the paroling practices of a board are related to inmate satisfaction or dissatisfaction, prison unrest, and the potential for prison disturbances, there has been little empirical study of such relations. Similarly, the role of the board's policy in possibly shaping inmate behavior toward desired program participation has been little studied. Whether the policies or decision making practices of parole boards are related generally to prison unrest or disorder, as many assert, is yet untested. And no paroling authority has yet, to our knowledge, linked a policy model to prison population constraints. Generally, the concept of the regulator function of parole boards poses important but as yet untested conjectures.

NOTES

1. Among the other correlates identified by Scott, controlling for offense seriousness, were institutional record and age (older offenders served longer terms). Prior criminal record and demographic variables (sex, race, socioeconomic status) were not found to be

related to these decisions. Another study of parole decisions for youthful offenders in the federal system is largely compatible with those cited in the text. Elion and Megargee (1979) were interested in determining the extent to which race was a factor in these decisions. Although race did not emerge as a significant predictor, their analysis of several legal, social, and personal factors discovered that entry sentence, violence of the offense, and institutional adjustment were related to the parole decision.

2. Portions of this section are drawn from Gottfredson, Flanagan, and Mitchell-Herzfeld (1982).

3. For discussions of the problems with predictive judgments with specific reference to parole, see Stanley (1976); von Hirsch and Hanrahan (1979).

Chapter 10

TOWARD MORE RATIONAL
DECISION MAKING

Before outlining our ideas about how rationality can be enhanced in the criminal justice system, we should first look back upon the preceding chapters to see what general statements may be made about the empirical work we have summarized. We have reviewed a large number of studies, united only by their focus on a decision point of interest to our analysis. Methods, analyses, and theoretical directions have varied considerably. The questions that the authors of these studies have asked of their data have been diverse. Can any general statements be made about the whole of the system on the basis of this impressive, yet quite heterogeneous, body of empirical research? Is there any consistency to be found in the ways in which these various actors in the system—citizens, police, judges, correctional officials—made their decisions?

We think some general statements are possible and perceive a good deal of consistency. Of the several recurring themes and common issues that appear in the previous pages, three issues, each supported by ample empirical study, merit special comment. They transcend the complexity and contradiction so often seen in the process from the report of a crime to the release of an offender from state custody. We can first state them briefly and then elaborate their significance to our model in the rest of the chapter.[1]

COMMON DECISION CORRELATES: THE TWO SYSTEMS OF JUSTICE

First, from the host of offender, offense, victim, decision-maker, and situational factors that potentially influence individual decision mak-

[handwritten margin note: factors that greatly influence decisions on all levels]

ing, three appear to play a persistent and major role throughout the system: <u>the seriousness of the offense,</u> the prior criminal conduct of the offender, and the personal relationship between the victim of the crime and the offender. Other factors are also influential (to a greater or lesser extent at various decision points), but none characterizes the process to a greater degree.

Given the widely observed conflicts over aims among the various components of the criminal justice system, it may surprise some to find considerable consistency with respect to major decision-making criteria. Yet, perhaps because they so readily are perceived to be of service simultaneously to so many masters (for example, crime control, retribution, efficiency), the factors of seriousness of offense, prior criminal record, and the personal relationship between victim and offender heavily influence nearly every decision in the process. In nearly every instance they are used as criteria to screen cases from further processing or for invoking severer sanctions.

Although operationalized differently in various studies, seriousness of offense, in the nature of bodily harm and property loss, has been shown to be a dominant factor in the decisions of victims, police, bail judges, sentencing judges, and parole boards.[2] The persistent finding is that *ceteris paribus* the more serious the event, the more likely it is that the offender (or alleged offender) will be reported to the police, will be arrested, and will be required to serve a lengthy prison term.

It is noteworthy that studies at each decision point report major effects for seriousness of offense. After all, each successive stage in the process views only those cases passed on by the previous stage—that is, only those cases that remain after screening for seriousness by earlier decision makers are required to be considered. Yet, at each decision point the cases are shifted again on the basis of seriousness. The power of this factor is thus difficult to overestimate; it survives to be used again and again, despite continuous truncation and selective sampling of the seriousness distribution. At each stage, the gravest dispositions are reserved for those cases, among those that are passed on from earlier stages, that are judged or classified as the most serious.

The consequences of the centrality of seriousness of offense are indeed many. One relates to the perceived <u>inconsistency of aims</u> among the components of the criminal justice system. Such inconsistency, we think, may be somewhat overstated given the empirically demonstrated regularity of some major decision criteria throughout the system. Another consequence has to do with the relations among the various components of the system. Perhaps much of the animosity often reported on the part of the police toward the courts, for example, reflects the fact that the courts, in shunting cases from the system, use criteria that the police themselves believe already have been applied adequately.

A second decision-making factor that appears throughout the system, again with great regularity and importance, is the prior criminal conduct of the offender. It appears to operate both in conjunction with and independent of seriousness of offense. That is, when an extensive prior record is present, even less serious offenses are, *ceteris paribus*, more likely to be given full processing and, when the offense seriousness is also great, to be given even greater attention. This influence is seen in relation to decisions to arrest, to require cash bail, to require incarceration, and to require lengthy prison terms.[3]

The persistence of this correlate of decisions also raises numerous critical issues. Does it signify, for example, simply another measure of "legal seriousness," whereby not the act but the person is regarded as more serious and thus deserving of greater state intervention?[4] Or is the repeated use of this factor related primarily to predictive aims of incapacitation and treatment? What are the implications for fairness of compounding decision after decision on the basis of the same data about previous conduct? We can only raise these questions here, noting that they arise from the consistency of the empirical findings reviewed in this book.

The third strikingly consistent major correlate of the decisions we have reviewed is the prior relationship between the victim and the offender. The major pattern may be stated succinctly: It is preferred that the criminal justice process not deal with criminal acts between nonstrangers. Nearly every decision maker in the process seeks alternatives for criminal acts between relatives, friends, and acquaintances. The gravest dispositions are reserved continuously for events between strangers. Victims report nonstranger events less frequently, police arrest less frequently, prosecutors charge less frequently, and so on through the system.

Perhaps, as with prior record, the victim–offender relationship is simply another aspect of "legal offense seriousness." Some empirical evidence suggests such an interpretation (Rossi *et al.*, 1974). Nevertheless, the issues raised by these empirical patterns are complex. Certainly, crimes among nonstrangers can be just as grave in their consequences to victims as stranger events—perhaps more so, given the increased opportunity for repetition. But the legal system shunts them away at every opportunity. Often it does so for obvious reasons; for example, it may be more difficult to obtain the required cooperation of the victim in prosecution of nonstranger crimes.

One significance of this finding relates to the development and evaluation of decision alternatives throughout the system. Nonstranger crimes comprise a major classification of events for which decision makers repeatedly seek alternatives to full processing. We discuss this implication later in this chapter in conjunction with proposals toward a model for improved rationality in decision making.

When the simultaneous influence of these correlates is considered, it appears to us that, in many respects, it is necessary to speak of two criminal justice "systems" rather one.[5] The first is characterized by what may be considered to be consensually defined very serious events. Here we speak of grave offenses (such as homicide, rape, aggravated assault, and robbery) committed by strangers, but the list must include also crimes of lesser seriousness committed by persons with extensive or serious prior criminal records. For events of these types there is very little discretion exhibited at any of the major criminal justice decision points. The decision virtually always is to proceed with full processing: to report crimes, to make arrests, to charge, to require bail, to sentence to grave dispositions. Although the reason for full processing undoubtedly varies among decision makers (from the victim's desire for retribution, to the bail judge's concern for incapacitation, to the sentencing judge's aim of general deterrence), the empirical result is the same: full processing, little decision variability.

The question immediately arises, therefore, for this first system, What difference would it make, as a matter of empirical reality, were a greater consistency of goals achieved among the decision-maker components of the system? Would the strength of these correlates diminish if one or the other of the commonly asserted aims of treatment, desert, deterrence, or incapacitation were to achieve superiority throughout the process? We think not. Would a lessened conflict of goals have the empirical result of a change in the factors most influential in characterizing the decision making of the whole of this system? We think not.

We think not, since it is precisely because seriousness of offense, prior criminal conduct, and the personal relationship between the victim and the offender are seen to be central features of each of these major decision goals that they are so influential. The harm done by an offense is seen simultaneously (or alternatively) as indicating a more compelling need for treatment, as more deserving of punishment, as in greater need of deterrence, and as more urgently requiring incapacitation. This perception applies similarly to those with demonstrated previous extensive or serious criminal conduct. And criminal acts committed by strangers are at once perceived as more reprehensible and as creative of the fear necessary for invoking crime control aims. Therefore, it may well be that for this system, the endless debates alleging the primacy of one or another of the classic decision aims of desert, deterrence, treatment, or incapacitation could be summarized from the standpoint of empirical reality as "It don't make no nevermind." The ends may be the same despite diverse justifications of means.

But things are quite different in the second system that the empirical studies reveal. This system is characterized by offenses of relatively low seriousness (such as larceny, minor assault, forgery), crimes committed by first-time offenders, and crimes between nonstrangers. Here the exhibition of discretion is vast. Here, too, alternatives to full processing are sought continuously; effort is expended to rid the criminal justice system of these cases everywhere and in any way that ingenuity can devise. Victims disproportionately fail to report them to the police; and police choose not to arrest, prosecutors not to charge, and judges to apply less severe sanctions.

It is within this system that factors other than the three mentioned so far play a larger role in decision making. As the reviews of empirical studies in earlier chapters have shown, when the offense is less serious, characteristics of the decision maker (for example, attitudes) and of the situation (such as complainant's preference) and extralegal characteristics (including demeanor) have a greater influence on the decision.[6] No doubt a part of the influence of these variables is a result of the desire by some to pursue alternatives to full processing when possible. Part may be assumed to be inconsistency arising from a lack of explicit guidelines designed to enhance evenhandedness among individual decision makers. Part may indeed result from the use of invidious decision criteria. It is within this second system that the challenge to control discretion is the greatest and for which the competition among the commonly held decision goals may be both most legitimate and most consequential.

We do not assert that the proper classification of cases into these two systems inevitably occurs. Which events or persons should be dealt with by full and formal processing in the criminal justice system and which events should be the object of vigorous pursuit of alternatives is largely a matter of values. Nor do we believe that the first system is entirely devoid of decision making on the basis of invidious criteria, a circumstance that should be relentlessly guarded against. We do not assert, then, that we have described an optimal state of affairs. Indeed, as we hope the following pages will amply demonstrate, we urge profound changes. What we do assert is that the data now available about the criminal justice process permit this analytical distinction. Although it results in a caricature, it has significant ramifications for conceptualization, for research, and, we believe, for modifications of the process.

THE OMNIPRESENCE OF PREDICTION

Another common feature of every major decision in the criminal justice system is the ubiquitous centrality of prediction. Often hidden, seldom verified, and increasingly denied justifiable relevance, the forecast of future behavioral states (of both persons and the system) is everywhere in evidence. It appears when the police decide that a person should be taken into custody, when the bail judge decides to release pending trial, when the prosecutor applies extra resources to habitual offenders, when the judge sentences for incapacitation (or for treatment or deterrence), and when the parole board considers parole risk in determining length of institutional stay. Goals of these diverse decisions makers may differ, but the evidence is compelling that they share the common problem of prediction.

Unfortunately, they share common problems with prediction as well. In elaborating a model for the enhancement of rationality one must take cognizance of the central role of predictive judgments throughout the system and include mechanisms by which they can be improved. (And it merits saying that those who seek to purge the justice process of predictive decisions scratch only the surface when they focus on sentencing or paroling decisions.) Utilitarian aims lie at the heart of every decision we have discussed. In the pages that follow we outline a defense of their inclusion and a method for their control and improvement.

THE ABSENCE OF FEEDBACK

The third recurring theme that we see emerging from the empirical literature we have summarized concerns the acquisition of knowledge by criminal justice decision makers. At every decision point in the process, decision makers lack the feedback required in the making of decisions that are consistent and rational. Two critical forms of feedback are especially noteworthy by their nearly universal absence. The first is information about how colleague decision makers (and the individual decision makers themselves) have decided similar cases in the past. Police, prosecutors, judges, and parole boards make routine decisions without the systematic provision of such experience. Little else is required for inconsistency. The empirical evidence demonstrates that at every decision point such inconsistency exists. Whenever researchers have attempted to define and measure the concepts of "equally situated offenders" and of "similar outcomes" and to relate them to one another, they repeatedly have found unwarranted variations in outcomes.

The second form of feedback routinely lacking is knowledge concerning the consequences of a decision choice. Given the goal of the decision in an individual case, was it achieved? Did the suspect appear for trial? Was the decision *nolle prosequi* correct? Was probation an appropriate disposition? The evidence reviewed in this book reveals quite clearly that virtually nowhere are decision makers provided with information of this kind, as a routine matter, in order to assist them to improve their decisions. Without such feedback there can be no informed use of experience, which, after all, is the hallmark of learning.

None of these three themes—common decision correlates, the omnipresence of prediction, and the absence of feedback—will startle those familiar with the empirical literature we have summarized. To be sure, exceptions to each may readily be discovered, even within these pages. Yet each warrants reflection and discussion; and each weighs heavily in our proposed model toward the enhancement of rationality, to which we now turn.

TOWARD RATIONALITY

Ten requisites for increased rationality in criminal justice decision making may be derived from the reviews and analyses of the previous chapters. They have to do first with the clarity and consistency of the aims of the criminal justice system. They also concern the adequacy of the available alternatives, that is, of the choices that criminal justice decision makers may make. These are matters of resource but also of the imagination. Another requisite is that of relevant information on which to base the choices. As we stress repeatedly, mere data are not sufficient; to reduce uncertainty, information is required.

The decision maker, besides a clear conception of purposes and in addition to information relevant to their achievement, needs sufficient flexibility—that is, discretion—to use the information in a prudent and humane manner. Some discretion is necessary for the attainment of aims that relate actions in individual cases to actions in other cases. This requires, in turn, a differentiation of policy and case decision making.

Moreover, it calls for explicit statements of policy at each decision point, including standards, rules, and procedures for both policy and individual decisions. The next requisite is that of feedback systems, concerning the application of both general policy and individual decision rules, in order that modifications may be made rationally on the basis of experience. In relation to each of these requirements, there is a need for improved measurement and classification. The final requisite (of the ten proposed) is that of an evolutionary system of policy and case decision making, monitoring, feedback, revision, and a repetition of this cycle—or, rather, a spiral of such cycles. The ten requisites will first be summarized briefly; then each will be reviewed in relation to some issues and evidence discussed in previous chapters. The requisites are:

- Clear, consistent aims
- Adequate alternatives
- Relevant information
- Flexible decision structures
- Controlled discretion
- Differentiation of policy and case decisions
- Explicit policy and decision rules
- Feedback systems
- Adequate measurement and classification
- Evolutionary processes

Clear, Consistent Aims

Are the purposes of victims, police, judges, and correctional officials or of the citizenry as a whole so diverse and conflicting that an increased clarity of internally consistent aims, with adequate consensus, is beyond reach? We think not.

The increased conceptual clarity needed requires, ideally, the development of an adequate theory of criminal justice, integrating the diverse perspectives of the presently fragmented system into a philosophically sound, internally consistent, morally justifiable whole that would allow, and indeed enhance, the learning from experience that is the *sine qua non* of science. No such theory is available. None may be expected soon. Nonetheless, apparently contradictory purposes leap out to call for a resolution, and a start must be made. The research we have reviewed in the previous chapters is, we believe, a foundation for an attempt at such a resolution. The often apparently conflicting purposes of the victim, the police, the prosecutor, the judge, the warden, and the parole board member also have a good deal in common. Therefore we may identify shared or similar objectives; and if a sound means may be found for reconciling the fundamental points of conflict, a beginning will have been made.

The objectives of the victim in deciding whether to report a crime are of central interest for two reasons. First, we have stressed an obvious but nevertheless often overlooked important aspect of the victim's decision: the victim is the principal gatekeeper of the system. Second, it may be assumed that the purposes of the victim may reflect general societal attitudes, beliefs, and values concerning criminal justice. Granted some probable distortion from personal investment, the victim's purpose still may reflect widely held citizen views of justice, of fairness, of equity, of incapacitation, of treatment, of deserved punishment, or of deterrence. Although these victim decisions have not been carefully studied to the extent deserved by their centrality, some evidence on victims' purposes is available.

We know, for example, that victims often decide not to report crimes, that there are marked differences in reporting by type of crime, and that the most commonly given reasons for not reporting have been that "nothing could be done" or that it was "not important enough." The first reason may be interpreted as a commentary on a perceived inefficiency and ineffectiveness of the system; the second is related to the concept of seriousness. Generally, the greater the gravity of the harm, the greater the likelihood that the victim will report the crime. Little is known (and what is known is largely from studies of particular types of crime) about the motivation or purposes of the victim when the crime is reported. But it appears from these studies that (in addition to personal utilitarian reasons) victims have many concerns similar to those expressed by later actors in the drama—for example, crime prevention (through deterrence or incapacitation, sometimes through treatment, or restitution or retribution) or the imposition of deserved punishment. Salient features of what is known about victims' purposes are thus that the gravity of the offense is a principal dimension of concern and that aside from personal (idiosyncratic) utility, the major utilitarian and desert goals of the system appear to be reflected in decisions as to whether to report a crime.

The purposes of the police, when effecting an arrest, embody utilitarian aims as well as that of desert. A principal concern in deciding to arrest is the perceived need for custody, an objective consistent with the goals of crime reduction. The arrest decision, it should be recalled, is one component of the primary function of daily policing, the maintenance of order.

As with victim decisions, the research suggests that seriousness of offense is a major determinant in police decisions to arrest. So, too, is the victim-offender relationship and the complaintant's preference concerning arrest. It was argued in Chapter 3 that such criteria may reflect each of the common aims of treatment, deterrence, incapacitation, and desert, in alternative circumstances.

Certainly, it cannot be argued that an arrest should be made in the absence of consideration of desert; the probable cause standard reflects such a concern. But, given alternative mechanisms for invoking the criminal law, such as summonses and citations, neither can it be argued that desert considerations *per se* indicate any need for custody before trial. Rather, custody functions of arrest decisions are viewed appropriately as being in pursuit of utilitarian aims (for example, to ensure the availability for further processing or to facilitate investigatory activities). It was found also that the decision to arrest may be made to accomplish temporary incapacitative aims: the cessation of an ongoing victimization is an example. And arrests often are made with treatment aims; the chronic inebriate may be a case in point.

Prosecution decisions to charge are influenced greatly by the weight of the evidence against the accused. To a lesser extent, the seriousness of the offense plays a role, yet not so significant a role as does the victim–offender relationship, judging from the studies reviewed in Chapter 5.

Although the use of the factor "weight of the evidence" is clearly commensurate with the personal utilitarian goals of prosecutors (for example, establishing a "winning record"), it may clearly be suitable to desert aims as well. Repeatedly in Chapter 5 we noted that prosecutors failed to prosecute unless they themselves were convinced of guilt. Beyond a concern for desert, however, the utilitarian aims of treatment, incapacitation, and deterrence were also in evidence in the charging decision. Emphasis on habitual offenders implies as much, as does the weight given to estimates of future crime risk in the emerging automated charging systems.

Pretrial release decisions by the courts highlight conflicting but widely supported goals of the entire system, namely, the preservation of liberty and community protection. Controversy in this area, like that concerning both sentencing and parole, centers especially on issues of prediction. The latter involves a fundamental issue of justice: Can confinement be justified by what a person *may* do rather than what he *has* done?

In the case of the avowed purpose of pretrial decisions, one objective appears to be clear and noncontroversial. That is the purpose of ensuring the appearance of the accused at trial. A second implicit but often denied purpose is confinement before conviction for incapacitation. The use of pretrial detention for the purpose of punishment, however, is clearly unconstitutional.

We have asserted that the purposes of the sentencing decision lie at the hub of the entire criminal justice system. The utilitarian aims of deterrence, of incapacitation, and of treatment have been contrasted with the fundamentally different ethical stance of just desert. Are these two radically opposed orientations irreconcilable?

Morris (1976), in a helpful discussion of sentencing aims, has distinguished among three types of principles of justice. He termed these *defining*, *limiting*, and *guiding*. The limiting and guiding types of principle may be contrasted with the precisely fixed punishment that would stem from the application of a defining principle. Concerning limiting principles, he explained that he meant one that "though it would rarely tell us the exact sanction to be imposed, . . . would give us the outer limits of leniency and severity which should not be exceeded. Desert, I will submit, is such a limiting principle" (1976:141–142).

If this concept is accepted—that is, if the aims of just desert are considered to provide the justifiable lower and upper bounds of the severity of sanctions to be imposed, but only that—then utilitarian aims may be sought within those limits. As Morris went on to say:

> The concept of "just desert" sets the maximum and minimum of the sentence that may be imposed for any offense and helps to define the punishment relations between offenses; it does not give any more fine tuning to the appropriate sentence than that. The fine tuning is to be done on utilitarian principles. (1976:159)

By a guiding principle, Morris (1976:142) meant "only a general value which should be respected unless other values sufficiently strongly justify its rejection in any case." He asserted that equality is such a guiding principle. (Although he did not say so, we would submit that the use of sentencing guidelines models, so far as their purpose is achievement of greater equity within a system permitting of deviation, is consistent with this conception of equality as a guiding principle.)

According to utilitarian principles, how can the fine tuning suggested by Morris take place? A general model may be proposed in which this and other aims may be achieved. This model incorporates, however, the requisites for more rational decision making that remain to be discussed. Its beginning point is to recognize that not all criminal justice functionaries (that is, police, prosecutors, judges, correctional administrators, and paroling authorities) must necessarily address the same aims, nor need it be assumed that they must give the same weight to the various systemwide goals.

Thus, the model proposed is based in part on the concept of a division of labor, especially among legislators, prosecutors, the judiciary, correctional administrators, and paroling authorities. Next, it assumes that a gradual reduction in discretion, as the offender is "processed" through the various stages of decision making, may have merit. Third, it is based on the concepts of explicit policy, guidelines models, feedback systems, and evolutionary processes that we include among the requisites for increased rationality.

What is the appropriate "division of labor" suggested? Is a different emphasis on the various aims of the criminal law warranted at different stages?

Legislators may be interested not only in desert but in deterrence, incapacitation, and treatment. But perhaps the emphasis given in prescribing sanctions ought to be on principles of desert, employing this concept as a limiting principle. Thus, in this model a principal function of the legislative decision makers is to determine both the least penalty necessary in order that the gravity of the harm not be depreciated and the maximum sanction that may be imposed as deserved for the crime. This suggests, of course, a presumptive sentencing model, but one with some degree of indeterminancy at the legislative stage. Clearly, we argue against strictly determinate, fixed, or "flat" penalties set by legislation.

If the legislature were to prescribe requirements for modification due to specific aggravating (for example, prior criminal record) or mitigating (for example, lessened culpability) factors, this would not be inconsistent, so long as these were related to the concept of deserved punishment.

Note that giving the emphasis to the aim of determining, within general bounds, the justifiable limits of deserved punishment does not in any way preclude the legislature from prescribing further procedures for the fine tuning necessary for utilitarian aims or from requiring the specific consideration of other factors later in the criminal justice decision process. Let us test whether the concept is sound in reference to the utilitarian purposes. Ought the legislature, in setting the limits of punishment, emphasize desert? Should they take account of treatment, incapacitation, and deterrence?

There appears to be widespread agreement that a person ought not to be sent to jail or prison for the purpose of treatment. This view does not require any diminished efforts toward rehabilitation in confinement when incarceration is deemed to be required; it merely asserts that imprisonment is punishment no matter what it is called and that a perceived need for treatment does not justify punishment. Judge Marvin E. Frankel (1976) described this view in these terms:

> The court agrees that this defendant should not be sent to prison for "rehabilitation." Apart from the patent inappositeness of the concept to this individual, this court shares the growing understanding that no one should

ever be sent to prison for rehabilitation. That is to say, nobody who would not otherwise be locked up should suffer that fate on the incongruous premise that it will be good for him or her. Facing that simple reality should help us to be civilized. It is less agreeable to confine someone when we deem it an affliction rather than a benefaction. If someone must be imprisoned—for other, valid reasons—we should seek to make rehabilitative resources available to him or her. But the goal of rehabilitation cannot fairly serve in itself as grounds for the sentencing to confinement.

Thus, there may be no necessary conflict between the aim of desert, if it is regarded as a limiting principle only, and the aim of voluntary, noncoercive treatment.

Similarly, there may be no necessary conflict between desert, considered as setting general bounds of deserved punishment, and the traditional aims of incapacitation and deterrence. Many will argue that a person may not justifiably be punished for the sole purpose of deterring others. Similarly, many will assert that it is justifiable to punish only for that which has been done and therefore not permissible to punish solely to prevent expected offenses that may or may not occur. But these arguments do not imply that these objectives are not justifiable if sought within the limits of deserved punishment. This is merely to argue that few, we expect, would claim that a person may not be punished in order to deter others even if he deserves it; nor do we think many would argue that a person may not be confined for what he may do if the confinement is first regarded as deserved in any case.

This general argument suggests, in very broad outline, appropriate roles for the legislature, the judges, and the paroling authorities. The legislature, in prescribing sanctions for crime, may reasonably be expected to establish the limits of punishment, principally from a desert perspective. The legislature would state the penalties above and below which punishment is deemed too much or too little to meet the criteria of proportionality of crime seriousness and sanction. According to our assessment, this does not imply that they may not state, as general purposes to be served by sentencing, the utilitarian aims that we have discussed. Given these legislatively fixed parameters, both the courts and the paroling authorities may—and we believe should—develop explicit policy models utilizing guidelines in systems for more rational control and development of decision making.

In such models, the aims of the judiciary, concerning both desert and utilitarian purposes, need not conflict. Even with respect to desert, the fine tuning suggested by Morris may be done in part by the judges. In this respect, it should be noted that guideline models for sentencing usually have included the seriousness of the offense as a major dimension. When such models include elements of discretion in sentencing, either within the guidelines themselves or by virtue of an ability to sentence outside the usual or expected values or sanctions, then there appears to be no inconsistency in allowing consideration of utilitarian purposes. If the limits of desert have been set by the legislature, the judiciary cannot exceed them.

Purposes of corrections are, as we have seen, extremely diverse. It is in jails and prisons particularly that the hard face of desert confronts the utilitarian aim of treatment. According to our analysis, however, a sentence, whether to confinement or not, by itself satisfies the aim of desert. It must, if it is within the limits prescribed as commensurate with the harm done. Within these limits, whatever is done with, for, or to the offender must be justified on other ethical principles and on the basis of the evidence with respect to utilitarian purposes. Thus, it is not necessarily inconsistent to seek, within the requirements of deserved punishment, either deterrence or incapacitation or treatment. In doing so, if rationality is desired, empirical evidence must be the guide.

In this framework, the correctional objectives of security are most directly related to the general goals of desert, incapacitation, and deterrence. All require secure custody when incarceration is the sentence. Therefore it is not surprising that correctional agency personnel ordinarily perceive this as a fundamental objective with a high (perhaps highest) priority. The responsibility for custody, however, stops at the fence of the institution. Beyond the fence there is a responsibility to the larger community, but within it the responsibility is to the welfare of the inmate body. This of course includes responsibilities for safety but also requires provision of services, whether medical, psychological, social, educational, or vocational. In part, these may be related to or justified by treatment purposes (that is, by the rehabilitation concept) when that is directed toward crime reduction goals. In part, however, such services may also be justified by objectives not necessarily related to crime reduction. If the desert aim is satisfied by incarceration and only incarceration (or other sentence), it may indeed be argued that a further deprivation of such services as are available to the free community goes beyond the limits of deserved punishment and therefore is unjust.

In addition, of course, it is clear that services offered in prison or jail need not be evaluated or assessed only in terms of the aims of crime prevention. If the purpose of educational programs is to promote learning, the evaluation of the program must be based principally on whether and to what extent learning occurs. If the education program were to reduce recidivism as well, then that clearly could be a welcome bonus.

The evaluation of vocational training surely should be based, at least in large part, on the future work careers of persons exposed to the training. The evaluation of psychotherapy ought to rely mainly on measures of mental health. This is not to argue that links between such program objectives and the more general aims of crime reduction should not be sought; rather, it is to argue that that is not necessarily the sole concern or even a necessary one.

In community corrections, the emphasis on custody (now termed surveillance) is lessened by the very nature of the enterprise, and the treatment aim is paramount. Indeed, were the surveillance functions of probation and parole to be turned over to the police, whose objectives clearly include the detection of crime as a central feature, this would not be inconsistent. Similar to correctional programs in confinement, the services provided probationers and parolees may be evaluated in part by crime reduction considerations but also in terms of other objectives of similar social services.

The aims of paroling authorities and those of the judiciary are strikingly similar, although different terms for central concepts tend to be used. Judges assign deserved punishments or exact retribution; parole boards apply sanctions. Judges seek rehabilitation; parole boards seek treatment. Judges seek due process, procedural regularity, equity; so do parole boards. Judges seek incapacitation; parole boards are also concerned with estimation of risk and seek to apply controls to prevent further criminal acts. The judge seeks deterrence; the parole board member may adopt in part a citizen frame of reference concerned with maintenance of the social order. The judge is concerned with equity, in part persuaded by the potential effects of unwarranted disparities on the populations of prisons; the parole board member, part regulator, may have the same concerns.

Generally, then, a set of purposes of the criminal justice system may be outlined within a framework in which much of the apparent inconsistency of aims of the various parts is eliminated or at least reduced. The principal difficulty heretofore has been the assumption that desert is a defining principle. If it is not, but rather can only set limits to the punishments that must be exacted, then within those limits there is still considerable potential for the achievement of utilitarian purposes.

When general goals have been defined adequately, then it may be expected that specific objectives *en route* to them may be defined as well. Much work remains to be done in order to specify such objectives and operational definitions of them, more adequately, and these concerns are discussed further on. No matter how clear the objectives, however, and no matter how informative in relation to them the data, there is no decision problem without alternative courses of action available to the decision maker. We turn next to an examination of alternatives.

Adequate Alternatives

The alternatives available to decision makers in the criminal justice system have one outstanding feature, an aspect that gives excitement and challenge to the entire decision-making fabric. It is feature that calls out for creativity and that reveals the philosophical bent, attitudes, and beliefs of those responsible for the decisions. This notable feature is that alternatives are invented.

The whole system, of course, has been invented in a rather chaotic and haphazard process of evolution as society's leaders have sought to provide a system of justice to control crime. Thus, police, courts, and jails came into being and more recently parole and probation. These are major structures, and it may appear that they are now relatively fixed, setting the parameters within which criminal justice decision making must henceforth be expected to take place. Not so: these structures themselves are still in a process of evolution. Much current debate, for example, centers upon issues of the appropriate role of legislation in prescribing the operation of the rest of the system; on the best division of labor of the courts in respect to criminal trials versus other mechanisms for resolution of disputes; on concepts of neighborhood justice centers to deal with disputes by means other than the criminal law and the courts; on the role of the police between service and law enforcement functions; and on whether the paroling function should be retained.

Fortunately for science, we may assume that change occurs slowly. If not, we could not find relations sufficiently stable over time that they might be reasonably depended upon. In the cases of decision-making structures, we could not identify stable relations among goals, alternatives, and information. Therefore we must expect change but we may expect also to find reasonably stable relations. At the same time we must be alert to system change, be prepared to evaluate rigorously the consequences of change, and regard what is known with a healthy skepticism.

Within the criminal justice system as now structured, even without major design changes (such as the abolition of paroling decisions), there is ample room for creation of alternatives to decisions. Examples of recent ones abound at every criminal justice decision point discussed in earlier chapters.

Assistance center programs for victims and witnesses and police community relations efforts may increase the tendency of citizens to report crimes or to seek police assistance in their problems without the invocation of the criminal justice system. The alternatives of the police were markedly changed when, largely through the efforts of one judge in New York City, a policy decision that drunks who were not disorderly would no longer be arrested was made by the police commissioner. An alternative was invented: a shelter and voluntary detoxification unit was established (Wilkins and Gottfredson, 1969).

Expanded use of the summons and of citations, in lieu of arrest, provides further examples of new alternatives. The recent development and expanded use of release on recognizance, discussed in Chapter 4, which markedly changed judicial pretrial release decision options, provides a dramatic example of change alternatives available for those decisions.

Probation as an alternative sentence available to the judge does not exist for many misdemeanor offenders, but it is possible that the availability of this alternative disposition may become more common. An expanded use of restitution and of community service as sanctions explicitly permissible might increase similarly the diversity of sentences that judges may select. Alternatively, the range of alternatives available to the prosecutor—as with pretrial intervention and supervision programs in some jurisdictions—may be increased.

The nature of alternatives available to corrections administrators is directly related to the degree of creativity exercised by them in program planning and development. Within institutions, a great variety of educational, vocational, work, counseling, and therapy programs have been developed in some settings; in others, work may be the only program provided. The development of halfway house programs, of school and work furlough programs, and of other placement alternatives designed to assist in the transition from confinement to life in the wider community provides other examples.

Thus, the development of alternatives may provide essential steps toward a more rational criminal justice system, but clearly the invention of such alternatives is not enough. Providing other choices does not ensure progress toward increased rationality. The police officer, the prosecutor, or the judge may have a wider selection of optional decision outcomes, but this does not yet mean that anything has been learned and does not give assurance of more effective decisions. If the choices are to be made rationally, that implies the presence of information such that the selections increase the likelihood of movement toward goals. This suggests, of course, the need for rigorous evaluations of the consequences of the new alternatives when they are put into place. In order for such evaluations to be most useful, new programs must be accompanied by clear, explicit statements of the programs' objectives; clear descriptions of the programs themselves not only as designed or intended but as actually implemented in practice; and the use of careful procedures to test whether and to what extent the integrity of the plan was maintained and the objectives achieved.

Thus, our use of the term *adequate alternatives* as a requisite of more rational decision making implies not only the need for choices but also the provision of informative evaluations of the consequences of selection of that option. Without this provision, we are not likely to increase the information available to the decision maker.

Relevant Information

A fundamental thesis of this book is that simply knowing that an alternative choice exists does not by itself provide the decision maker with information. That is, the availability of the alternative does not reduce his or her uncertainty about the probable consequences of the selection; that requires knowledge also of the relation of the choice to the decision objective. This is a principal reason for the need for program evaluation at each stage in criminal justice processes, and it is why such research is critical to the improvement of individual decision making.

The general problem of program evaluation is a very large and complex one. Generally, however, it may be said that either experimental or quasi-experimental (statistical) designs are used with the aim of determining how much, if any, of the variance in outcomes (that is, consequences related to objectives) may be attributed reasonably to the program under study. That is the kind of information needed by the decision maker, and each available alternative should be assessed in this way.

The circumstance exists at each stage of the criminal justice system. The victim of crime must assess the likely consequences of reporting it, and on this assessment rests the principal activating event for the rest of the process. The police officer must know the expected consequences of arrest versus citation versus summons, and the estimate should be based on systematic study rather than guesswork. The judge must know, from empirical study, the likelihood that the offender will appear for trial if released on his or her own recognizance. The juvenile judge must know, from the evidence after follow-up study, whether detention versus foster home placement makes any difference in the probability of later delinquency. The prosecutor must know, from examination of prior cases, how assessments of offense seriousness, of the weight of the evidence, of the probability of winning the case, and of prior criminality may best be used in setting priorities for prosecution. The judge of the criminal court must know empirically whether placement on probation, in jail, or a combination changes the probabilities of future crimes, compared with other alternatives. The probation officer must know whether persons placed in treatment category A will respond in better or worse ways than persons placed in category B. The classification committee in the prison reception center must be aware, from follow-up study, of the probable consequences of their placements.

These examples only hint at the complexity of the general problem. Before much progress can be made in examining rigorously the interrelated decisions along the continuum from arrest of offenders to their final discharge, we will need reliable, comparable data about the persons involved, the decisions made about them, and a wide range of consequences of these decisions. Therefore there is a pressing need for data that are uniformly collected along this continuum. Then we can begin to examine consequences of decisions in one sector upon other justice areas and to provide administrators with the tools necessary for their policies and programs.

In order to make a start toward dealing adequately with this complexity and begin to improve the information available to guide decisions, systems are needed that meet three fundamental requirements:

1. Agency information systems are needed, with sufficient sophistication to permit program evaluation feedback routinely.
2. Since it is not feasible to provide such feedback routinely from experimental designs for all alternatives of concern, the systems developed must provide for statistical control of nontreatment variables related to outcome.
3. The integrated nature of the criminal justice system is such that the necessary feedback can be obtained only by the coordination of each agency's components.

Flexibility

A problem frequently encountered with specific decision-making policy is that it does not always fit the individual case. Indeed, the arguments against any general policy often have involved the concept of the uniqueness of the individual, with the argument that such uniqueness implies that no general institutional policy can be formulated to specify adequately the best choice in individual cases. The argument overlooks, of course, the fact that no individual case is entirely unique and also the fact that in dealing with the unique factors of the individual case there can be no experience to guide one in making the decision. Some persons who argue forcefully against any classifications of persons on grounds of uniqueness often also argue that in case decision making it is experience that counts, and they then fail to perceive the error in logic. Yet the diversity of cases—in nature and circumstances of offenses, in offenders, and in resources available—is indeed extensive. Decision-making structures are needed that are sufficiently flexible to permit reasonable responsiveness to this diversity. The policy control methods using guideline models, as discussed in Chapters 1, 4, 6 and 9, appear to be useful because they permit deviation and indeed because it is the deviations that enable the system to provide a learning process.

Discretionary Control

Even though some discretion (that is, flexibility) is required in the decisions discussed in this book, adequate mechanisms for control of the exercise of that discretion is also a requisite for more rational decision making. If discretion implies a lack of control—that is, the freedom to choose from among available alternatives completely unfettered by constraints of law or policy—then the idea of controlled discretion may seem to be a self-contradiction. But discretion can be limited, depending upon circumstances, in such a way as to provide considerable freedom within constraints of policy, and this is what is meant here by controlled discretion.

Consider the bail, paroling and sentencing policy, and guidelines models as described in Chapters 4, 6, and 9. In each, there are two levels at which discretion may be (and is expected to be) exercised consistently with an articulated policy. First, the parole hearing examiner, commission member, or judge has some limited discretion within the guidelines themselves. Second, although the judge may deviate from the usually expected guideline decision, if that is done, then explicit written reasons are required. Thus, there are the two levels of discretion. The first is a limited degree of choice within the guidelines. The second is within boundaries prescribed by policy but outside the guidelines. In the second level there is a further control, that of requiring reasons for deviation. It is this feature that permits, and indeed may enhance, the judge's ability to learn from experience in application of the guidelines. The deviations and reasons are important elements in the feedback system that is essential to the rational review and assessment of the guidelines system.

If unfettered discretion is an ill, but some discretion is a value, then perhaps the decision makers involved may thus fetter their own area of discretion. This could occur in a reasonable way that does not completely bind them within a smaller scope of choices than permitted by the appropriate legal structure. Indeed, *fettered* is too strong a word for the constraints of the guidelines as described here; they do not shackle, but they do add a degree of constraint.

Differentiation of Policy and Case Decisions

Implicit in much of the discussion herein is the need for a clear distinction between decisions of general institutional policy and individual case decision making. Some decisions are made, in any agency, that provide a general framework within which decisions about persons are made. Examples of policy decisions would include decisions to develop or to implement decision guidelines of the type discussed in the previous section. Similarly, the structure of the guidelines, the admissible information for consideration within the model, and the permissible ranges of decision outcomes are all matters of policy. They are not directed specifically toward any individual. The police commissioner may set rules for the use of citations as opposed to arrest; the prosecutor may issue directives to prosecutorial staff as to the selection of cases for prosecution; the administrative office of the courts may establish guidelines for bail amounts; the jail superintendent may require screening procedures to identify inmates for suicide prevention; the director of corrections may define criteria for differential assignment to levels of custody; the probation officer may devise rules for assignment of probationers to differing levels of supervision. These policy decisions establish the context within which individual decisions are made.

Although this distinction may seem obvious, it is clear that it is not apparent to all and that, indeed, decision makers may not always readily agree that a general policy exists concerning their decisions. They may assert not only that no general policy exists but that this is a value. This may be expected particularly when the concept of a general policy is seen as conflicting with an aim of individualized decision making within which each decision is assumed to be made on the merits of each individual (and unique) case. As shown by the reviews in the previous chapters, however, experience demonstrates that analyses of decisions may be expected to reveal an implicit policy even in such instances. It may be asserted that the implicit policy, if made explicit, may afford a greater degree of control and hence an increased opportunity for attaining a greater degree of rationality. Individual uniqueness may not be denied, but the fact of uniqueness should not be a straw man set up to hide either unwritten, merely implicit policy or sloppy procedures conducive to bias and unfair treatment in decision making. People are, in some respect, all different; and in some ways they are similar to others and may be classified into groups; and in other ways they are all alike. The establishment of general policies requires use of the facts of similarities, that is, the use of classification. Individual differences, even after such classifications have been established, require some opportunity for the exercise of discretion.

It may be assumed, therefore, that neither the language of the law nor general policy statements can differentiate persons and criminal acts to such a degree that the infinite variety of offenders and offenses will be described adequately for all decision situations. No matter how clear the law, no matter how explicit the policy, some interpretive functions are required in decision making by the complexity and variety of the persons and behaviors concerned. At some point there must be provision for consideration of the individuality of the offender and the idiosyncratic nature of the criminal act.

Explicit Policy

Discretion is needed in order to provide an opportunity for the diverse response required by the variety of persons, acts, alternatives, and objectives of a given criminal justice decision. The improved rationality in decision making that is sought, however—as well as fairness—requires clear statements of established policy within which that discretion is to be exercised. Otherwise, there is no general guide for examination of the consequences of the decisions made and no avenue toward increased effectiveness of the general pattern of decision making. Therefore there is no mechanism for utilization of information discovered to be relevant to the achievement of the criminal justice goals.

Examples have been provided in this book, in the areas of bail, sentencing and paroling, of the development of more explicit policy. It is not asserted that these examples suggest the only means for development of decision policy models. It may be claimed, however, that there are values present in the decision-making processes of the jurisdictions studied that were not present before the development of policy guidelines. The procedures are clearer, and the nature of the information used is revealed. Therefore they may be debated on ethical or scientific grounds; the process is more open to review and criticism; and the increased articulation of the bases for decisions sets the stage for assessment with respect to the decision objectives. In order that such assessment may be accomplished, feedback systems are needed to inform the policymakers of the actual use of the model.

Feedback Systems

The development of adequate feedback systems, which are also claimed to be a requisite to more rational planning, policy formulation, policy review, and individual case decision making, requires coordinated research and management operations. Models for decision making (for example, the guidelines systems previously discussed) may be developed through a collaboration of research workers and those responsible for and actively engaged in the decisions. The collaboration is initially important at the first step of problem formulation and analysis.

We have seen in these pages that the objectives of decisions may not always be defined readily and that they may vary over differing points in the criminal justice decision process and over jurisdictions (or among decision makers in one jurisdiction). Furthermore, they may conflict. A first step in research and operational collaboration is to clarify the objectives of the decision and to define how these are to be measured. This is of course critical to the later assessment of both the policy model to be devised and the individual decisions taken, with or without the model.

Similarly, we have seen that available alternatives differ among jurisdictions, legal structures, and available resources. These, too, must be defined, from observations of the decisions or from discussions with the decision makers. Also, the data resources providing information relevant to the decisions may vary markedly among criminal justice decision problems. These must be identified as well, or if necessary, they must be created.

Either a descriptive analysis of the decisions or hypothesis testing about them requires a research function that may enable the invention, guided by the empirical results, of a tentative model of the decision. This calls for further collaboration by the decision makers themselves and the research staff, possible revision, and a test of the model in order to determine how well it "fits" as a description of the present decision processes. The policy model may be implemented in practice when it is acceptable to the decision makers. The research operation may proceed to examine the implications of the model, while the operational monitoring of its use sets the stage for further examination and possible revision.

Thus, a policy development, implementation, examination, and revision cycle may be established in which a process of repeated examination and revision is a central feature. An evolutionary process has been designed that is a requisite to more rational policy development.

A second evolutionary process, distinct from that just described but related to it, is also essential. It has to do with the utilitarian aims of the criminal justice system and the central issues of effectiveness in achieving those crime control purposes.

We have found it necessary to assert repeatedly throughout this book that demonstrably relevant information with respect to the utilitarian aims of treatment, deterrence, and incapacitation is simply not available to guide decisions toward greater rationality. This lack is not a function of unavailable technology; procedures for assessing relevance are available. It is not a result of inability to conceptualize the problem adequately; the utilitarian aims are reasonably clear and may be defined readily. It is not due to inadequate funding of the criminal justice system; large sums are spent annually to detect, arrest, convict, confine, or supervise offenders against the law. It does not arise from a lack of caring; the public and criminal justice functionaries all decry the ineffectiveness of present crime control measures. Rather, it is due to a lack of data, information systems, and analyses adequate to the task of informing decision makers, through feedback systems. Only with such feedback systems can there be an increase in the rationality of decision making.

Decision makers throughout the criminal justice process have in common that they all make decisions about offenders against the law. What they share in addition is a frustrating lack of feedback on the consequences of their decisions. Although it has been known for half a century that learning does not occur in the absence of knowledge of the results of one's actions, adequate information systems have not yet been developed to provide such feedback.

Individual-based tracking systems are needed to enable the adequate follow-up and analyses of offenders and of decisions affecting their placement, from start to finish, in the criminal justice process. Some good starts toward such a system have been made, and we have described some of them elsewhere (Gottfredson and Gottfredson, 1980). But the necessary integrated system of accounting that could provide a sound basis in reliable data to permit the needed analyses has not yet been developed.

Adequate Measurement

A first illustration of the yet unshaped state of the measurement art in criminal justice may be given by pointing to the concept of seriousness of offense. The idea that criminal acts vary in seriousness has appeared in each of the chapters of this book as a concept that provides an important dimension in many critical criminal justice decisions. Variation in seriousness of the offense appears to be an important factor for understanding the gatekeeping decisions of victims as to whether to invoke the criminal justice process. It appears to be a key consideration in the decision making of police, judges, corrections administrators, and parole boards. Yet only crude measures based on assumptions that may be questioned are available for its assessment (Gottfredson, Young, and Laufer, 1980).

A related concept, equally important to decision making in criminal justice (and especially sentencing and parole), is that of the severity of sanctions. In the case of this concept, measurement is still more primitive than in the matter of seriousness of the offense. Until more adequate measures are available, the lofty concepts and high ideals of requiring sanctions commensurate with the gravity of harm done may gain philosophical acceptance but are certain to be frustrated in application. How can harm and punishment be evaluated adequately if the measurement of both is flawed or primitive?

These are but striking examples. The general problems of measurement, even of key concepts, call for research at every stage of decision making in the criminal justice process. Given the importance and complex purposes of these decisions, it is remarkable that the objectives still must be so crudely measured.

Similarly, the need for development of more useful procedures for offender classifications is apparent. The general problems of what works for deterrence, incapacitation, or treatment may not be solved for decision making until the requisite classification methods have been developed, shown to be demonstrably relevant, and incorporated into routine agency information systems. Work toward improvement of classification for predictive purposes must continue as well. Besides adding potentially relevant information for both policy and individual decisions, such classification tools are needed in order to aid in evaluation of the effectiveness of decisions.

Evolutionary Processes

Both science and criminal justice management must proceed toward a greater rationality by successive approximations. The increased rationality desired is not apt to come by revolution; it can be achieved by evolution. This requires, however, attention to establishing a framework within which acceptable decision processes may evolve and from which gains in knowledge can be made. The process envisioned is a dynamic one, with no firm answers and only partial perhaps temporary, gains. Its central features are the articulation of problems and of policies, procedures to structure and control decision making while assessing the consequences of alternative actions, repeated analysis of the relations of the alternative choices to the purposes of the decisions, and a continuous search for knowledge to inform those responsible for the entire process.

FRAIL WAND, PROFOUND SPELL

These aspirations toward greater rationality may, at this stage of our ignorance, seem at worst grandiose and at best unfeasible. The requisites specified are easy to recite but exceedingly difficult to achieve. Yet we have asserted the need mainly for application of scientific methods to the analysis of decisions throughout the criminal justice process. In a world of values and ethics, science may play only a part, but that part may be profound.

PARADOX

Not truth, nor certainty. These I foreswore
In my novitiate, as young men called
To holy orders must abjure the world.
"If . . . , then . . . ," this only I assert;
And my successes are but pretty chains
Linking twin doubts, for it is vain to ask
If what I postulate be justified,
Or what I prove possess the stamp of fact.
Yet bridges stand, and men no longer crawl
In two dimensions. And such triumphs stem
In no small measure from the power this game,
Played with the thrice-attenuated shades
Of things, has over their originals.
How frail the wand, but how profound the spell![7]

—C. Wylie, Jr.

NOTES

1. The empirical support for the assertions that follow is to be found throughout the earlier chapters, to which the reader is referred.
2. As discussed in Chapter 5, the prosecutor's decision to charge may stand in contrast to the general finding that seriousness of offense is a persistent major criterion in decision making.
3. The influence of known prior criminal conduct has not been studied in relation to victims' decisions to report a crime.
4. Several desert theorists, most notably von Hirsch, argue that prior criminal conduct does indeed make an offense more blameworthy and thus, from the point of view purely of desert, can be a factor legitimately used to increase penalties. This position

has been criticized on the grounds that prior record is a characteristic of persons, not acts, and therefore is antithetical to the desert perspective. Also, it has been noted that von Hirsch's position to let prior record enhance penalties could provide simply a rationalization for the use of the best predictive data while eschewing any role for prediction in sentencing.

5. For a comparable distinction predating our own, see Vorenberg (1976).

6. We suspect that the controversy in the sociological literature that argues the relative importance of *legal* versus *extralegal* attributes in criminal justice decisions may be resolved by the distinction made here.

7. C. Wylie, Jr., "Paradox," *Scientific Monthly*, 67:63 (1948, July 1). Reprinted by permission.

BIBLIOGRAPHY

Abrams, N. "Internal Policy: Guiding the Exercise of Prosecutorial Discretion." *U.C.L.A. Law Review* 19:1 (1971).

———. "Prosecutorial Charge Decisions Systems." *University of California Law Review* 21:1 (1975).

Adams, S. "Some Findings From Correctional Caseload Research." *Federal Probation* 31:48 (1967).

Aichhorn, A. *Wayward Youth*. New York: Viking Press, 1938.

Albanese, J. S. "Predicting Probation Outcomes: An Assessment of Critical Issues." In D. M. Gottfredson, J. O. Finckenauer, and C. Rauh, *Probation on Trial*, ch. 4. Newark, New Jersey: School of Criminal Justice, Rutgers University, 1977.

Alexander, G.; M. Glass; P. King; J. Palermo; J. Roberts; and A. Schury. "A Study of the Administration of Bail in New York City." *University of Pennsylvania Law Review* 106:685 (1958).

Alschuler, A. "The Prosecutor's Role in Plea Bargaining." *University of Chicago Law Review* 36:50 (1968).

American Bar Association. *Standards Relating to the Prosecution and the Defense Function*. Approved draft. New York: Institute for Judicial Administration, 1971.

———. *Standards Relating to the Urban Police Function*. Approved Draft. Chicago, 1973.

American Law Institute. *Model Penal Code*. Philadelphia, 1972.

Angel, A.; E. Green; H. Kaufman; and E. Van Loon. "Preventive Detention: An Empirical Analysis." *Harvard Civil Rights–Civil Liberties Law Review* 6:301 (1971).

Ares, C.; A. Rankin; and H. Sturz. "The Manhattan Bail Project: An Interim Report on the Use of Pre-Trial Parole." *New York University Law Review* 38:67 (1963).

Asher and Orleans. "Criminal Citation as a Post-Arrest Alternative to Custody for Certain Offenses." Paper cited in M. Berger, "Police Field Citations in New Haven." *Wisconsin Law Review*, 2:382 (1972).

Attorney General's Task Force on Violent Crime, Final Report. Washington, D.C.: U.S. Department of Justice, 1981.

Babst, D. V., and J. W. Mannering. "Probation versus Imprisonment for Similar Types of Offenders: A Comparison by Subsequent Violators." *Journal of Research in Crime and Delinquency* 2:60 (1965).

Bailey, W. C. "Correctional Outcome: An Evaluation of 100 Reports." *Journal of Criminal Law, Criminology, and Police Science* 57:153–60 (1966).

Banks, E. "Reconviction of Young Offenders." *Current Legal Problems* 17:74 (1964).

Barry, D., and A. Greer. "Sentencing Versus Prosecutorial Discretion: The Application of a New Disparity Measure." *Journal of Research in Crime and Delinquency* 18:254 (1981).

Beeley, A. *The Bail System in Chicago*. Chicago: University of Chicago Press, 1927.

Bercal, T. "Calls for Police Assistance: Consumer Demands for Governmental Service." *American Behavioral Scientist* 13:681 (1970).

Berk, R.; S. Berk; P. Newton; and D. Loseke. "Cops on Call: Summoning the Police to the Scene of Spousal Violence," *Law and Society Review* 18–3:479–498 (1984).

Bernstein, I.; E. Kick; J. Leung; and B. Schulz. "Charge Reduction: An Intermediary Stage in the Process of Labeling Criminal Defendants." *Social Forces* 56:363 (1977).

Bernstein, I.; W. Kelly; and P. Doyle. "Societal Reaction to Deviants: The Case of Criminal Defendants." *American Sociological Review* 42:743 (1977).

Bittner, E. "The Police on Skid-Row: A Study of Peacekeeping." *American Sociological Review* 32:699 (1967).

———. *The Functions of the Police in Modern Society*. Chevy Chase, Maryland: Center for Studies in Crime and Delinquency, Public Health Service Publication No. 2059, 1970.

———. "Florence Nightingale in Pursuit of Willie Sutton: A Theory of the Police." In H. Jacob, ed., *The Potential for Reform in Criminal Justice*. Beverly Hills: Sage, 1974.

———. *The Functions of the Police in Modern Society*. New York: Aronson, 1975.

Black, D. "Police Control of Juveniles." *American Sociological Review* 35:63 (1970).

———. "The Social Organization of Arrest." *Stanford Law Review* 23:1087 (1971).

———. *The Behavior of Law*. New York: Academic Press, 1976.

Black, D., and A. Reiss. "Patterns of Behavior in Police and Citizen Transactions." In *Studies of Crime and Law Enforcement in Major Metropolitan Areas*. Washington, D.C.: Government Printing Office, 1967.

Bloch, R. "Why Notify the Police? The Victim's Decision to Notify the Police of An Assault." *Criminology* 11:555 (1974).

Block, H. A., and F. T. Flynn. *Delinquency*. New York: Random House, 1956.

Blumstein, A. "Sentencing Reforms: Impacts and Implications." *Judicature* 68:129 (1984).

Blumstein, A.; J. Cohen; and D. Nagin, eds. *Deterrence and Incapacitation: Estimating the Effects of Criminal Sanctions on Crime Rates.* Washington, D.C.: National Academy of Sciences, 1978.

———; J. Cohen; S. Martin; and M. Tonry, eds. *Research on Sentencing: The Search for Reform.* Washington, D.C.: National Academy Press, 1983.

Bock, E., and C. Frazier. "Official Standards versus Actual Criteria in Bond Dispositions." *Journal of Criminal Justice* 5:321 (1977).

Boland, B. *The Prosecution of Felony Arrests.* Cited in Bureau of Justice Statistics (1983).

Brereton D., and J. Casper. "Does It Pay To Plead Guilty? Differential Sentencing and the Functioning of Criminal Courts." *Law and Society Review* 16:1:45–70 (1981–1982).

Brosi, K. *A Cross-City Comparison of Felony Case Processing.* Washington, D.C.: Institute for Law and Social Research, 1979.

Bruce, A. A.; E. W. Burgess; and A. J. Harno. *The Working of the Indeterminate Sentence Law and the Parole System in Illinois.* Springfield: Illinois Parole Board, 1928.

———; A. J. Harno; E. W. Burgess; and J. Landesco. *Parole and the Indeterminate Sentence.* Springfield: Illinois Parole Board, 1928.

Burdman, M. Increased Correctional Effectiveness Progress Statement. Memorandum from the California Department of Correction to the California Senate Finance Subcommittee and the California Assembly Ways and Means Subcommittee. January 1, 1983. Unpublished.

Bureau of Justice Statistics. *Setting Prison Terms.* Washington, D.C.: U.S. Department of Justice. 1983.

———. *The Prevalence of Guilty Pleas.* Washington, D.C.: U.S. Department of Justice. 1984.

———. *Probation and Parole 1983.* Washington, D.C.: U.S. Department of Justice. 1984.

———. *Prisoners in 1984.* Washington, D.C.: U.S. Department of Justice. 1985.

Burnham, R. W. "Modern Decision Theory and Corrections." In D. M. Gottfredson, ed., *Decision-Making in the Criminal Justice System: Reviews and Essays,* ch. 7. Washington, D.C.: U.S. Government Printing Office, 1975.

Bynum, T. "An Empirical Exploration of the Factors Influencing Release on Recognizánce," Ph.D. dissertation, Florida State University, 1976.

Carter, R. M. *Presentence Report Handbook.* Washington, D.C.: U.S. Government Printing Office, 1978.

Carter, R., and M. Klein. *Back on the Street—The Diversion of Juvenile Offenders.* Englewood Cliffs, New Jersey: Prentice-Hall, 1976.

———, and L. T. Wilkins. "Some Factors in Sentencing Policy." *Journal of Criminal Law, Criminology, and Police Science* 58:503 (1967).

Casper, J. *American Criminal Justice: The Defendant's Perspective.* Englewood Cliffs: Prentice-Hall, 1972.

———. "Reformers Versus Abolitionists: Some Notes For Further Research on Plea Bargaining." *Law and Society Review,* 13:567 (1979).

Casper, J.; D. Brereton; and D. Neal. *The Implementation of the California Deter-minate Sentencing Law.* Washington, D.C.: U.S. Department of Justice, 1982.

Chiricos, T., and G. Waldo. "Socioeconomic Status and Criminal Sentencing: An Empirical Assessment of a Conflict Proposition." *American Sociological Review* 40:753 (1975).

Chute, C. L. "Probation and Suspended Sentence." *Journal of the American In-stitute of Criminal Law and Criminology* 12:558 (1922).

Clarke, S. *The Bail System in Charlotte: 1971–1973.* Charlotte-Mecklenburg Crim-inal Justice Pilot Project. Chapel Hill, North Carolina: Institute of Govern-ment, 1974.

———. "North Carolina's Determinate Sentencing Legislation." *Judicature* 68(4):141 (1984).

Clarkson, J. S. "Probation Improvement Program." Southfield, Michigan: Forty-Sixth District Court, 1974. Mimeograph.

Cohen, J. "Selective Incapacitation: An Assessment." *University of Illinois Law Review* 1984(2):253 (1984).

Cohen, J., and M. Tonry. "Sentencing Reforms and Their Impacts." In A. Blum-stein *et al., Research on Sentencing.* Washington, D.C.: National Academy Press, 1983.

Cohen, L., and J. Kluegel. "Determinants of Juvenile Court Dispositions: As-criptive and Achieved Factors in Two Metropolitan Courts." *American So-ciological Review* 43:162 (1978).

———. "Selecting Delinquents for Adjudication." *Journal of Research in Crime and Delinquency* 16:143 (1979).

Cohen, L., and R. Stark. "Discriminatory Labeling and the Five-Finger Dis-count." *Journal of Research in Crime and Delinquency* 11:25 (1974).

Cole, G. "The Decision to Prosecute." *Law and Society Review* 4:313 (1970).

Comment. "Prosecutorial Discretion in the Initiation of Criminal Complaints." *Southern California Law Review* 42:518 (1969).

Comptroller General of the United States. *The Federal Bail Process Fosters Inequities.* Report to the Congress, GGD-78-105. October 18, 1978.

Conklin, J., and D. Meagher. "The Percentage Deposit Bail System: An Alter-native to the Professional Bondsman." *Journal of Criminal Justice* 1:299 (1973).

Cormack, R. "A Review of Classification." *Journal of the Royal Statistical Society* 4:321 (1971).

Cronback, L., and G. C. Gleser. *Psychological Tests and Personnel Decisions.* Urbana: University of Illinois Press, 1957.

Cumming, E.; I. Cumming; and L. Edel. "Policeman as Philosopher, Guide, and Friend." *Social Problems* 12:276 (1965).

Cureton, E. E. "Recipe for a Cookbook." *Psychological Bulletin* 54:494 (1957).

Daudistel, H. "On the Elimination of Plea-Bargaining: The El Paso Experiment." In McDonald and Cramer, eds., *Plea Bargaining.* Lexington: D.C. Heath, 1980.

Davis, K. *Police Discretion.* St. Paul: West Publishing, 1975. Discretionary Justic-

Dawson, R. *Sentencing: The Decision as to Type, Length and Conditions of Sen-tence.*Chicago: Little, Brown, 1969.

Dershowitz, A. "Imprisonment on Judicial Hunch: The Case Against Pretrial Prevention Detention." *Prison Journal* 1:12 (1970a).

―――. "The Law of Dangerousness: Some Fictions About Prediction." *Journal of Legal Studies* 23:24 (1970b).

―――. *Fair and Certain Punishment: Report of the Twentieth Century Fund Task Force on Criminal Sentencing.* New York: McGraw-Hill, 1976.

Dill, F. "Bail and Bail Reform: A Sociological Study." Ph.D. dissertation, University of California at Berkeley, 1972.

Dunbar, W. "Provision of Base Expectancy Information to the Adult Authority." *California Department of Corrections Administrative Bulletin* 61/115. Sacramento: Department of Correction, December, 1961.

Dunford, F. "Police Diversion: An Illusion?" *Criminology 15:335 (1977).*

Ebbesen, E., and V. Konecni. "Decisionmaking and Information Integration in the Courts: The Setting of Bail." *Journal of Personality and Social Psychology* 32:805 (1975).

Eisenstein, J., and H. Jacob. *Felony Justice.* Boston: Little, Brown, 1977.

Elion, V., and E. Megargee. "Racial Identity, Length of Incarceration, and Parole Decisionmaking." *Journal of Research in Crime and Delinquency* 16:232 (1979).

Ennis, P. *Criminal Victimization in the United States.* Field Surveys II. President's Commission on Law Enforcement and Administration of Justice. Washington, D.C.: Government Printing Office, 1967.

Feeley, M. *Court Reform on Trial: Why Simple Solutions Fail.* New York: Basic Books, 1983.

―――. "Plea Bargaining and the Structure of the Criminal Process." in G. Cole, ed., *Criminal Justice,* 4th ed. Monterey, California: Brooks/Cole, 1984.

Feeley, M., and J. McNaughton. "The Pre-Trial Process in the Sixth Circuit." New Haven, 1974. Mimeograph.

Feeney, F. "Citation in Lieu of Arrest: The New California Law." *Vanderbilt Law Review* 25:36 (1972).

Feinberg, J. *Doing and Deserving: Essays on the Theory of Responsibility.* Princeton, New Jersey: Princeton University Press, 1970.

Ferry, J., and M. Kravitz. *Issues in Sentencing: A Selected Bibliography.* Washington, D.C.: National Institute on Law Enforcement and Criminal Justice, 1978.

Figueira-McDonough, J. "Gender Differences in Informal Processing." *Journal of Research in Crime and Delinquency* 22:2:101–133 (1985).

Finckenauer, J. "Some Factors in Police Discretion and Decisionmaking." *Journal of Criminal Justice* 4:29 (1976).

Fleming, R. *Punishment Before Trial.* New York: Longman, 1982.

Fogel, D. *We Are the Living Proof: The Justice Model for Corrections.* Cincinnati: Anderson, 1975.

Foote, C. "The Coming Constitutional Crisis in Bail." *University of Pennsylvania Law Review* 113:959 (1965).

―――. "Deceptive Determinate Sentencing." In National Institute on Law Enforcement and Criminal Justice, *Determinate Sentencing.* Washington, D.C.: U.S. Department of Justice, 1978.

Foote, C.; J. Markle; and E. Woolley. "Compelling Appearance in Court: Administration of Bail in Philadelphia." *University of Pennsylvania Law Review* 102:1031 (1954).

Ford, R. C., and S. R. Johnson. "Probation Prediction Models and Recidivism." Geneva, Illinois: Kane County Diagnostic Center, 1976. Mimeograph.

Forst, B. "Prosecution and Sentencing." In J. Q. Wilson, ed., *Crime and Public Policy*. San Francisco: Institute for Contemporary Studies, 1983.

———. "Selective Incapacitation: A Sheep in Wolf's Clothing? *Judicature* 68:4:153 (1984).

Forst, B., and K. Brosi. "A Theoretical and Empirical Analysis of the Prosecutor." *Journal of Legal Studies* 6:177 (1977).

Forst, B.; J. Lucianovic; and S. Cox. *What Happens After Arrest?* Institute for Law and Social Research. Washington, D.C.: U.S. Government Printing Office, 1977.

Frankel, M. E. Sentencing Memorandum 75 Cr. 785, U.S. District Court, Southern District of New York, June 17, 1976, as cited in N. Morris (1976) at 142–143.

Frase, R. "The Decision to File Federal Criminal Charges." *University of Chicago Law Review* 47:246 (1980).

Frazier, C.; E. Block; and J. Hensetta. "Pretrial Release and Bail Decisions: The Effects of Legal, Community, and Personal Variables." *Criminology* 18:2:162–181 (1980).

Freed, D., and P. Wald. *Bail in the United States: 1964*. Washington, D.C.: U.S. Department of Justice and the Vera Foundation, 1964.

Friedman, L. "Plea Bargaining in Historical Perspective." *Law and Society Review*, 13:247 (1979).

Friedrich, R. "The Impact of Organizational, Individual, and Situational Factors on Police Behavior." Ph.D. dissertation, University of Michigan, 1977.

Garofalo, J. *The Police and Public Opinion*. National Criminal Justice Information and Statistics Service. Washington, D.C.: U.S. Government Printing Office, 1977.

———, and M. Hindelang. *An Introduction to the National Crime Survey*. Washington, D.C.: U.S. Government Printing Office, 1977.

Gaudet, F.; G. Harris; and C. St. John. "Individual Differences in the Sentencing Tendencies of Judges." *Journal of Criminal Law and Criminology* 23:811 (1933).

Geason, D., and F. Hangren. "Predicting the Adjustment of Federal Probationers." *National Probation and Parole Association Journal* 4:265 (1958).

Gibbs, J. J. "Psychological and Behavioral Pathology in Jails: A Review of the Literature." Paper prepared for the Special National Workshop on Mental Health Services in Local Jails, Baltimore, Maryland, September, 1978.

Glaser, D. *Routinizing Evaluation: Getting Feedback on Effectiveness of Crime and Delinquency Programs*. Washington, D.C.: National Institute of Mental Health, 1973.

Glaser, D.; F. Cohen; and V. O'Leary. "The Sentencing and Parole Process." Washington, D.C.: U.S. Department of Health, Education, and Welfare, Office of Juvenile Delinquency and Youth Development, 1966.

Goldfarb, R. *Ransom.* New York: Harper & Row, 1965.

Goldkamp, J. *Two Classes of Accused: A Study of Bail and Detention in America.* Cambridge, Massachusetts: Ballinger, 1979.

———. "Questioning the Practice of Pretrial Detention." *Journal of Criminal Law and Criminology* 74(4):1556–1588 (1983).

———. "Danger and Detention." *Journal of Criminal Law and Criminology* 76:1(1985).

———, and M. Gottfredson. "Bail Decisionmaking and Pretrial Detention: Surfacing Judicial Policy." *Law and Human Behavior* 3:227 (1979).

———, and M. Gottfredson. *Guidelines for Bail: The Philadelphia Experiment.* Philadelphia: Temple University Press, 1985.

Goldkamp, J.; M. Gottfredson; and S. Mitchell-Herzfeld. *Bail Decisionmaking: A Study of Policy Guidelines,* Washington, D.C.: National Institute of Corrections, 1981.

Goldstein, H. "Setting High Bail to Prevent Pretrial Release." In *Proceedings,* National Conference on Bail and Criminal Justice, Washington, D.C., 1964.

———. "Administrative Problems in Controlling the Exercise of Police Authority." *Journal of Criminal Law, Criminology and Police Science* 58:160 (1967).

———. *Policing A Free Society.* Cambridge, Massachusetts: Ballinger, 1977.

Goldstein, J. "Police Discretion Not to Invoke the Criminal Process: Low Visibility Decisions in the Administration of Justice." *Yale Law Journal* 69:543 (1969).

Gottfredson, D. M. "Comparing and Combining Subjective and Objective Parole Predictions." *Research Newsletter 3.* Vacaville: California Medical Facility, California Department of Corrections, September–December, 1961.

———. "The Practical Application of Research." *Canadian Journal of Corrections* 5:212 (1963).

———. "One Approach to Social Agency Self-Study." *Canadian Journal of Corrections* 5:271 (1965).

———. "Assessment and Prediction Methods in Crime and Delinquency." In President's Commission on Law Enforcement and Administration of Justice, *Task Force Report: Juvenile Delinquency and Youth Crime.* Washington, D.C.: U.S. Government Printing Office, 1967.

———. "Sentencing Trends in the United States: Implications for Clinical Criminology." Paper presented at the Sixth International Seminar on clinical Criminology, Santa Margharita, Italy, May, 1975a.

———. "Some Positive Changes in the Parole Process." Paper delivered at the annual meeting of the American Society of Criminology, Toronto, Canada, 1975b.

Gottfredson, D. M., and J. A. Bonds. "A Manual for Intake Base Expectancy Scoring." Sacramento: California Department of Corrections. Mimeograph (1961).

———, and M. R. Gottfredson. "Data for Criminal Justice Evaluations: Some Resources and Pitfalls." In M. Klein and K. Teilman, eds., *Handbook of Criminal Justice Evaluation.* Beverly Hills, California: Sage, 1980.

———, and B. Stecher. "Sentencing Policy Models." Newark, New Jersey: School of Criminal Justice, Rutgers University, 1979. Manuscript.

Gottfredson, D. M.; M. G. Neithercutt; J. Nuffield; and V. O'Leary. *Four Thousand Lifetimes: A Study of Time Served and Parole Outcomes*. Davis, California: National Council on Crime and Delinquency Research Center, 1973.

———, J. O. Finckenauer; and C. Rauh. *Probation on Trial*. Newark, New Jersey: School of Criminal Justice, Rutgers University, 1977.

———; M. R. Gottfredson; and J. Garofalo. "Time Served in Prison and Parole Outcomes Among Parolee Risk Categories." *Journal of Criminal Justice* 5:1 (197).

———; C. A. Cosgrove; L. T. Wilkins; J. Wallerstein; and C. Rauh. *Classification for Parole Decision Policy*. Washington, D.C.: U.S. Government Printing Office, 1978.

———; L. T. Wilkins; and P. B. Hoffman. *Guidelines for Parole and Sentencing: A Policy Control Method*. Lexington, Massachusetts: Lexington Books, 1978.

Gottfredson, M. R. "An Empirical Analysis of Pre-Trial Release Decisions." *Journal of Criminal Justice* 2:287 (1974).

———. "The Classification of Crimes and Victims." Ph.D. dissertation, State University of New York at Albany, 1976.

———. "Substantive Contributions of Victimization Surveys." *Crime and Justice: An Annual Review of Research* 6:251 (1986).

Gottfredson, M. R., and K. Adams. "Prison Behavior and Release Performance: Empirical Reality and Public Policy." *Law and Policy Quarterly* 4:373 (1982).

———, and D. M. Gottfredson. "Guidelines for Incarceration Decisions: A Partisan Review." *University of Illinois Law Review*, 2:291–317 (1984).

———, and M. J. Hindelang. "A Study of the Behavior of Law." *American Sociological Review* 44:1 (1979a).

———. "Theory and Research in the Sociology of Law." *American Sociological Review* 44:27 (1979b).

———. "Trite But True." *American Sociological Review* 45:338 (1980).

Gottfredson, M. R.; T. Flanagan; and S. Mitchell-Herzfeld. "Another Look at the Effectiveness of Parole Supervision." *Journal of Research in Crime and Delinquency* 19:277–298 (1982).

Gottfredson, S.; K. Young; and W. Laufer. "Additivity and Interaction in Offense Seriousness Scales." *Journal of Research in Crime and Delinquency* 17:26 (1980).

Gough, H. G. "Clinical versus Statistical Prediction in Psychology." In L. Postman, ed., *Psychology in the Making*. New York: Knopf, 1962.

Green, E. *Judicial Attitudes in Sentencing*. London: MacMillan, 1961.

Greenwood, P. with A. Abrahamse. *Selective Incapacitation*. Santa Monica: Rand Corporation, 1982.

Greenwood, P.; S. Wildhorn; E. Poggin; M. Strumwasser; and P. DeLeon. *Prosecution of Adult Felony Defendants in Los Angeles County: A Policy Perspective*. Washington, D.C.: U.S. Department of Justice, 1973.

Hagan, J. "Extra-Legal Attributes and Criminal Sentencing: An Assessment of a Sociological Viewpoint." *Law and Society Review* 8:357 (1974).

Hamilton, W., and C. Work. "The Prosecutor's Role in the Urban Court System: The Case for Management Consciousness." *Journal of Criminal Law and Criminology* 64:183 (1973).

Hanley, C. "The Gauging of Criminal Predispositions." In H. Toch, *Legal and Criminal Psychology*. New York: Holt, Rinehart & Winston, 1961.

Harris, M. K. "Disquisition on the Need for a New Model for Criminal Sanctioning Systems." *West Virginia Law Review* 77:263 (1975).

Hart, H. L. A. *Punishment and Responsibility: Essays in the Philosophy of Law*. New York: Oxford University Press, 1968.

Havel, J. *Special Intensive Parole Unit, Phase IV: A High Base Expectancy Study.* Sacramento: California Department of Correction, June 1963.

Heinz, A.; J. Heinz; S. Senderowitz; and M. Vance. "Sentencing by Parole Board: An Evaluation." *Journal of Criminal Law and Criminology* 67:1 (1976).

Heumann, M. "A Note on Plea Bargaining and Case Pressure." *Law and Society Review*, 9:3:515 (1975).

———. *Plea Bargaining.* Chicago: University of Chicago Press, 1978.

Heumann, M., and C. Loftin. "Mandatory Sentencing and the Abolition of Plea Bargaining." *Law and Society Review*. 13:393 (1979).

———. "On the Methodological Rigor of the Bellamy Memorandum." *Criminal Law Bulletin* 8:507 (1972).

———. "Decisions of Shoplifting Victims to Invoke the Criminal Justice Process." *Social Problems* 21:580 (1974).

Hindelang, M. J. *Criminal Victimization in Eight American Cities: A Descriptive Analysis of Common Theft and Assault.* Cambridge, Massachusetts: Ballinger, 1976.

Hindelang, M., and M. R. Gottfredson. "The Victim's Decision Not to Invoke the Criminal Process." In W. McDonald, ed., *Criminal Justice and the Victim.* Beverly Hills: Sage, 1976.

Hindelang, M.; M. R. Gottfredson; and J. Garofalo. *Victims of Personal Crime: Am Empirical Foundation for a Theory of Personal Victimization.* Cambridge, Massachusetts: Ballinger, 1978.

Hirschi, T. "Labelling Theory and Juvenile Delinquency: An Assessment of the Evidence." In W. Gove, ed., *The Labelling of Deviance.* New York: Halsted Press, 1975.

Hoffman, P.; B. Stone-Meierhoefer; and J. Beck. "Salient Factor Score and Release Behavior: Three Validation Samples." *Law and Human Behavior* 2:47 (1978).

Hogarth, J. *Sentencing as a Human Process.* Toronto: University of Toronto Press, 1971.

Hopkinson, C. C., and S. Adams. "The Specialized Alcoholic Caseload Project: A Study of the Effectiveness of Probation with Alcoholic Offenders." Los Angeles: Los Angeles County Probation Department, 1964. Mimeograph.

Hough, M., and Mayhew, P. *The British Crime Survey: First Report.* London: HMSO, 1983.

Institute for Law and Social Research. *Uniform Case Evaluation and Rating.* INSLAW Briefing Paper Number 3. Washington, D.C.: INSLAW, 1976.

Irish, J. F. "Assessment of Adult Division Supervision Program Effectiveness." Mineola, New York: Adult Probation Department, 1976. Mimeograph.

Jackson, R. "The Federal Prosecutor." *Journal of American Judicature Society* 24:18 (1940).

Jacoby, J. *The Prosecutor's Charging Decision: A Policy Perspective.* Washington, D.C.: U.S. Government Printing Office, 1977.

Kadish, S. "Legal Norms and Discretion in the Police and Sentencing Process." *Harvard Law Review* 75:904 (1962).

Kant, I. *The Philosophy of Law, Part II.* Trans. W. Hastic. Edinburgh: T. T. Clar, 1887.

Kaplan, J. "The Prosecutorial Discretion—A Comment." *Northwestern University Law Review* 60:174 (1965).

Kaput, T. A., and M. E. Santese. "Evaluation of General Caseload Drug Unit." Hartford, Connecticut: Department of Adult Probation, 1972. Mimeograph.

Kassebaum, G.; D. A. Ward; and D. M. Wilner. *Prison Treatment and Parole Survival.* New York: Wiley, 1971.

Kastenmeier, R. W., and H. C. Eglit. "Parole Release Decisionmaking: Rehabilitation, Expertise, and the Demise of Mythology." *American University Law Review* 22:477–88 (1975).

Klein, M.; K. Teilman; J. Styles; S. Lincoln; and S. Labin-Rosensweig. "The Explosion in Police Diversion Programs: Evaluating the Structural Dimensions of a Social Fad." In M. Klein, ed., *The Juvenile Justice System.* Beverly Hills: Sage, 1976.

Knapp, K. "What Sentencing Reform in Minnesota Has and Has Not Accomplished." *Judicature* 68:181 (1984).

Kolodney, S. *Parole Board Reform in California: Order Out of Chaos.* Report of the Select Committee on the Administration of Justice. Sacramento Assembly of the State of California, 1970.

Lafave, W. "The Police and Nonenforcement of the Law." *Wisconsin Law Review* 104 (1962).

———. *Arrest: The Decision to Take a Suspect into Custody.* Boston: Little, Brown, 1965.

———. "The Prosecutor's Discretion in the United States." *American Journal of Comparative Law* 18:532 (1970).

LaFree G. "Official Reactions to Social Problems: Police Decisions in Sexual Assault Cases." *Soc. Problems* 28(5): 582–594 (1981).

Landes, W. "Legality and Reality: Some Evidence on Criminal Procedure." *Journal of Legal Studies* 3:287 (1974).

Laub, J. "Ecological Considerations in Victim Reporting to the Police." *Journal of Criminal Justice* 9:419 (1981).

Lerner, M. "The Effectiveness of a Definite Sentence Parole Program." *Criminology* 15 (2):211–224 (1977).

Lipton, D.; R. Martinson; and J. Wilks. *The Effectiveness of Correctional Treatment: A Survey of Evaluation Studies.* New York: Praeger, 1975.

Locke, J.; R. Penn; R. Rock; E. Bunten; and G. Hare. *Compilation and Use of Criminal Court Data in Relation to Pretrial Release of Defendants: Pilot Study.* Washington, D.C.: U.S. Government Printing Office, 1970.

Loftin, C. and M. Heumann. "Mandatory Sentencing and Firearms Violence: Evaluating One Alternative to Gun Control." *Law and Society Review* 17:2:287 (1983).

Lohman, J. D.; A. Wahl; and R. M. Carter. "The Intensive Supervision Caseload: A Preliminary Evaluation." Berkeley: University of California School of Criminology, 1966. Mimeograph.

Lundman, R. "Routine Police Arrest Practices: A Commonweal Perspective." *Social Problems* 22:127 (1974).

———. "Shoplifting and Police Referral: A Re-examination." *Journal of Criminal Law and Criminology* 69:395 (1978).

Lundman, R.; R. Sykes; and J. Clarke. "Police Control of Juveniles: A Replication." *Journal of Research in Crime and Delinquency* 15:74 (1978).

Mannheim, H., and L. T. Wilkins. *Prediction Methods in Relation to Borstal Training.* London: Her Majesty's Stationery Office, 1955.

Martinson, R. "What Works? Questions and Answers about Prison Reform." *The Public Interest* 35:22 (1974).

Mather, L. *Plea Bargaining or Trial?* Lexington: D.C. Heath, 1979.

Mattick, H. "The Contemporary Jail in the United States." In D. Glaser, ed., *Handbook of Criminology.* Chicago: Rand McNally, 1974.

McCarthy, D., and J. Wohl. "The District of Columbia Bail Project: An Illustration of Experimentation and a Brief for Change." *Georgetown Law Journal* 55:218 (1965).

McCord, J. "A Thirty-Year Follow-Up of Treatment Effects." *American Psychologist* 33:284 (1978).

McDonald, W., and J. Cramer, eds. *Plea Bargaining.* Lexington: D.C. Heath 1980.

McIntyre, D., ed., *Law Enforcement in the Metropolis.* Chicago: American Bar Foundation, 1967.

McIntyre, D., and D. Lippman. "Prosecutors and Early Disposition of Felony Cases." *American Bar Association Journal* 56:1154 (1970).

Meehl, P. E. *Clinical versus Statistical Prediction.* Minneapolis: University of Minnesota Press, 1954.

Meehl, P. E., and A. Rosen. "Antecedent Probability and the Efficiencies of Psychometric Signs, Patterns, or Cutting Scores." *Psychological Bulletin* 52:215 (1955).

Megargee, E. L. "Psychological Assessment in Jails: Implementation of the Standards Recommended by the National Advisory Commission on Criminal Justice Standards." Paper prepared for the Special Workshop on Mental Health Services in Local Jails, Baltimore, Maryland, September, 1978.

Mellon, L.; J. Jacoby, and M. Brewer. "The Prosecutor Constrained by His Environment." *Journal of Criminal Law and Criminology* 72:1:52 (1981).

Miller, F. *Prosecution: The Decision to Charge a Suspect With a Crime.* Boston: Little, Brown, 1970.

Miller, F.; R. Dawson; G. Dix; and R. Parnas. *Criminal Justice Administration and Related Processes*. Mineola, New York: Foundation Press, 1971.

Mills, R. "The Prosecutor: Charging and 'Bargaining'." *Illinois Criminal Proceedings* 1966:511 (1966).

Minnesota Sentencing Guidelines Commission. *The Impact of the Minnesota Sentencing Guidelines: Three Year Evaluation*. St. Paul Minnesota (1984).

Missouri Division of Probation and Parole. "Probation in Missouri, July 1, 1986 to June 30, 1970." Jefferson City, Mo. Mimeograph (1976).

Moos, R. *Evaluating Treatment Environments: A Social Ecological Approach*. New York: John Wiley, 1974.

Morris, N. *The Future of Imprisonment*. Chicago: University of Chicago Press, 1974.

———. "Punishment, Desert and Rehabilitation." In U.S. Department of Justice, *Equal Justice Under Law*, Bicentennial Lecture Series. Washington, D.C.; U.S. Government Printing Office, 1976.

Morse, W., and R. Beattie. *Survey of the Administration of Criminal Justice in Oregon*. New York: Arno Press, 1974.

Mott, J. "Police Decisions for Dealing with Juvenile Offenders." *British Journal of Criminology* 23(3):249–262 (1983).

Mueller, G. *Sentencing: Process and Purpose*. Springfield, Illinois: Charles C Thomas, 1977.

Mueller, P. *Advanced Release to Parole*. Research Report No. 20. Sacramento: Department of Corrections, Youth and Adult Corrections Agency, 1965.

Muir, W. *Police: Streetcorner Politicians*. Chicago: University of Chicago Press, 1977.

Nardulli, P. *The Courtroom Elite*, Cambridge, Massachusetts: Ballinger, 1978.

Nardulli, P. "The Caseload Controversy and the Study of the Criminal Courts." *Journal of Criminal Law and Criminology* 70:125 (1979).

National Advisory Commission on Criminal Justice Standards and Goals. *Corrections*. Washington, D.C.: U.S. Government Printing Office, 1973a.

———. *Police*. Washington, D.C.: U.S. Government Printing Office, 1973b.

National Association of Pretrial Services Agencies. *Performance Standards and Goals for Pretrial Release and Diversion, Pretrial Release*. Washington, D.C.: Author, 1978.

National Council on Crime and Delinquency. *Standards and Goals for Adult Probation*. New York: Author, 1962.

Neithercutt, M. G., and D. M. Gottfredson. *Caseload Size Variation and Difference in Probation/Parole Performance*. Pittsburgh: National Center for Juvenile Justice, 1973.

———. "Caseload Size Variation and Difference in Probation and Parole Performance." In W. Amos and C. Newman, eds., *Parole*. New York: Federal Legal Publications (1975).

———, and W. Mosley. *Arrest Decisions as Preludes to? An Evaluation of Policy Related Research*. Vol. III. Davis, California: National Council on Crime and Delinquency Research Center, 1974.

Nettler, G. *Explaining Crime,* 2nd ed. New York: McGraw-Hill, 1978.

Newman, D. *Conviction: The Determination of Guilt or Innocence Without Trial.* Boston: Little, Brown, 1966.

———. "Role and Process in the Criminal Court." In D. Glaser, ed., *Handbook of Criminology,* ch. 15. Chicago: Rand McNally, 1974.

Newman, G. *The Punishment Response.* New York: Lippincott, 1978.

Nuttall, C. P., and Associates. *Parole In England and Wales.* Home Office Research Studies No. 38. London: Her Majesty's Stationery Office (1977).

Ohlin, L. E. *Selection for Parole: A Manual of Parole Prediction.* New York: Russell Sage Foundation, 1951.

———, and F. Remington. "Sentencing Structure: Its Effects Upon Systems for the Administration of Criminal Justice," *Law and Contemporary Problems* 23:495 (1958).

O'Leary, V., and D. Glaser. "The Assessment of Risk in Parole Decisionmaking." In J. D. West, ed., *The Future of Parole.* London: Duckworth, 1972.

———, and J. Hall. *Frames of Reference in Parole.* Hackensack, New Jersey: National Council on Crime and Delinquency Training Center, National Parole Institutes Training Document, n.d. (ca. 1976).

———, and K. J. Hanrahan. *Parole Systems in the United States.* Hackensack, New Jersey: National Council on Crime and Delinquency, 1976.

O'Leary, V.; M. R. Gottfredson; and A. Gelman. "Contemporary Sentencing Proposals." *Criminal Law Bulletin* 11:55 (1975).

Packer, H. "Two Models of the Criminal Process." *University of Pennsylvania Law Review* 113:1 (1964).

Palmer, T. "The Youth Authority's Community Treatment Project." *Federal Probation* 38:3 (1974).

———. "Martinson Revisited." *Journal of Research in Crime and Delinquency* 12:133 (1975).

Parnas, R. "The Police Response to Domestic Disturbance." *Wisconsin Law Review* 1967:914 (1967).

———. "Police Discretion and Diversion of Incidents of Intra-Family Violence." *Law and Contemporary Problems* 36:539 (1971).

Parole and Community Services Division. *The Work Unit Parole Program: 1969.* Sacramento: California Department of Correction, December 5, 1969.

Petersen, D. "Police Disposition of the Petty Offender." *Sociology and Social Research* 56:320 (1972).

Petersilia, J.; S. Turner, J. Kahan, and J. Peterson. *Granting Felons Probation.* Santa Monica: Rand, 1985.

Piliavin, I., and S. Briar. "Police Encounters with Juveniles." *American Journal of Sociology* 70:206 (1964).

Pope, C. *Offender-Based Transaction Statistics: New Directions in Data Collection and Reporting.* Washington, D.C.: National Criminal Justice Information and Statistics Service, 1975.

———. "The Influence of Social and Legal Factors on Sentence Dispositions: A Preliminary Analysis of Offender-Based Transaction Statistics." *Journal of Criminal Justice* 4:203 (1976).

————. "Postarrest Release Decisions: An Empirical Examination of Social and Legal Criteria." *Journal of Research in Crime and Delinquency* 15:35 (1978a).

————. "Sentence Dispositions Accorded Assault and Burglary Offenders: An Exploratory Study in Twelve California Counties." *Journal of Criminal Justice* 6:151 (1978b).

Powell, J. "Critical Assessment of Revocation/Recidivism Statistics." In D. Gottfredson, J. Finckenauer, and C. Rauh eds., *Probation on Trial.* Newark, School of Criminal Justice, Rutgers, 1977.

President's Commission on Law Enforcement and Administration of Justice. *The Challenge of Crime in a Free Society.* Washington, D.C.: U.S. Government Printing Office, 1967.

Rankin, A. "The Effect of Pretrial Detention." *New York University Law Review* 39:641 (1964).

Rawls, J. *A Theory of Justice.* Cambridge, Massachusetts: Belknap Press of Harvard University Press, 1971.

Reiss, A. *The Police and the Public.* New Haven: Yale University Press, 1971.

Reiss, A., and D. Bordua. "Environment and Organization: A Perspective on the Police." In D. Bordua, ed., *The Police: Six Sociological Essays.* New York: Wiley, 1967.

Remington, F.; D. Newman; E. Kimball; M. Melli; and H. Goldstein. *Criminal Justice Administration.* Indianapolis: Bobbs-Merrill, 1969.

Roberts, D. "The Changing Structure of Criminal Sentencing." *Land and Water Law Review* 18:2:591 (1983).

Robison, J., and G. Smith. "The Effectiveness of Correctional Programs." *Crime and Delinquency* 17:67 (1971).

Rosett, A., and D. Cressey. *Justice By Consent: Plea-Bargains in the American Courthouse.* Philadelphia: Lippincott, 1976.

Rossi, P., *et al.* "The Seriousness of Crimes: Normative Structure and Individual Differences." *American Sociological Review* 39:224 (1974).

Rossman, H., W. McDonald, and J. Cramer. "Some Patterns and Determinants of Plea-Bargaining Decisions: A Simulation and Quasi-Experiment." In W. McDonald and J. Cramer, eds., *Plea Bargaining.* Lexington: D.C. Heath, 1980.

Roth, J., and P. Wice. "Pretrial Release and Misconduct in the District of Columbia." PROMIS Research Project Publication 16. Washington, D.C.: IN-SLAW, 1978.

Rubenstein, M., and T. White. "Alaska's Ban on Plea-Bargaining. In W. McDonald and J. Cramer, eds., *Plea Bargaining.* Lexington: D.C. Heath, 1980.

Rubin, S.; Weihofen; Edwards; and Rosenzweig. *The Law of Criminal Correction.* St. Paul: West.

Russell, B., "An Outline of Intellectual Rubbish." In *Unpopular Essays.* New York: Simon & Schuster, 1962.

————. *The Scientific Outlook.* New York: W. W. Norton, 1962.

Sacks, H., and C. Logan. *Does Parole Make A Difference?* Storrs: University of Connecticut School of Law Press, 1979.

————. *Parole: Crime Prevention or Crime Postponement?* Storrs, Connecticut: University of Connecticut School of Law Press (1980).

Schneider, A.; J. Burcart; and L. Wilson. "The Role of Attitudes in the Decision to Report Crimes to the Police." In W. McDonald, ed., *Criminal Justice and the Victim.* Beverly Hills: Sage, 1976.

Scott, J. "The Use of Discretion in Determining the Severity of Punishment for Incarcerated Offenders." *Journal of Criminal Law and Criminology* 65:214 (1974).

Sechrest, L., S. White, and E. Brown, eds. *The Rehabilitation of Criminal Offenders: Problems and Prospects.* Washington, D.C.: National Academy of Sciences, 1979.

Sellin, T., and M. Wolfgang. *The Measurement of Delinquency.* New York: Wiley, 1964.

Sheppard, D. J. "Denver High-Impact Anti-Crime Program: Intensive Probation and Parole." Denver: State Judicial Department, 1975. Mimeograph.

Sherman, L. "Causes of Police Behavior: The Current State of Quantitative Research." *Journal of Research in Crime and Delinquency* 17:69 (1980a).

————. "Execution without Trial: Police Homicide and the Constitution." *Vanderbilt Law Review* 33:71 (1980b).

————. "Patrol Strategies for Police." In J. Q. Wilson, ed., *Crime and Public Policy.* San Francisco: ICS, 1983.

Sherman, L., and R. Berk. "The Specific Deterrent Effects of Arrest for Domestic Assault," *American Sociological Review,* 49(2):261–172 (1984).

Simon, F. H. *Prediction Methods in Criminology.* London: Her Majesty's Stationery Office, 1971.

Single, E. "The Unconstitutional Administration of Bail: *Bellamy* v. *the Judges of New York City.*" *Criminal Law Bulletin* 8:459 (1972).

Skogan, W. *Issues in the Measurement of Victimization.* Washington, D.C.: U.S. Government Printing Office, 1981.

————. "Reporting Crimes to the Police: The Status of World Research." *Journal of Research in Crime and Delinquency* 21:2:113–137 (1984).

Smith, A., and D. Maness. "The Decision to Call the Police." In W. McDonald, ed., *Criminal Justice and the Victim.* Beverly Hills: Sage Publications, 1976.

Smith, Douglas. "The Organizational Context of Legal Control." *Criminology* 22(1)19–38 (1984).

Sparks, R. "Surveys of Victimization—An Optimistic Assessment." In M. Tonry and N. Morris, eds., *Crime and Justice,* 3. Chicago: University of Chicago Press, 1981.

————. *Research on Victims of Crime.* Washington, D.C.: U.S. Government Printing Office, 1982.

Sparks, R.; H. Genn; and D. Dodd. *Surveying Victims: A Study of the Measurement of Criminal Victimization.* New York: Wiley, 1977.

Sperlak, D. "Bail: A Legal Analysis of the Bond-Setting Behavior of Holiday Court Judges in Chicago." *Chicago-Kent Law Review* 51:757 (1974).

Stanley, D. *Prisoners among Us.* Washington, D.C.: Brookings Institution, 1976.

Steele, E. "Fraud, Dispute, and the Consumer: Responding to Consumer Complaints." *University of Pennsylvania Law Review* 173:1107 (1975).

Suffet, F. "Bail Setting: A Study of Courtroom Interaction." *Crime and Delinquency* 12:318 (1966).

Sullivan, D., and L. Siegal. "How Police Use Information to Make Decisions." *Crime and Delinquency* 18:253 (1972).

Sutherland, E. H. *Principles of Criminology.* Philadelphia: J. B. Lippincott, 1934.

Sutton, L. *Variations in Federal Criminal Sentences: A Statistical Assessment at the National Level.* Washington, D.C.: National Criminal Justice Information and Statistics Service, 1978.

Swanson, C. "A Comparison of Organizational and Environmental Influences in Arrest Policies." In F. Meyer and R. Baker, eds., *Determinants of Law-Enforcement Policies.* Lexington, Massachusetts: Lexington Books, 1979.

Sykes, R., and J. Clarke. "A Theory of Deference Exchange in Police–Citizen Encounters." *American Journal of Sociology* 81:58 (1975).

Sykes, R.; J. Fox; and J. Clarke. "A Socio-Legal Theory of Police Discretion." In A. Niederhoffer and A. Blumberg, eds., *The Ambivalent Force,* 2nd ed. Hinsdale, Illinois: Dryden Press, 1976.

Talarico, S., and C. Swanson. "Styles of Policing: An Exploration of Compatibility and Conflict." In F. Meyer and R. Baker, eds., *Determinants of Law-Enforcement Policies.* Lexington, Massachusetts: Lexington Books, 1979.

Thomas, W. *Bail Reform in America.* Berkeley: University of California Press, 1976.

Tiffany, L.; Y. Avichai; and G. Peters. "A Statistical Analysis of Sentencing in Federal Courts: Defendants Convicted After Trial, 1967–68." *Journal of Legal Studies* 4:369 (1975).

Toborg, M. and M. Sorin. "Pretrial Release and Selected Findings and Issues from a National Evaluation." Paper presented at the 1980 Annual Meeting of the American Society of Criminology, San Francisco, California (1980).

Toch, H. *Living in Prison.* New York: Free Press, 1977.

Uhlman, T., and N. Walker. "He Takes Some of My Time; I Take Some of His: An Analysis of Judicial Sentencing Patterns in Jury Cases." *Law and Society Review,* 14:23 (1980).

Utz, P. "Determinate Sentencing in Two California Courts." Cited by J. Cohen and M. Tonry, "Sentencing Reforms and Their Impacts," in A. Blumstein, ed., *Research on Sentencing: The Search for Reform,* ch. 7. Washington, D.C.: National Academy Press, 1983.

Vera Institute of Justice. *Felony Arrests: Their Prosecution and Disposition in New York City's Courts.* New York: Author, 1977.

Vetter, H. J., and R. Adams. "Effectiveness of Probation Caseload Size: A Review of the Empirical Literature." *Criminology* 8:33 (1971).

von Hirsch, A. "Prediction of Criminal Conduct and Preventive Confinement of Convicted Persons." *Buffalo Law Review* 21:717 (1972).

———. *Doing Justice: The Choice of Punishment.* New York: Hill & Wang, 1976.

————. "Constructing Guidelines for Sentencing: The Critical Choices for the Minnesota Sentencing Guidelines Commission." *Hamline Law Review*, 5:2:164 (1982).

————, A. and D. M. Gottfredson. "Selective Incapacitation." *New York University Review of Law and Social Change* 12:1 (1984).

von Hirsch, A., and K. Hanrahan. *Abolish Parole?* Washington, D.C.: U.S. Government Printing Office, 1978.

————. *The Question of Parole*, Cambridge, Massachusetts: Ballinger, 1979.

————. *Past and Future Crimes*. New Brunswick: Rutgers University Press (1985).

Vorenberg, J. "Narrowing the Discretion of Criminal Justice Officials." *Duke Law Journal* 4:651 (1976).

Wald, P. "Pretrial Detention and Ultimate Freedom: A Statistical Study." *New York University Law Review* 39:631 (1964).

Waller, I. *Men Released From Prison*. Toronto: University of Toronto Press, 1974.

Walters, A. A. "A Note on Statistical Methods in Predicting Delinquency." *British Journal of Delinquency* 6:297 (1956).

Weiler, P. C. "The Reform of Punishment." In Law Reform Commission of Canada, *Studies on Sentencing*. Ottawa: Information Canada, 1974.

Welsh, J., and D. Viets. *The Pretrial Offender in the District of Columbia*. Washington, D.C.: District of Columbia Bail Agency, 1977.

Wheeler, S.; D. Weisburd; and N. Bode. "Sentencing the White Collar Offender: Rhetoric and Reality." *American Sociological Review* 47:641 (1982).

Wice, P. *Freedom for Sale*. Lexington, Mass: Lexington Books (1974).

————. "Perspectives on Court Decision-Making." In D.M. Gottfredson, ed., *Decision-Making in the Criminal Justice System: Reviews and Essays*, ch. 5. Washington, D.C.: U.S. Government Printing Office, 1975a.

————. "Some Philosophical Issues: Values and the Parole Decision." In W. E. Amos and C. L. Newman, eds., *Parole: Legal Issues, Decision-making and Research*. New York: Federal Legal Publications, 1975b.

Wilkins, L. T. *Evaluation of Penal Measures*. New York: Random House, 1969.

Wilkins, L. T., and A. Chandler. "Confidence and Competence in Decision-making." *British Journal of Delinquency* 5:22 (1965).

————, and D. M. Gottfredson. *Research, Demonstration and Social Action*. Davis, California: National Council on Crime and Delinquency, 1969.

Williams, K. *The Role of the Victim in the Prosecution of Violent Offenses*. Institute for Law and Social Research, Publication Number 12. Washington, D.C.: U.S. Government Printing Office, 1978.

Wilson, J. Q. *Varieties of Police Behavior*. Cambridge, Massachusetts: Harvard University Press, 1965.

————. *Thinking About Crime*. New York: Basic Books, 1975.

Worden, R. and A. Pollitz. "Police Arrests in Domestic Disturbances: A Further Look." *Law and Society Review* 18(1):103–119 (1984).

Wylie C., Jr. "Paradox." *Scientific Monthly*, 67:63 (1948).

AUTHOR INDEX

SUBJECT INDEX